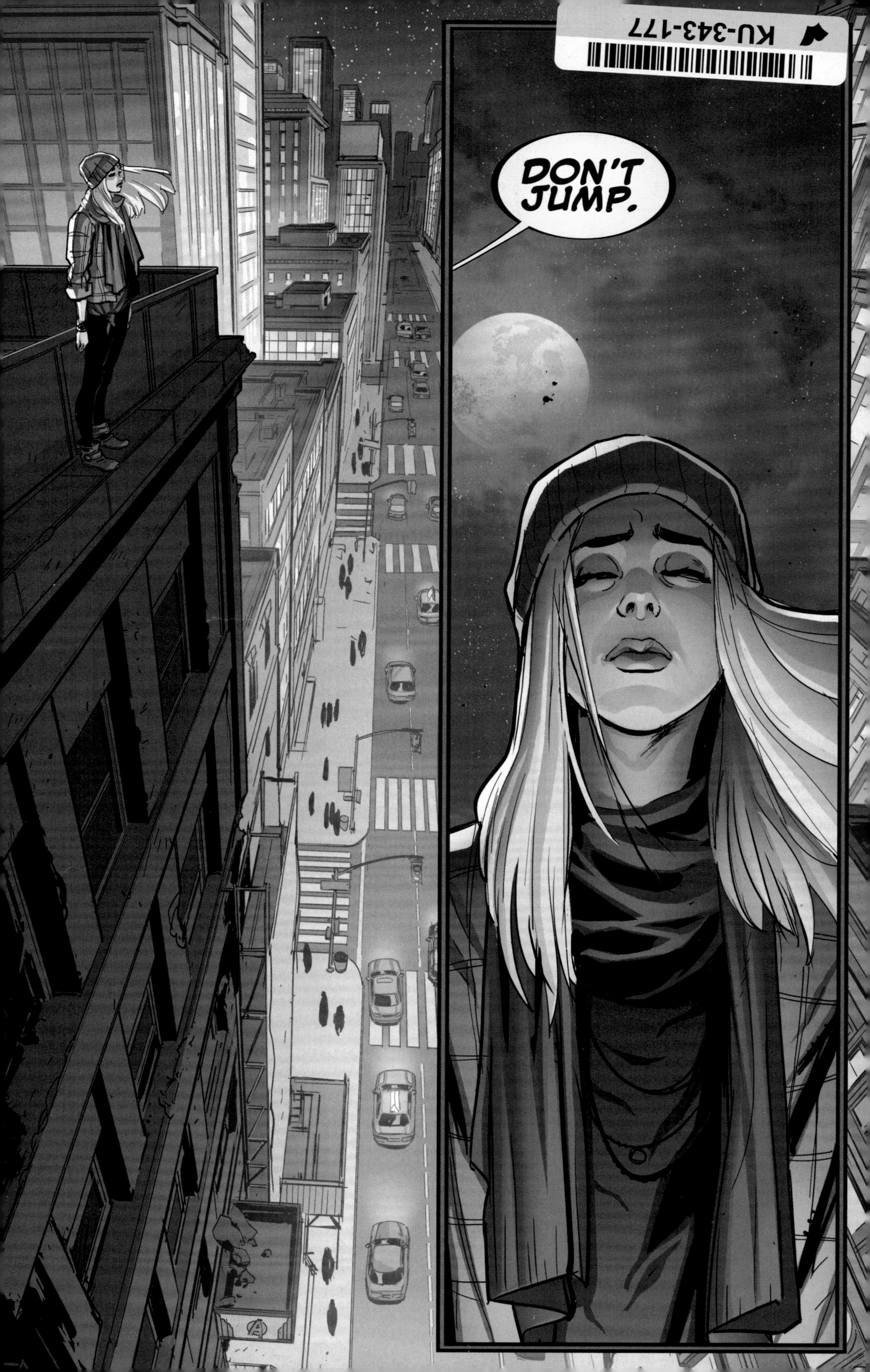
DON'T JUMP.

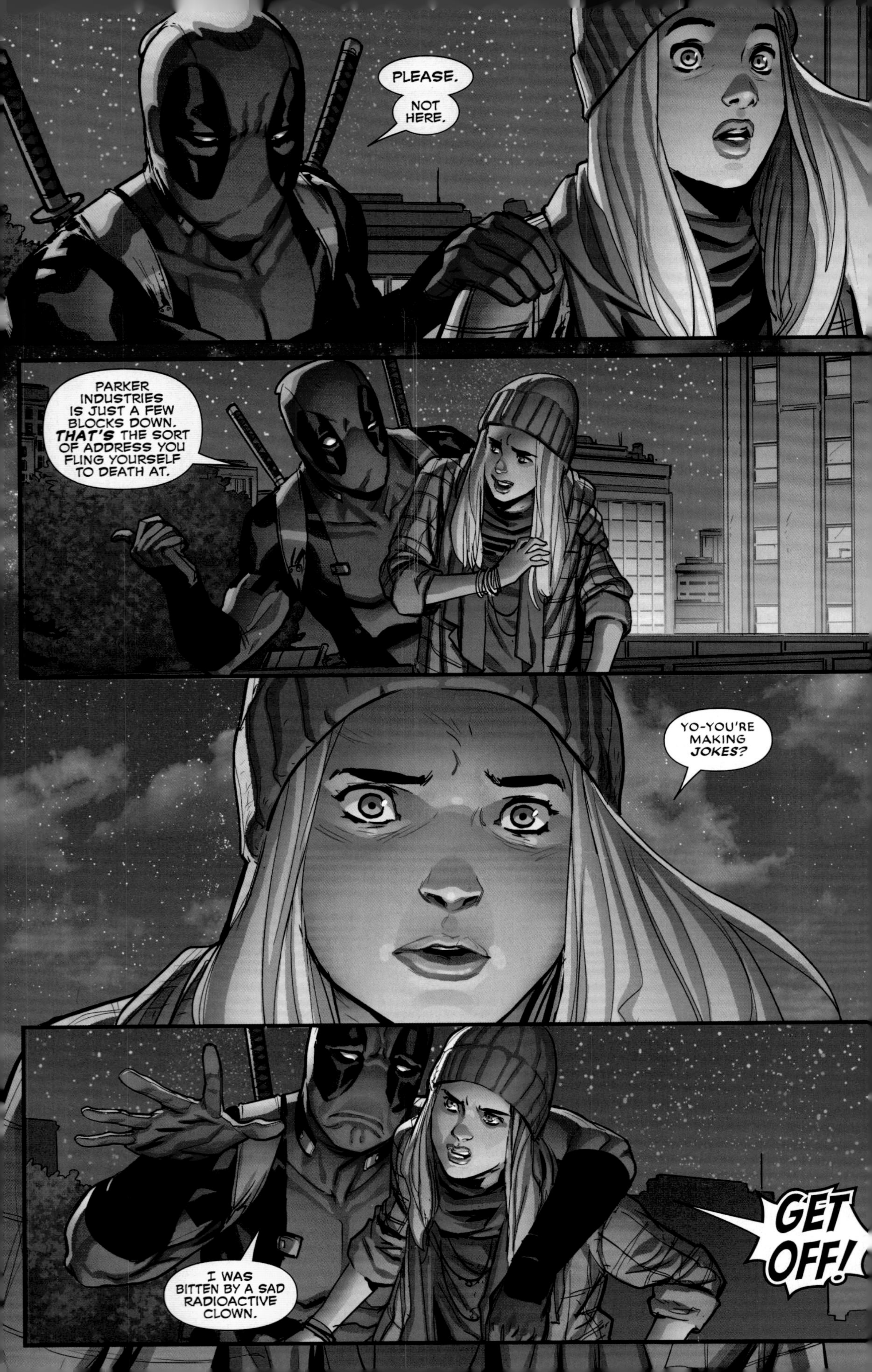
PLEASE.
NOT HERE.
PARKER INDUSTRIES IS JUST A FEW BLOCKS DOWN. THAT'S THE SORT OF ADDRESS YOU FLING YOURSELF TO DEATH AT.
YO-YOU'RE MAKING JOKES?
I WAS BITTEN BY A SAD RADIOACTIVE CLOWN.
GET OFF!

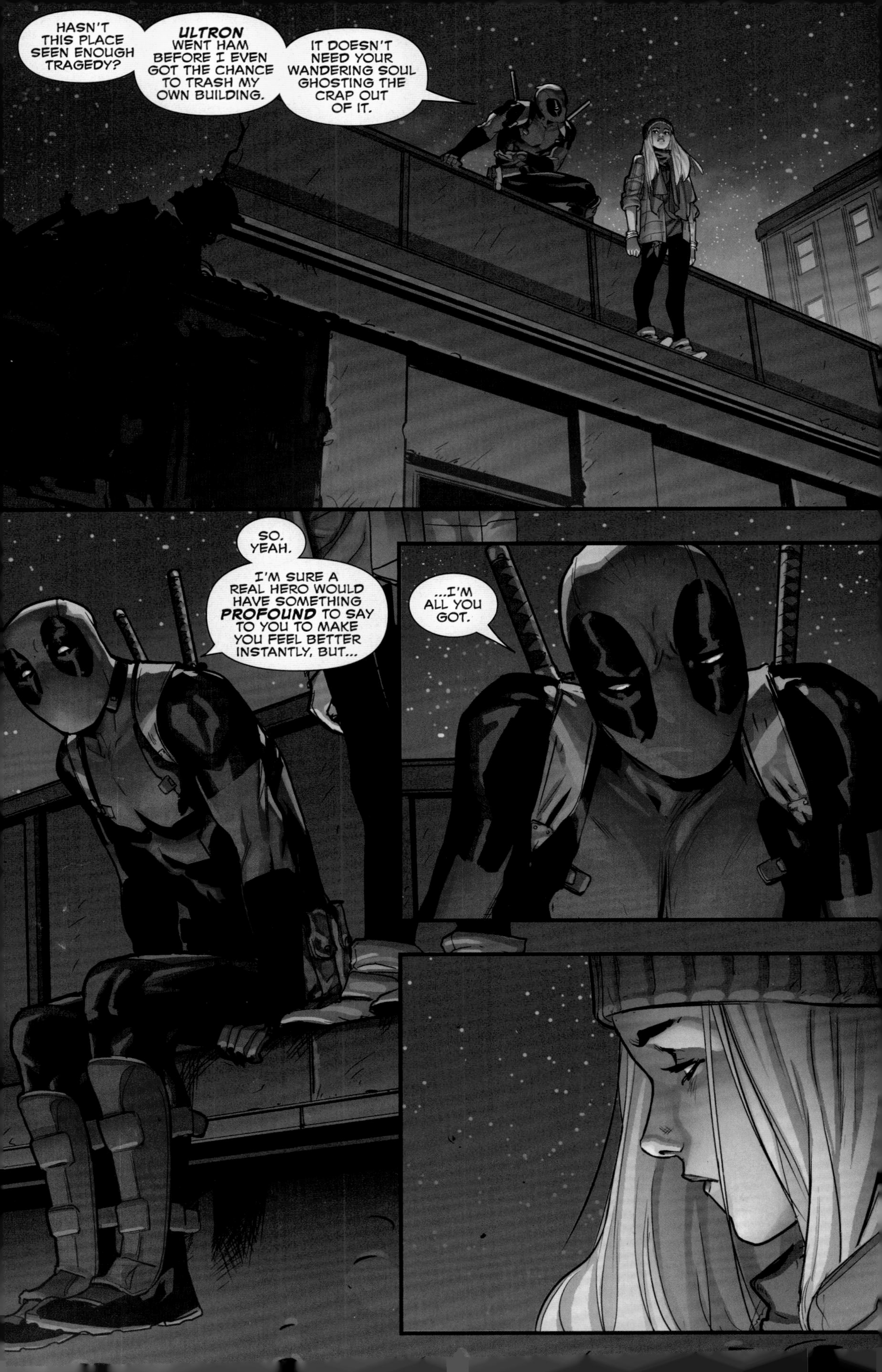
HASN'T THIS PLACE SEEN ENOUGH TRAGEDY?
ULTRON WENT HAM BEFORE I EVEN GOT THE CHANCE TO TRASH MY OWN BUILDING.
IT DOESN'T NEED YOUR WANDERING SOUL GHOSTING THE CRAP OUT OF IT.
SO, YEAH.
I'M SURE A REAL HERO WOULD HAVE SOMETHING PROFOUND TO SAY TO YOU TO MAKE YOU FEEL BETTER INSTANTLY, BUT...
...I'M ALL YOU GOT.

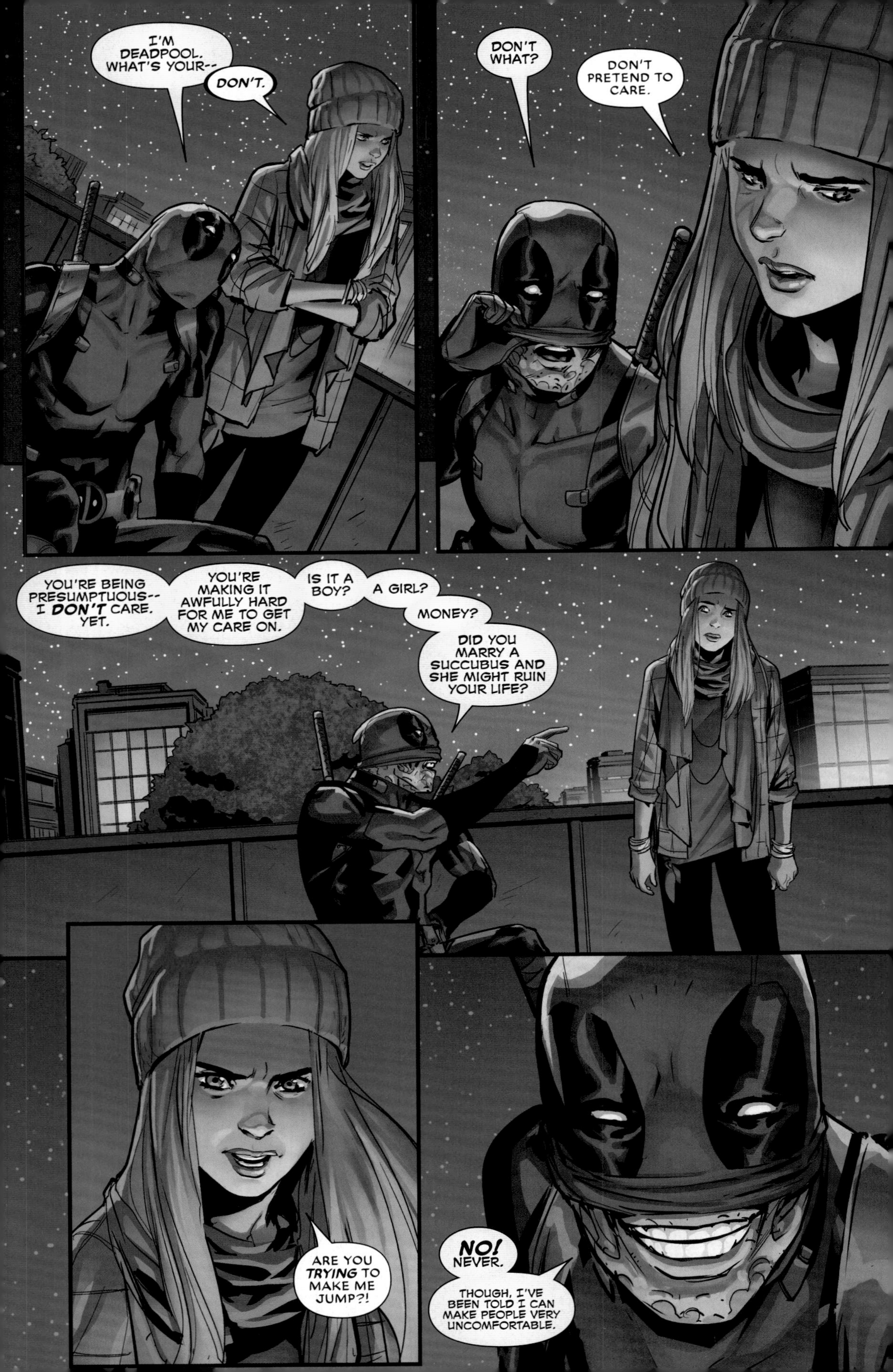
I'M DEADPOOL. WHAT'S YOUR--
DON'T.
DON'T WHAT?
DON'T PRETEND TO CARE.
YOU'RE BEING PRESUMPTUOUS-- I DON'T CARE. YET.
YOU'RE MAKING IT AWFULLY HARD FOR ME TO GET MY CARE ON.
IS IT A BOY?
A GIRL?
MONEY?
DID YOU MARRY A SUCCUBUS AND SHE MIGHT RUIN YOUR LIFE?
ARE YOU TRYING TO MAKE ME JUMP?!
NO! NEVER.
THOUGH, I'VE BEEN TOLD I CAN MAKE PEOPLE VERY UNCOMFORTABLE.

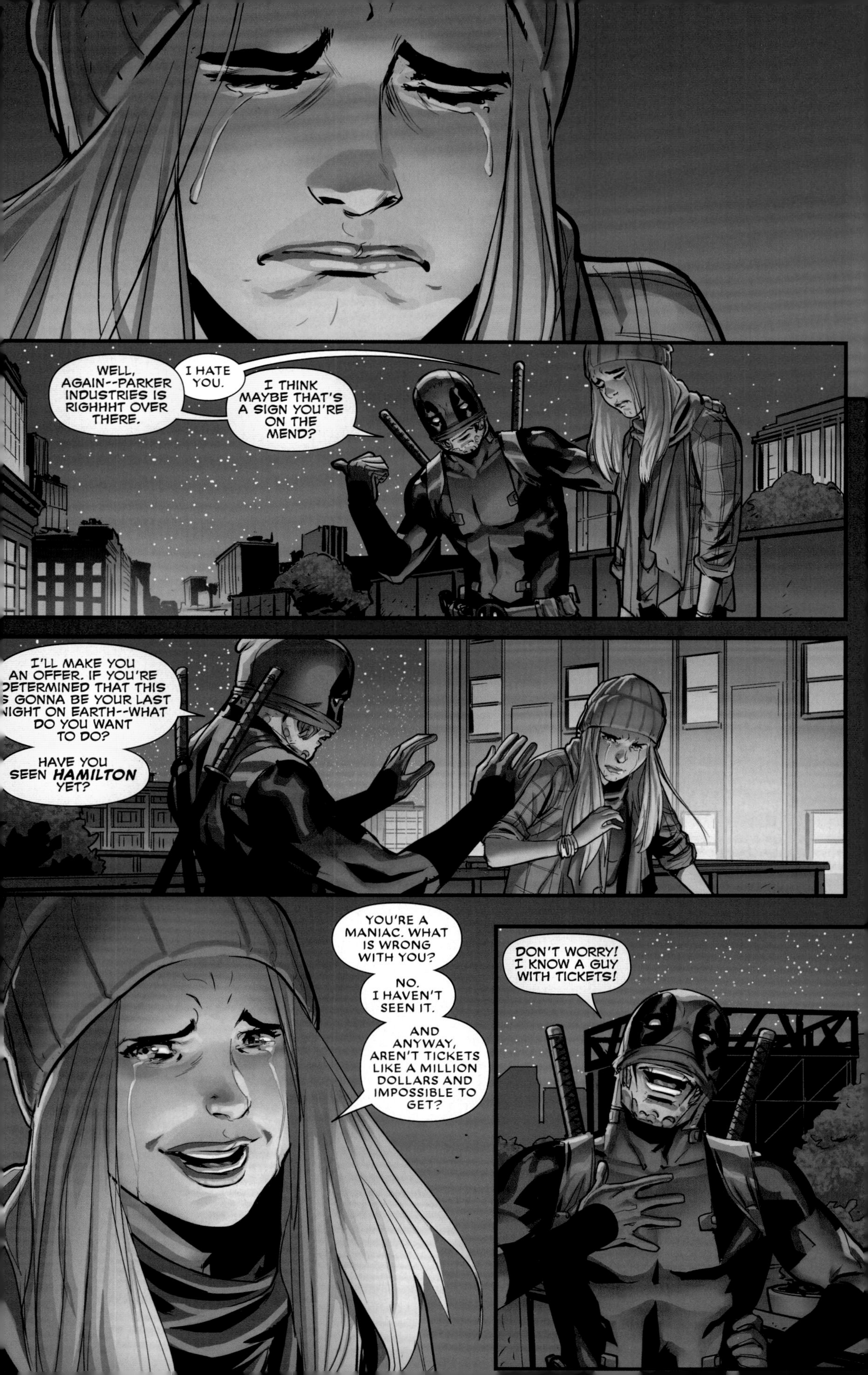

WELL, AGAIN--PARKER INDUSTRIES IS RIGHHHT OVER THERE.
I HATE YOU.
I THINK MAYBE THAT'S A SIGN YOU'RE ON THE MEND?
I'LL MAKE YOU AN OFFER. IF YOU'RE DETERMINED THAT THIS IS GONNA BE YOUR LAST NIGHT ON EARTH--WHAT DO YOU WANT TO DO?
HAVE YOU SEEN HAMILTON YET?
YOU'RE A MANIAC. WHAT IS WRONG WITH YOU?
NO. I HAVEN'T SEEN IT.
AND ANYWAY, AREN'T TICKETS LIKE A MILLION DOLLARS AND IMPOSSIBLE TO GET?
DON'T WORRY! I KNOW A GUY WITH TICKETS!

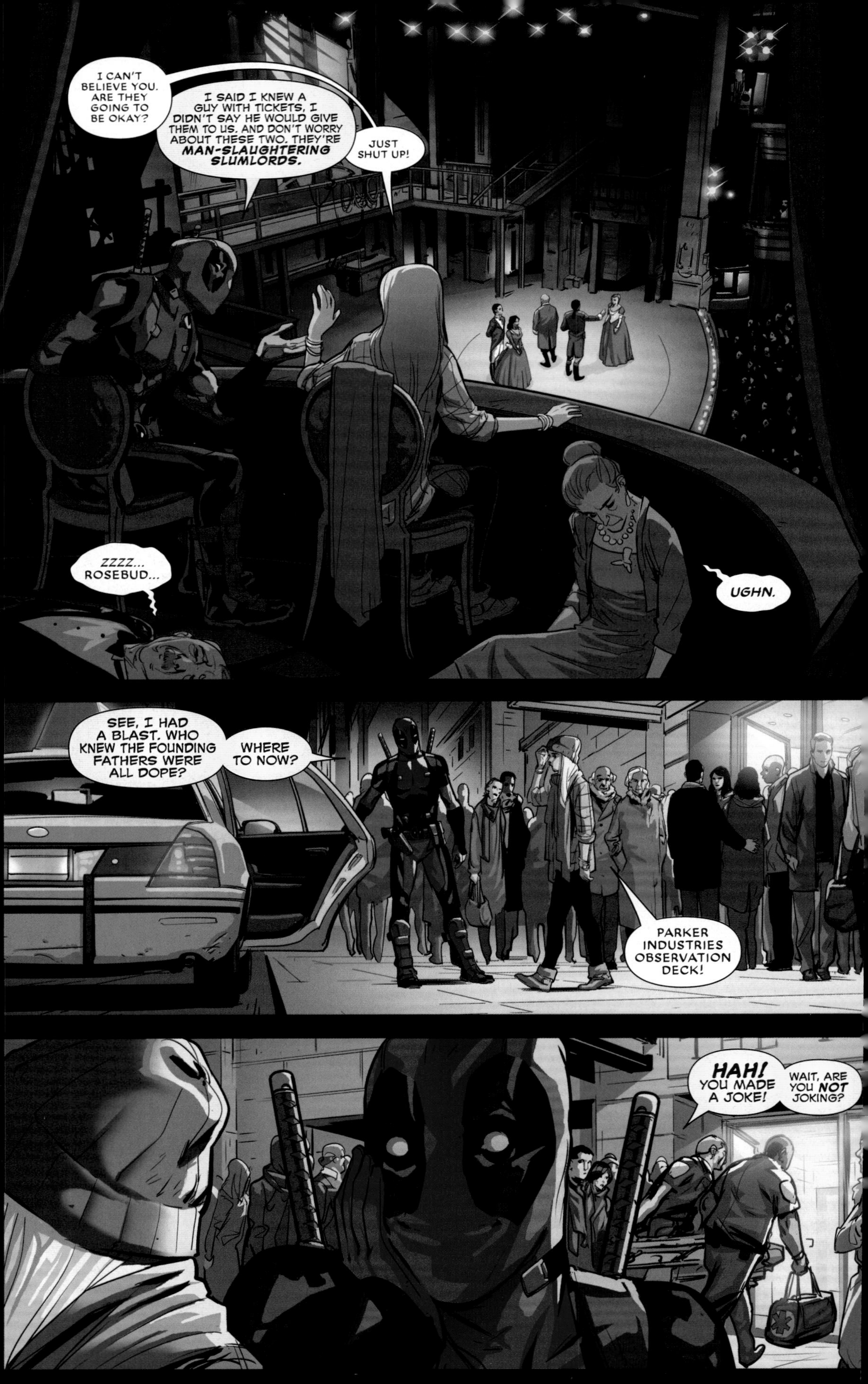
I CAN'T BELIEVE YOU. ARE THEY GOING TO BE OKAY?
I SAID I KNEW A GUY WITH TICKETS, I DIDN'T SAY HE WOULD GIVE THEM TO US. AND DON'T WORRY ABOUT THESE TWO. THEY'RE MAN-SLAUGHTERING SLUMLORDS.
JUST SHUT UP!
ZZZZ... ROSEBUD...
UGHN.
SEE, I HAD A BLAST. WHO KNEW THE FOUNDING FATHERS WERE ALL DOPE?
WHERE TO NOW?
PARKER INDUSTRIES OBSERVATION DECK!
HAH! YOU MADE A JOKE!
WAIT, ARE YOU NOT JOKING?

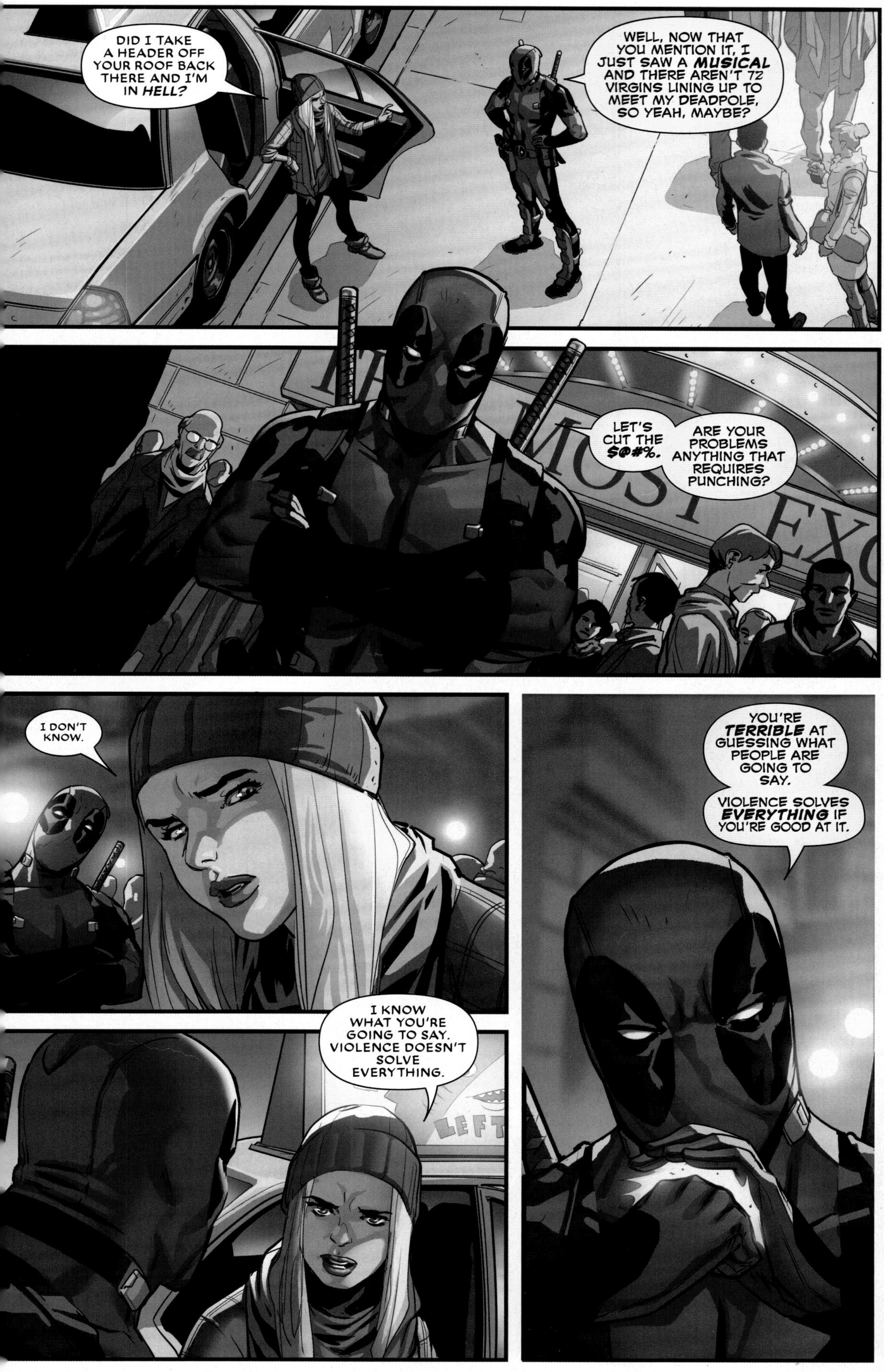
DID I TAKE A HEADER OFF YOUR ROOF BACK THERE AND I'M IN HELL?
WELL, NOW THAT YOU MENTION IT, I JUST SAW A MUSICAL AND THERE AREN'T 72 VIRGINS LINING UP TO MEET MY DEADPOLE, SO YEAH, MAYBE?
LET'S CUT THE $@#%.
ARE YOUR PROBLEMS ANYTHING THAT REQUIRES PUNCHING?
I DON'T KNOW.
I KNOW WHAT YOU'RE GOING TO SAY. VIOLENCE DOESN'T SOLVE EVERYTHING.
YOU'RE TERRIBLE AT GUESSING WHAT PEOPLE ARE GOING TO SAY.
VIOLENCE SOLVES EVERYTHING IF YOU'RE GOOD AT IT.

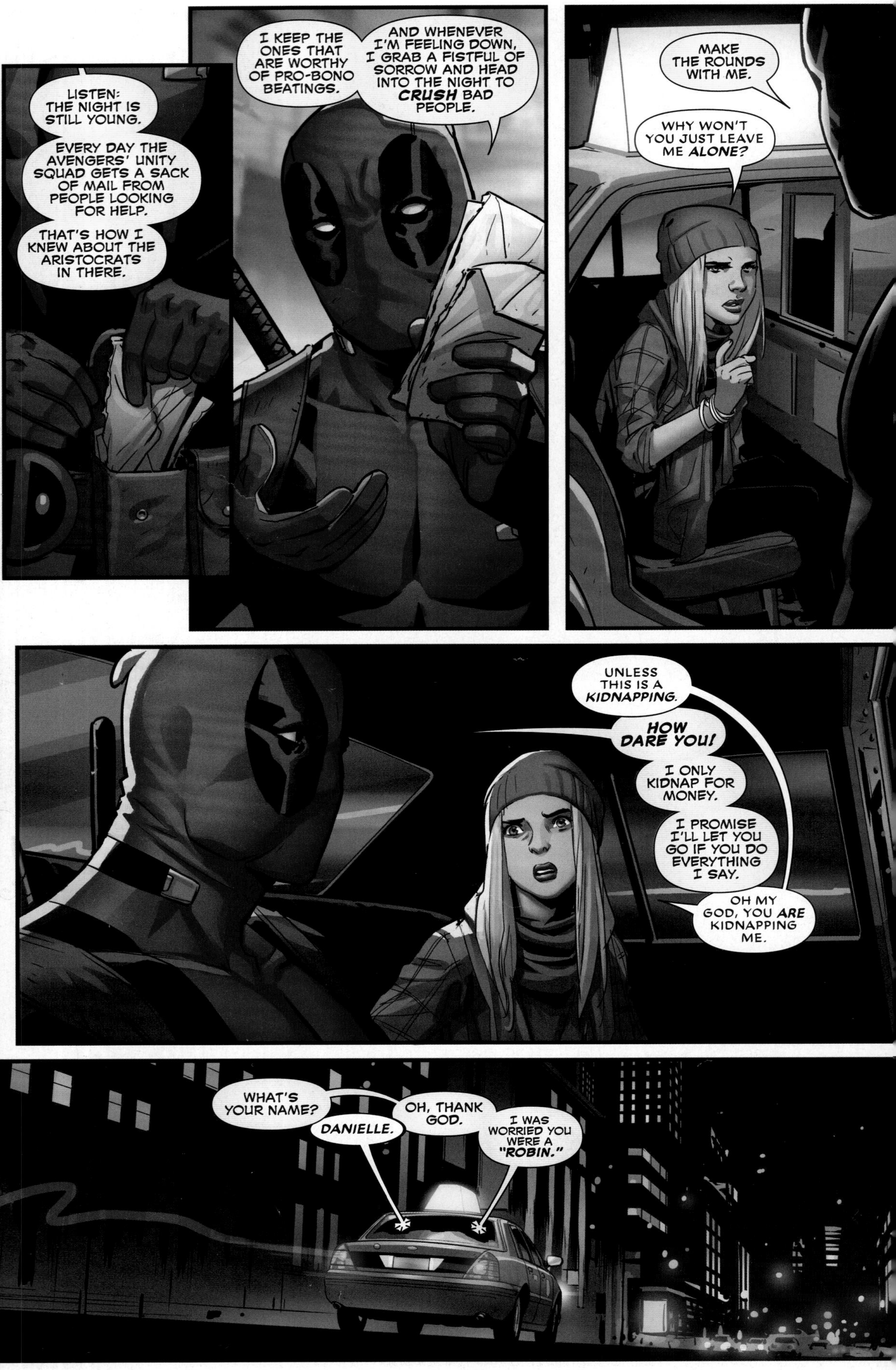
LISTEN: THE NIGHT IS STILL YOUNG.
EVERY DAY THE AVENGERS' UNITY SQUAD GETS A SACK OF MAIL FROM PEOPLE LOOKING FOR HELP.
THAT'S HOW I KNEW ABOUT THE ARISTOCRATS IN THERE.
I KEEP THE ONES THAT ARE WORTHY OF PRO-BONO BEATINGS.
AND WHENEVER I'M FEELING DOWN, I GRAB A FISTFUL OF SORROW AND HEAD INTO THE NIGHT TO CRUSH BAD PEOPLE.
MAKE THE ROUNDS WITH ME.
WHY WON'T YOU JUST LEAVE ME ALONE?
UNLESS THIS IS A KIDNAPPING.
HOW DARE YOU!
I ONLY KIDNAP FOR MONEY.
I PROMISE I'LL LET YOU GO IF YOU DO EVERYTHING I SAY.
OH MY GOD, YOU ARE KIDNAPPING ME.
WHAT'S YOUR NAME?
DANIELLE.
OH, THANK GOD.
I WAS WORRIED YOU WERE A "ROBIN."

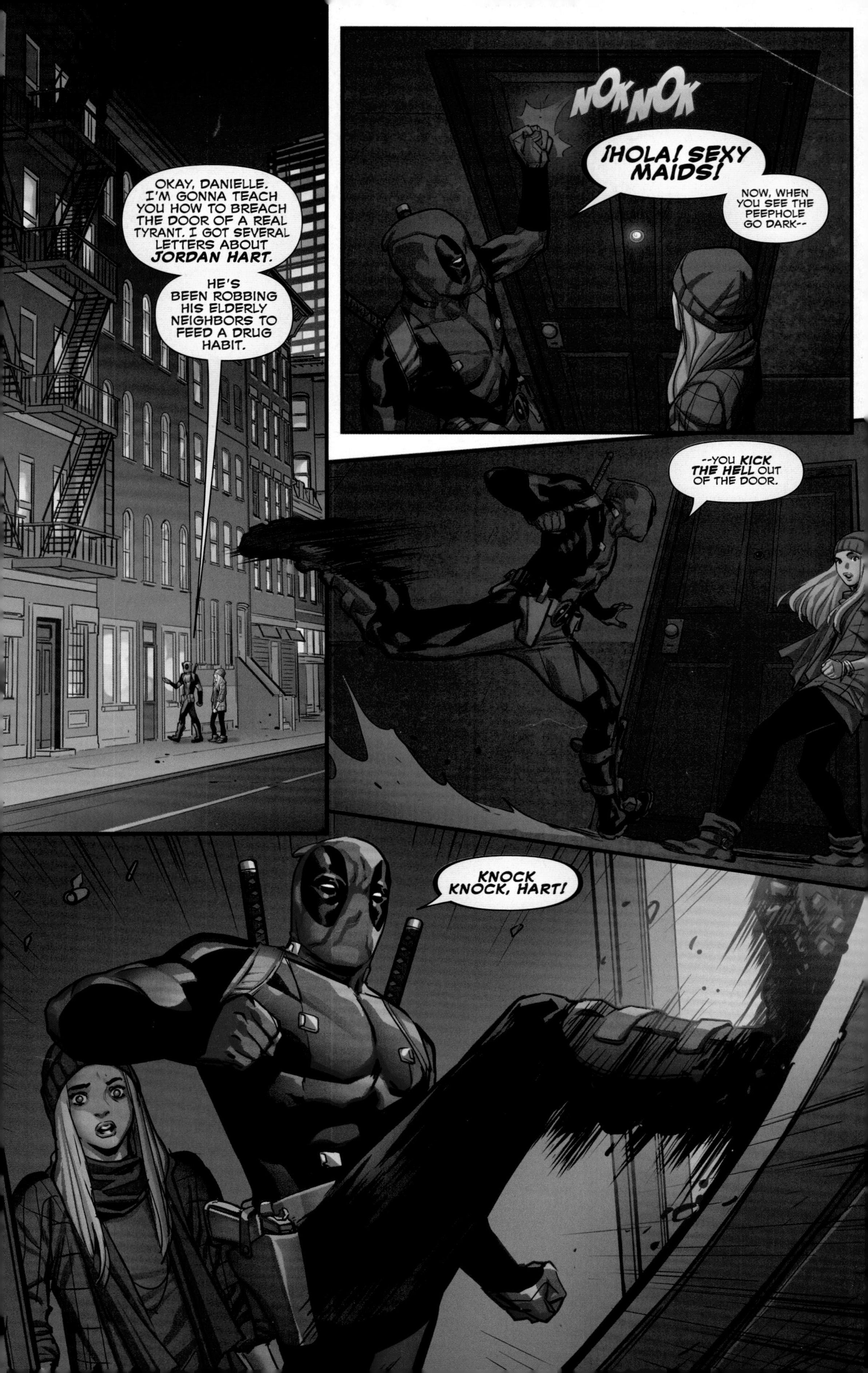

OKAY, DANIELLE. I'M GONNA TEACH YOU HOW TO BREACH THE DOOR OF A REAL TYRANT. I GOT SEVERAL LETTERS ABOUT JORDAN HART.
HE'S BEEN ROBBING HIS ELDERLY NEIGHBORS TO FEED A DRUG HABIT.
NOK NOK
¡HOLA! SEXY MAIDS!
NOW, WHEN YOU SEE THE PEEPHOLE GO DARK--
--YOU KICK THE HELL OUT OF THE DOOR.
KNOCK KNOCK, HART!

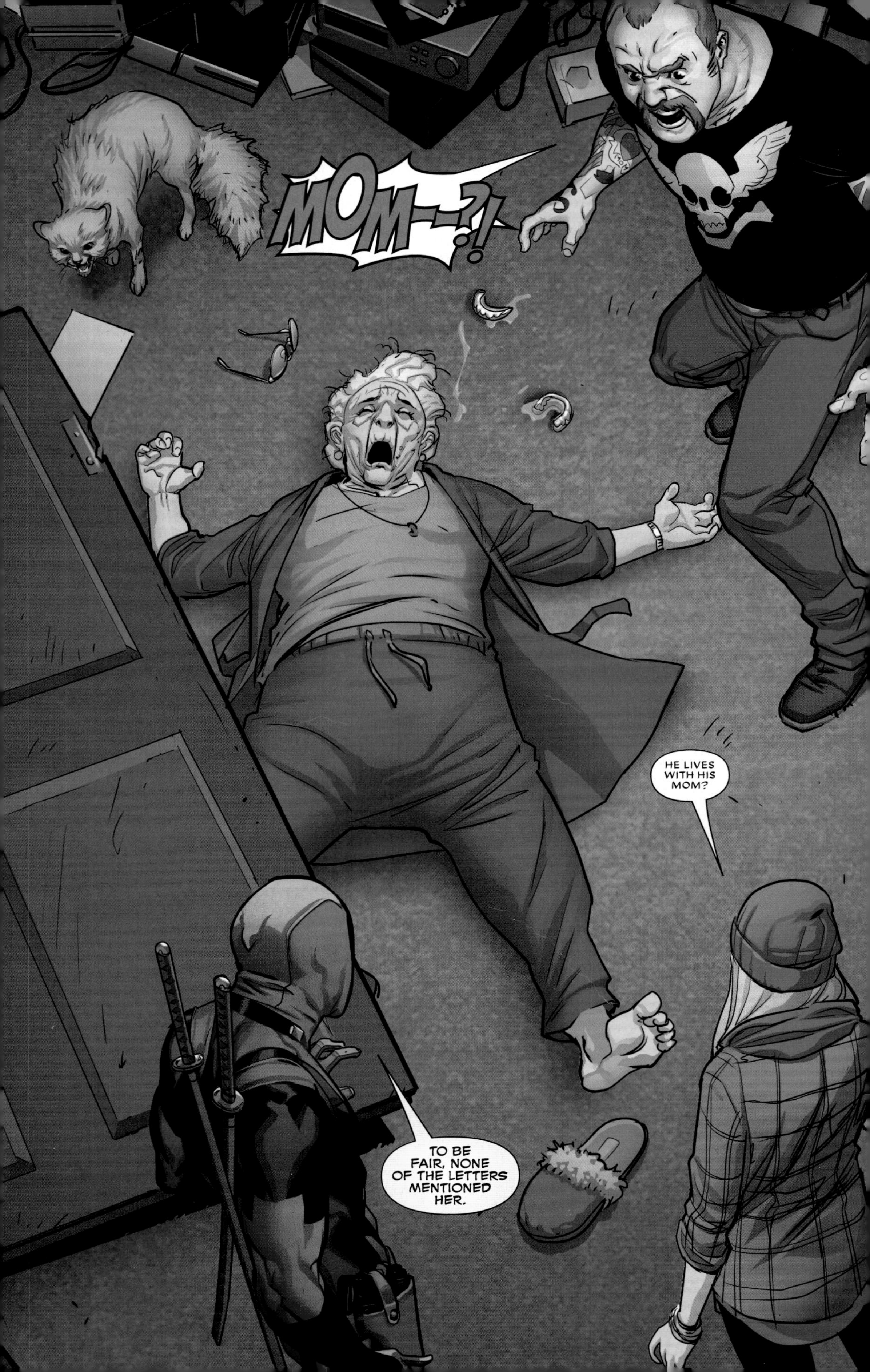
MOM--?!
HE LIVES WITH HIS MOM?
TO BE FAIR, NONE OF THE LETTERS MENTIONED HER.

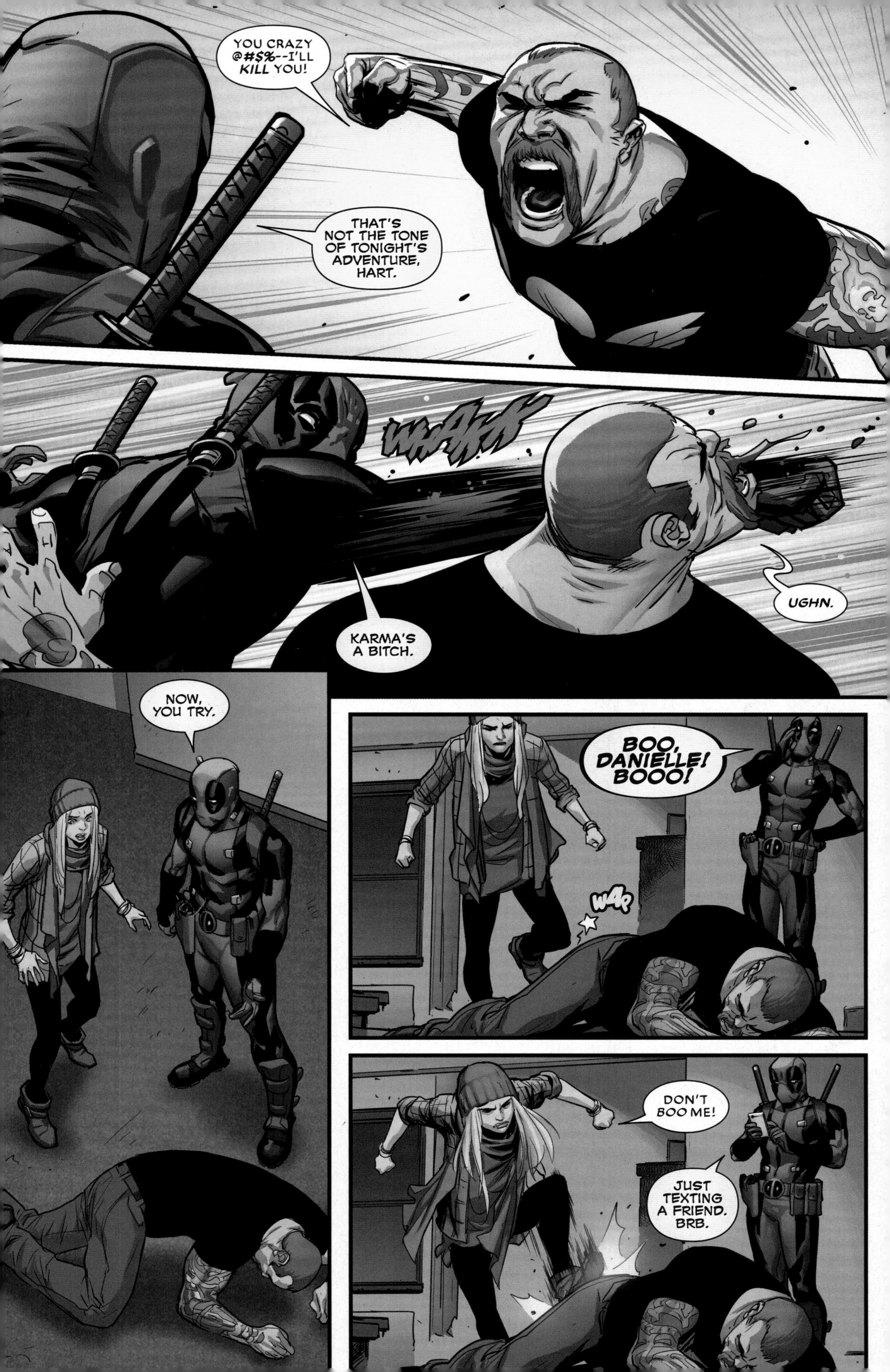
YOU CRAZY @#$%--I'LL KILL YOU!
THAT'S NOT THE TONE OF TONIGHT'S ADVENTURE, HART.
WHAKK
KARMA'S A BITCH.
UGHN.
NOW, YOU TRY.
BOO, DANIELLE! BOOO!
WAP
DON'T BOO ME!
JUST TEXTING A FRIEND. BRB.

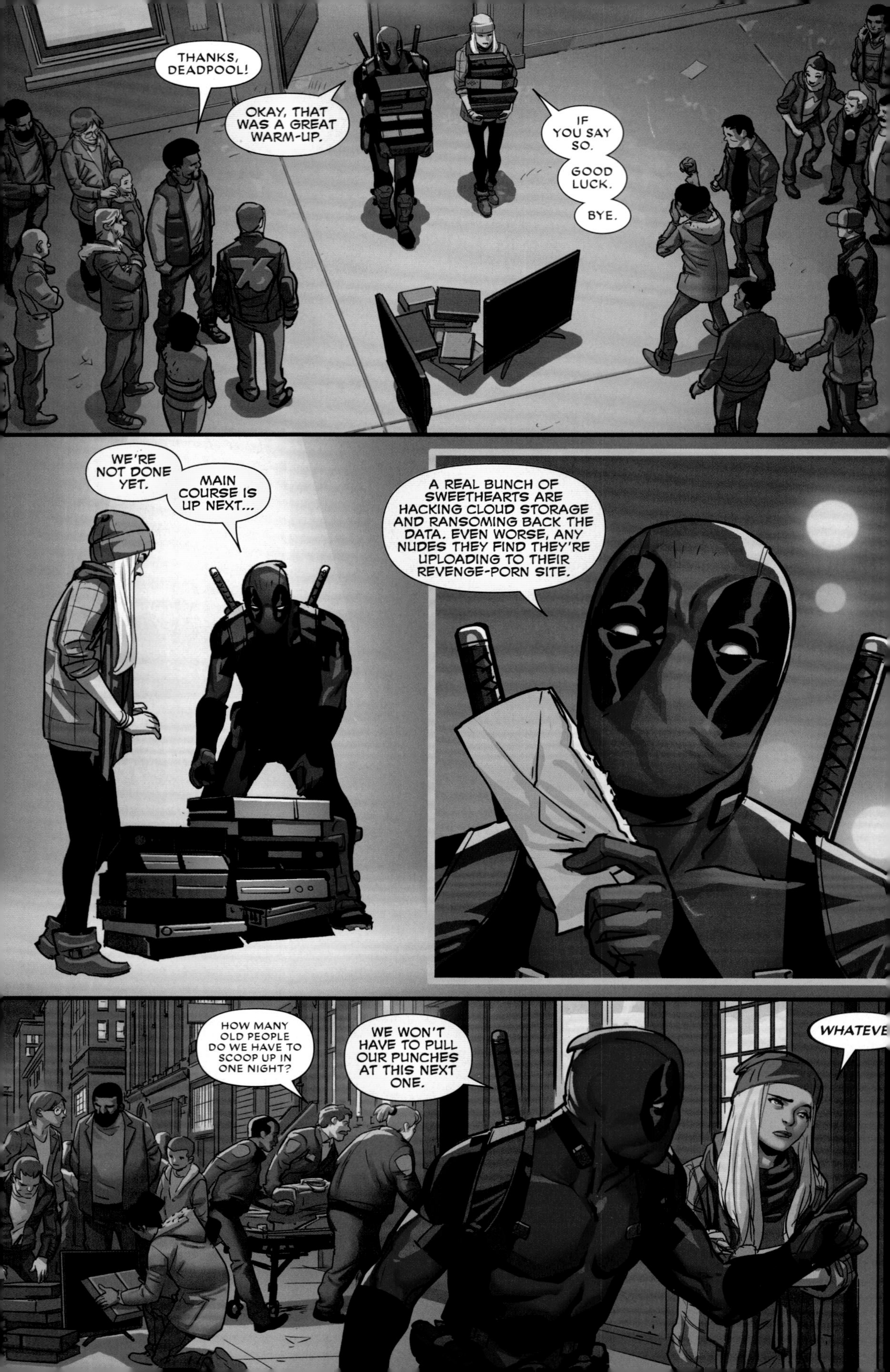
THANKS, DEADPOOL!
OKAY, THAT WAS A GREAT WARM-UP.
IF YOU SAY SO.
GOOD LUCK.
BYE.
WE'RE NOT DONE YET.
MAIN COURSE IS UP NEXT...
A REAL BUNCH OF SWEETHEARTS ARE HACKING CLOUD STORAGE AND RANSOMING BACK THE DATA. EVEN WORSE, ANY NUDES THEY FIND THEY'RE UPLOADING TO THEIR REVENGE-PORN SITE.
HOW MANY OLD PEOPLE DO WE HAVE TO SCOOP UP IN ONE NIGHT?
WE WON'T HAVE TO PULL OUR PUNCHES AT THIS NEXT ONE.
WHATEVE

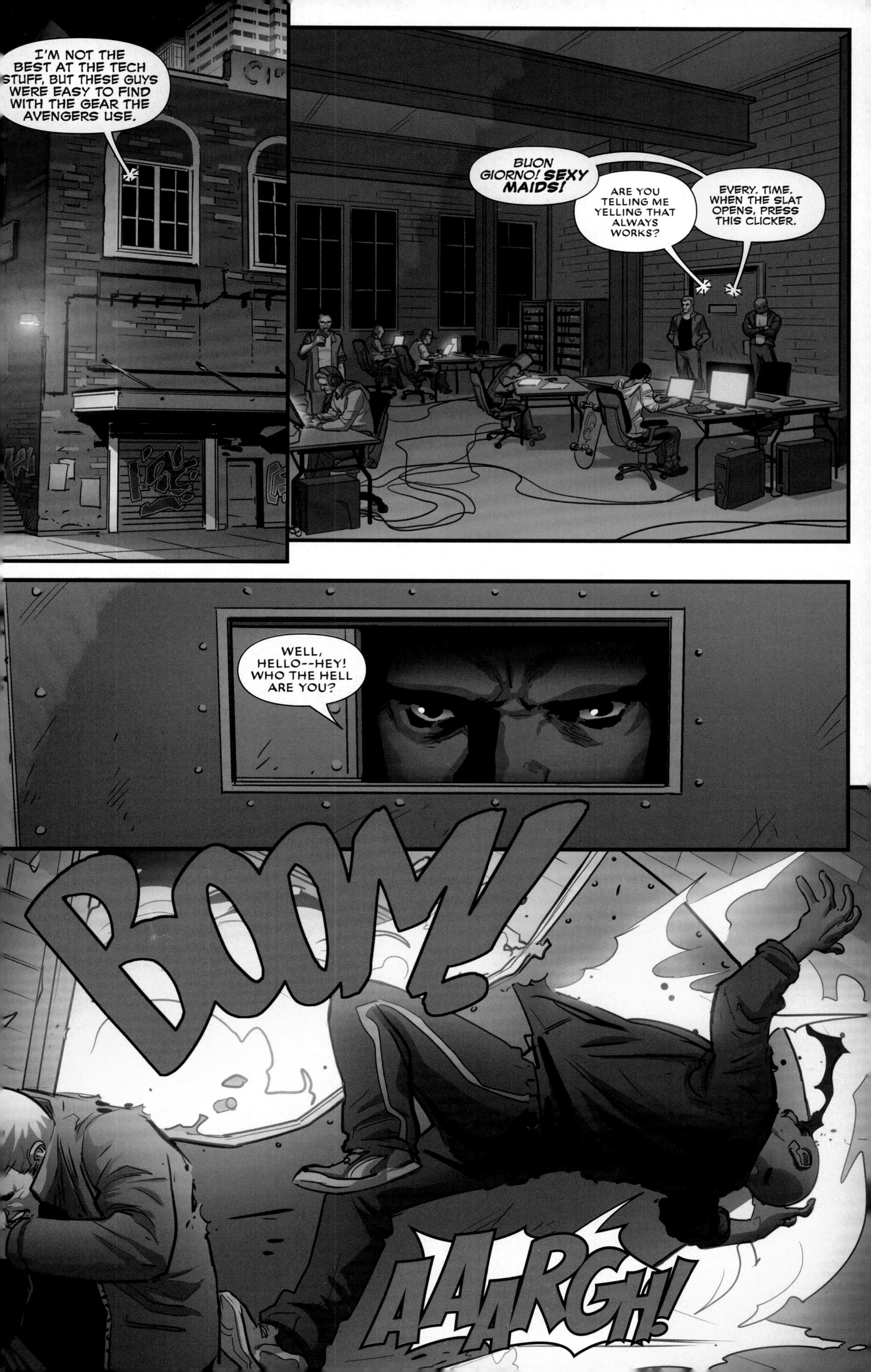
I'M NOT THE BEST AT THE TECH STUFF, BUT THESE GUYS WERE EASY TO FIND WITH THE GEAR THE AVENGERS USE.
BUON GIORNO! **SEXY MAIDS!**
ARE YOU TELLING ME YELLING THAT ALWAYS WORKS?
EVERY. TIME. WHEN THE SLAT OPENS, PRESS THIS CLICKER.
WELL, HELLO--HEY! WHO THE HELL ARE YOU?
BOOM!
AAARGH!

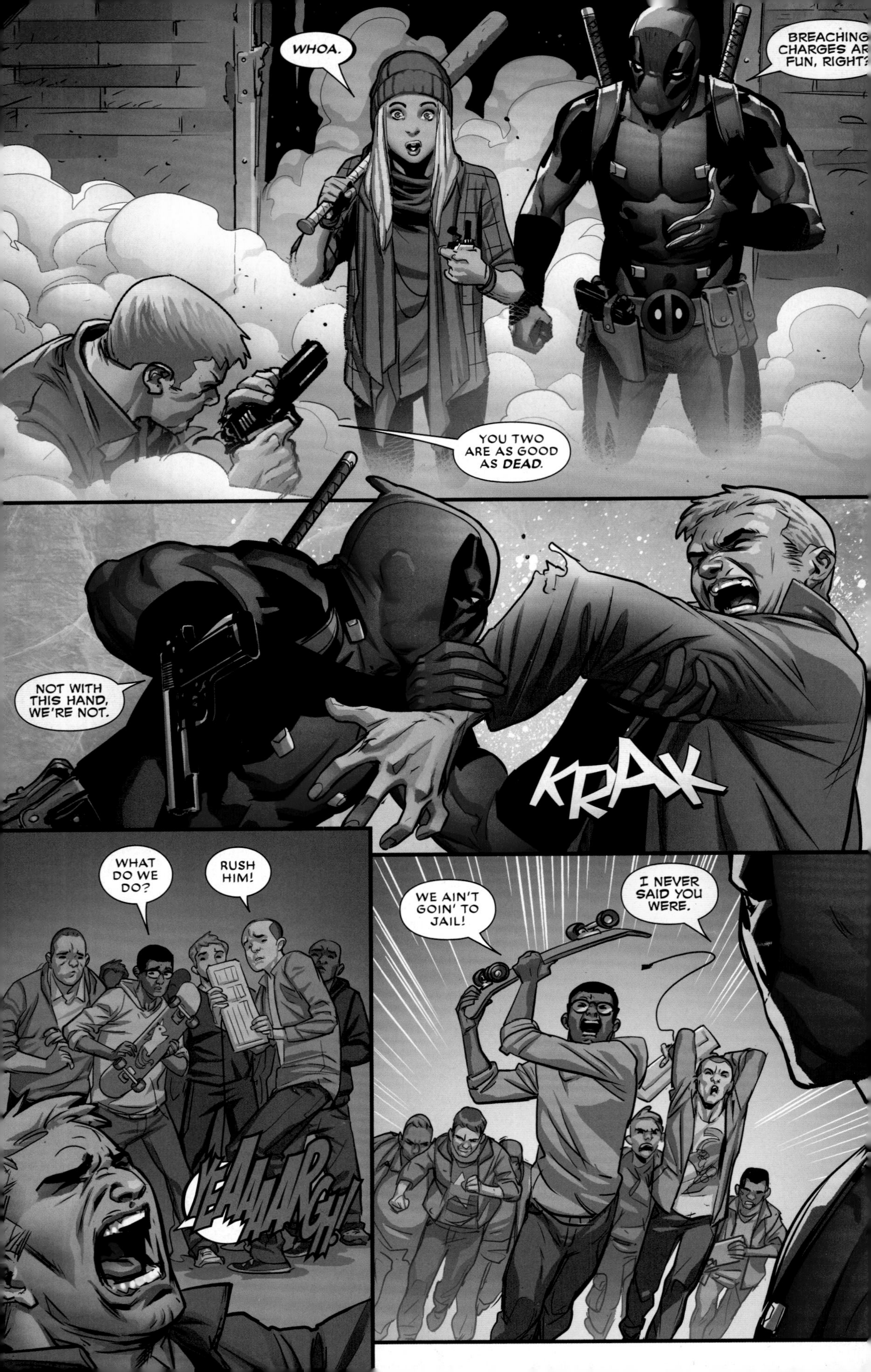
WHOA.
BREACHING CHARGES ARE FUN, RIGHT?
YOU TWO ARE AS GOOD AS *DEAD*.
NOT WITH THIS HAND, WE'RE NOT.
KRAK
WHAT DO WE DO?
RUSH HIM!
YEAAARGH!
WE AIN'T GOIN' TO JAIL!
I NEVER SAID YOU WERE.

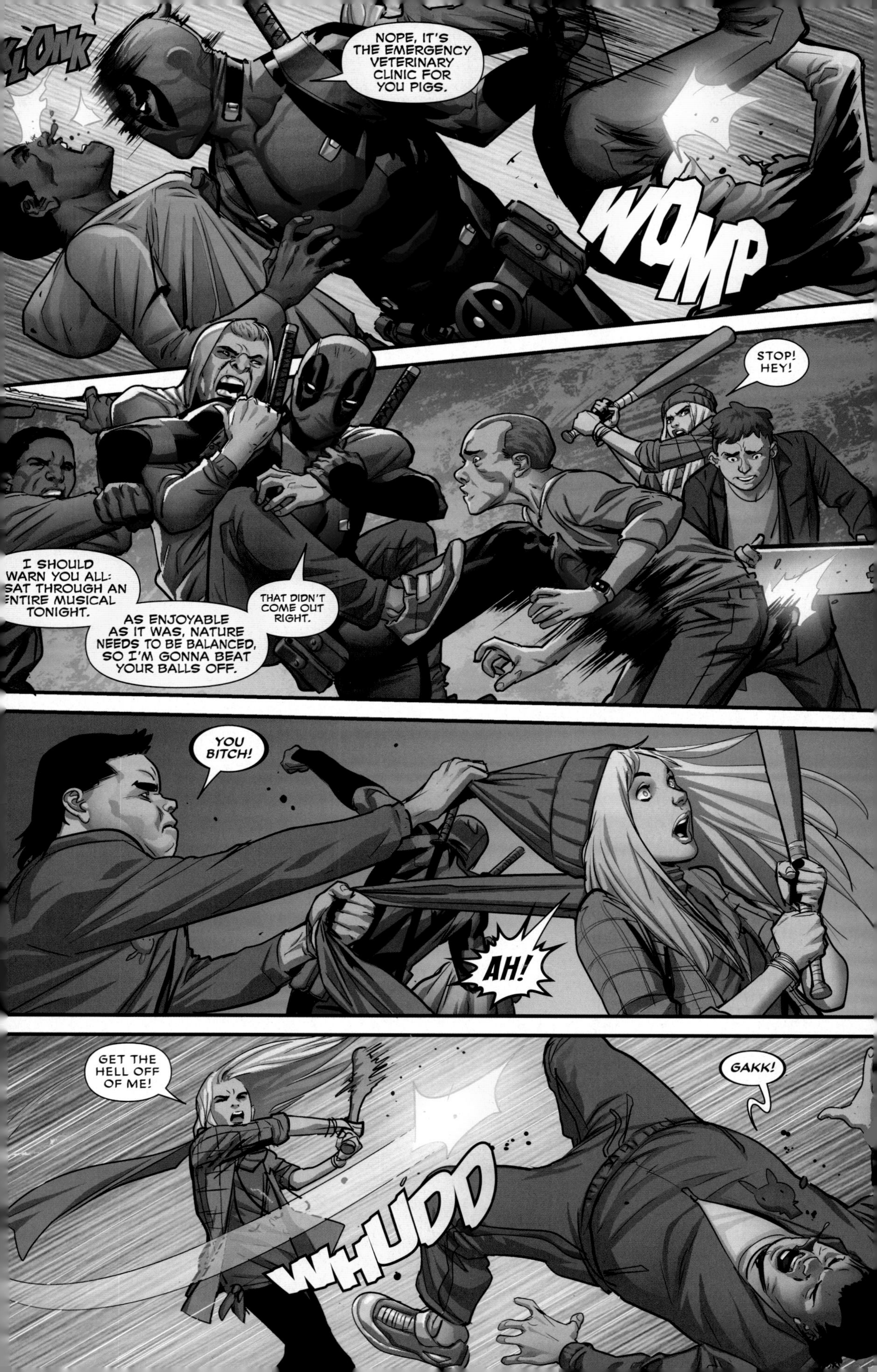
KLONK
NOPE, IT'S THE EMERGENCY VETERINARY CLINIC FOR YOU PIGS.
WOMP
STOP! HEY!
I SHOULD WARN YOU ALL: SAT THROUGH AN ENTIRE MUSICAL TONIGHT.
AS ENJOYABLE AS IT WAS, NATURE NEEDS TO BE BALANCED, SO I'M GONNA BEAT YOUR BALLS OFF.
THAT DIDN'T COME OUT RIGHT.
YOU BITCH!
AH!
GET THE HELL OFF OF ME!
GAKK!
WHUDD

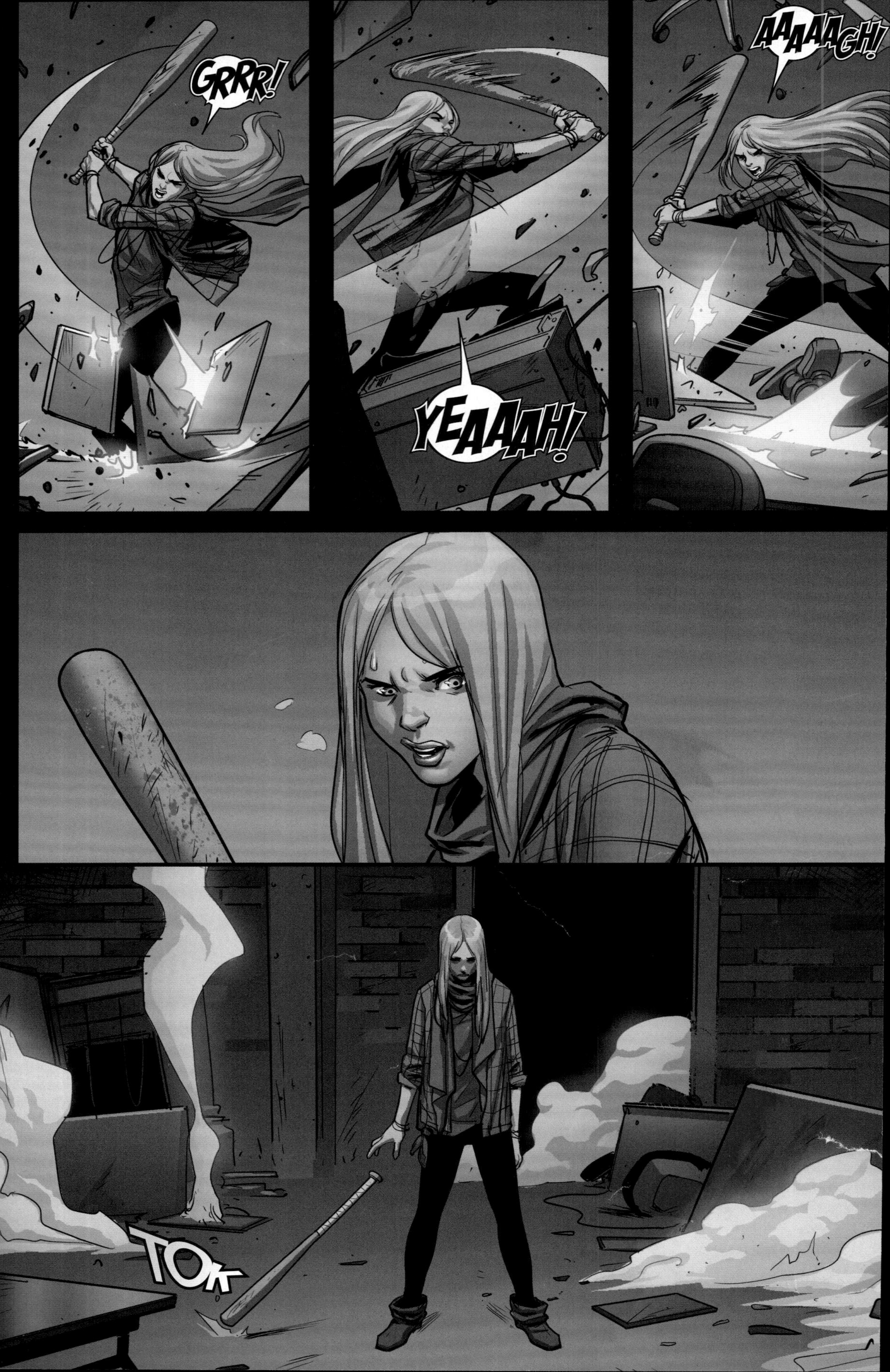
GRRR!
YEAAAH!
AAAAAGH!
TOK

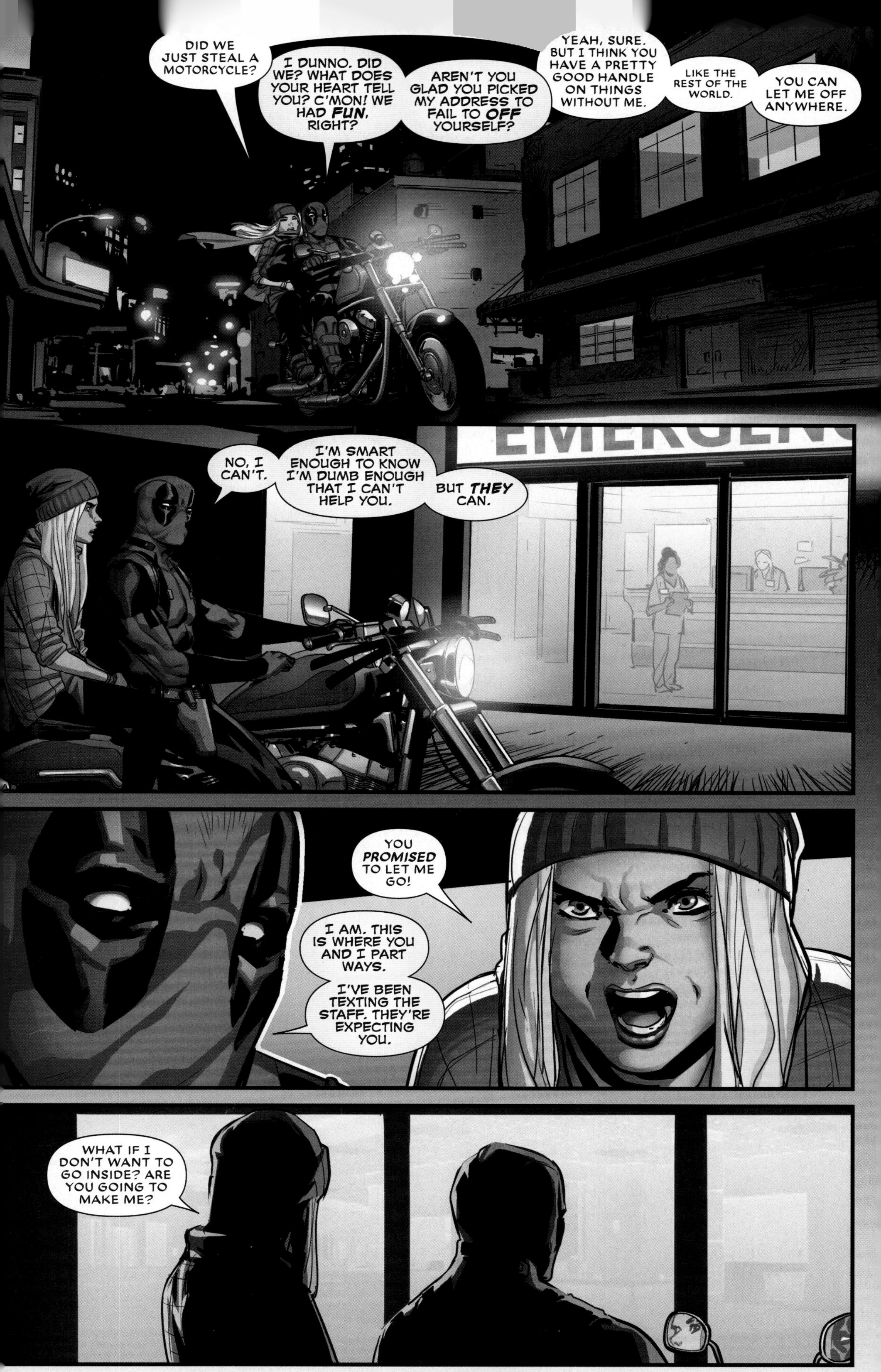
DID WE JUST STEAL A MOTORCYCLE?
I DUNNO. DID WE? WHAT DOES YOUR HEART TELL YOU? C'MON! WE HAD FUN, RIGHT?
AREN'T YOU GLAD YOU PICKED MY ADDRESS TO FAIL TO OFF YOURSELF?
YEAH, SURE. BUT I THINK YOU HAVE A PRETTY GOOD HANDLE ON THINGS WITHOUT ME.
LIKE THE REST OF THE WORLD.
YOU CAN LET ME OFF ANYWHERE.
NO, I CAN'T.
I'M SMART ENOUGH TO KNOW I'M DUMB ENOUGH THAT I CAN'T HELP YOU.
BUT THEY CAN.
YOU PROMISED TO LET ME GO!
I AM. THIS IS WHERE YOU AND I PART WAYS.
I'VE BEEN TEXTING THE STAFF. THEY'RE EXPECTING YOU.
WHAT IF I DON'T WANT TO GO INSIDE? ARE YOU GOING TO MAKE ME?

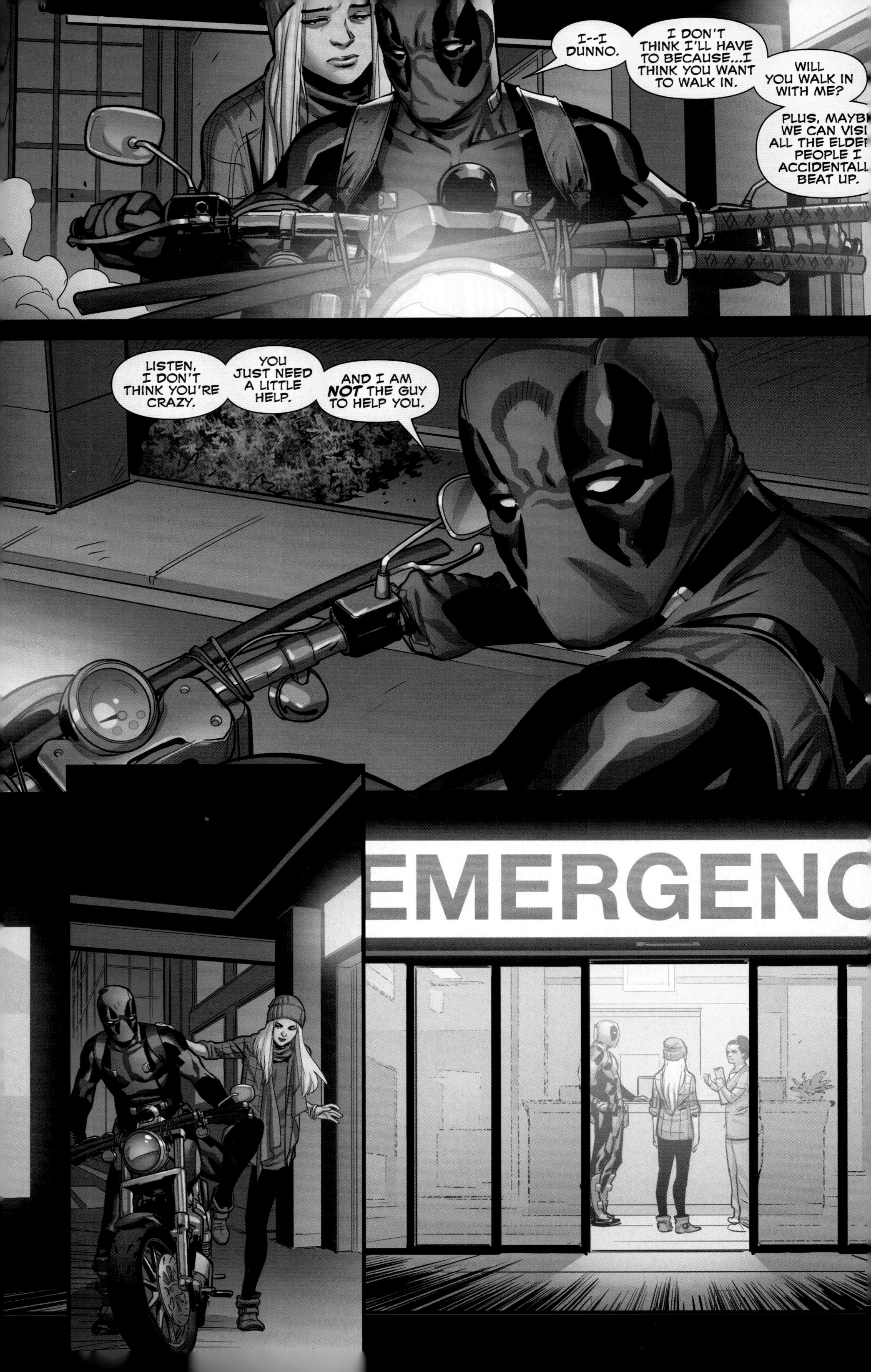
I--I DUNNO.
I DON'T THINK I'LL HAVE TO BECAUSE...I THINK YOU WANT TO WALK IN.
WILL YOU WALK IN WITH ME?
PLUS, MAYB WE CAN VISI ALL THE ELDE PEOPLE I ACCIDENTALL BEAT UP.
LISTEN, I DON'T THINK YOU'RE CRAZY.
YOU JUST NEED A LITTLE HELP.
AND I AM **NOT** THE GUY TO HELP YOU.
EMERGENC

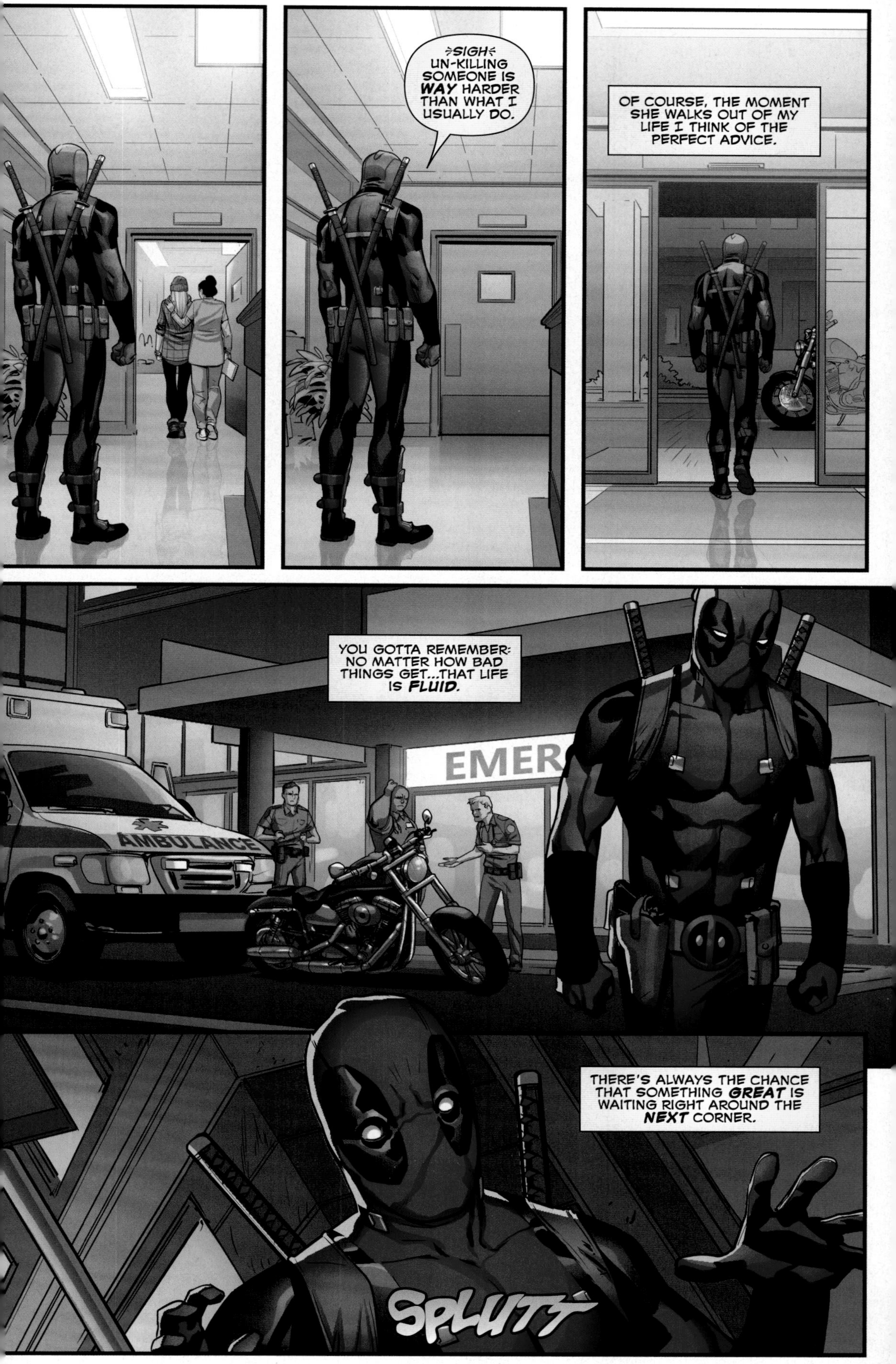

SIGH UN-KILLING SOMEONE IS WAY HARDER THAN WHAT I USUALLY DO.
OF COURSE, THE MOMENT SHE WALKS OUT OF MY LIFE I THINK OF THE PERFECT ADVICE.
YOU GOTTA REMEMBER: NO MATTER HOW BAD THINGS GET...THAT LIFE IS FLUID.
EMER
AMBULANCE
THERE'S ALWAYS THE CHANCE THAT SOMETHING GREAT IS WAITING RIGHT AROUND THE NEXT CORNER.
SPLUTT

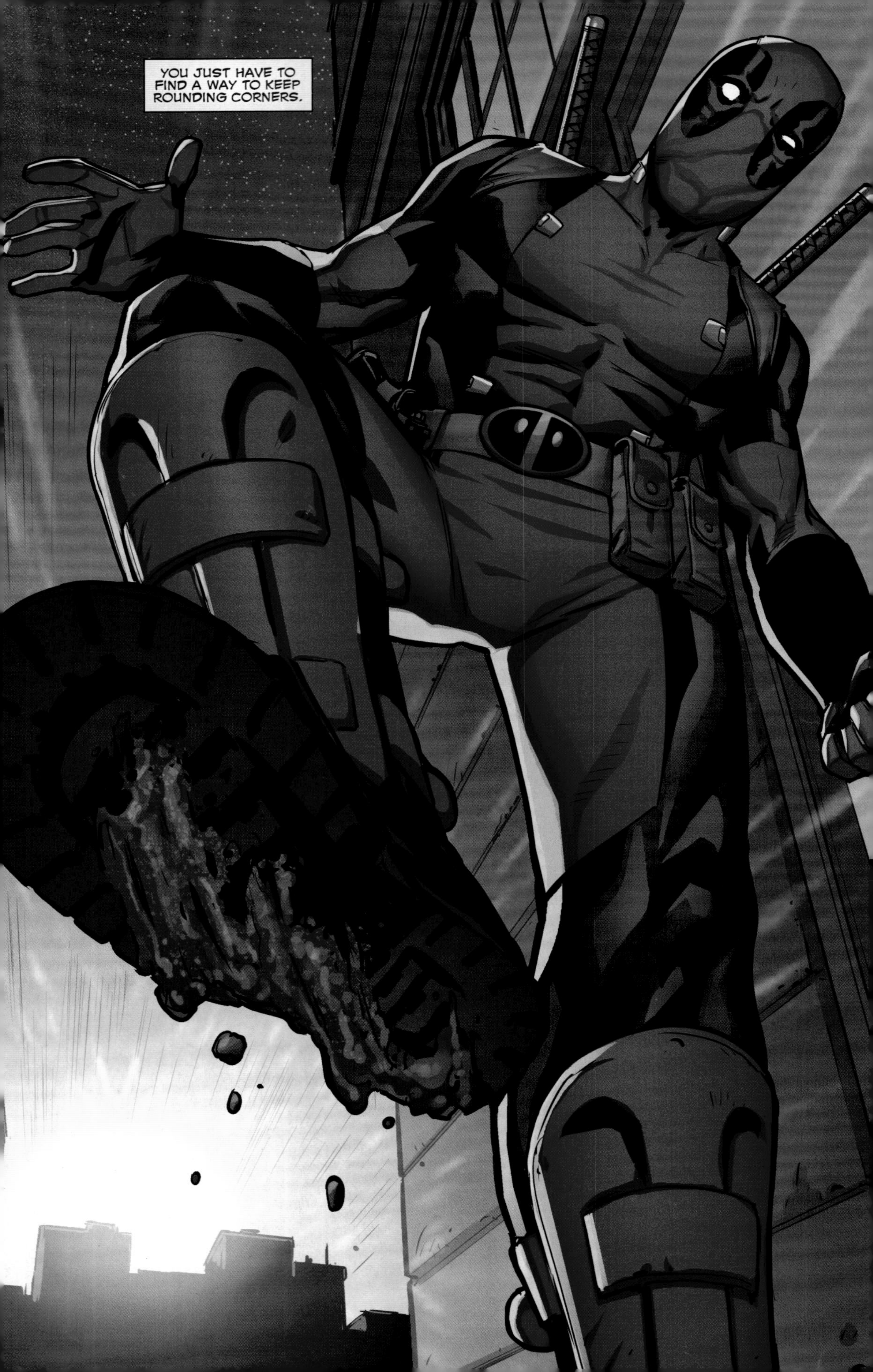
YOU JUST HAVE TO FIND A WAY TO KEEP ROUNDING CORNERS.

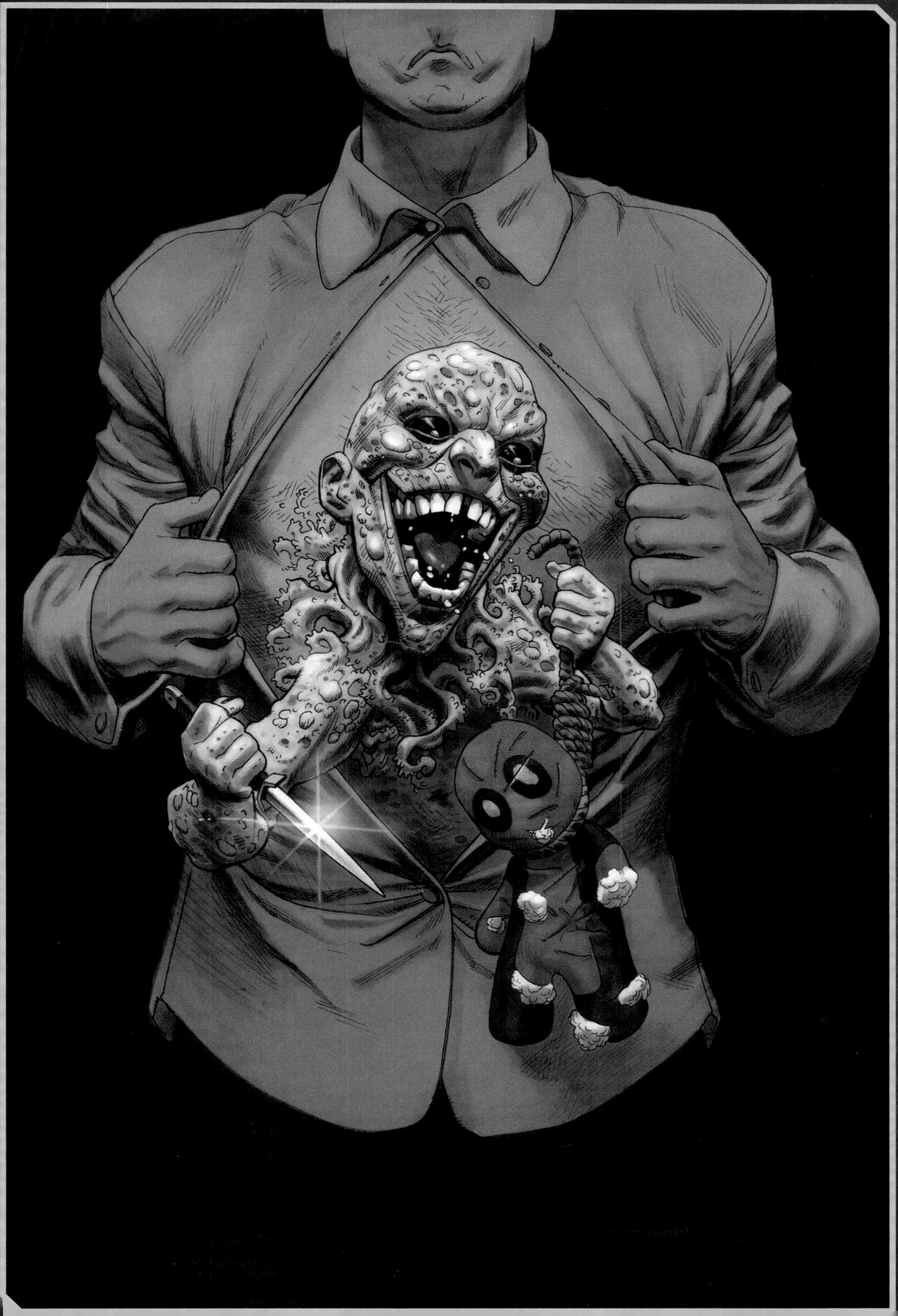

Avenger...Assassin...Superstar...Smelly person...Possibly the world's most skilled mercenary, definitel the world's most annoying, Wade Wilson was chosen for a top-secret government program that gav him a healing factor allowing him to heal from any wound. Somehow, despite making his money as gun for hire, Wade has become one of the most beloved "heroes" in the world. Call him the Merc wit the Mouth...call him the Regeneratin' Degenerate...call him...

DEADPOOL

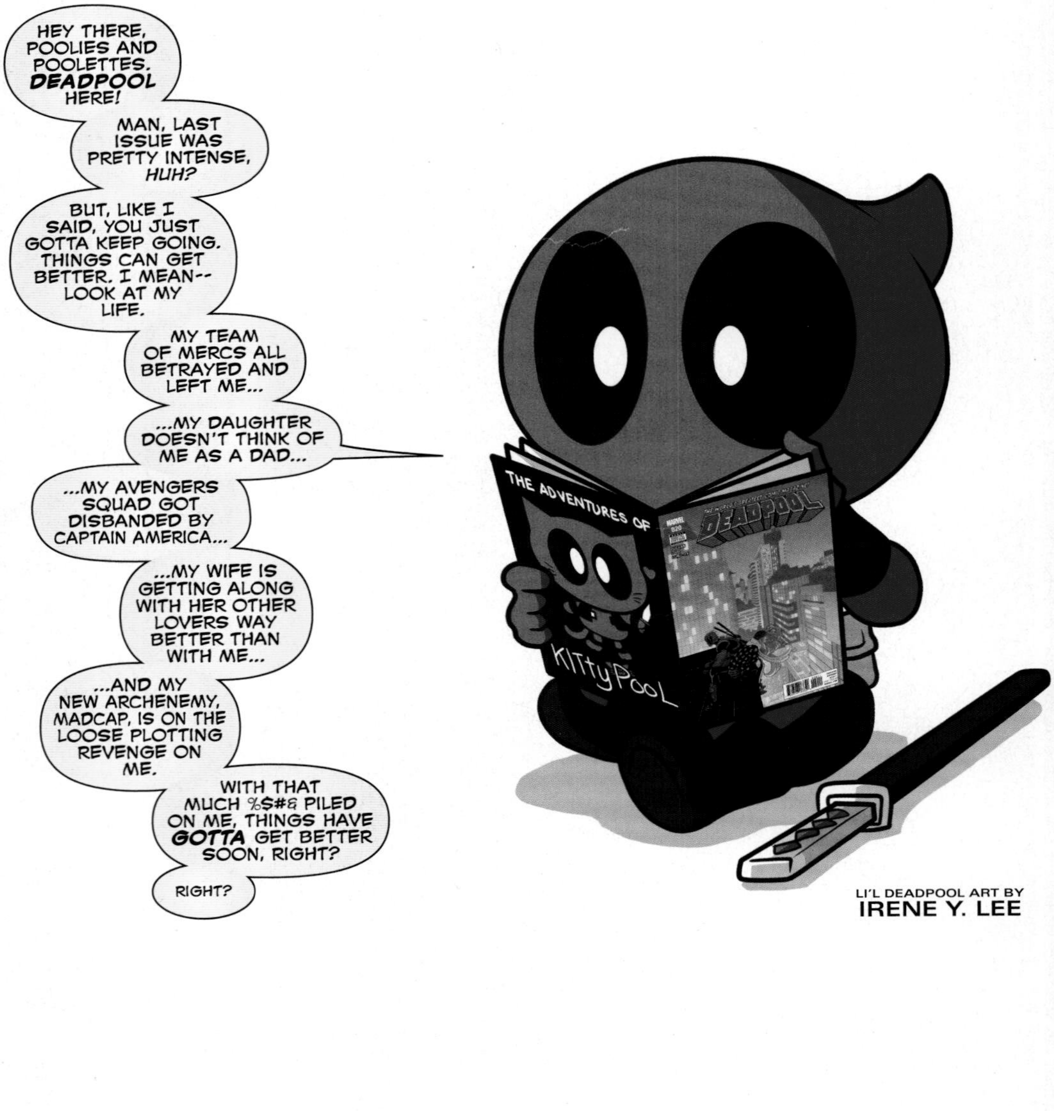

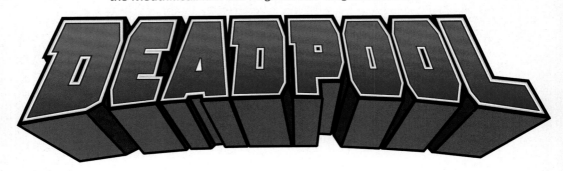

HEY THERE, POOLIES AND POOLETTES. DEADPOOL HERE!
MAN, LAST ISSUE WAS PRETTY INTENSE, HUH?
BUT, LIKE I SAID, YOU JUST GOTTA KEEP GOING. THINGS CAN GET BETTER. I MEAN-- LOOK AT MY LIFE.
MY TEAM OF MERCS ALL BETRAYED AND LEFT ME...
...MY DAUGHTER DOESN'T THINK OF ME AS A DAD...
...MY AVENGERS SQUAD GOT DISBANDED BY CAPTAIN AMERICA...
...MY WIFE IS GETTING ALONG WITH HER OTHER LOVERS WAY BETTER THAN WITH ME...
...AND MY NEW ARCHENEMY, MADCAP, IS ON THE LOOSE PLOTTING REVENGE ON ME.
WITH THAT MUCH %$#& PILED ON ME, THINGS HAVE GOTTA GET BETTER SOON, RIGHT?
RIGHT?
THE ADVENTURES OF
KITtyPooL
DEADPOOL

LI'L DEADPOOL ART BY
IRENE Y. LEE

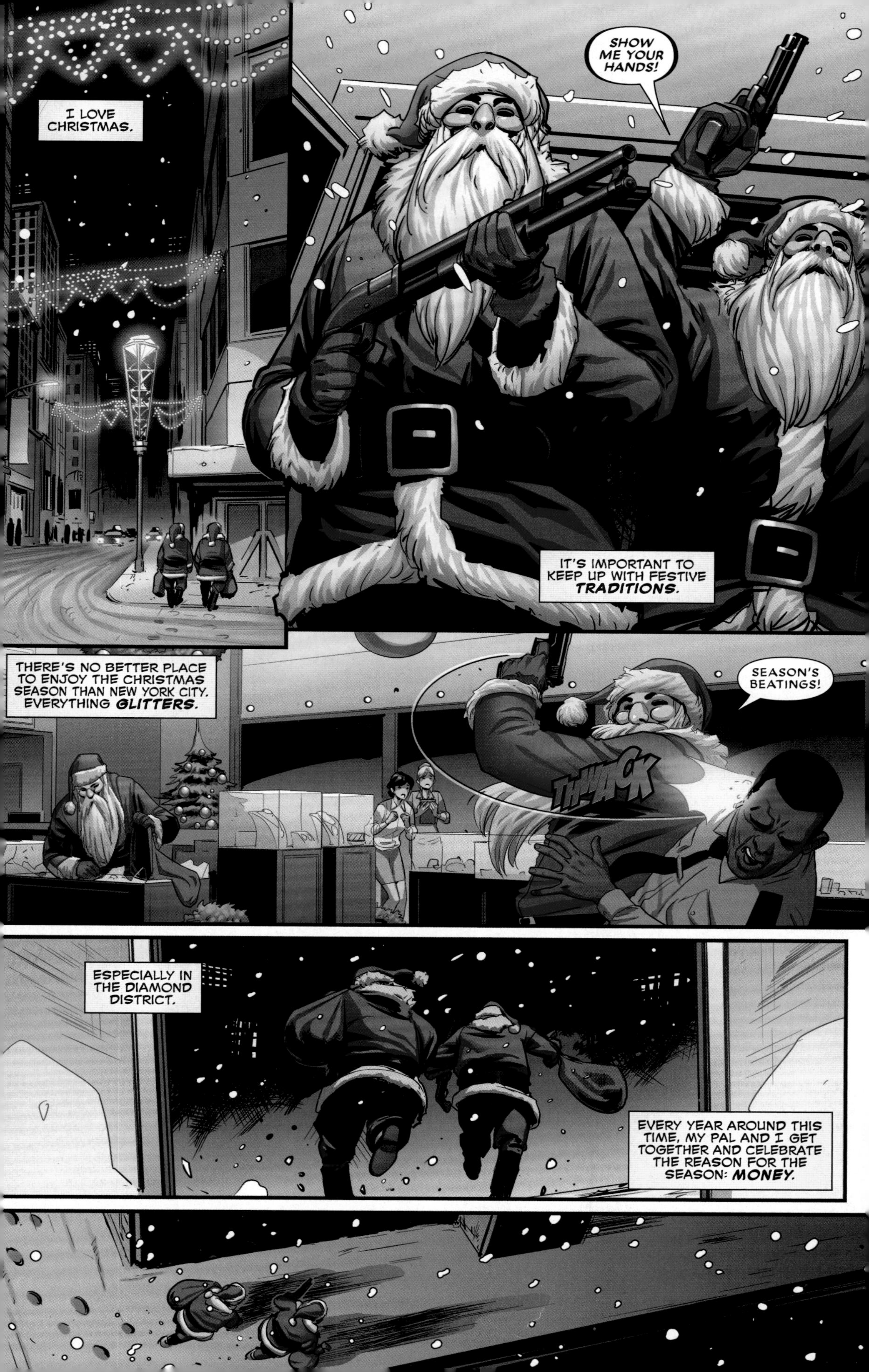
I LOVE CHRISTMAS.
SHOW ME YOUR HANDS!
IT'S IMPORTANT TO KEEP UP WITH FESTIVE TRADITIONS.
THERE'S NO BETTER PLACE TO ENJOY THE CHRISTMAS SEASON THAN NEW YORK CITY. EVERYTHING GLITTERS.
SEASON'S BEATINGS!
THWACK
ESPECIALLY IN THE DIAMOND DISTRICT.
EVERY YEAR AROUND THIS TIME, MY PAL AND I GET TOGETHER AND CELEBRATE THE REASON FOR THE SEASON: MONEY.

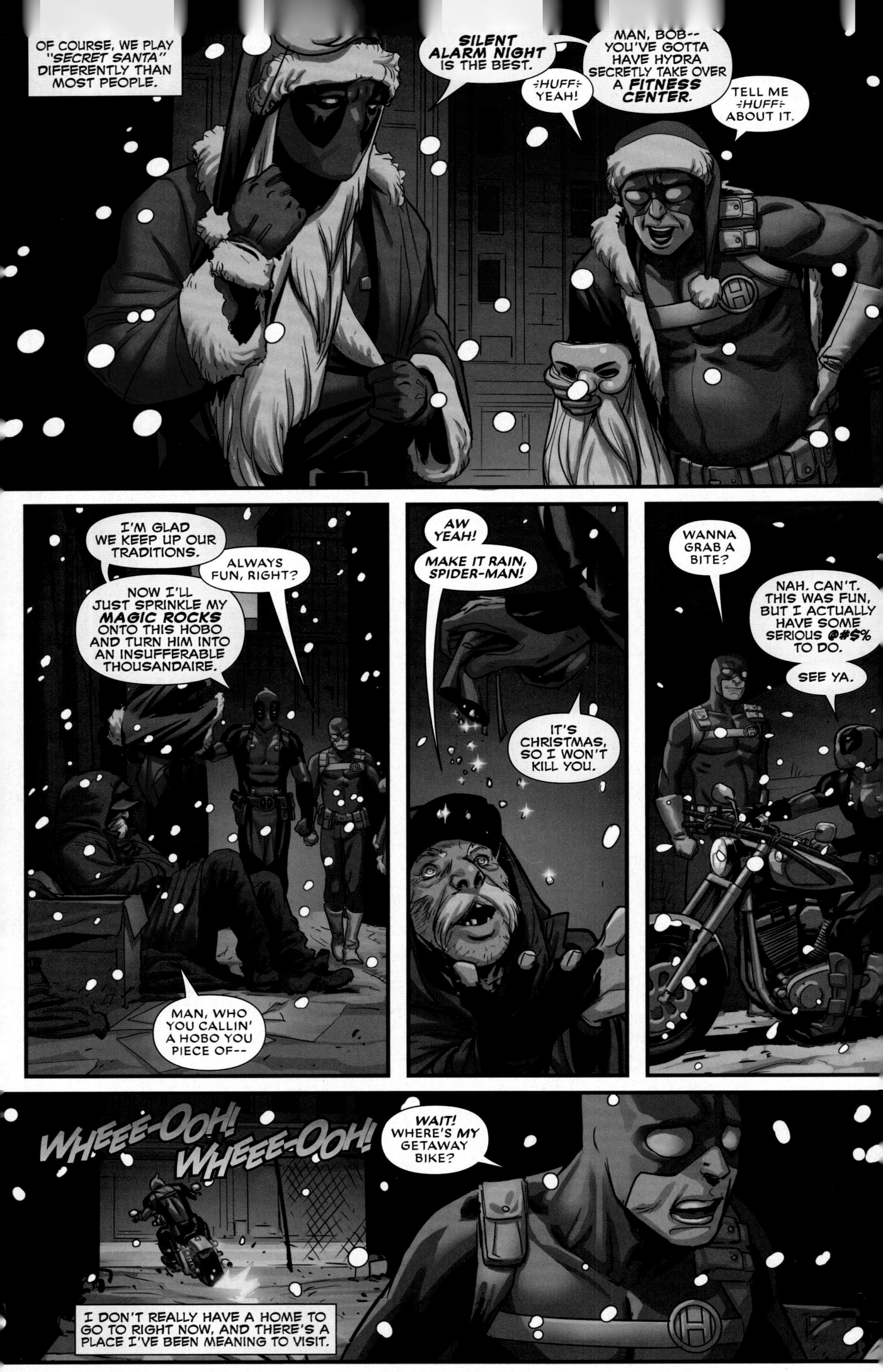

OF COURSE, WE PLAY "SECRET SANTA" DIFFERENTLY THAN MOST PEOPLE.
SILENT ALARM NIGHT IS THE BEST.
HUFF YEAH!
MAN, BOB-- YOU'VE GOTTA HAVE HYDRA SECRETLY TAKE OVER A FITNESS CENTER.
TELL ME *HUFF* ABOUT IT.
I'M GLAD WE KEEP UP OUR TRADITIONS.
ALWAYS FUN, RIGHT?
NOW I'LL JUST SPRINKLE MY MAGIC ROCKS ONTO THIS HOBO AND TURN HIM INTO AN INSUFFERABLE THOUSANDAIRE.
MAN, WHO YOU CALLIN' A HOBO YOU PIECE OF--
AW YEAH!
MAKE IT RAIN, SPIDER-MAN!
IT'S CHRISTMAS, SO I WON'T KILL YOU.
WANNA GRAB A BITE?
NAH. CAN'T. THIS WAS FUN, BUT I ACTUALLY HAVE SOME SERIOUS @#$% TO DO.
SEE YA.
WHEEE-OOH! WHEEE-OOH!
WAIT! WHERE'S MY GETAWAY BIKE?
I DON'T REALLY HAVE A HOME TO GO TO RIGHT NOW, AND THERE'S A PLACE I'VE BEEN MEANING TO VISIT.

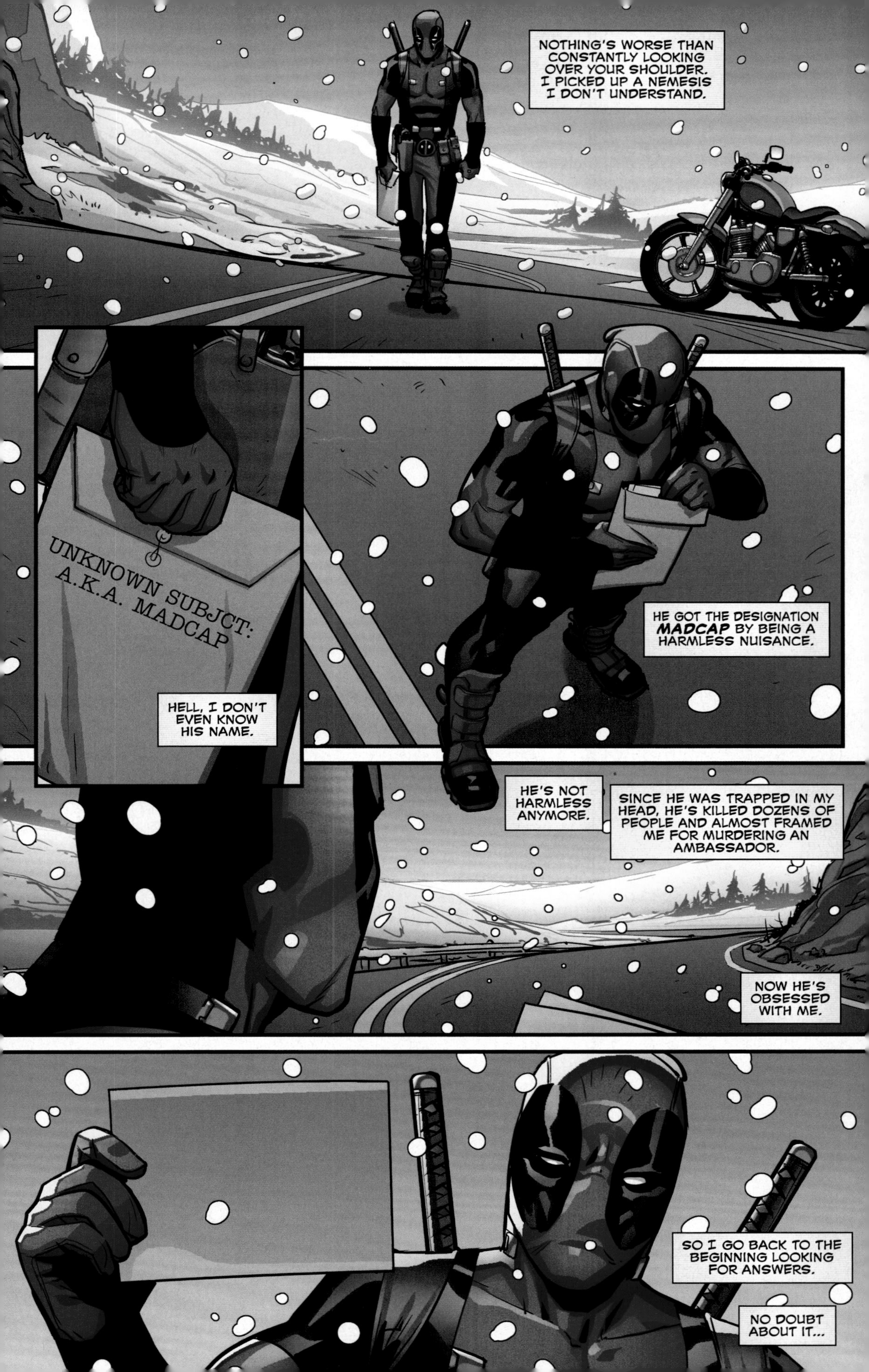
NOTHING'S WORSE THAN CONSTANTLY LOOKING OVER YOUR SHOULDER. I PICKED UP A NEMESIS I DON'T UNDERSTAND.
UNKNOWN SUBJCT: A.K.A. MADCAP
HELL, I DON'T EVEN KNOW HIS NAME.
HE GOT THE DESIGNATION MADCAP BY BEING A HARMLESS NUISANCE.
HE'S NOT HARMLESS ANYMORE.
SINCE HE WAS TRAPPED IN MY HEAD, HE'S KILLED DOZENS OF PEOPLE AND ALMOST FRAMED ME FOR MURDERING AN AMBASSADOR.
NOW HE'S OBSESSED WITH ME.
SO I GO BACK TO THE BEGINNING LOOKING FOR ANSWERS.
NO DOUBT ABOUT IT...

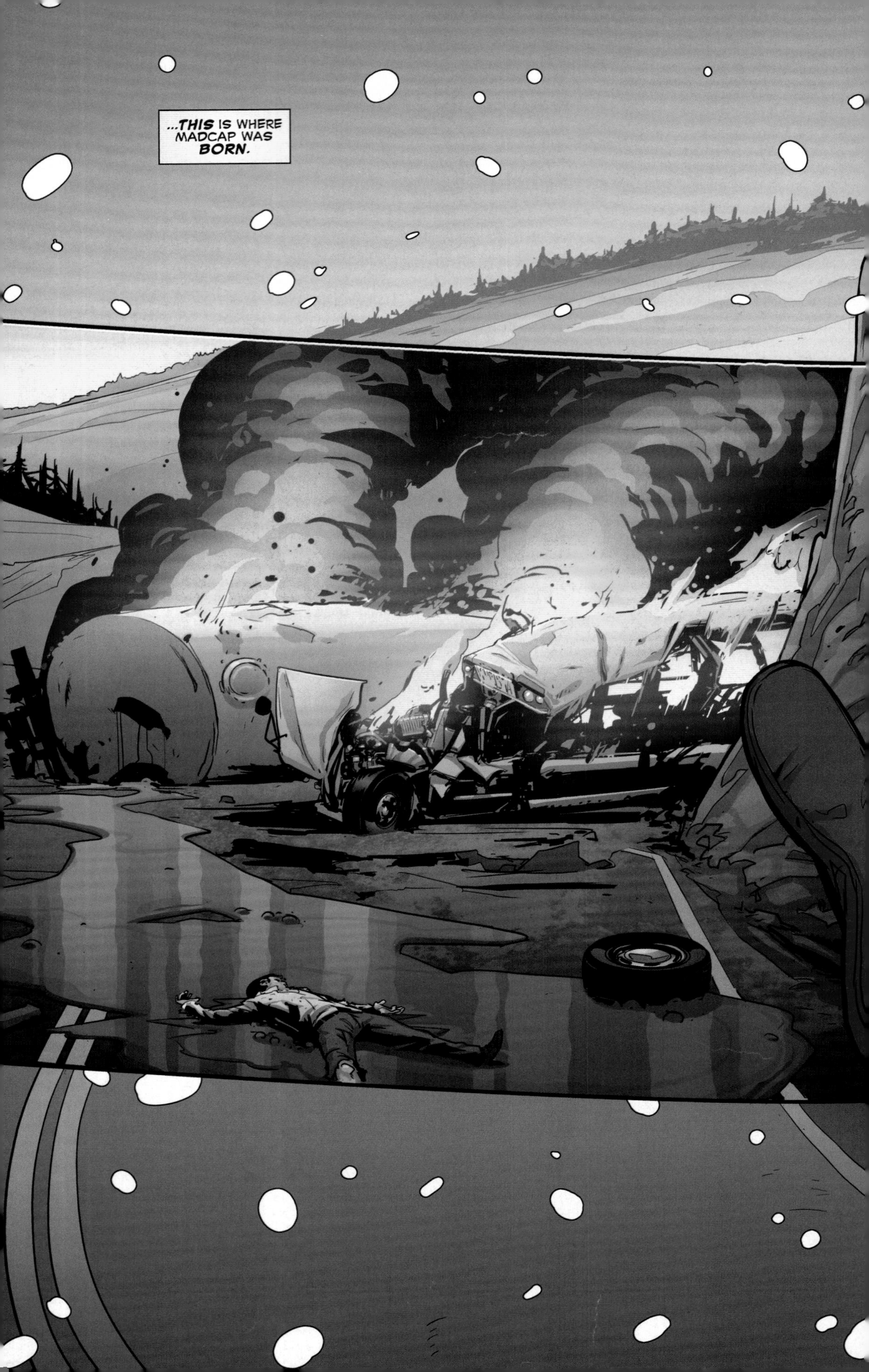
...THIS IS WHERE MADCAP WAS BORN.

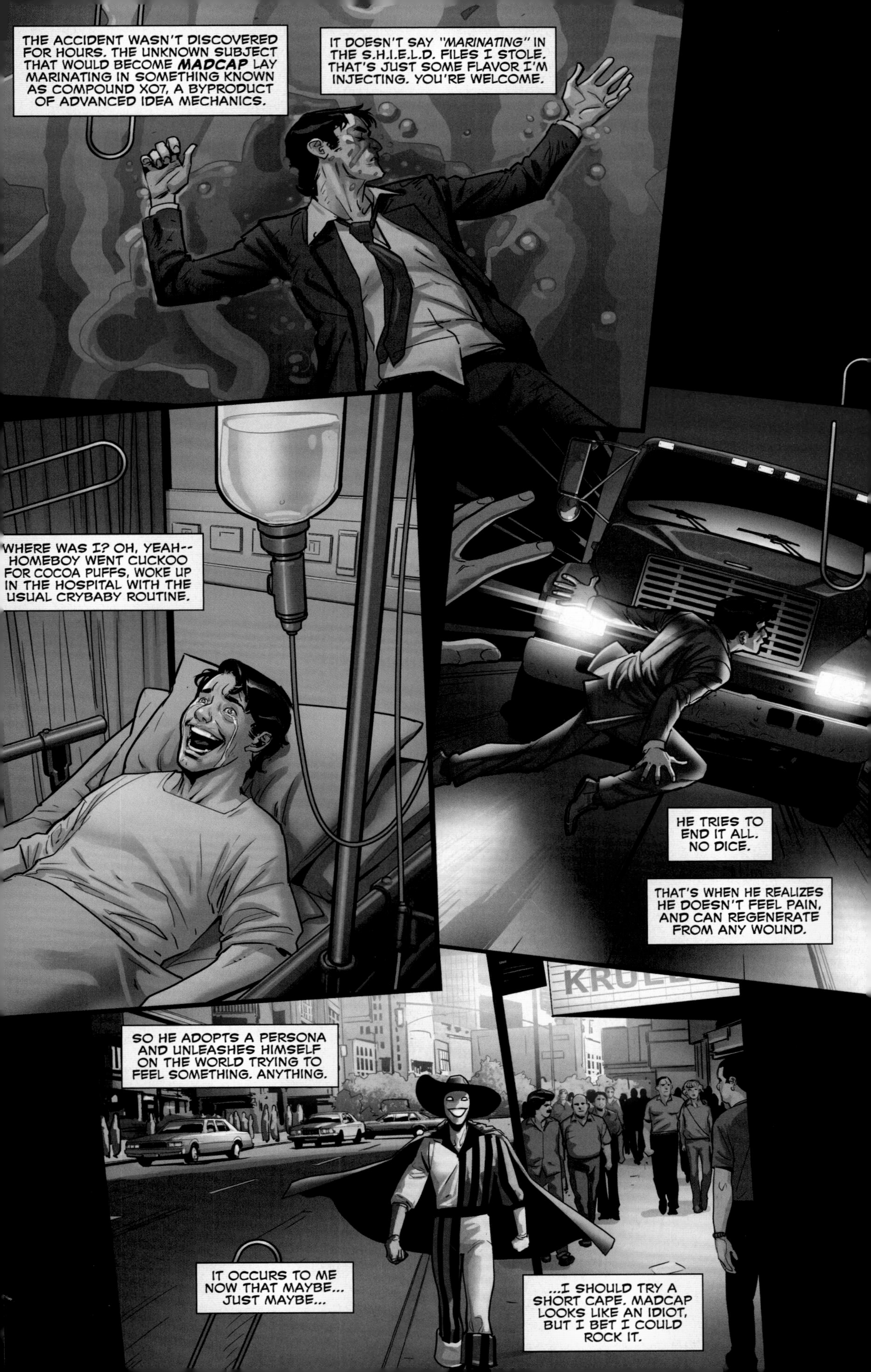
THE ACCIDENT WASN'T DISCOVERED FOR HOURS. THE UNKNOWN SUBJECT THAT WOULD BECOME MADCAP LAY MARINATING IN SOMETHING KNOWN AS COMPOUND XO7, A BYPRODUCT OF ADVANCED IDEA MECHANICS.
IT DOESN'T SAY "MARINATING" IN THE S.H.I.E.L.D. FILES I STOLE. THAT'S JUST SOME FLAVOR I'M INJECTING. YOU'RE WELCOME.
WHERE WAS I? OH, YEAH-- HOMEBOY WENT CUCKOO FOR COCOA PUFFS, WOKE UP IN THE HOSPITAL WITH THE USUAL CRYBABY ROUTINE.
HE TRIES TO END IT ALL. NO DICE.
THAT'S WHEN HE REALIZES HE DOESN'T FEEL PAIN, AND CAN REGENERATE FROM ANY WOUND.
KRULL
SO HE ADOPTS A PERSONA AND UNLEASHES HIMSELF ON THE WORLD TRYING TO FEEL SOMETHING. ANYTHING.
IT OCCURS TO ME NOW THAT MAYBE... JUST MAYBE...
...I SHOULD TRY A SHORT CAPE. MADCAP LOOKS LIKE AN IDIOT, BUT I BET I COULD ROCK IT.

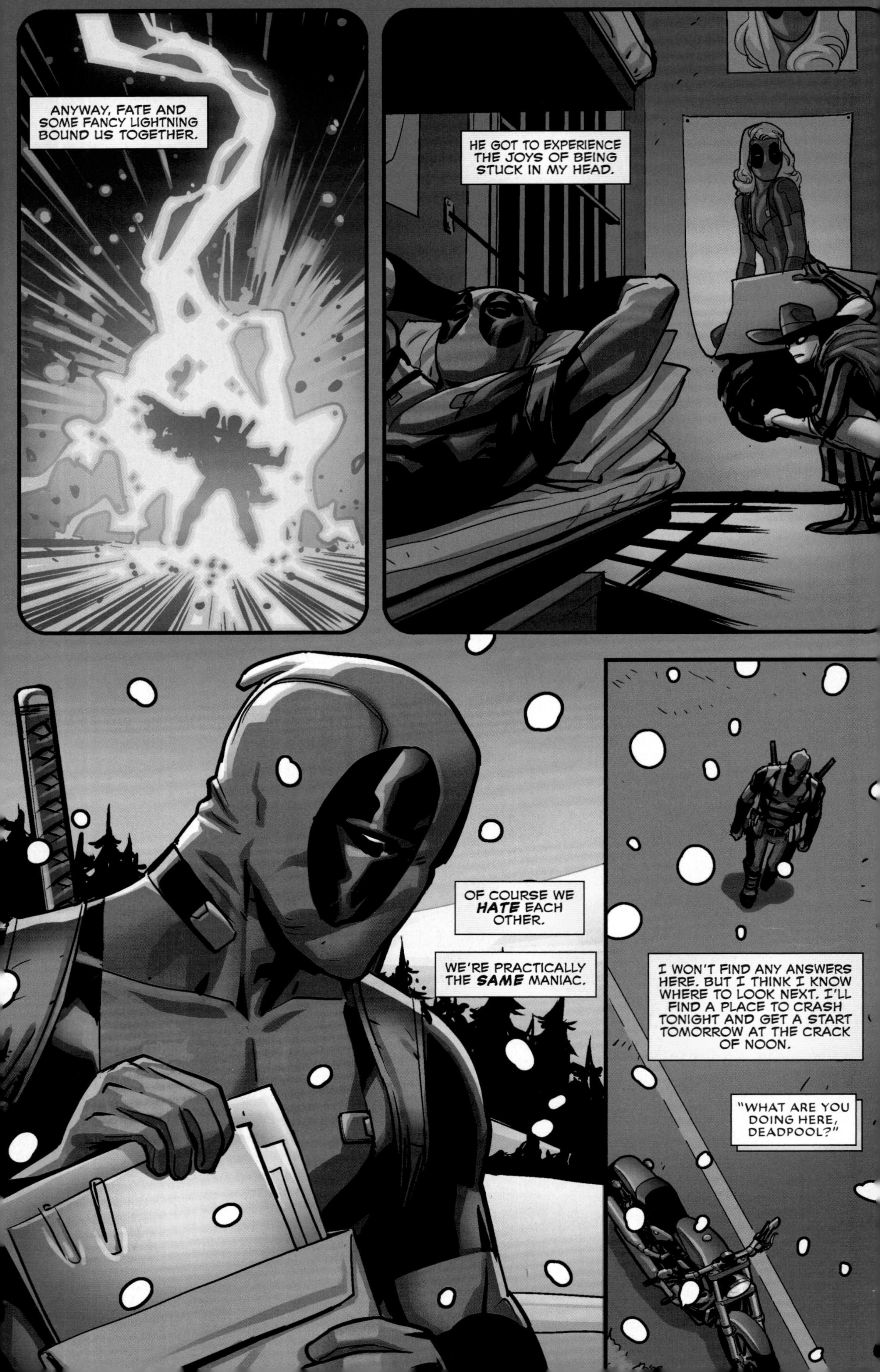
ANYWAY, FATE AND SOME FANCY LIGHTNING BOUND US TOGETHER.
HE GOT TO EXPERIENCE THE JOYS OF BEING STUCK IN MY HEAD.
OF COURSE WE *HATE* EACH OTHER.
WE'RE PRACTICALLY THE *SAME* MANIAC.
I WON'T FIND ANY ANSWERS HERE. BUT I THINK I KNOW WHERE TO LOOK NEXT. I'LL FIND A PLACE TO CRASH TONIGHT AND GET A START TOMORROW AT THE CRACK OF NOON.
"WHAT ARE YOU DOING HERE, DEADPOOL?"

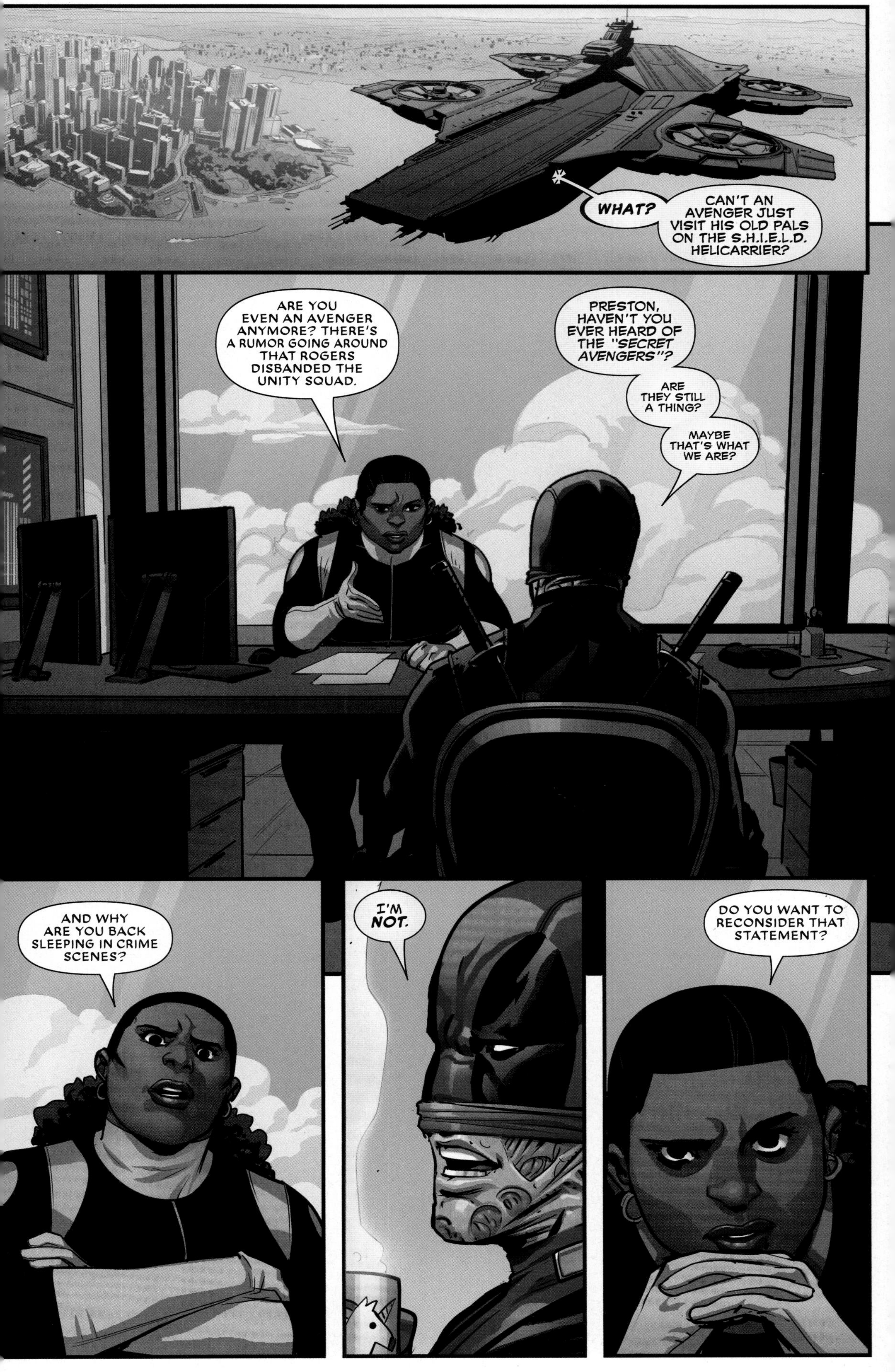
WHAT?
CAN'T AN AVENGER JUST VISIT HIS OLD PALS ON THE S.H.I.E.L.D. HELICARRIER?
ARE YOU EVEN AN AVENGER ANYMORE? THERE'S A RUMOR GOING AROUND THAT ROGERS DISBANDED THE UNITY SQUAD.
PRESTON, HAVEN'T YOU EVER HEARD OF THE "SECRET AVENGERS"?
ARE THEY STILL A THING?
MAYBE THAT'S WHAT WE ARE?
AND WHY ARE YOU BACK SLEEPING IN CRIME SCENES?
I'M NOT.
DO YOU WANT TO RECONSIDER THAT STATEMENT?

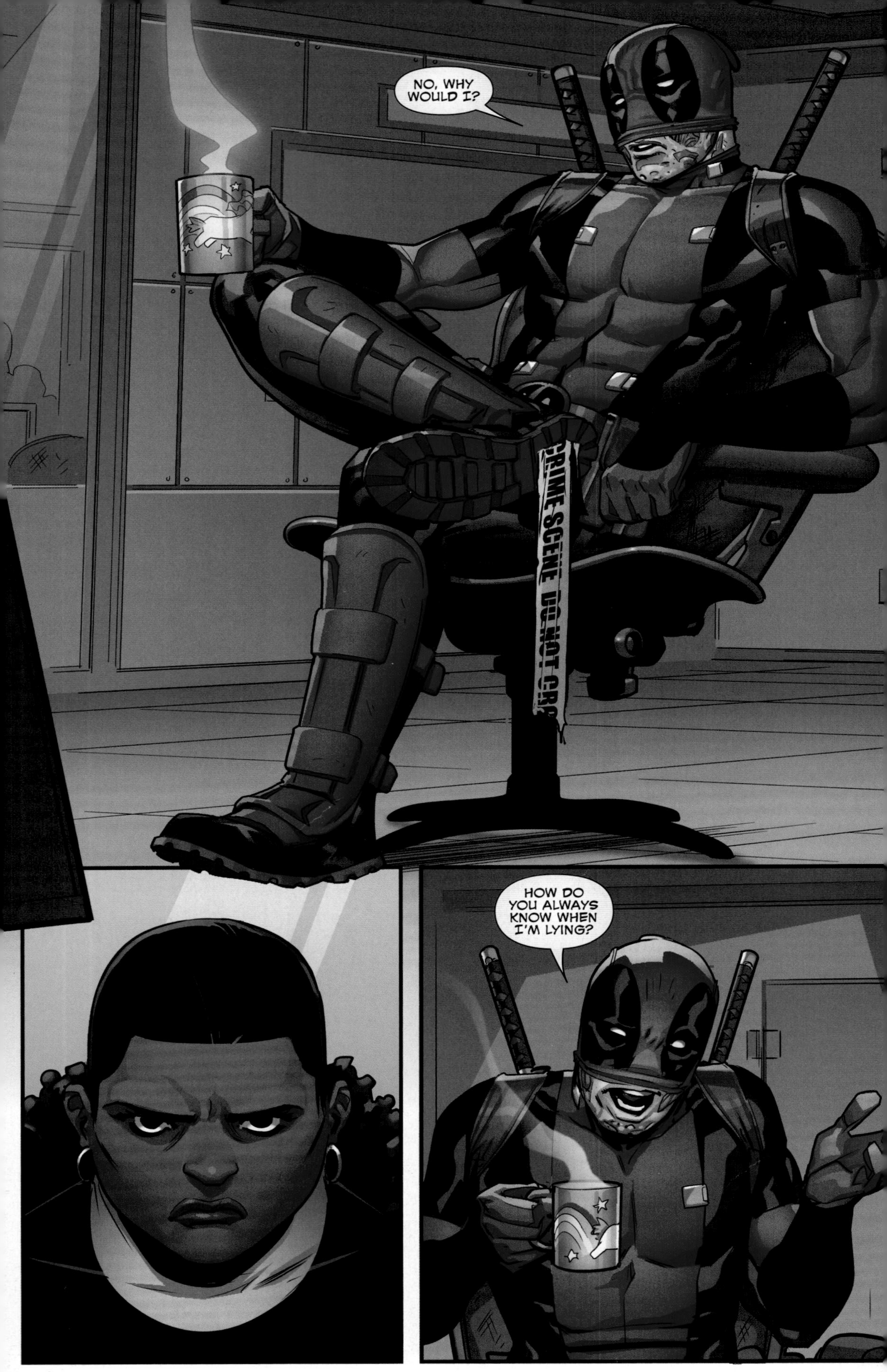
NO, WHY WOULD I?
CRIME SCENE DO NOT CR
HOW DO YOU ALWAYS KNOW WHEN I'M LYING?

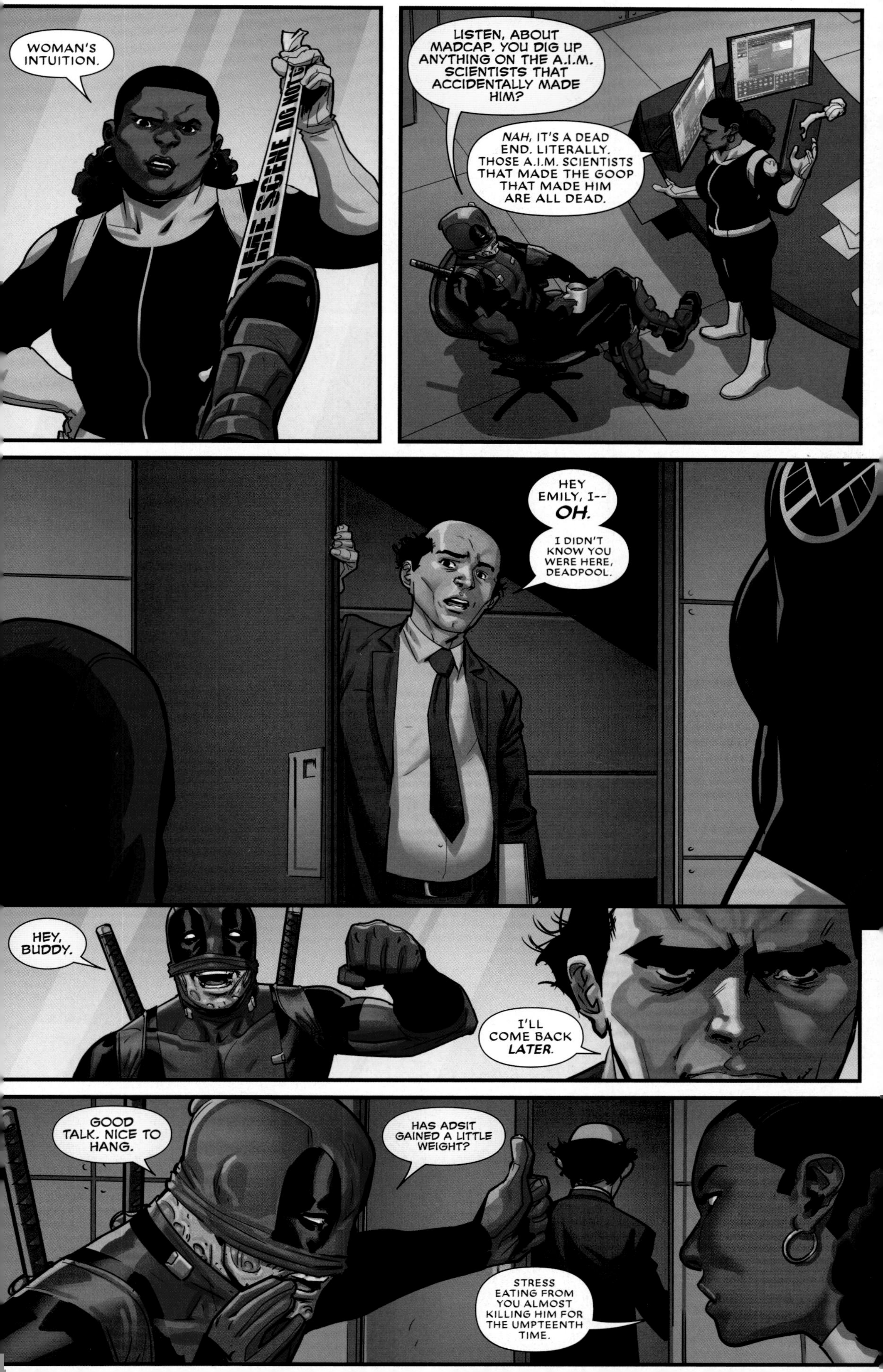
WOMAN'S INTUITION.
CRIME SCENE DO NOT
LISTEN, ABOUT MADCAP. YOU DIG UP ANYTHING ON THE A.I.M. SCIENTISTS THAT ACCIDENTALLY MADE HIM?
NAH, IT'S A DEAD END. LITERALLY. THOSE A.I.M. SCIENTISTS THAT MADE THE GOOP THAT MADE HIM ARE ALL DEAD.
HEY EMILY, I-- OH.
I DIDN'T KNOW YOU WERE HERE, DEADPOOL.
HEY, BUDDY.
I'LL COME BACK LATER.
GOOD TALK. NICE TO HANG.
HAS ADSIT GAINED A LITTLE WEIGHT?
STRESS EATING FROM YOU ALMOST KILLING HIM FOR THE UMPTEENTH TIME.

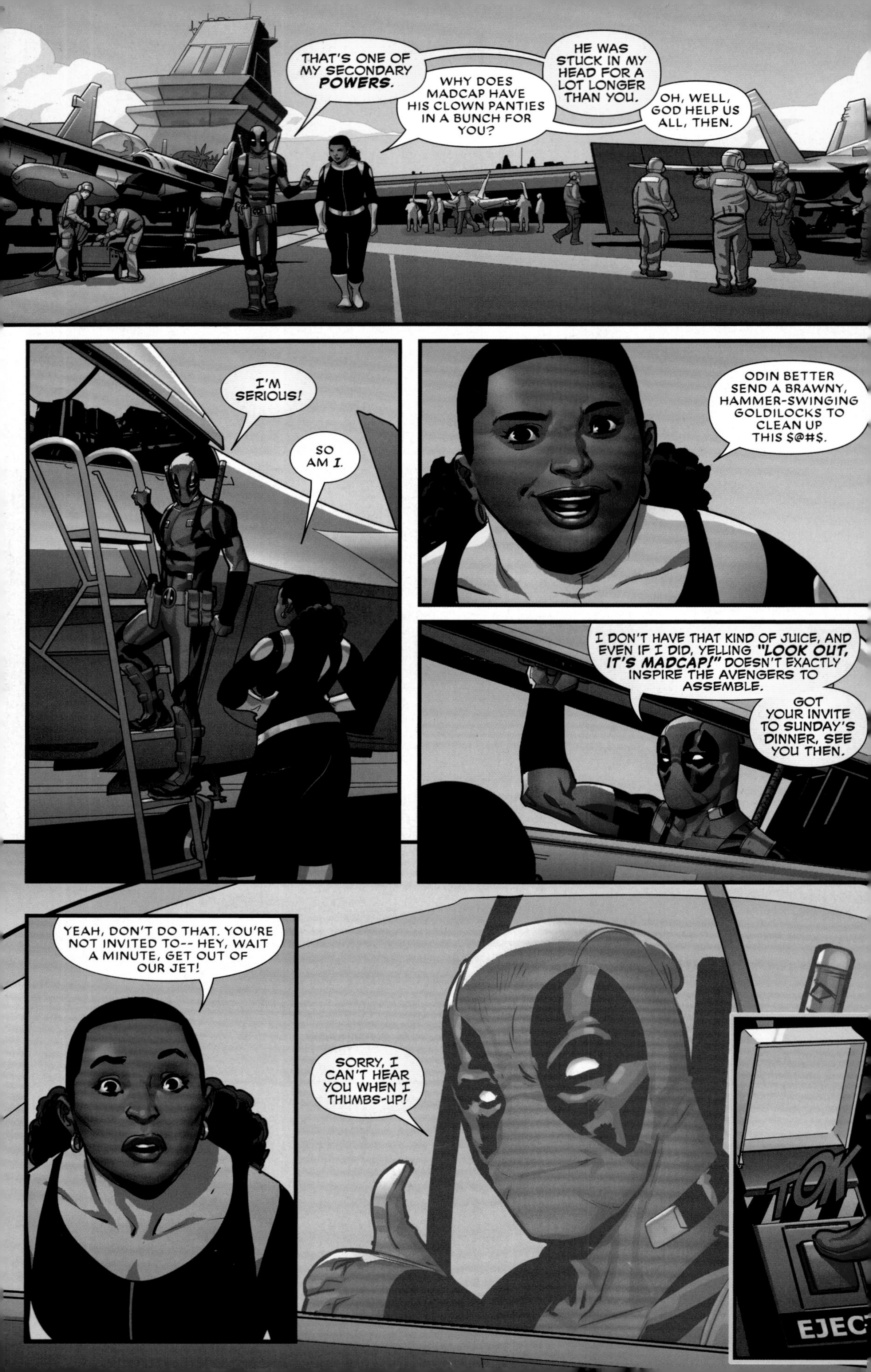
THAT'S ONE OF MY SECONDARY POWERS.
WHY DOES MADCAP HAVE HIS CLOWN PANTIES IN A BUNCH FOR YOU?
HE WAS STUCK IN MY HEAD FOR A LOT LONGER THAN YOU.
OH, WELL, GOD HELP US ALL, THEN.
I'M SERIOUS!
SO AM I.
ODIN BETTER SEND A BRAWNY, HAMMER-SWINGING GOLDILOCKS TO CLEAN UP THIS $@#$.
I DON'T HAVE THAT KIND OF JUICE, AND EVEN IF I DID, YELLING "LOOK OUT, IT'S MADCAP!" DOESN'T EXACTLY INSPIRE THE AVENGERS TO ASSEMBLE.
GOT YOUR INVITE TO SUNDAY'S DINNER, SEE YOU THEN.
YEAH, DON'T DO THAT. YOU'RE NOT INVITED TO-- HEY, WAIT A MINUTE, GET OUT OF OUR JET!
SORRY, I CAN'T HEAR YOU WHEN I THUMBS-UP!
TOK
EJEC

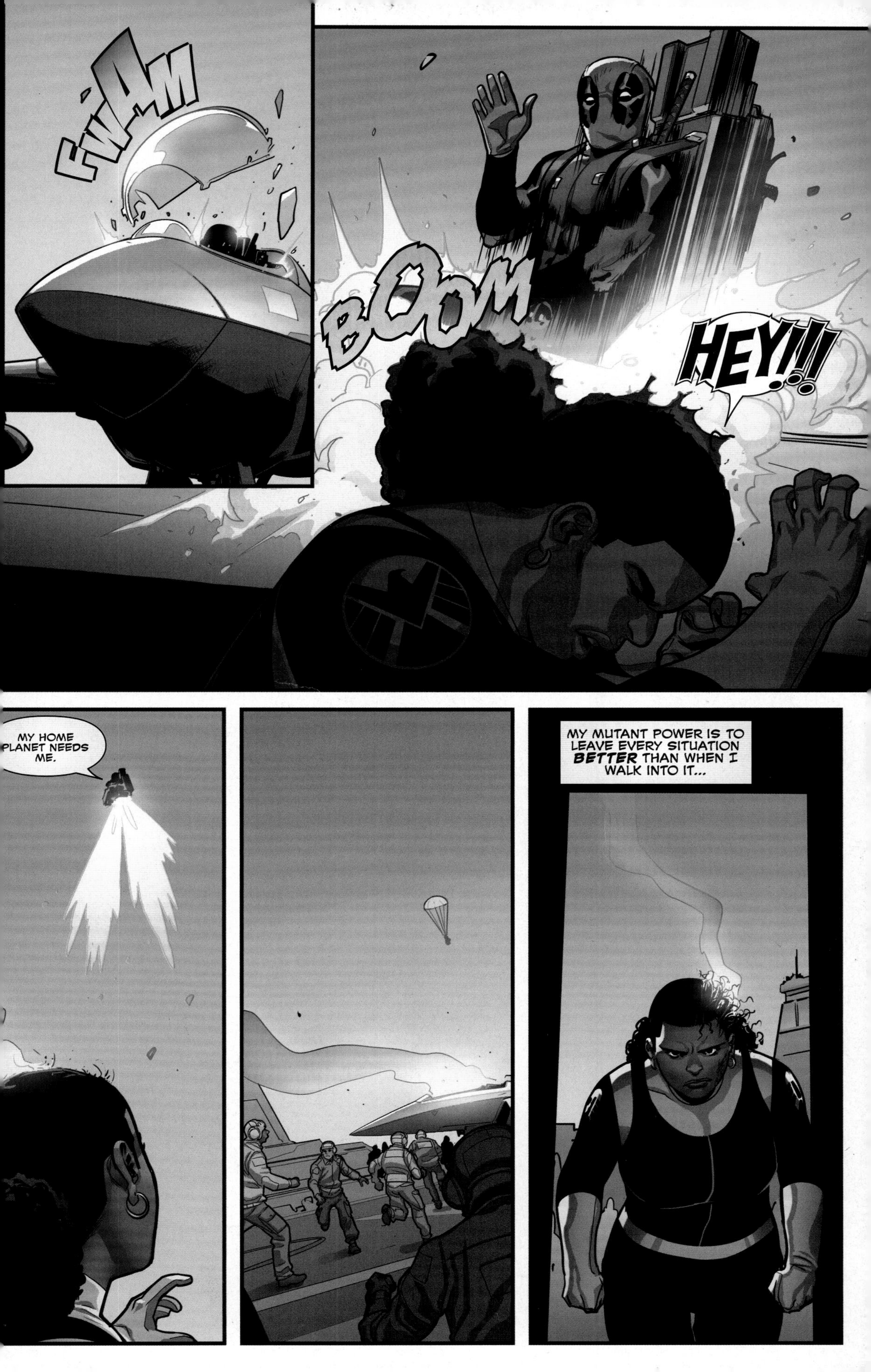
FWAM
BOOM
HEY!!!
MY HOME PLANET NEEDS ME.
MY MUTANT POWER IS TO LEAVE EVERY SITUATION BETTER THAN WHEN I WALK INTO IT...

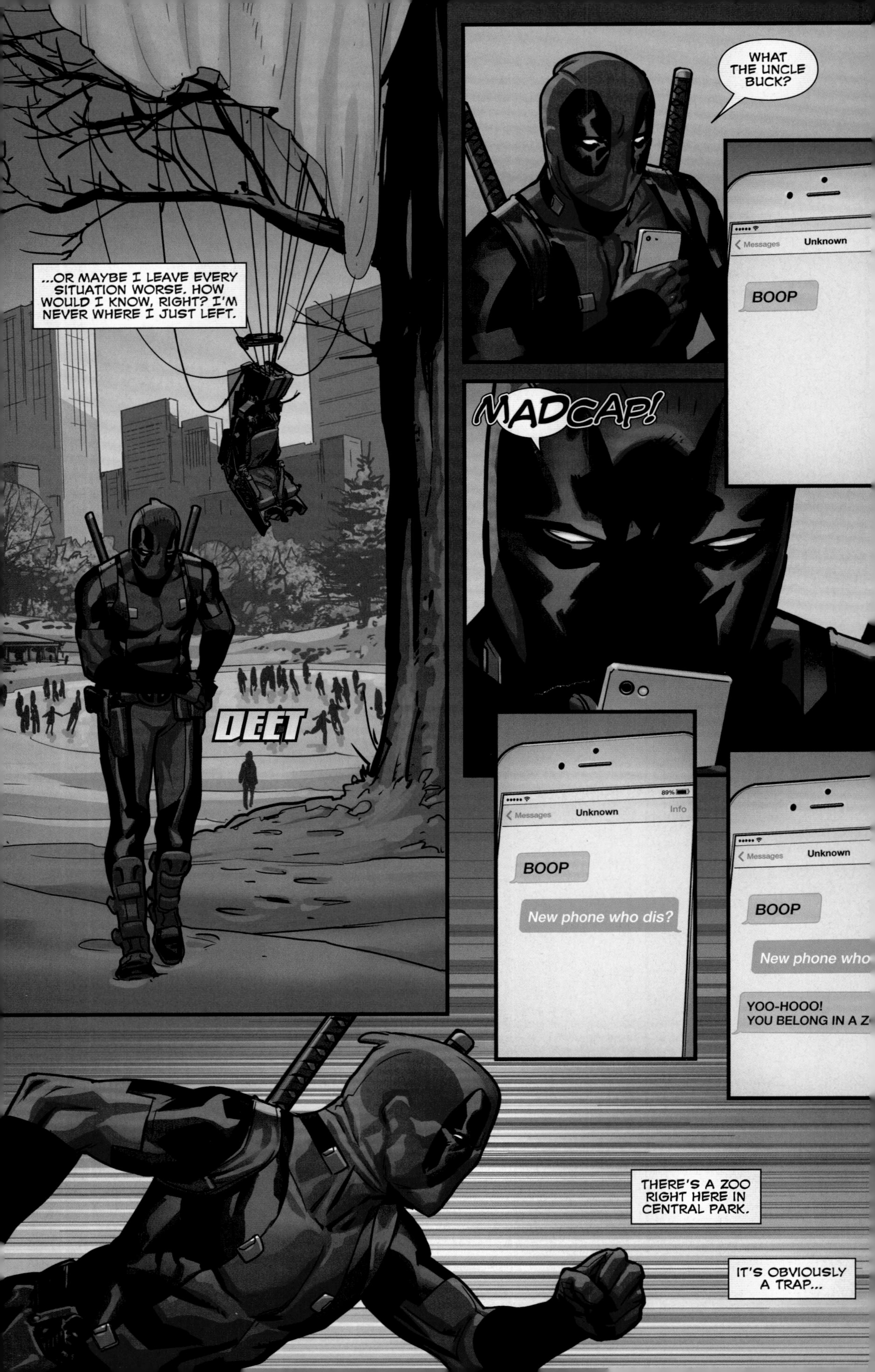
...OR MAYBE I LEAVE EVERY SITUATION WORSE. HOW WOULD I KNOW, RIGHT? I'M NEVER WHERE I JUST LEFT.
DEET
WHAT THE UNCLE BUCK?
Messages
Unknown
BOOP
MADCAP!
89%
Messages
Unknown
Info
BOOP
New phone who dis?
Messages
Unknown
BOOP
New phone who
YOO-HOOO!
YOU BELONG IN A Z
THERE'S A ZOO RIGHT HERE IN CENTRAL PARK.
IT'S OBVIOUSLY A TRAP...

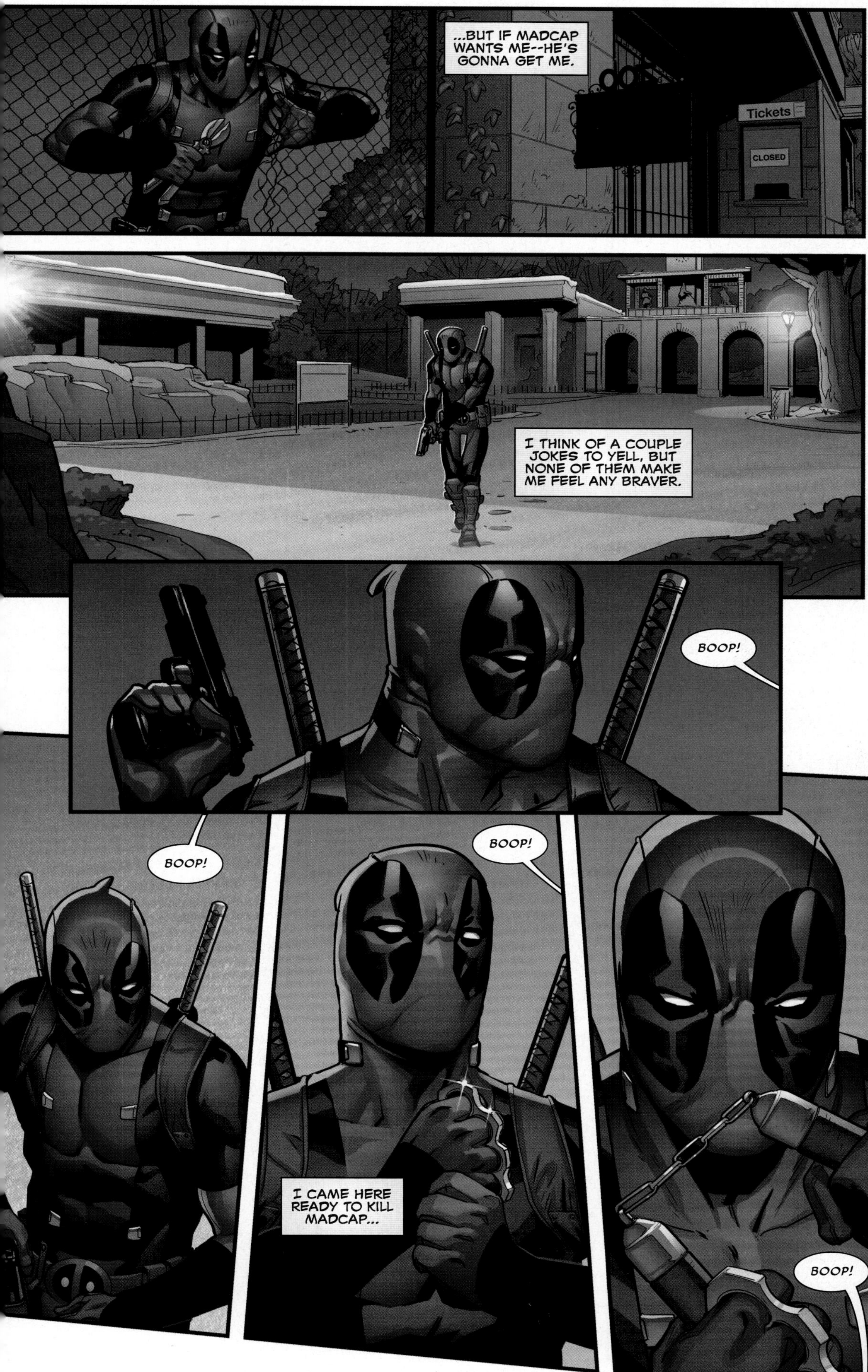

...BUT IF MADCAP WANTS ME--HE'S GONNA GET ME.
Tickets
CLOSED
I THINK OF A COUPLE JOKES TO YELL, BUT NONE OF THEM MAKE ME FEEL ANY BRAVER.
BOOP!
BOOP!
BOOP!
I CAME HERE READY TO KILL MADCAP...
BOOP!

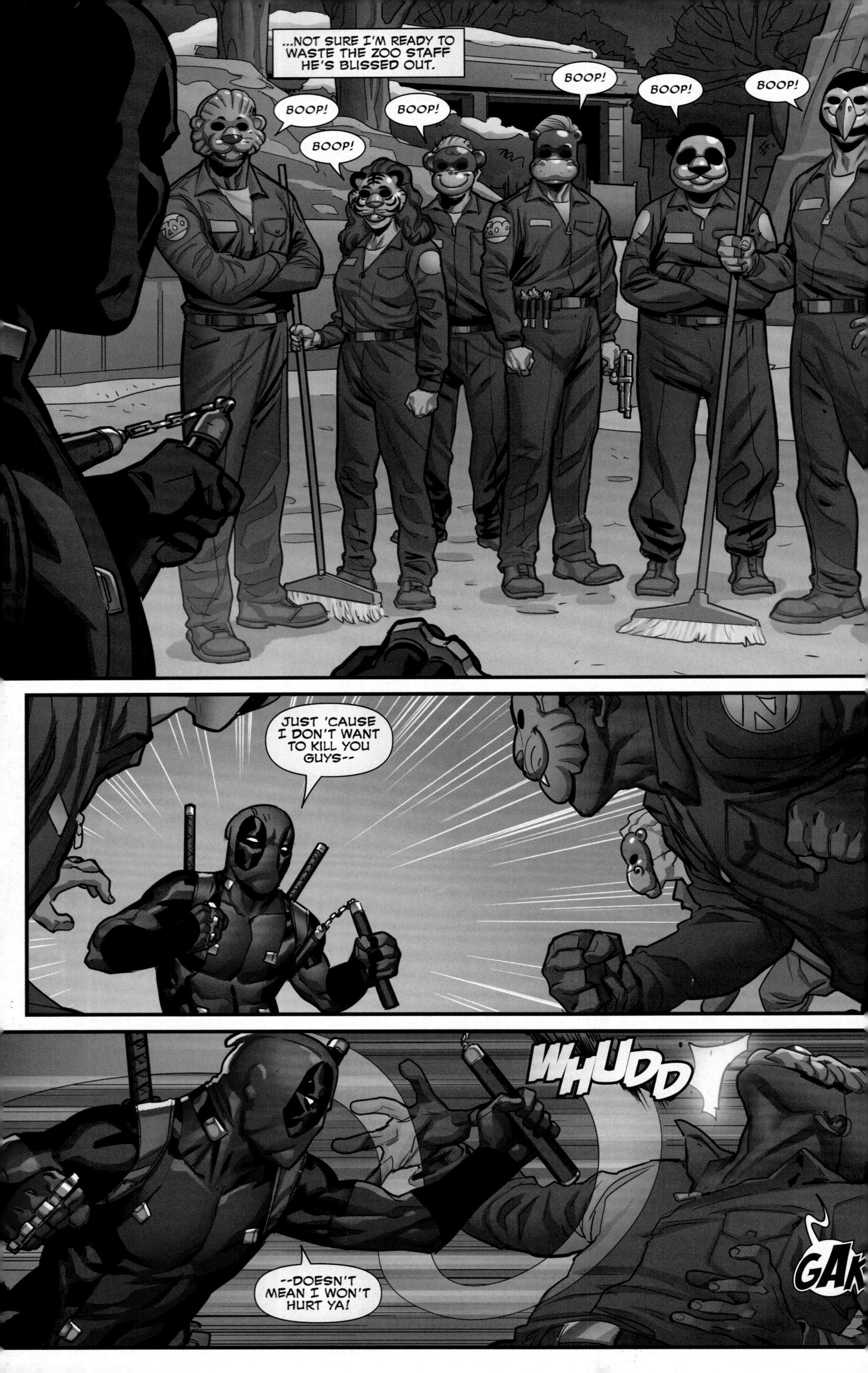
...NOT SURE I'M READY TO WASTE THE ZOO STAFF HE'S BLISSED OUT.
BOOP!
BOOP!
BOOP!
BOOP!
BOOP!
BOOP!
BOOP!
JUST 'CAUSE I DON'T WANT TO KILL YOU GUYS--
WHUDD
--DOESN'T MEAN I WON'T HURT YA!
GAK

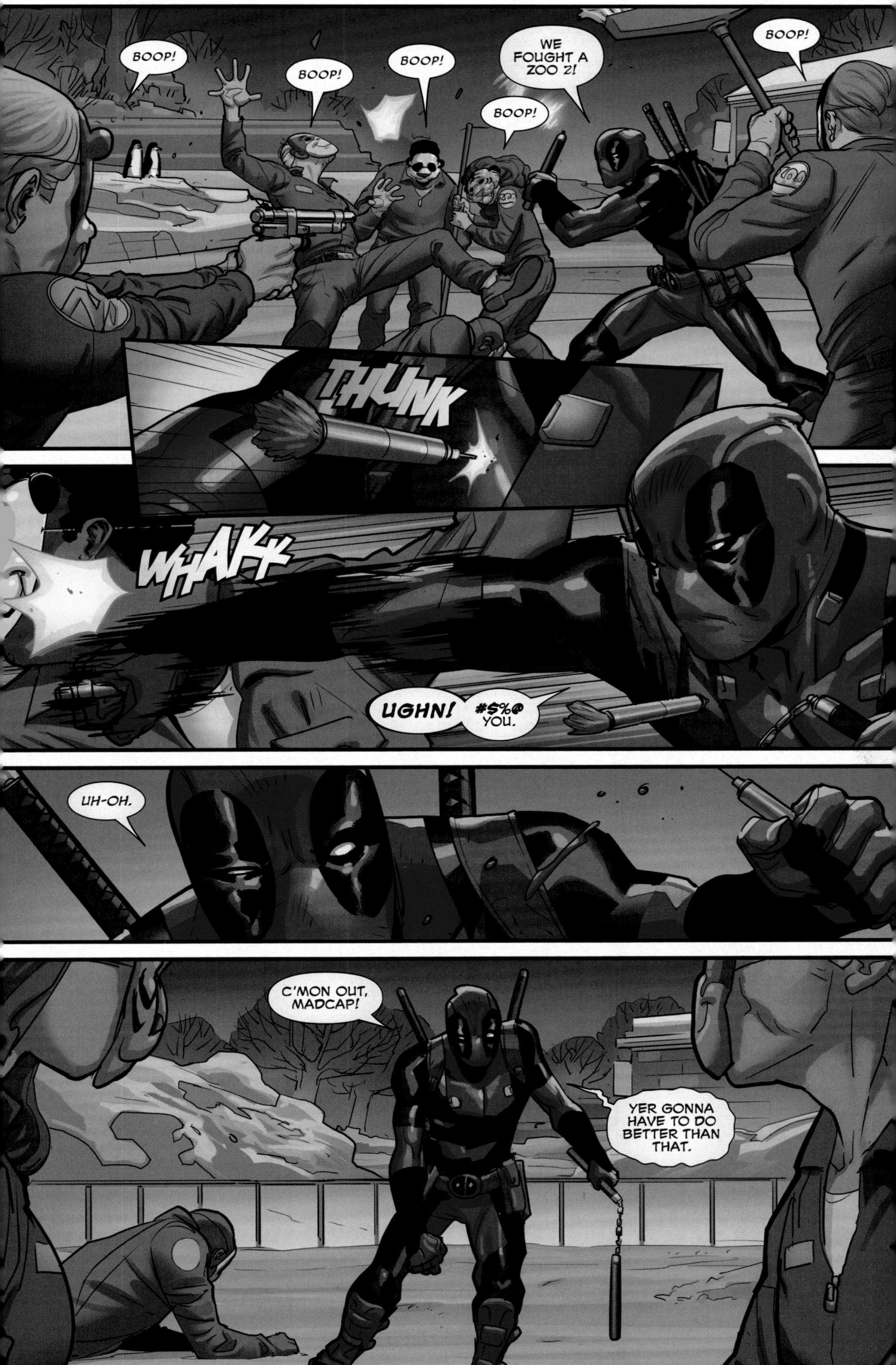
BOOP!
BOOP!
BOOP!
WE FOUGHT A ZOO Z!
BOOP!
BOOP!
THUNK
WHAKK
UGHN!
#$%@ YOU.
UH-OH.
C'MON OUT, MADCAP!
YER GONNA HAVE TO DO BETTER THAN THAT.

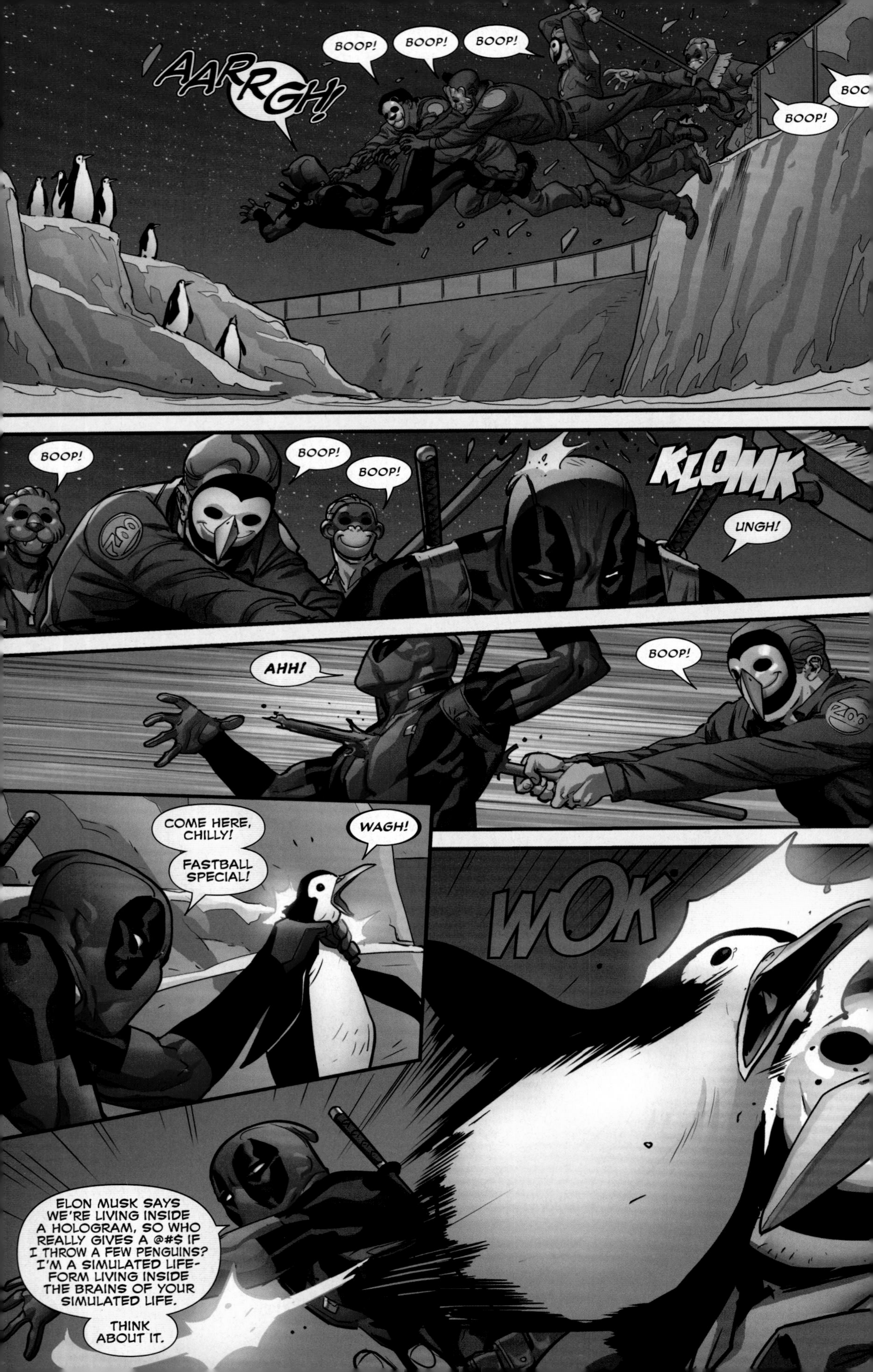
AARRGH!
BOOP!
BOOP!
BOOP!
BOOP!
BOOP!
BOOP!
BOOP!
KLOMK
UNGH!
AHH!
BOOP!
COME HERE, CHILLY!
FASTBALL SPECIAL!
WAGH!
WOK
ELON MUSK SAYS WE'RE LIVING INSIDE A HOLOGRAM, SO WHO REALLY GIVES A @#$ IF I THROW A FEW PENGUINS? I'M A SIMULATED LIFE-FORM LIVING INSIDE THE BRAINS OF YOUR SIMULATED LIFE.
THINK ABOUT IT.

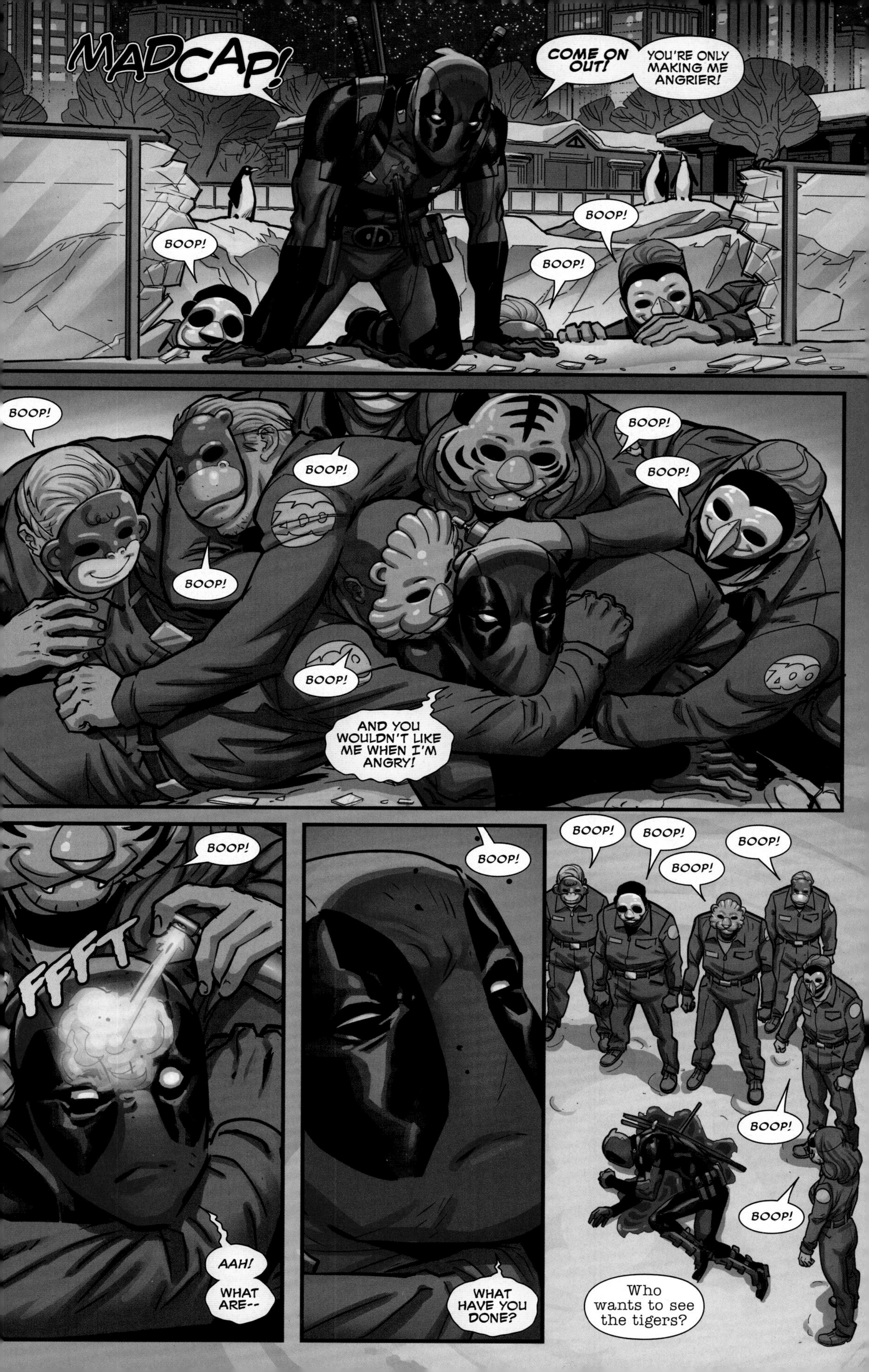
MADCAP!
COME ON OUT!
YOU'RE ONLY MAKING ME ANGRIER!
BOOP!
BOOP!
BOOP!
BOOP!
BOOP!
BOOP!
BOOP!
BOOP!
BOOP!
BOOP!
AND YOU WOULDN'T LIKE ME WHEN I'M ANGRY!
BOOP!
FFFT
AAH!
WHAT ARE--
BOOP!
WHAT HAVE YOU DONE?
BOOP!
BOOP!
BOOP!
BOOP!
BOOP!
BOOP!
Who wants to see the tigers?

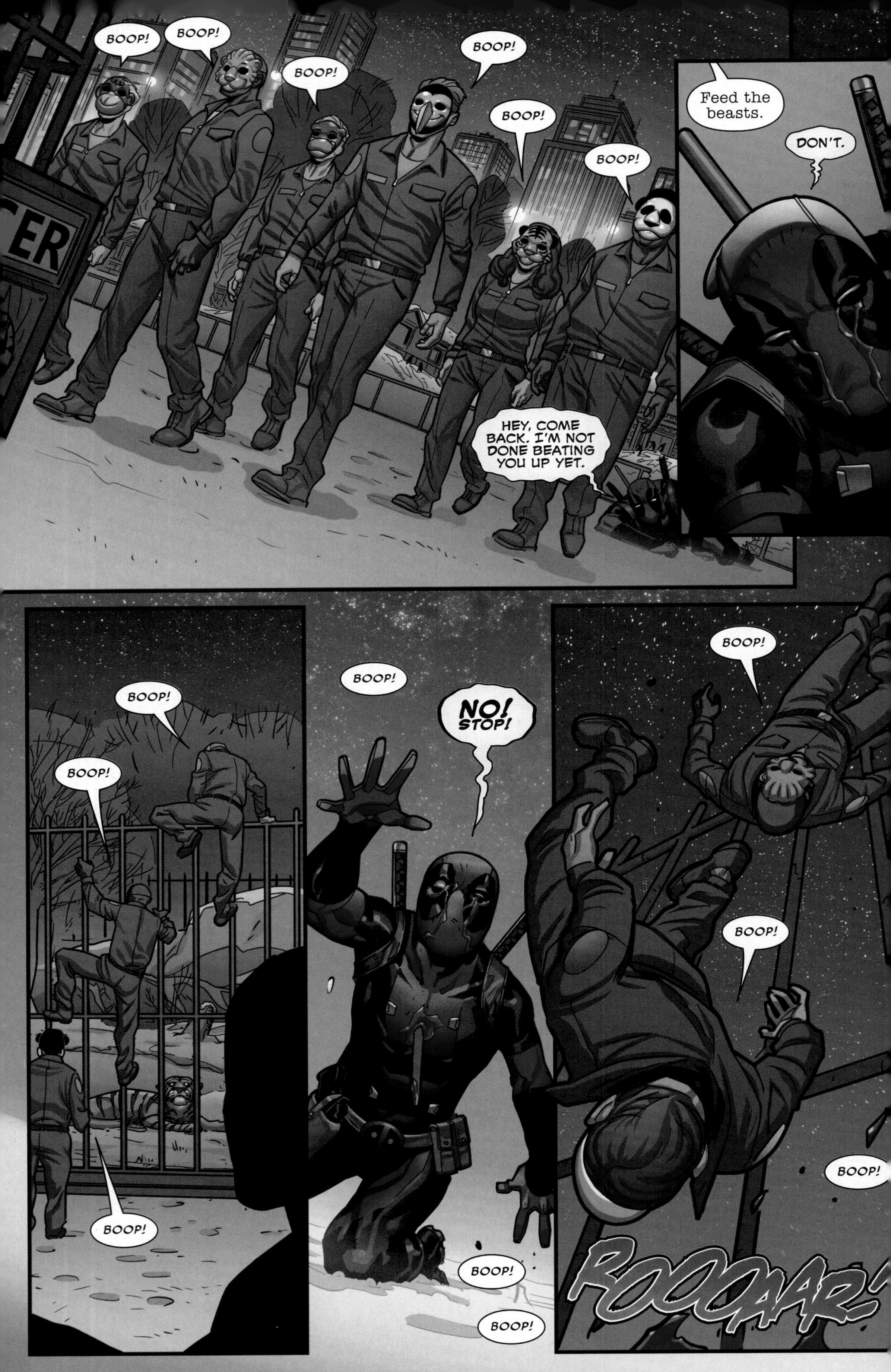
BOOP!
BOOP!
BOOP!
BOOP!
BOOP!
BOOP!
ER
HEY, COME BACK. I'M NOT DONE BEATING YOU UP YET.
Feed the beasts.
DON'T.
BOOP!
BOOP!
BOOP!
BOOP!
NO! STOP!
BOOP!
BOOP!
BOOP!
BOOP!
BOOP!
ROOOAAR!

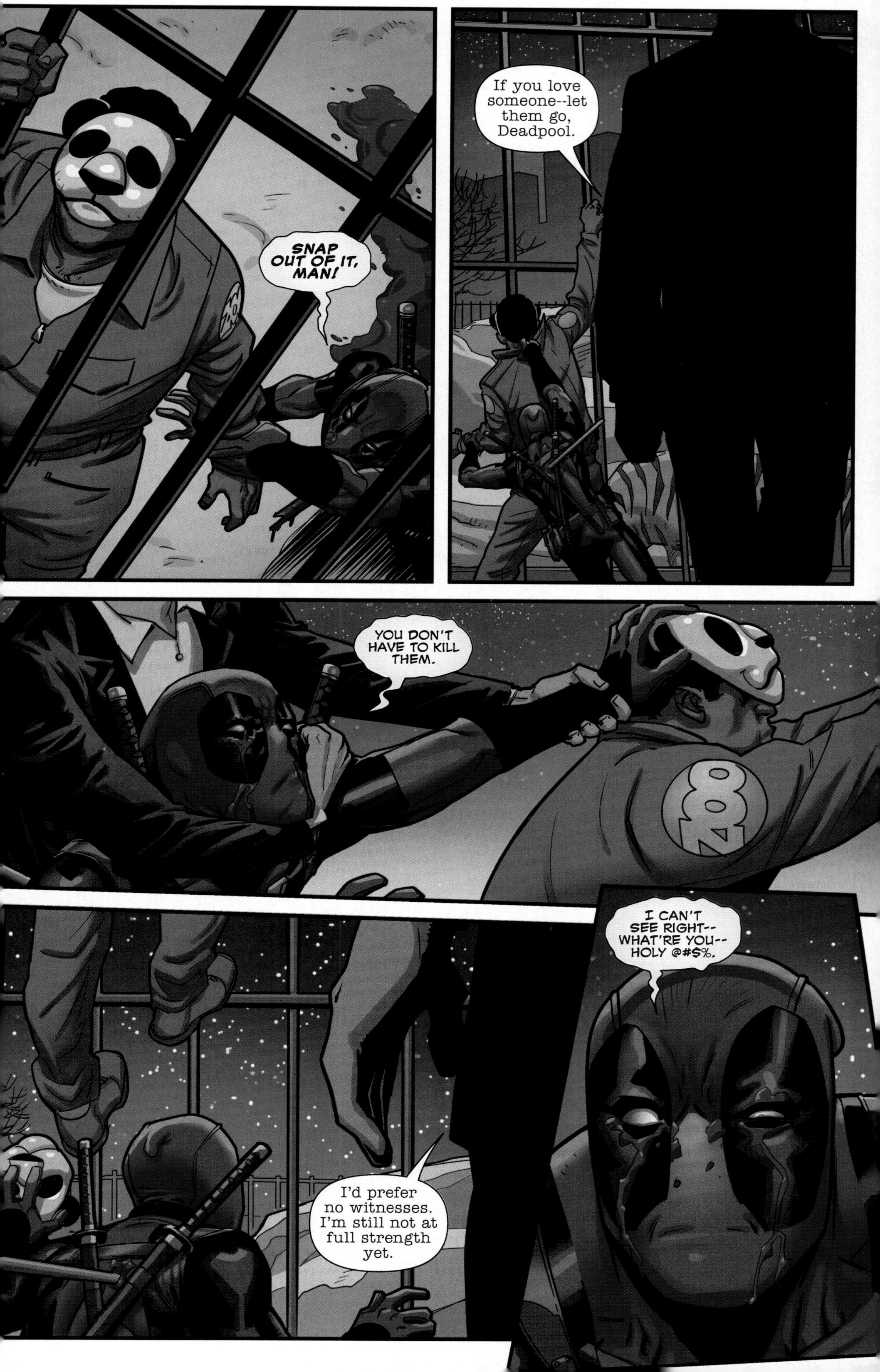
SNAP OUT OF IT, MAN!
If you love someone--let them go, Deadpool.
YOU DON'T HAVE TO KILL THEM.
I CAN'T SEE RIGHT-- WHAT'RE YOU-- HOLY @#$%.
I'd prefer no witnesses. I'm still not at full strength yet.

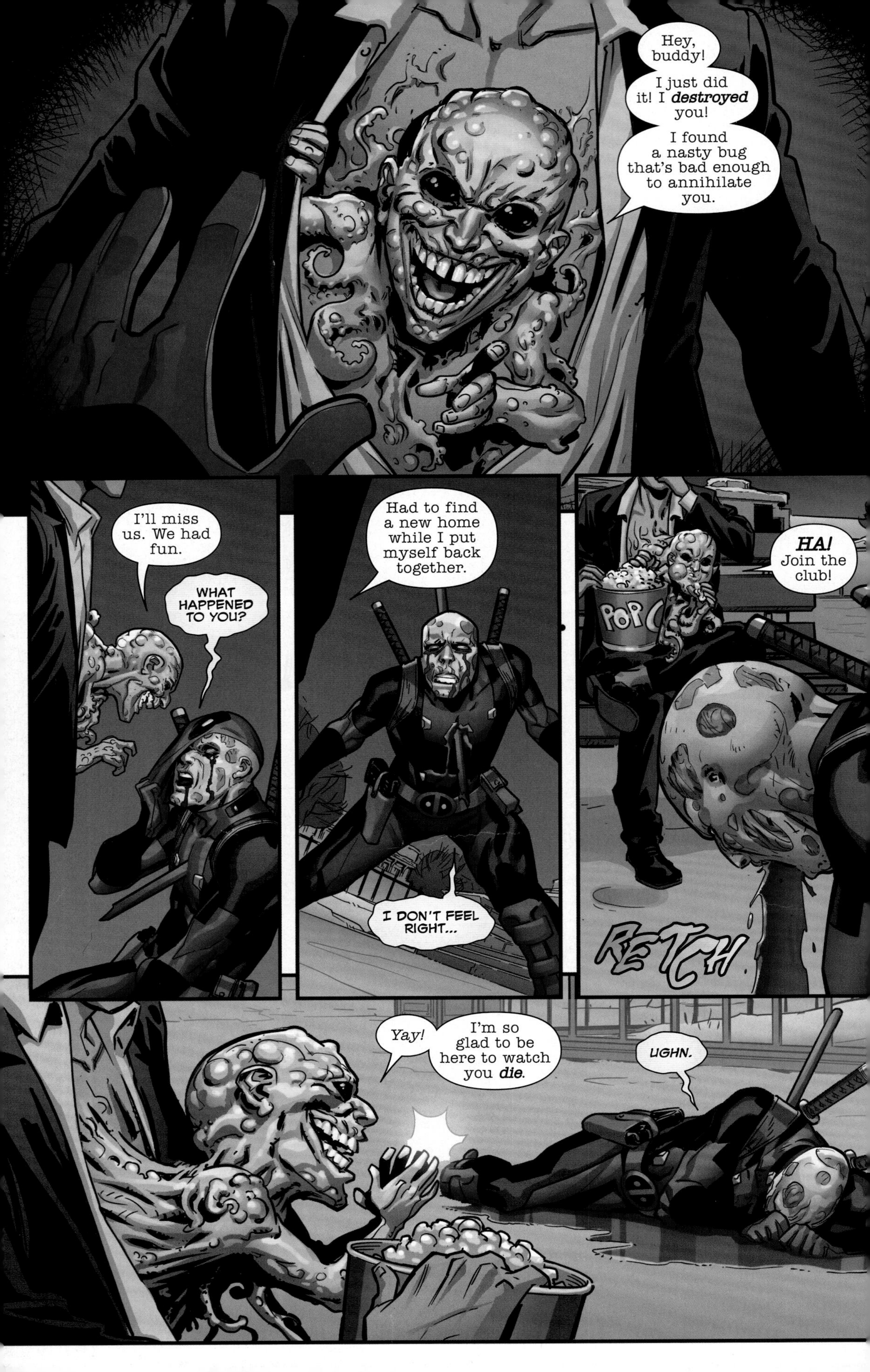
Hey, buddy!
I just did it! I *destroyed* you!
I found a nasty bug that's bad enough to annihilate you.
I'll miss us. We had fun.
WHAT HAPPENED TO YOU?
Had to find a new home while I put myself back together.
I DON'T FEEL RIGHT...
HA! Join the club!
POP C
RETCH
Yay!
I'm so glad to be here to watch you *die*.
UGHN.

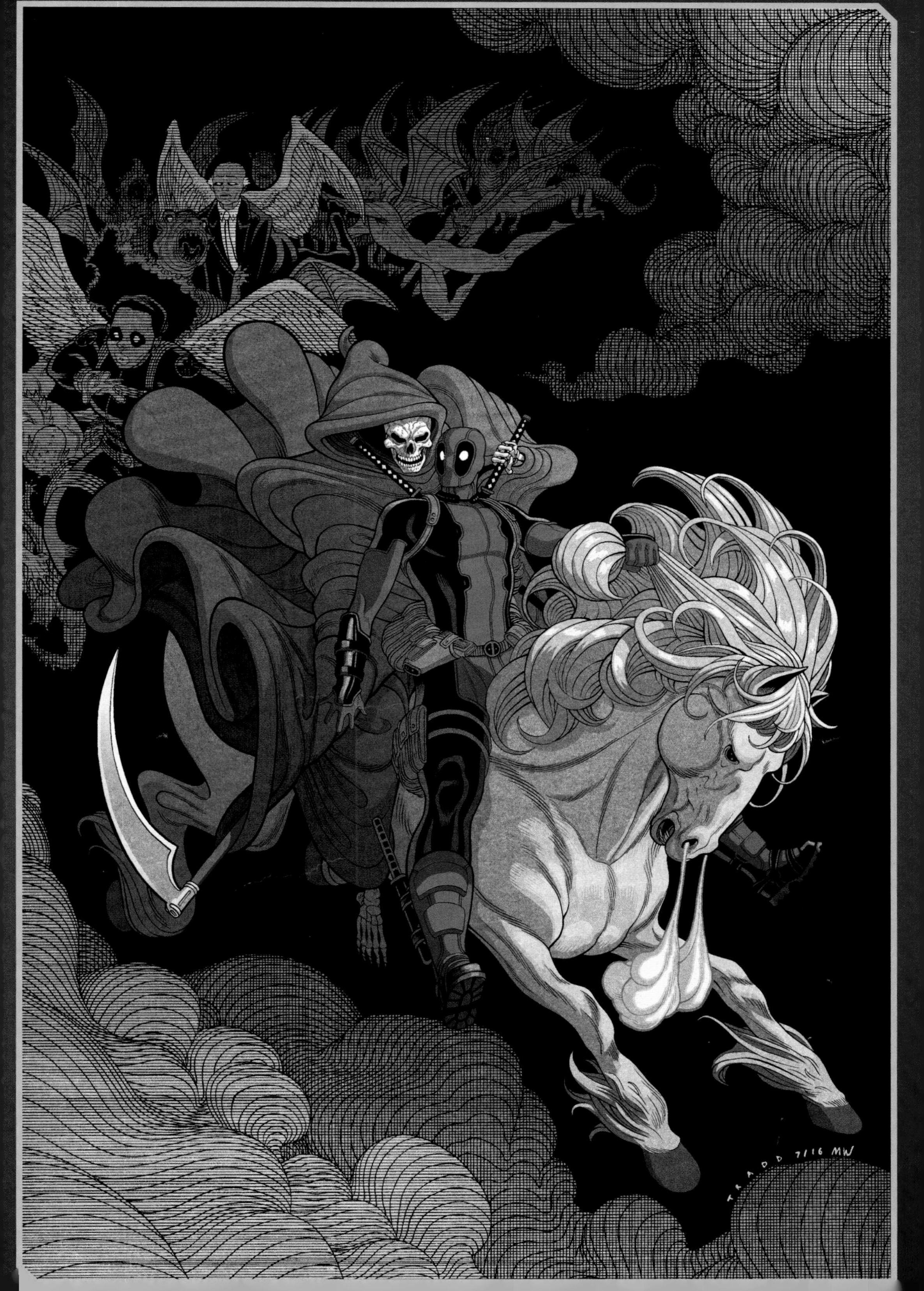
TRADD 7/16 MW

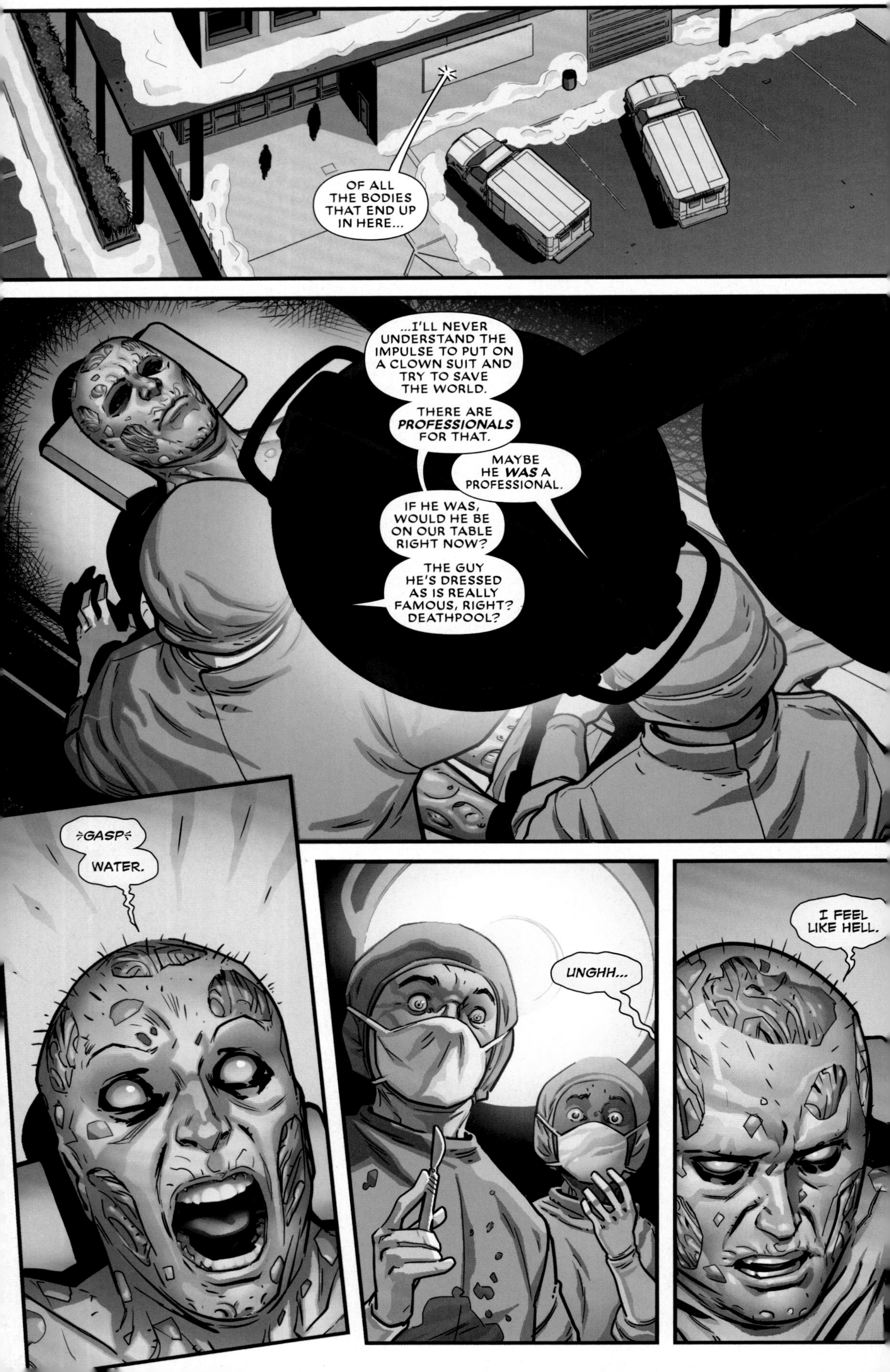
OF ALL THE BODIES THAT END UP IN HERE...
...I'LL NEVER UNDERSTAND THE IMPULSE TO PUT ON A CLOWN SUIT AND TRY TO SAVE THE WORLD.
THERE ARE **PROFESSIONALS** FOR THAT.
MAYBE HE ***WAS*** A PROFESSIONAL.
IF HE WAS, WOULD HE BE ON OUR TABLE RIGHT NOW?
THE GUY HE'S DRESSED AS IS REALLY FAMOUS, RIGHT? DEATHPOOL?
GASP
WATER.
UNGHH...
I FEEL LIKE HELL.

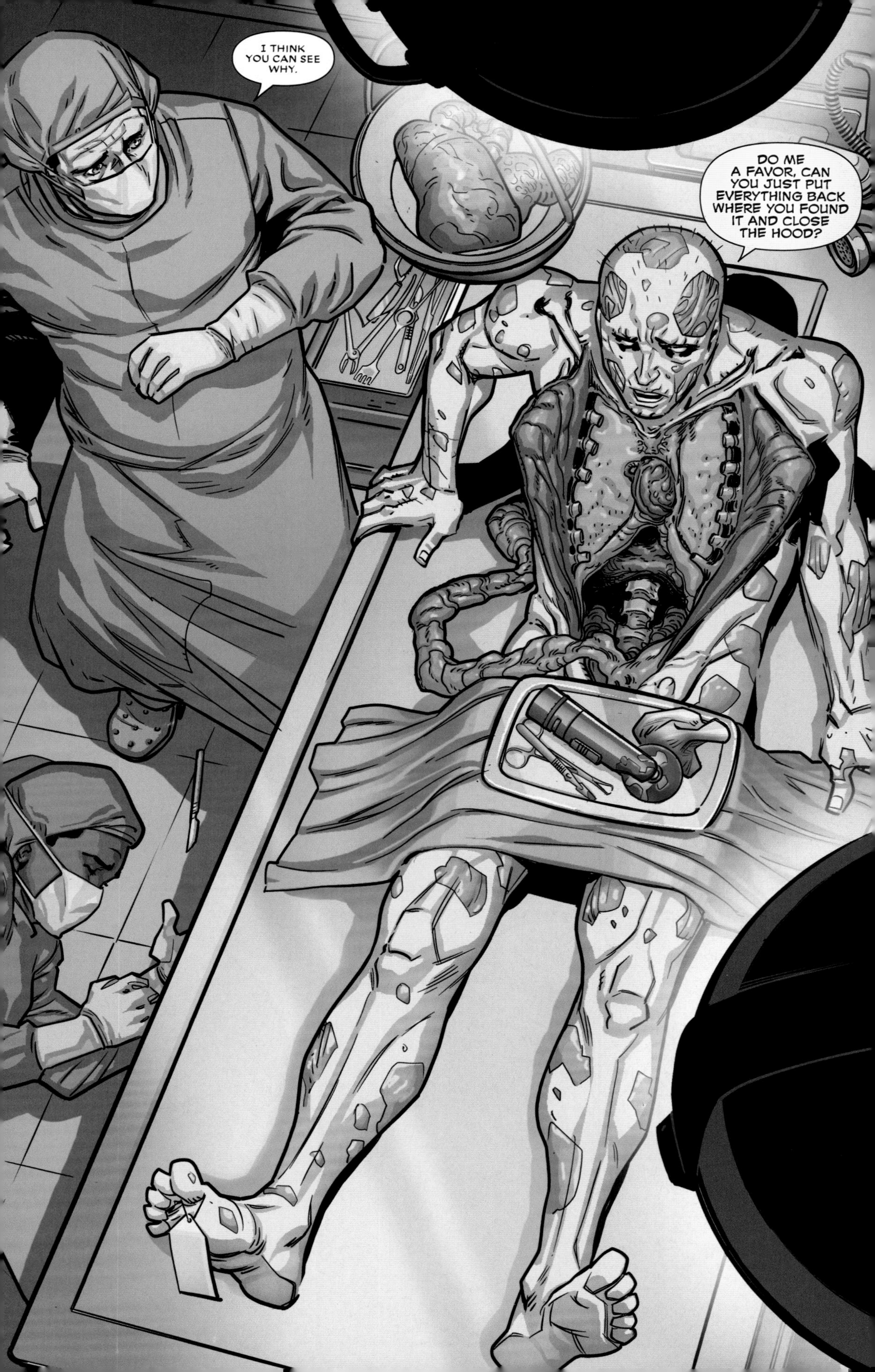
I THINK YOU CAN SEE WHY.
DO ME A FAVOR, CAN YOU JUST PUT EVERYTHING BACK WHERE YOU FOUND IT AND CLOSE THE HOOD?

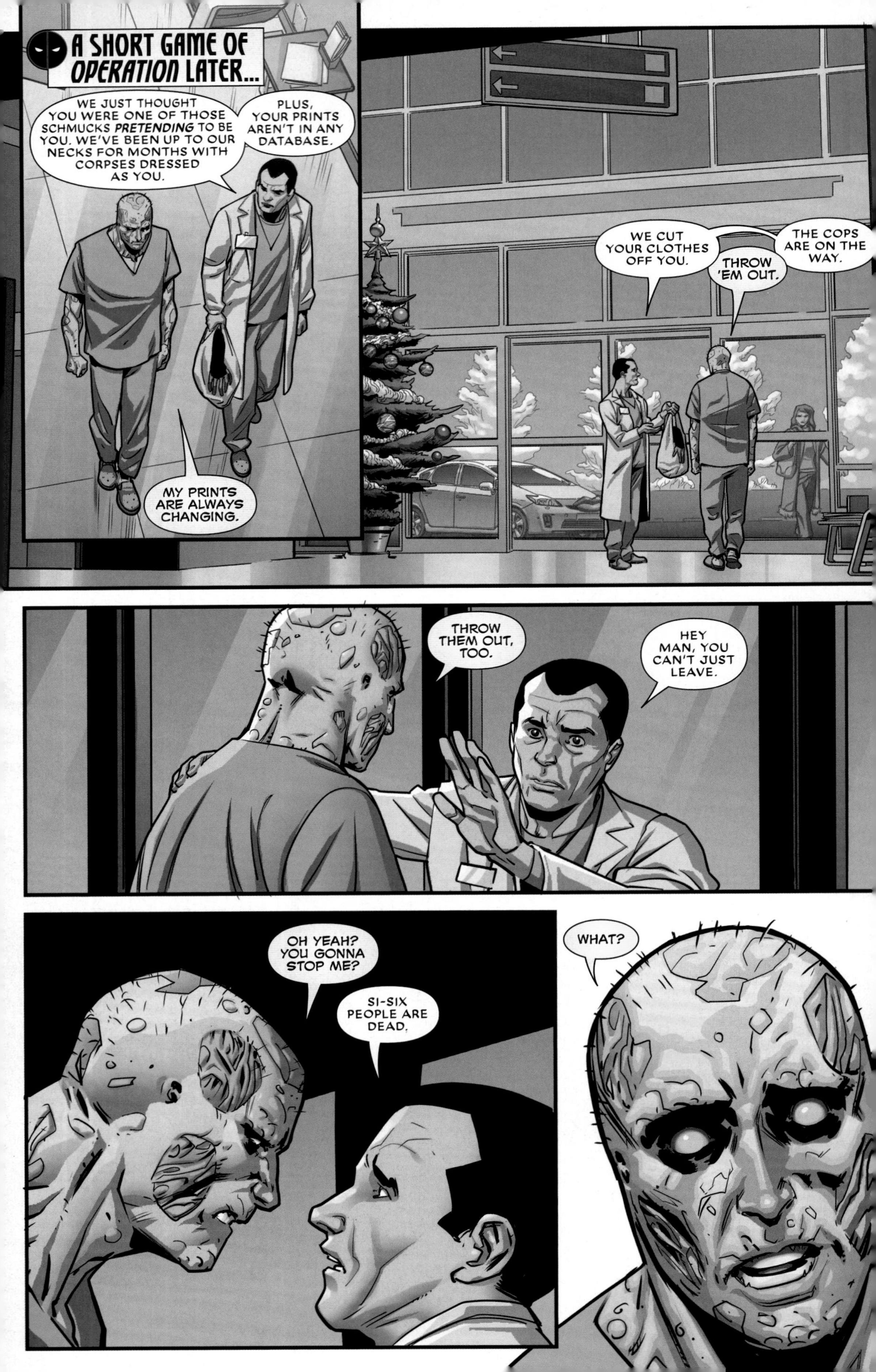
A SHORT GAME OF *OPERATION* LATER...
WE JUST THOUGHT YOU WERE ONE OF THOSE SCHMUCKS *PRETENDING* TO BE YOU. WE'VE BEEN UP TO OUR NECKS FOR MONTHS WITH CORPSES DRESSED AS YOU.
PLUS, YOUR PRINTS AREN'T IN ANY DATABASE.
MY PRINTS ARE ALWAYS CHANGING.
WE CUT YOUR CLOTHES OFF YOU.
THE COPS ARE ON THE WAY.
THROW 'EM OUT.
THROW THEM OUT, TOO.
HEY MAN, YOU CAN'T JUST LEAVE.
OH YEAH? YOU GONNA STOP ME?
SI-SIX PEOPLE ARE DEAD.
WHAT?

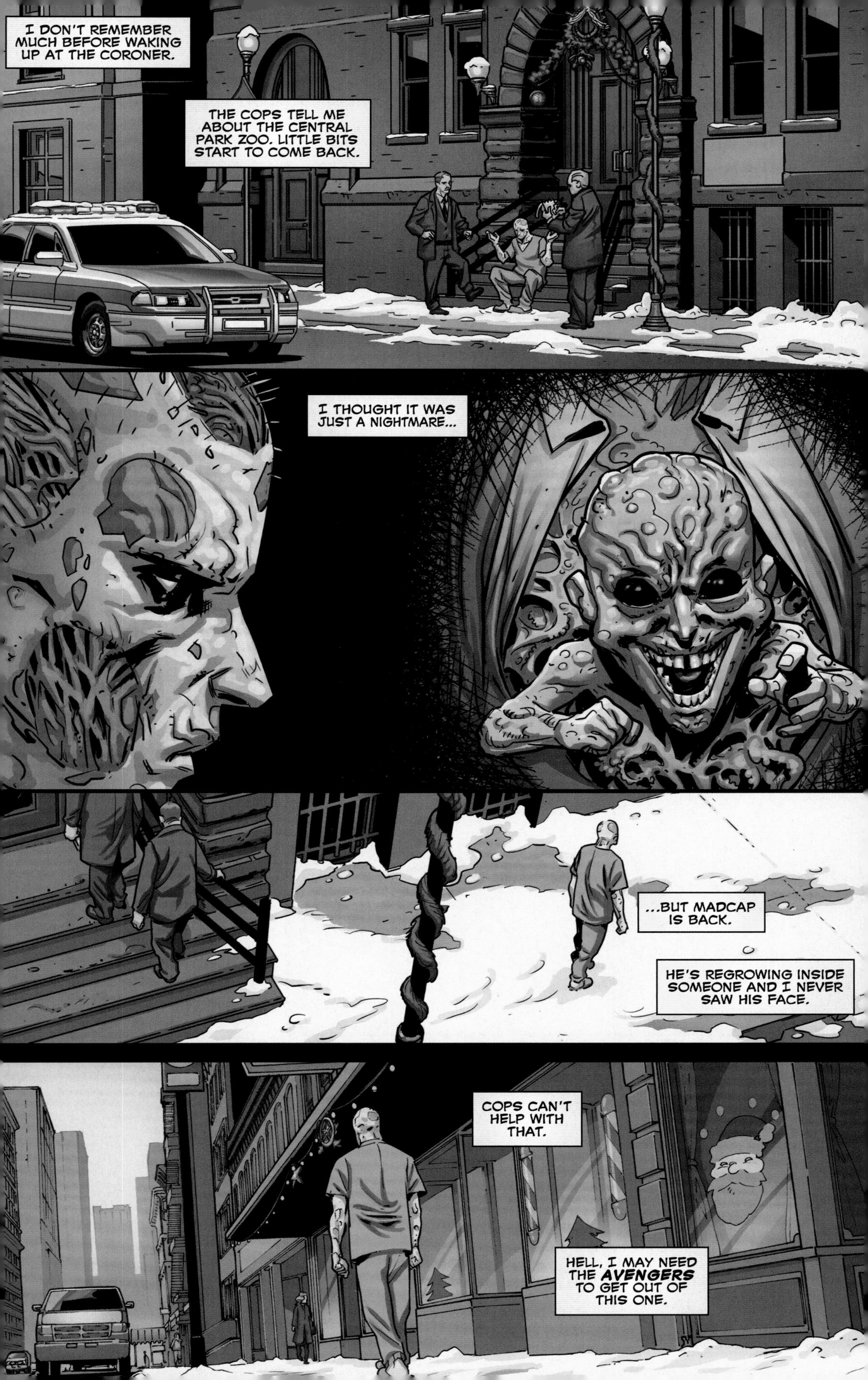
I DON'T REMEMBER MUCH BEFORE WAKING UP AT THE CORONER.
THE COPS TELL ME ABOUT THE CENTRAL PARK ZOO. LITTLE BITS START TO COME BACK.
I THOUGHT IT WAS JUST A NIGHTMARE...
...BUT MADCAP IS BACK.
HE'S REGROWING INSIDE SOMEONE AND I NEVER SAW HIS FACE.
COPS CAN'T HELP WITH THAT.
HELL, I MAY NEED THE AVENGERS TO GET OUT OF THIS ONE.

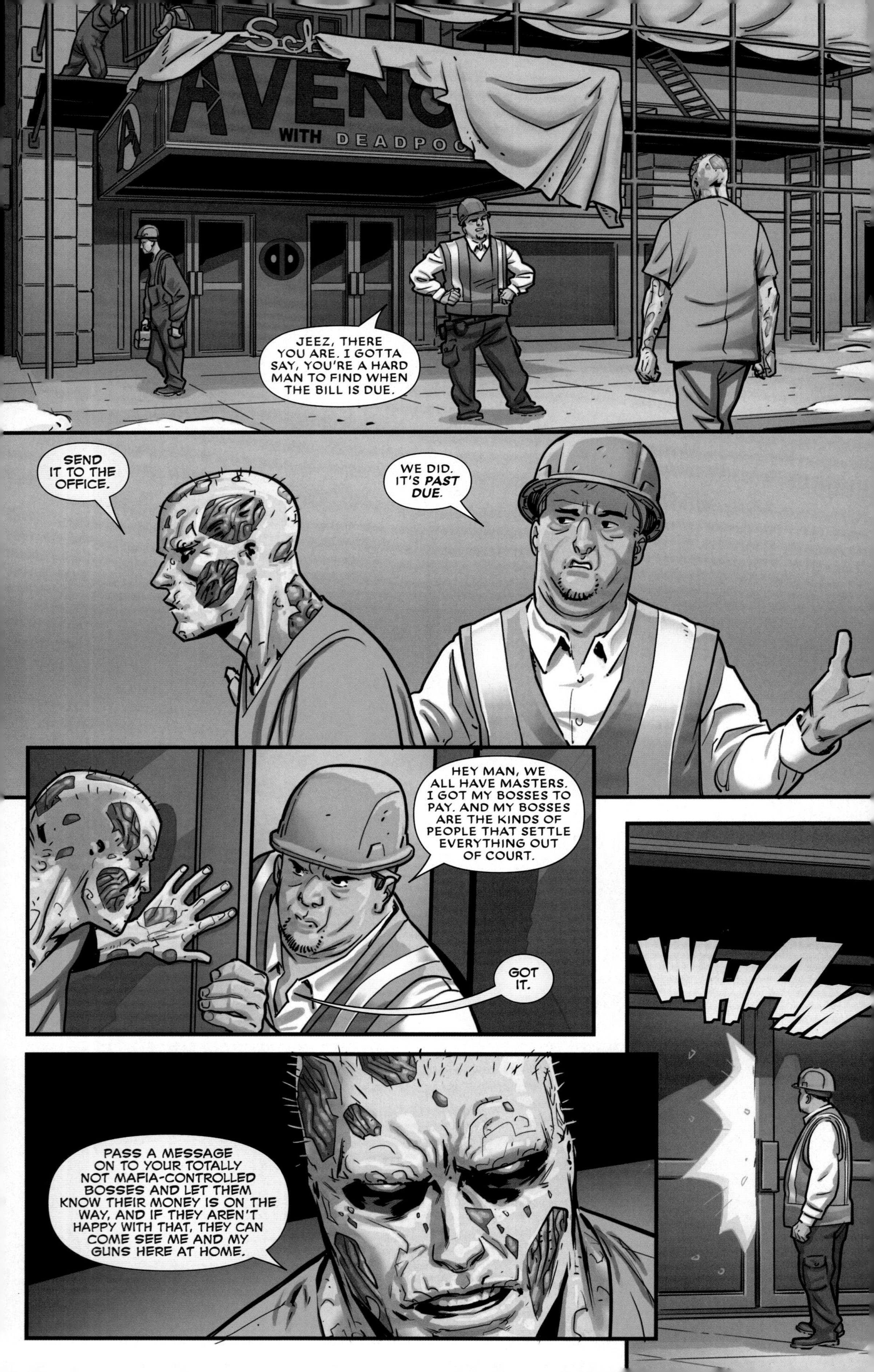

AVENG
WITH DEADPOO
JEEZ, THERE YOU ARE. I GOTTA SAY, YOU'RE A HARD MAN TO FIND WHEN THE BILL IS DUE.
SEND IT TO THE OFFICE.
WE DID. IT'S *PAST DUE*.
HEY MAN, WE ALL HAVE MASTERS. I GOT MY BOSSES TO PAY. AND MY BOSSES ARE THE KINDS OF PEOPLE THAT SETTLE EVERYTHING OUT OF COURT.
GOT IT.
PASS A MESSAGE ON TO YOUR TOTALLY NOT MAFIA-CONTROLLED BOSSES AND LET THEM KNOW THEIR MONEY IS ON THE WAY, AND IF THEY AREN'T HAPPY WITH THAT, THEY CAN COME SEE ME AND MY GUNS HERE AT HOME.
WHAM

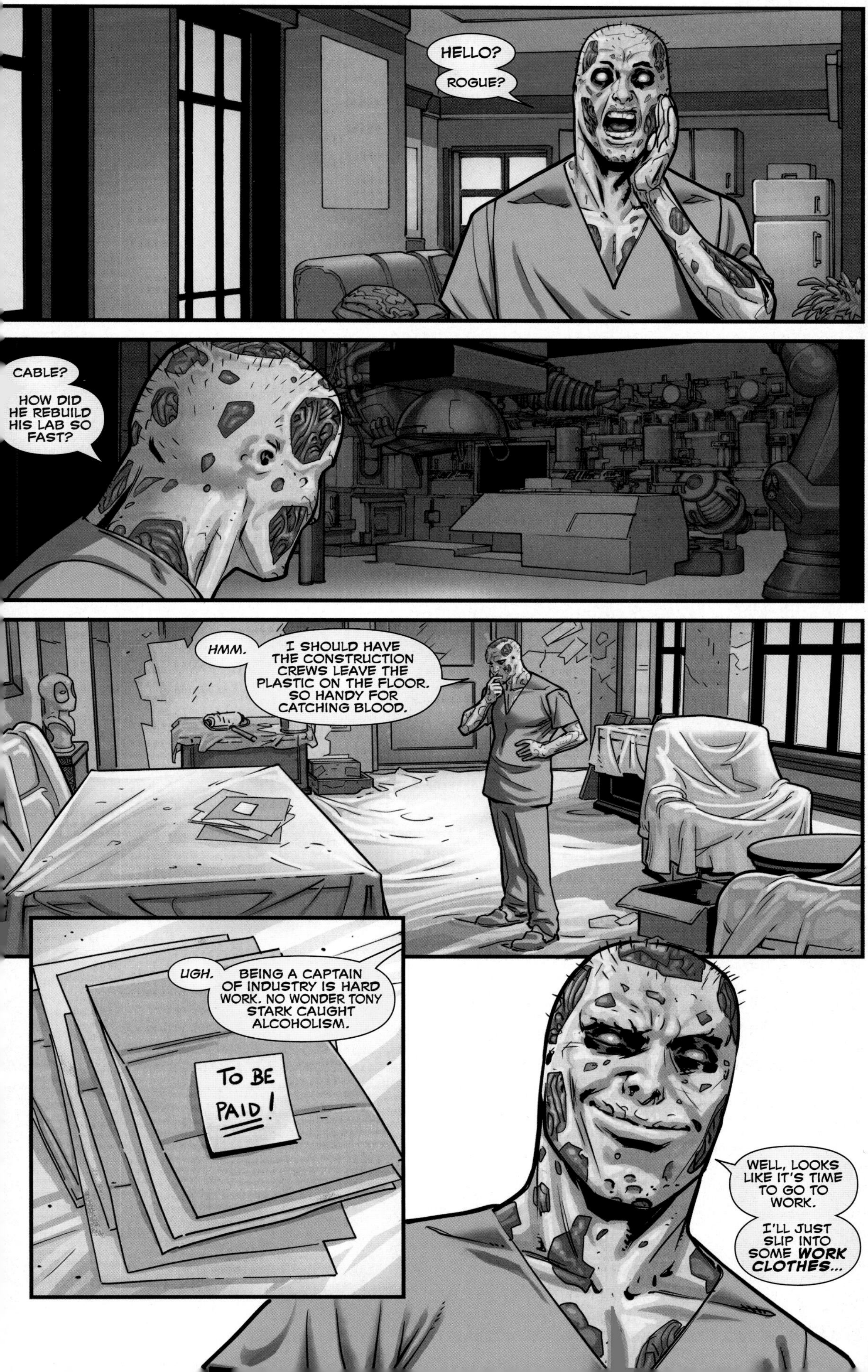
HELLO?
ROGUE?
CABLE?
HOW DID HE REBUILD HIS LAB SO FAST?
HMM.
I SHOULD HAVE THE CONSTRUCTION CREWS LEAVE THE PLASTIC ON THE FLOOR. SO HANDY FOR CATCHING BLOOD.
UGH.
BEING A CAPTAIN OF INDUSTRY IS HARD WORK. NO WONDER TONY STARK CAUGHT ALCOHOLISM.
TO BE PAID!
WELL, LOOKS LIKE IT'S TIME TO GO TO WORK.
I'LL JUST SLIP INTO SOME WORK CLOTHES...

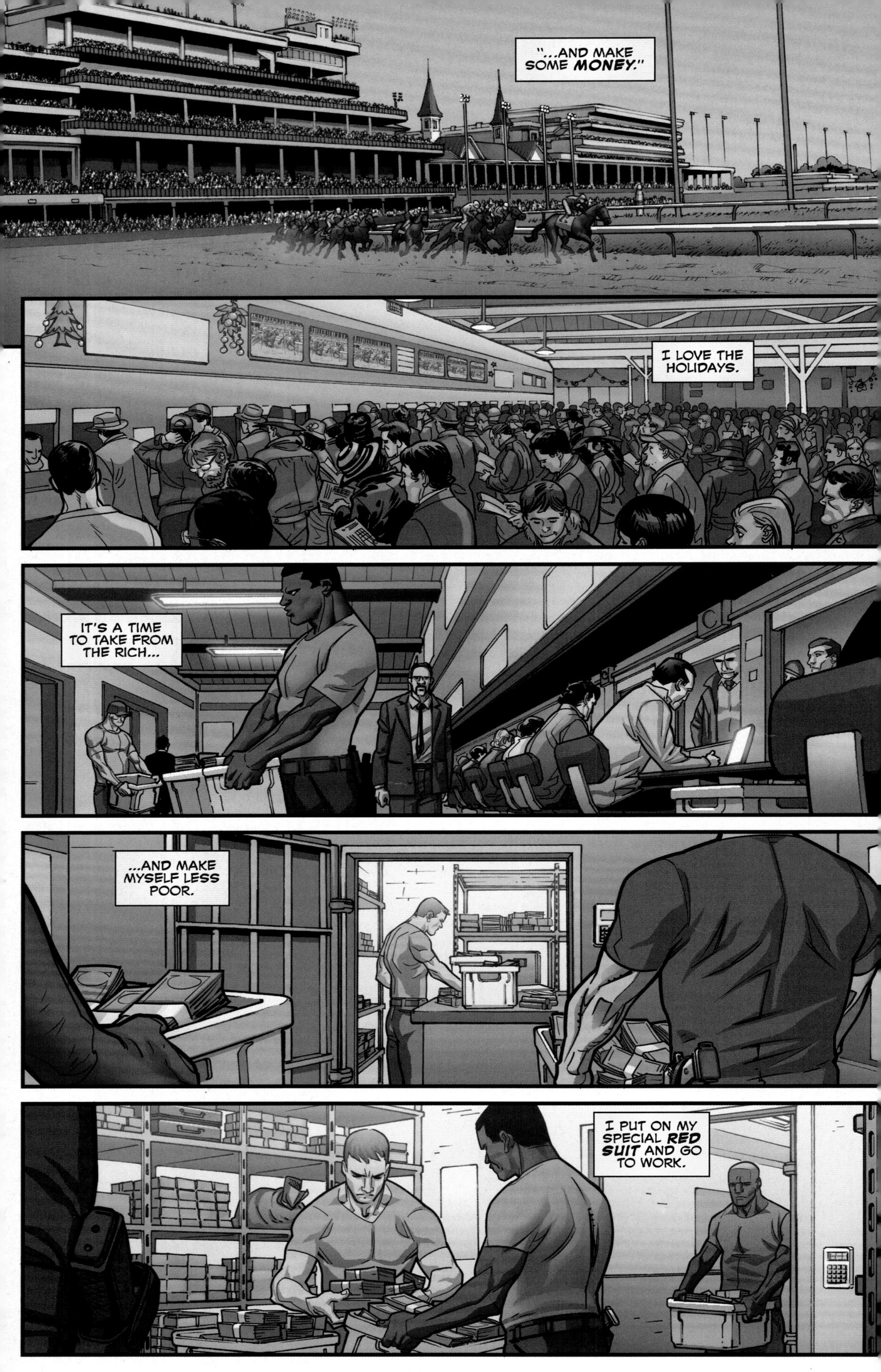
"...AND MAKE SOME MONEY."
I LOVE THE HOLIDAYS.
IT'S A TIME TO TAKE FROM THE RICH...
...AND MAKE MYSELF LESS POOR.
I PUT ON MY SPECIAL RED SUIT AND GO TO WORK.

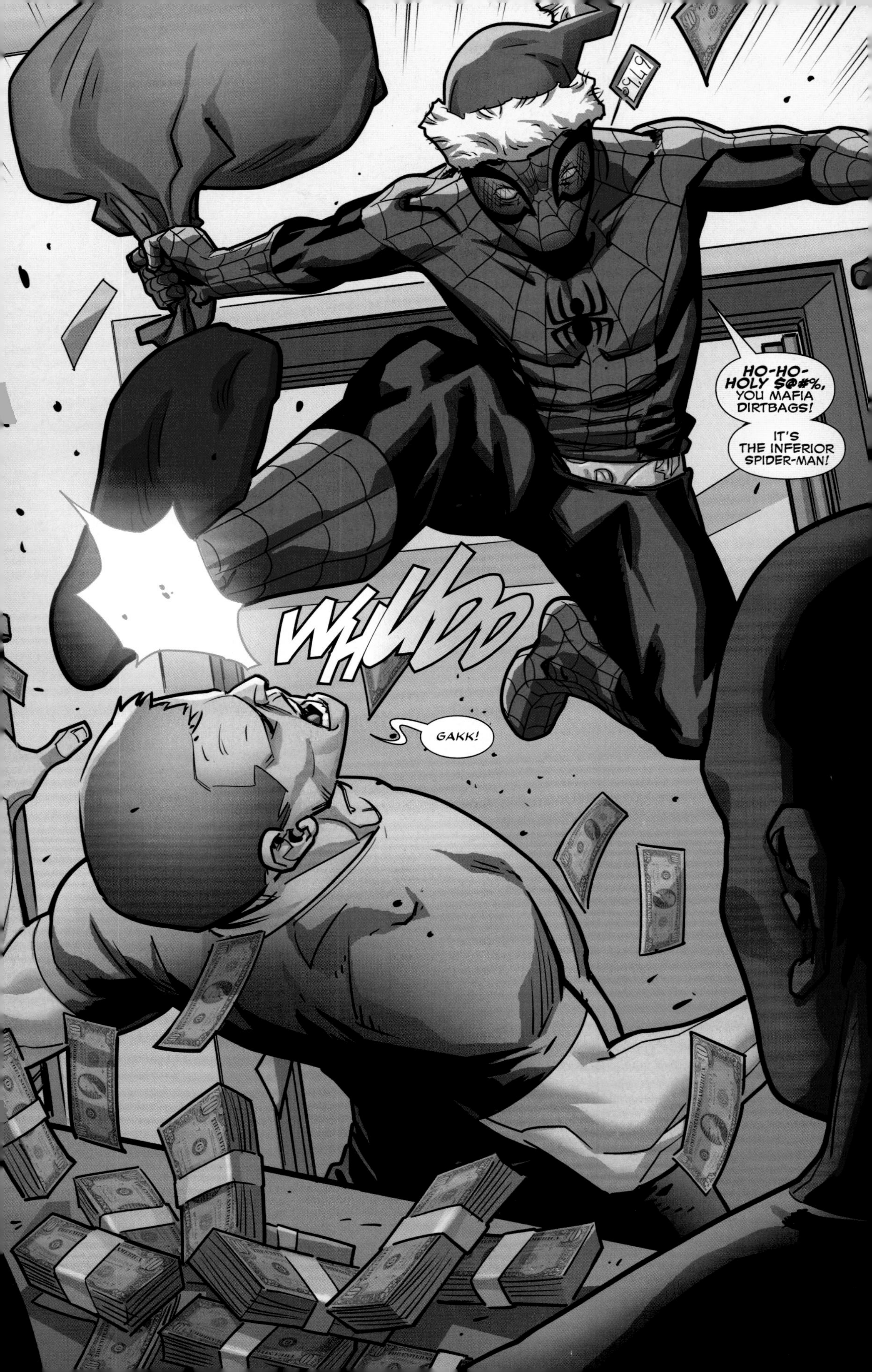
HO-HO-HOLY $@#%, YOU MAFIA DIRTBAGS!
IT'S THE INFERIOR SPIDER-MAN!
WHUDD
GAKK!

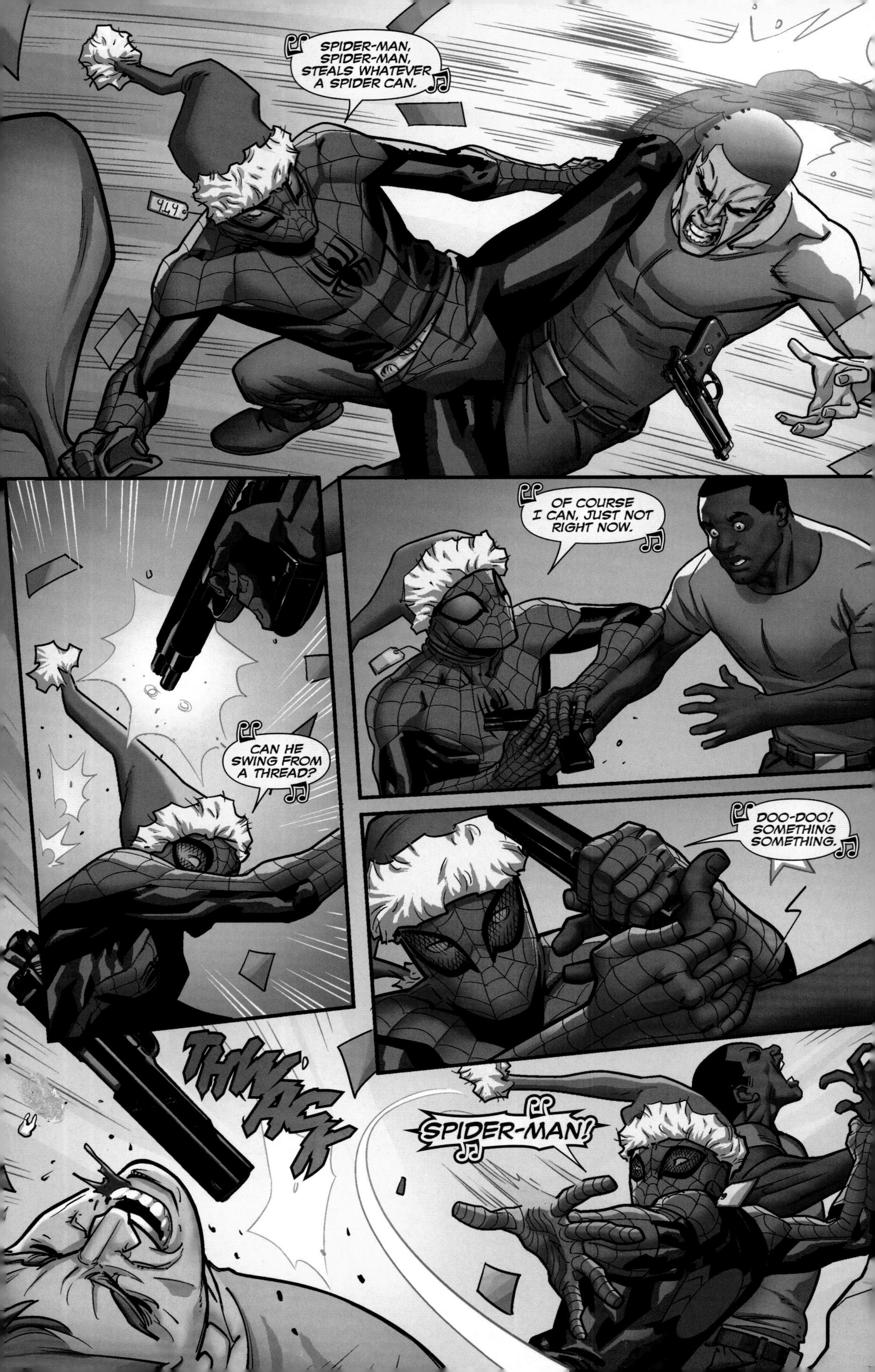
SPIDER-MAN, SPIDER-MAN, STEALS WHATEVER A SPIDER CAN.
976
CAN HE SWING FROM A THREAD?
OF COURSE I CAN, JUST NOT RIGHT NOW.
DOO-DOO! SOMETHING SOMETHING.
THWACK
SPIDER-MAN!

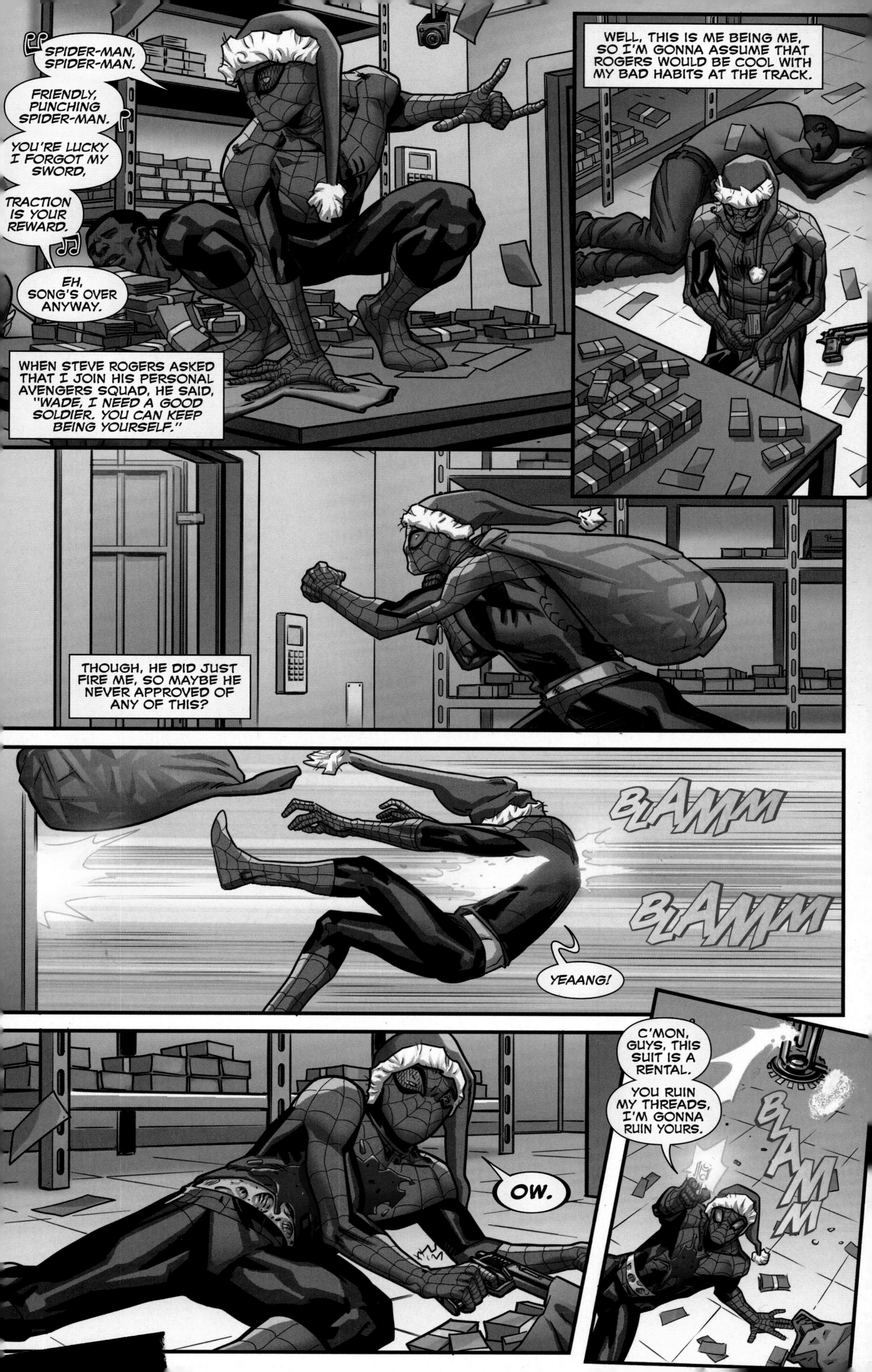
SPIDER-MAN, SPIDER-MAN.
FRIENDLY, PUNCHING SPIDER-MAN.
YOU'RE LUCKY I FORGOT MY SWORD,
TRACTION IS YOUR REWARD.
EH, SONG'S OVER ANYWAY.
WHEN STEVE ROGERS ASKED THAT I JOIN HIS PERSONAL AVENGERS SQUAD, HE SAID, "WADE, I NEED A GOOD SOLDIER. YOU CAN KEEP BEING YOURSELF."
WELL, THIS IS ME BEING ME, SO I'M GONNA ASSUME THAT ROGERS WOULD BE COOL WITH MY BAD HABITS AT THE TRACK.
THOUGH, HE DID JUST FIRE ME, SO MAYBE HE NEVER APPROVED OF ANY OF THIS?
BLAMM
BLAMM
YEAANG!
OW.
C'MON, GUYS, THIS SUIT IS A RENTAL.
YOU RUIN MY THREADS, I'M GONNA RUIN YOURS.
BLAMM

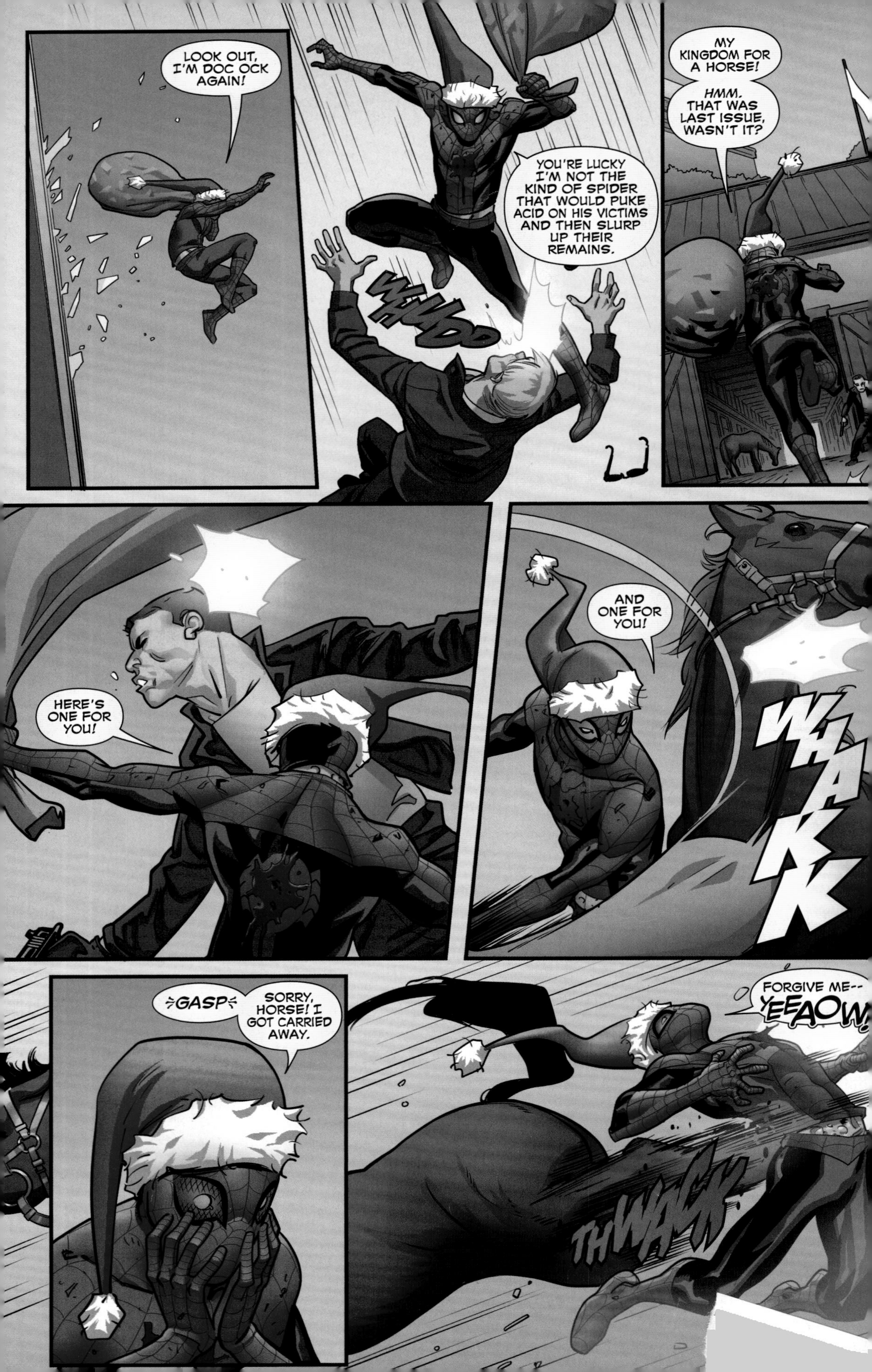

LOOK OUT, I'M DOC OCK AGAIN!
YOU'RE LUCKY I'M NOT THE KIND OF SPIDER THAT WOULD PUKE ACID ON HIS VICTIMS AND THEN SLURP UP THEIR REMAINS.
WHUD
MY KINGDOM FOR A HORSE!
HMM. THAT WAS LAST ISSUE, WASN'T IT?
HERE'S ONE FOR YOU!
AND ONE FOR YOU!
WHAKK
GASP
SORRY, HORSE! I GOT CARRIED AWAY.
FORGIVE ME-- YEEAOW!
THWACK

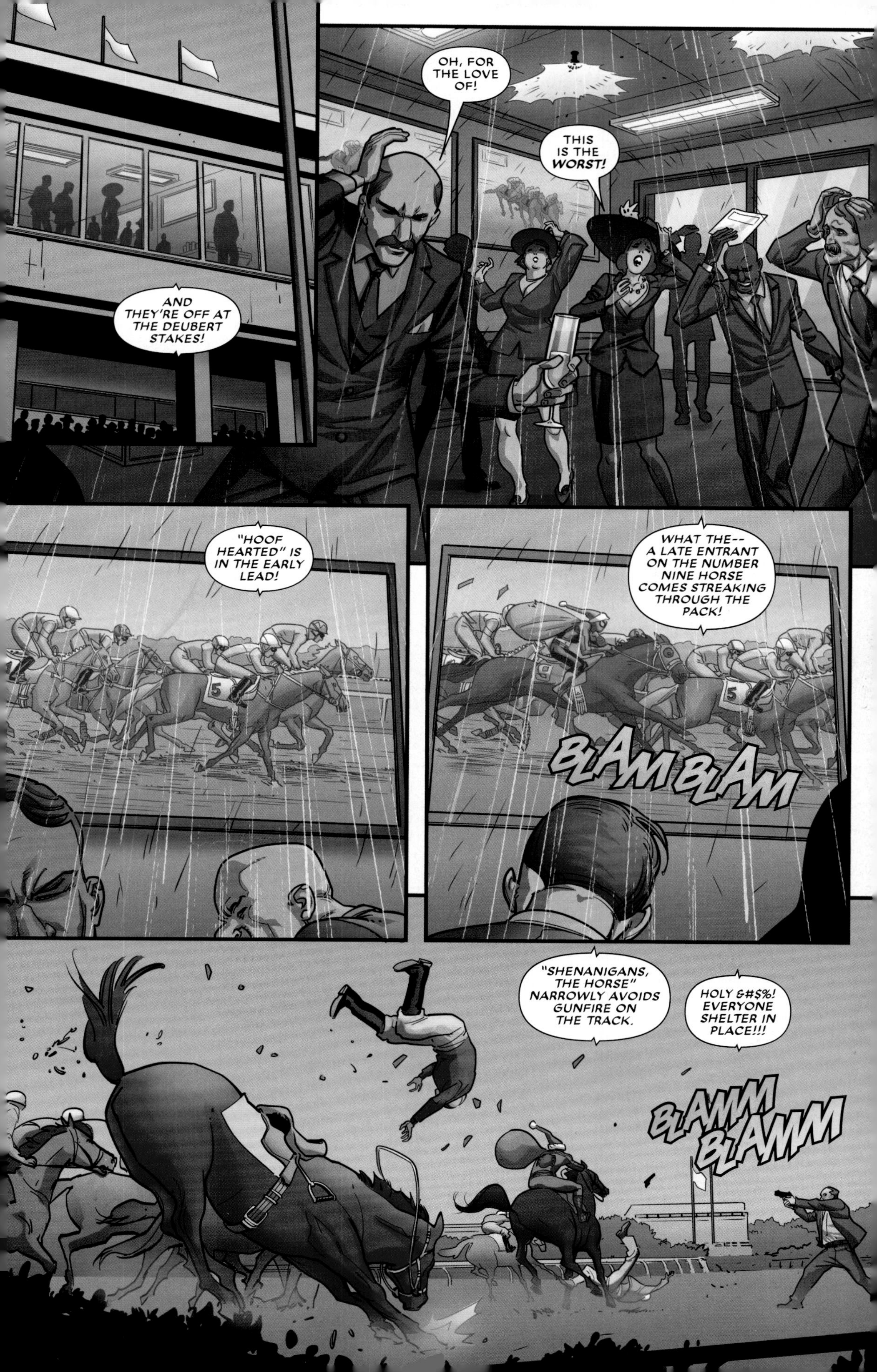
AND THEY'RE OFF AT THE DEUBERT STAKES!
OH, FOR THE LOVE OF!
THIS IS THE WORST!
"HOOF HEARTED" IS IN THE EARLY LEAD!
WHAT THE-- A LATE ENTRANT ON THE NUMBER NINE HORSE COMES STREAKING THROUGH THE PACK!
BLAM BLAM
"SHENANIGANS, THE HORSE" NARROWLY AVOIDS GUNFIRE ON THE TRACK.
HOLY &#$%! EVERYONE SHELTER IN PLACE!!!
BLAMM BLAMM

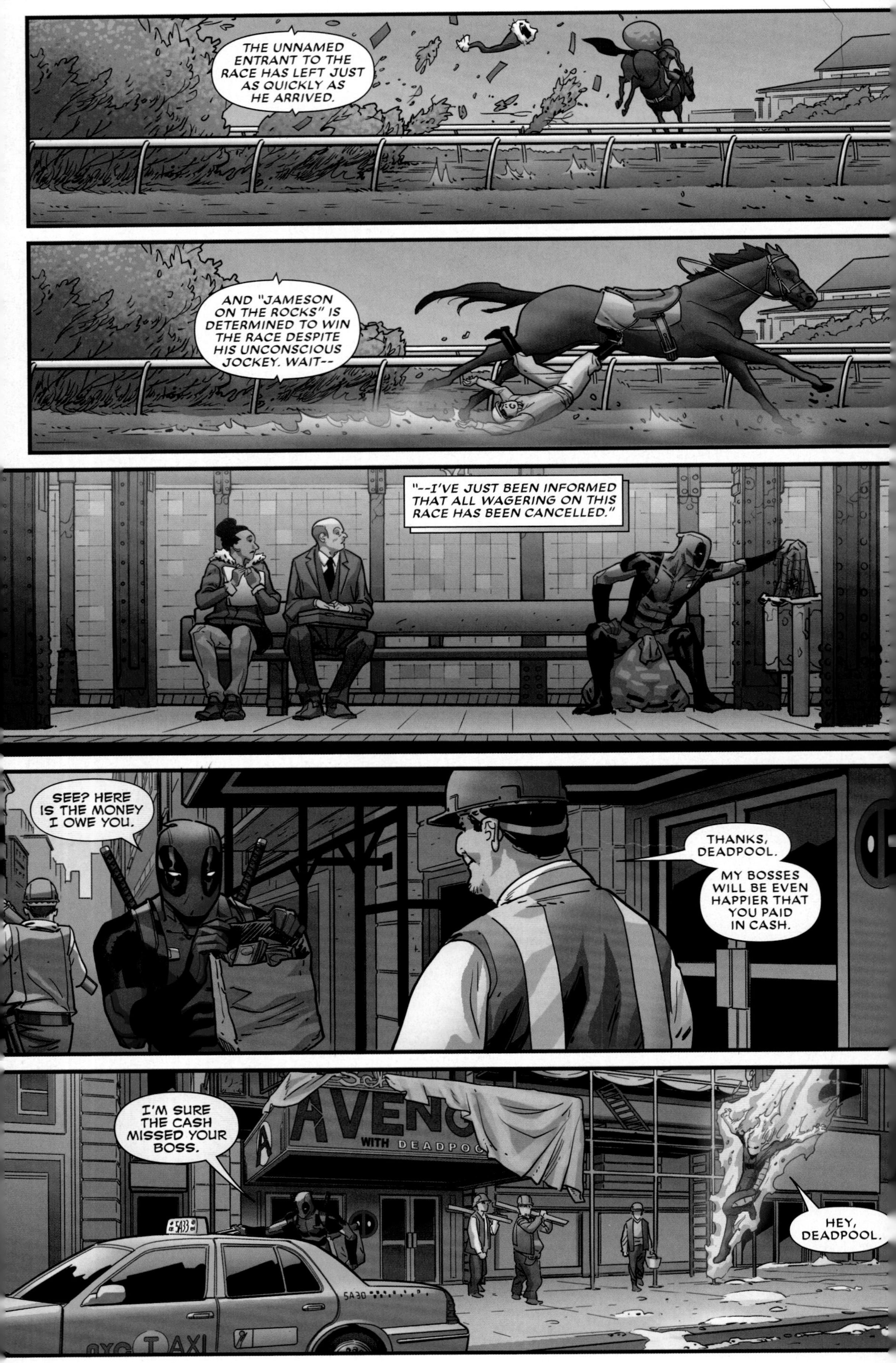

THE UNNAMED ENTRANT TO THE RACE HAS LEFT JUST AS QUICKLY AS HE ARRIVED.
AND "JAMESON ON THE ROCKS" IS DETERMINED TO WIN THE RACE DESPITE HIS UNCONSCIOUS JOCKEY. WAIT--
"--I'VE JUST BEEN INFORMED THAT ALL WAGERING ON THIS RACE HAS BEEN CANCELLED."
SEE? HERE IS THE MONEY I OWE YOU.
THANKS, DEADPOOL.
MY BOSSES WILL BE EVEN HAPPIER THAT YOU PAID IN CASH.
I'M SURE THE CASH MISSED YOUR BOSS.
AVENG
WITH DEADPOO
NYC TAXI
HEY, DEADPOOL.

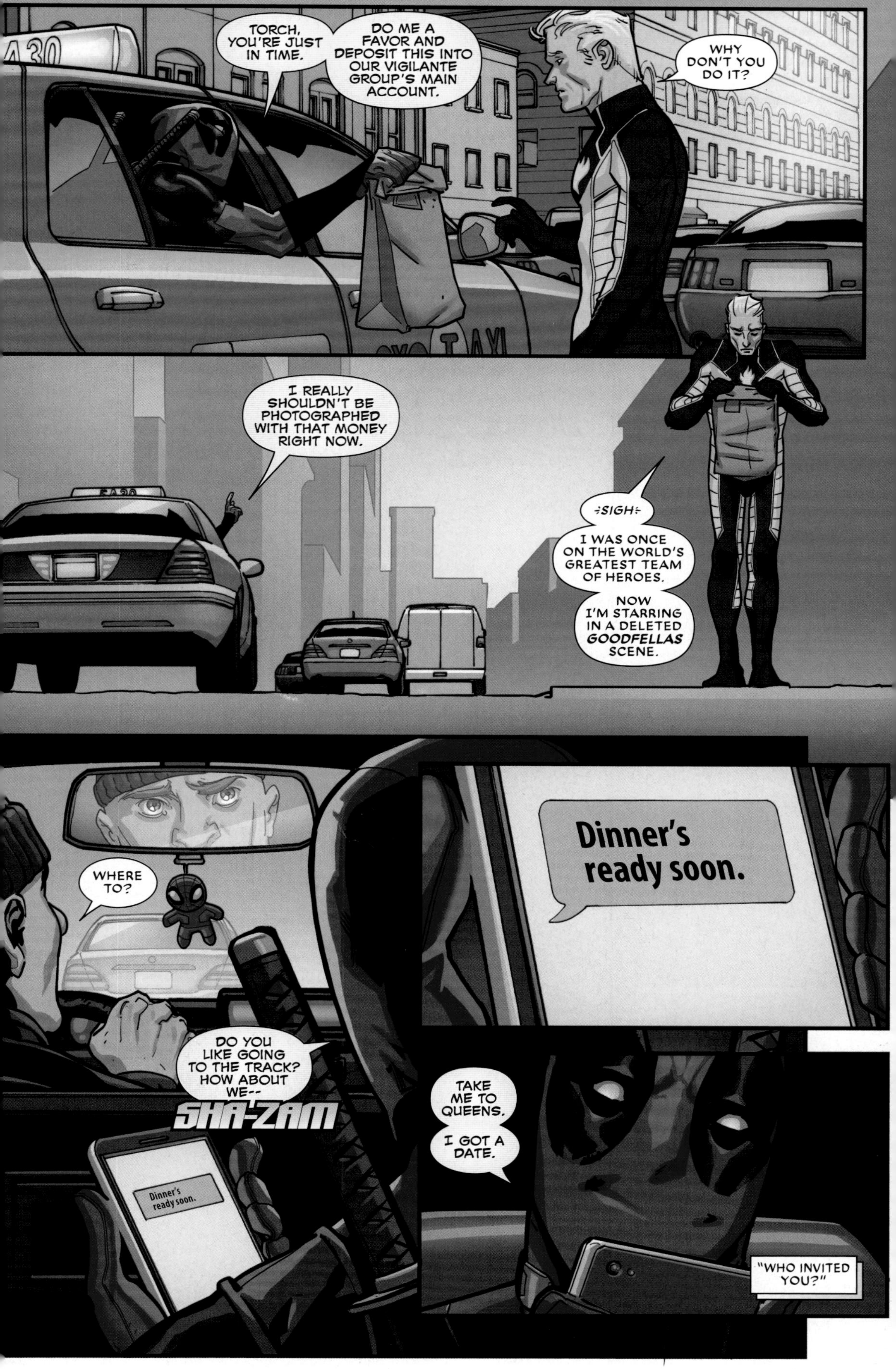
TORCH, YOU'RE JUST IN TIME.
DO ME A FAVOR AND DEPOSIT THIS INTO OUR VIGILANTE GROUP'S MAIN ACCOUNT.
WHY DON'T YOU DO IT?
I REALLY SHOULDN'T BE PHOTOGRAPHED WITH THAT MONEY RIGHT NOW.
SIGH
I WAS ONCE ON THE WORLD'S GREATEST TEAM OF HEROES.
NOW I'M STARRING IN A DELETED GOODFELLAS SCENE.
WHERE TO?
DO YOU LIKE GOING TO THE TRACK? HOW ABOUT WE--
SHA-ZAM
Dinner's ready soon.
Dinner's ready soon.
TAKE ME TO QUEENS.
I GOT A DATE.
"WHO INVITED YOU?"

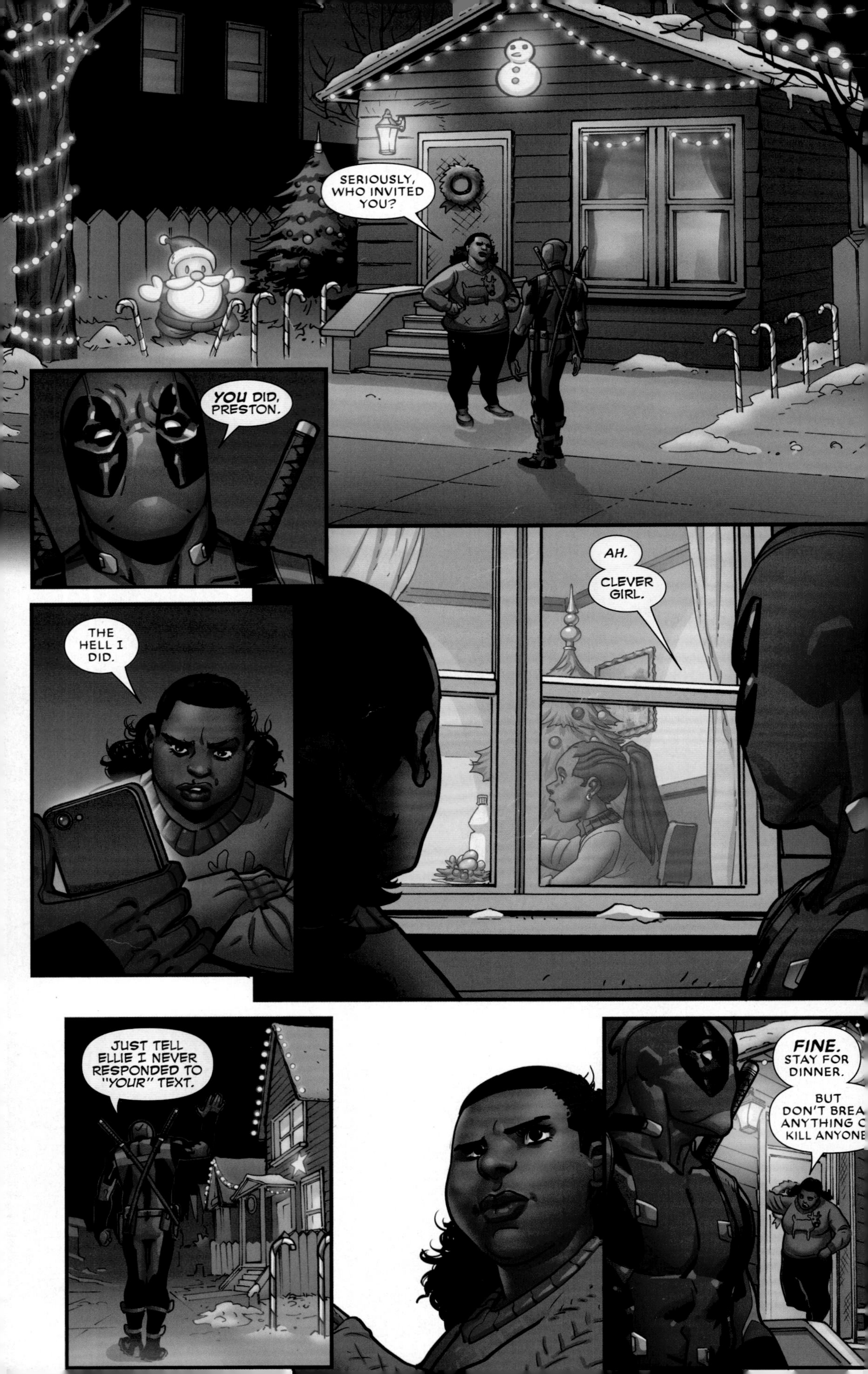
SERIOUSLY, WHO INVITED YOU?
YOU DID, PRESTON.
THE HELL I DID.
AH.
CLEVER GIRL.
JUST TELL ELLIE I NEVER RESPONDED TO "YOUR" TEXT.
FINE. STAY FOR DINNER.
BUT DON'T BREA ANYTHING C KILL ANYONE

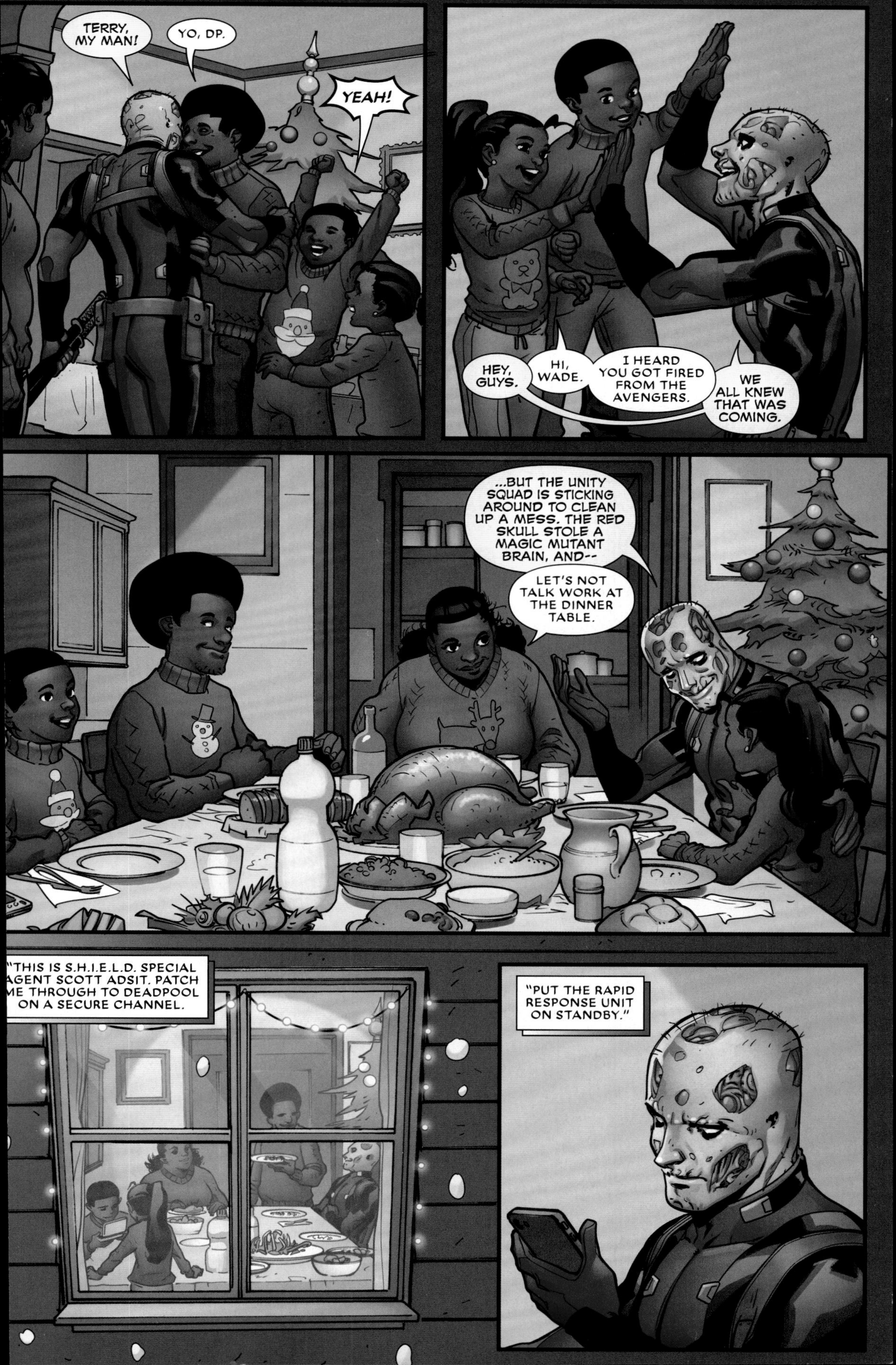
TERRY, MY MAN!
YO, DP.
YEAH!
HEY, GUYS.
HI, WADE.
I HEARD YOU GOT FIRED FROM THE AVENGERS.
WE ALL KNEW THAT WAS COMING.
...BUT THE UNITY SQUAD IS STICKING AROUND TO CLEAN UP A MESS. THE RED SKULL STOLE A MAGIC MUTANT BRAIN, AND--
LET'S NOT TALK WORK AT THE DINNER TABLE.
"THIS IS S.H.I.E.L.D. SPECIAL AGENT SCOTT ADSIT. PATCH ME THROUGH TO DEADPOOL ON A SECURE CHANNEL.
"PUT THE RAPID RESPONSE UNIT ON STANDBY."

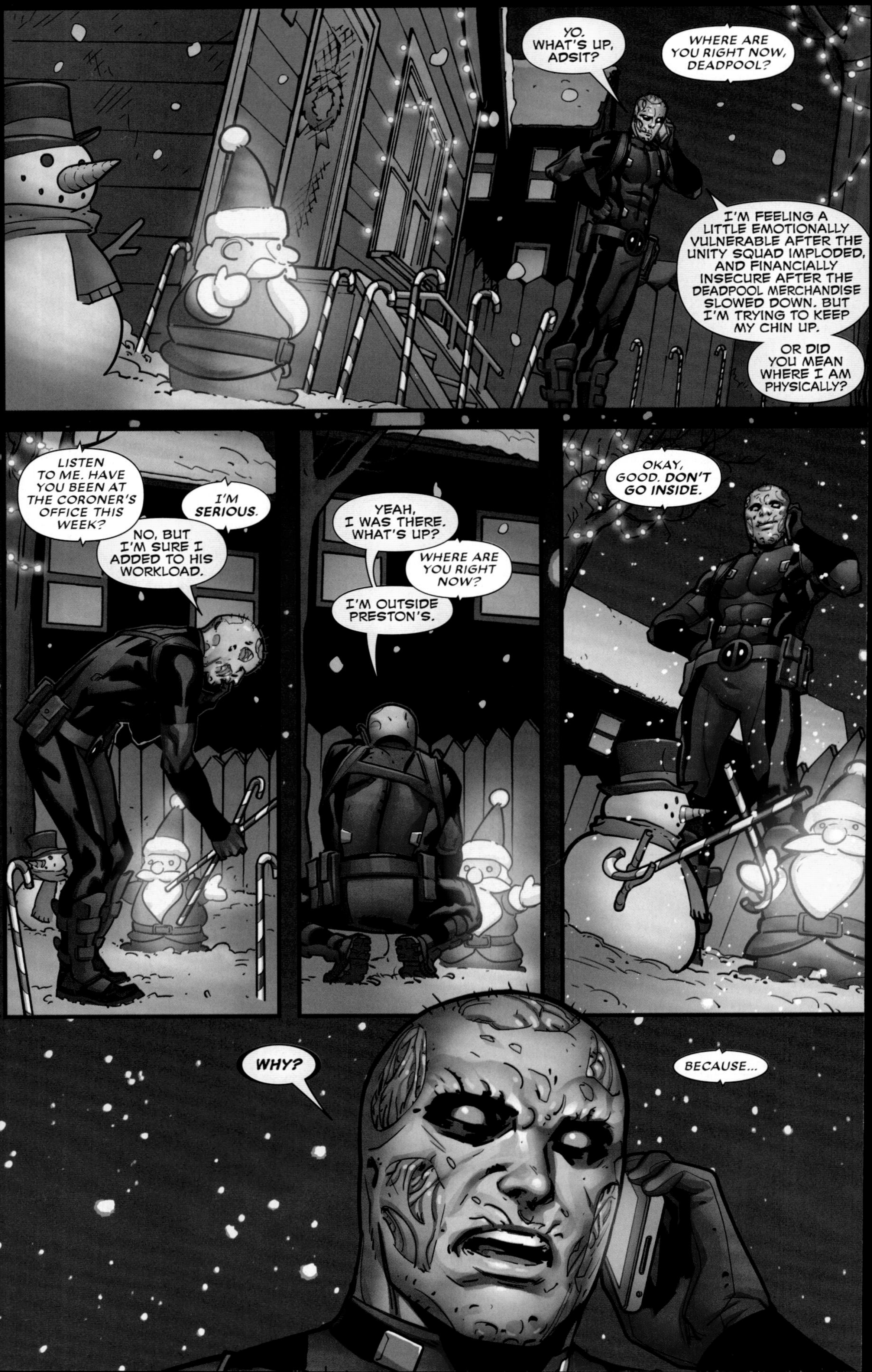
YO. WHAT'S UP, ADSIT?
WHERE ARE YOU RIGHT NOW, DEADPOOL?
I'M FEELING A LITTLE EMOTIONALLY VULNERABLE AFTER THE UNITY SQUAD IMPLODED, AND FINANCIALLY INSECURE AFTER THE DEADPOOL MERCHANDISE SLOWED DOWN. BUT I'M TRYING TO KEEP MY CHIN UP.
OR DID YOU MEAN WHERE I AM PHYSICALLY?
LISTEN TO ME. HAVE YOU BEEN AT THE CORONER'S OFFICE THIS WEEK?
I'M SERIOUS.
NO, BUT I'M SURE I ADDED TO HIS WORKLOAD.
YEAH, I WAS THERE. WHAT'S UP?
WHERE ARE YOU RIGHT NOW?
I'M OUTSIDE PRESTON'S.
OKAY, GOOD. DON'T GO INSIDE.
WHY?
BECAUSE...

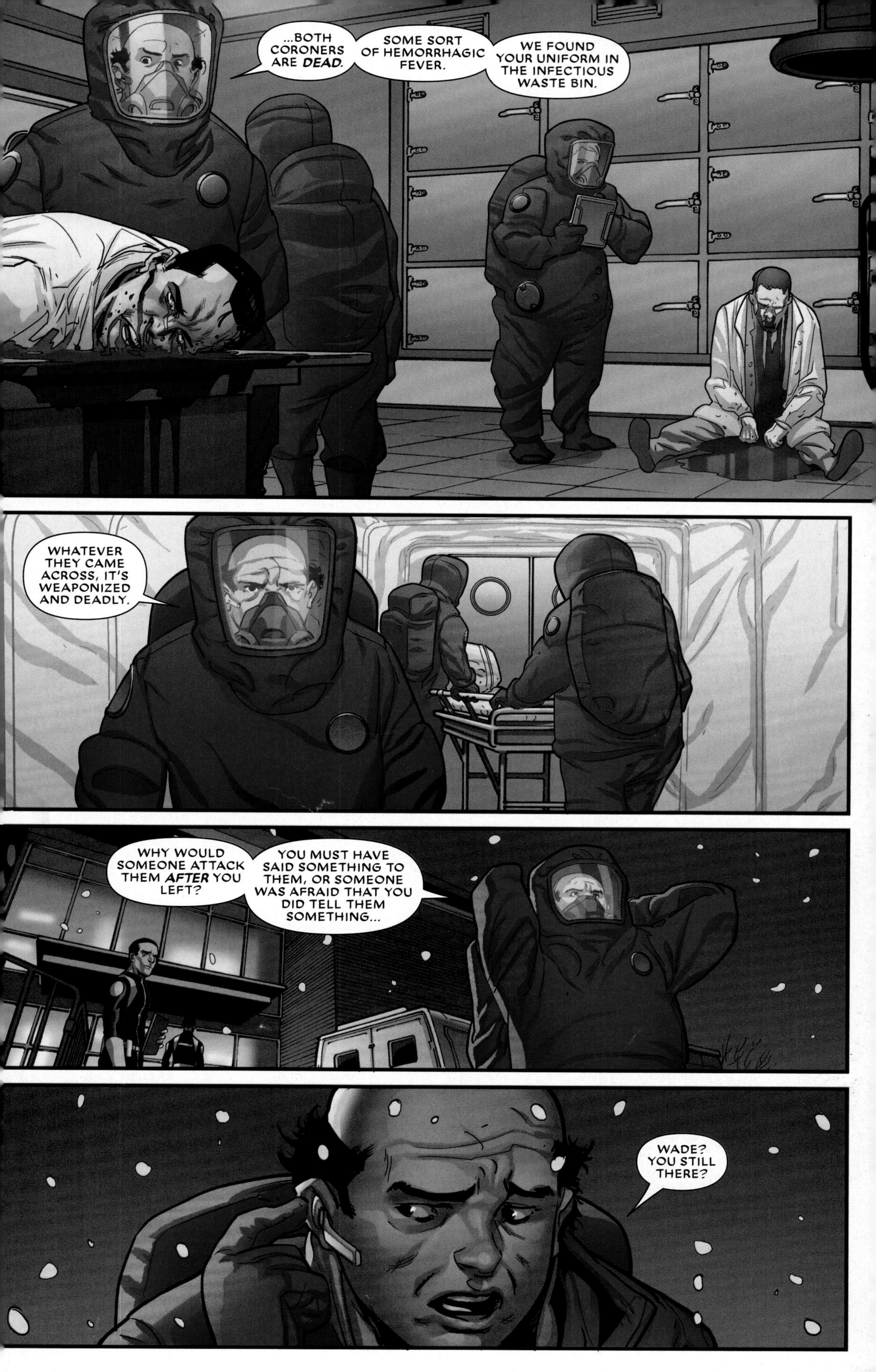
...BOTH CORONERS ARE *DEAD*.
SOME SORT OF HEMORRHAGIC FEVER.
WE FOUND YOUR UNIFORM IN THE INFECTIOUS WASTE BIN.
WHATEVER THEY CAME ACROSS, IT'S WEAPONIZED AND DEADLY.
WHY WOULD SOMEONE ATTACK THEM *AFTER* YOU LEFT?
YOU MUST HAVE SAID SOMETHING TO THEM, OR SOMEONE WAS AFRAID THAT YOU DID TELL THEM SOMETHING...
WADE? YOU STILL THERE?

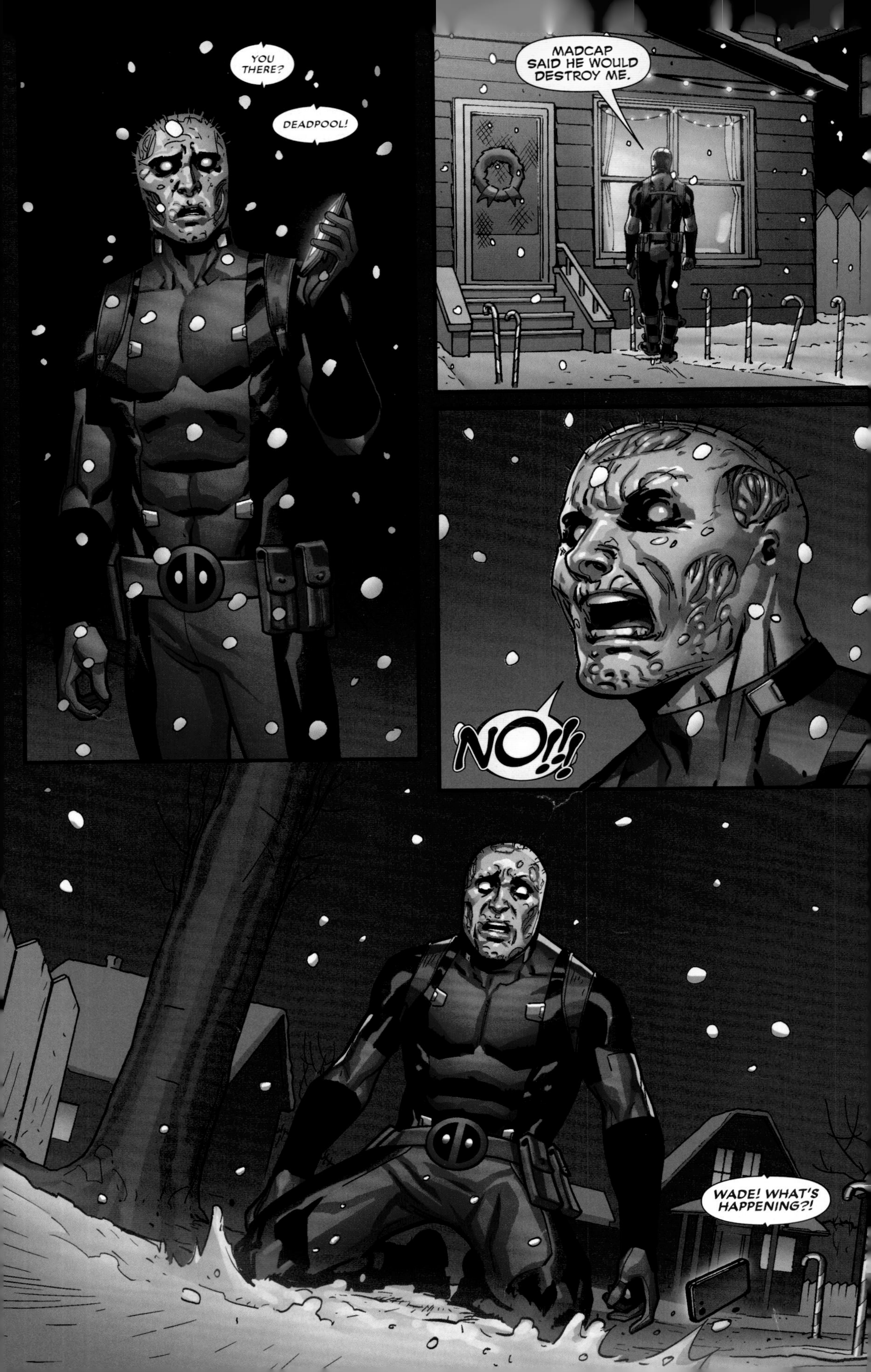
YOU THERE?
DEADPOOL!
MADCAP SAID HE WOULD DESTROY ME.
NO!!!
WADE! WHAT'S HAPPENING?!

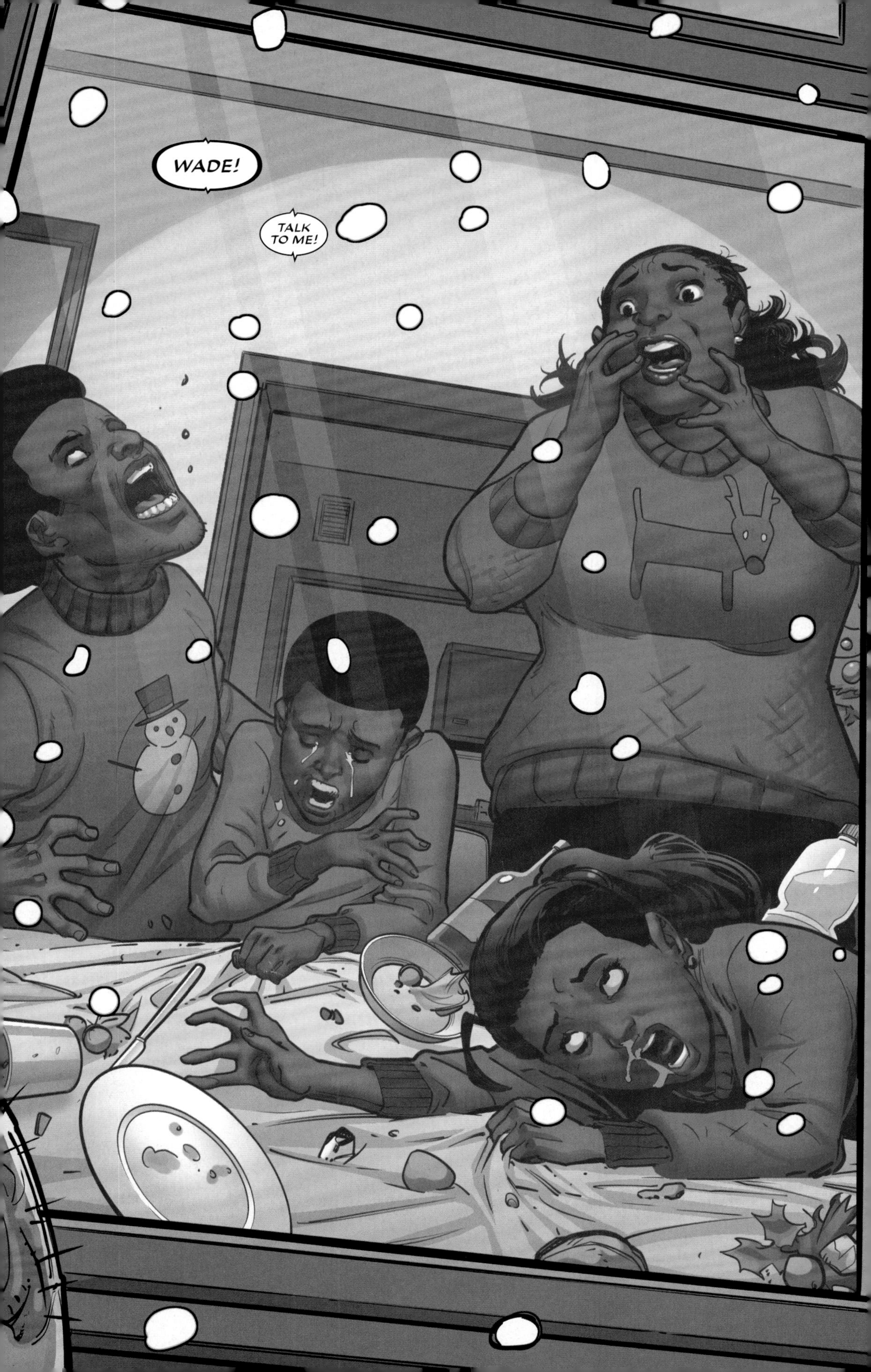
WADE!
TALK TO ME!

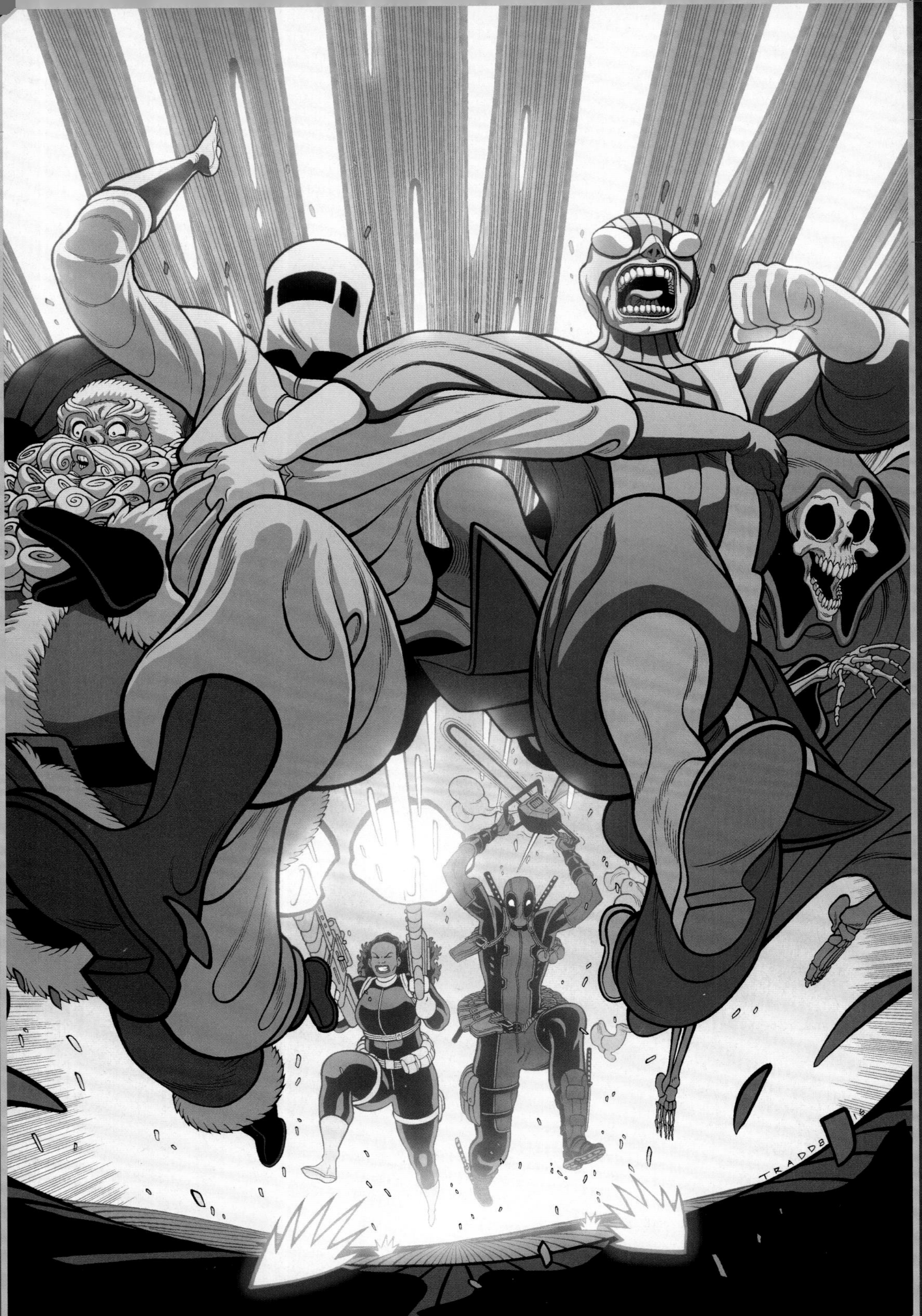

23 | DO THE TRUFFLE SHUFFLE

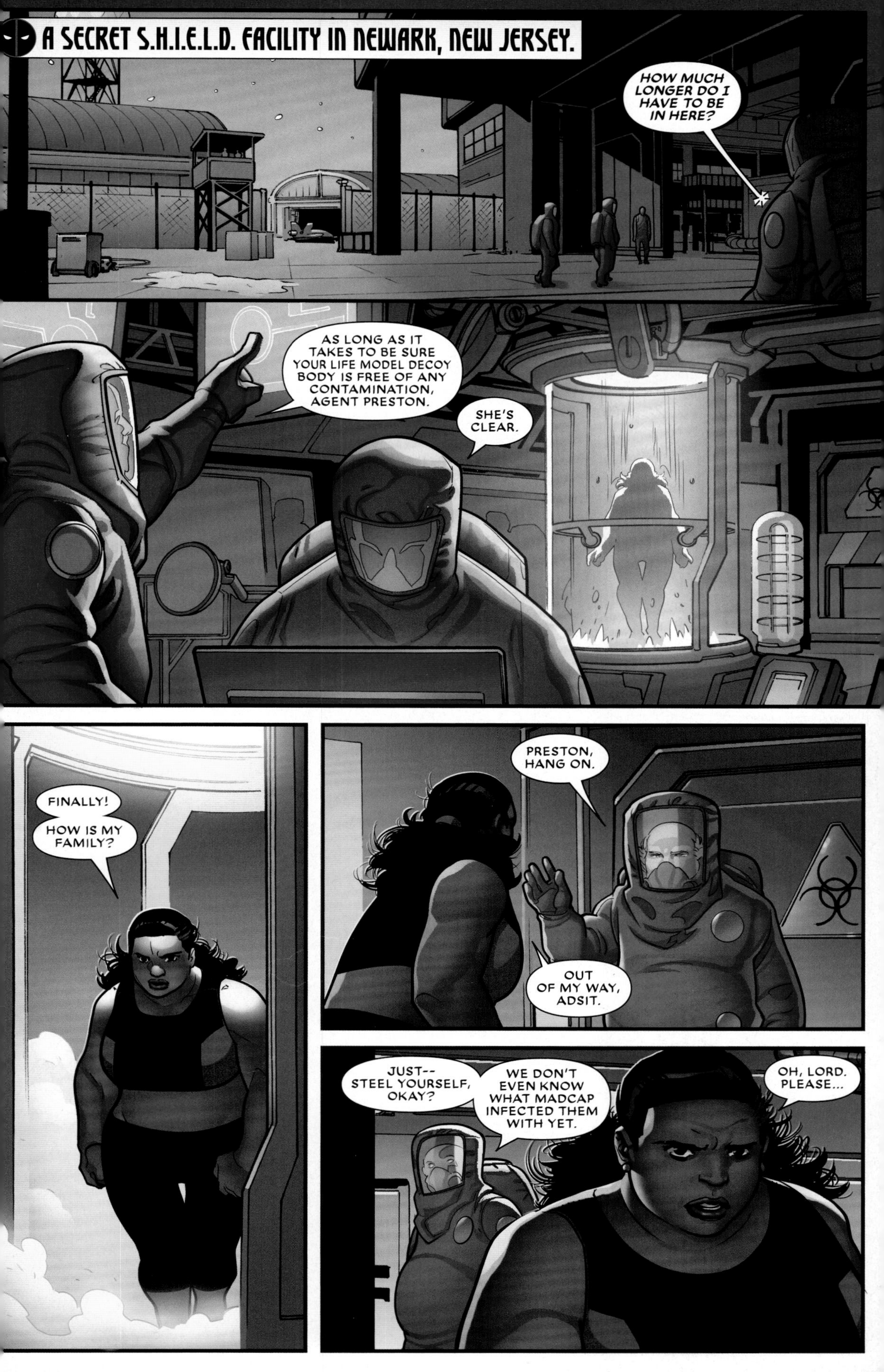
A SECRET S.H.I.E.L.D. FACILITY IN NEWARK, NEW JERSEY.
HOW MUCH LONGER DO I HAVE TO BE IN HERE?
AS LONG AS IT TAKES TO BE SURE YOUR LIFE MODEL DECOY BODY IS FREE OF ANY CONTAMINATION, AGENT PRESTON.
SHE'S CLEAR.
FINALLY!
HOW IS MY FAMILY?
PRESTON, HANG ON.
OUT OF MY WAY, ADSIT.
JUST-- STEEL YOURSELF, OKAY?
WE DON'T EVEN KNOW WHAT MADCAP INFECTED THEM WITH YET.
OH, LORD. PLEASE...

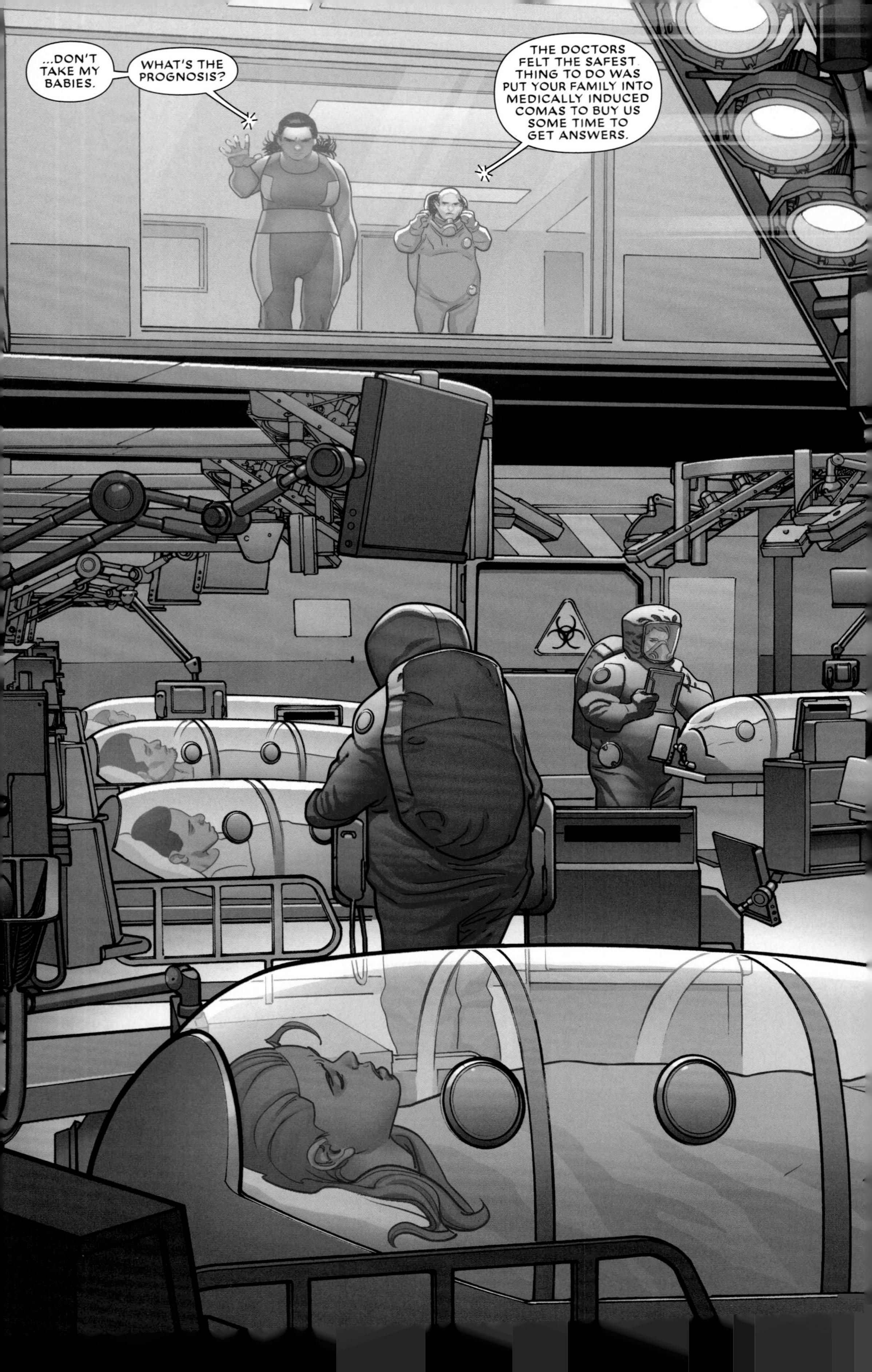
...DON'T TAKE MY BABIES.
WHAT'S THE PROGNOSIS?
THE DOCTORS FELT THE SAFEST THING TO DO WAS PUT YOUR FAMILY INTO MEDICALLY INDUCED COMAS TO BUY US SOME TIME TO GET ANSWERS.

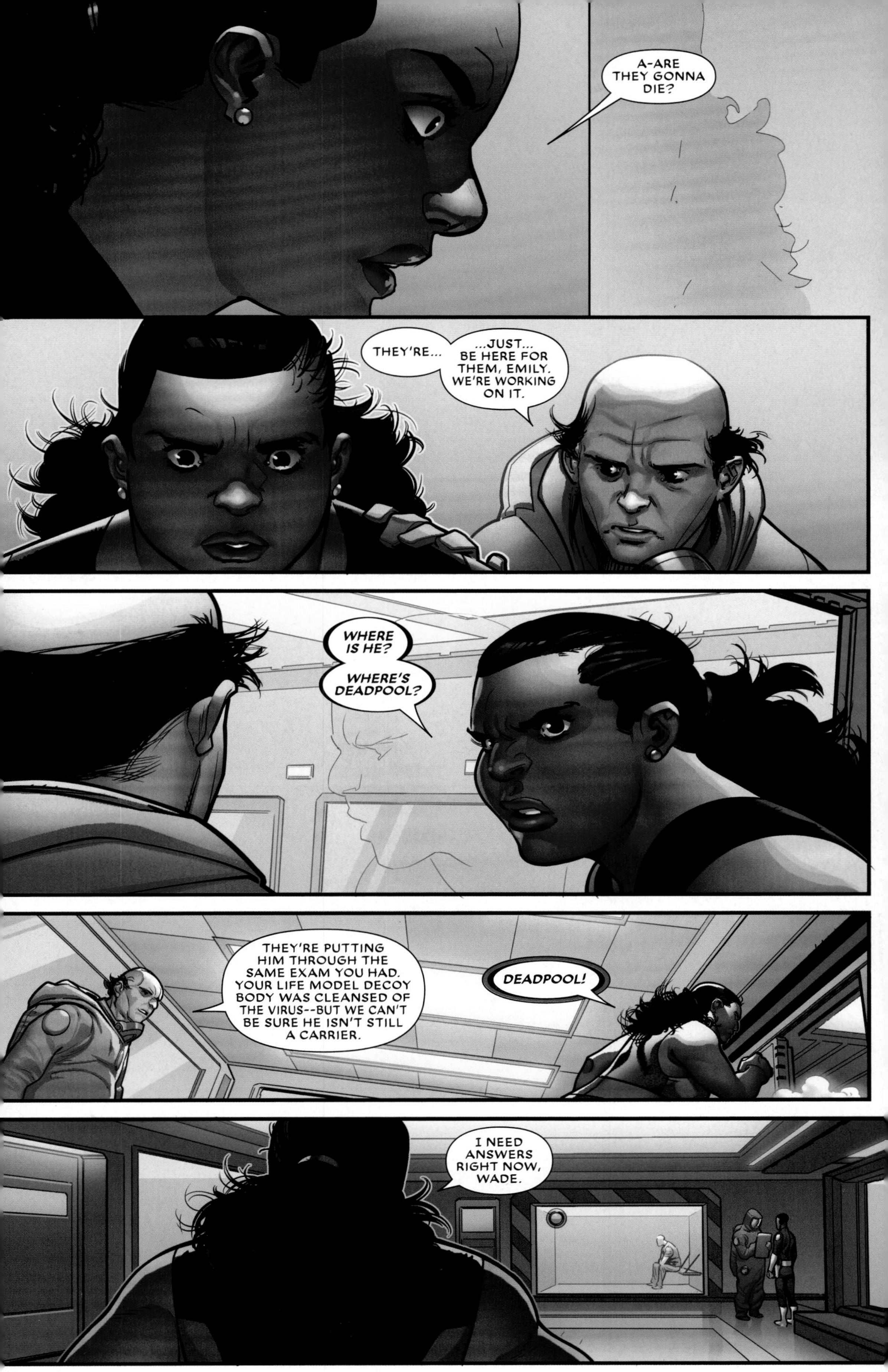
A-ARE THEY GONNA DIE?
THEY'RE...
...JUST... BE HERE FOR THEM, EMILY. WE'RE WORKING ON IT.
WHERE IS HE?
WHERE'S DEADPOOL?
THEY'RE PUTTING HIM THROUGH THE SAME EXAM YOU HAD. YOUR LIFE MODEL DECOY BODY WAS CLEANSED OF THE VIRUS--BUT WE CAN'T BE SURE HE ISN'T STILL A CARRIER.
DEADPOOL!
I NEED ANSWERS RIGHT NOW, WADE.

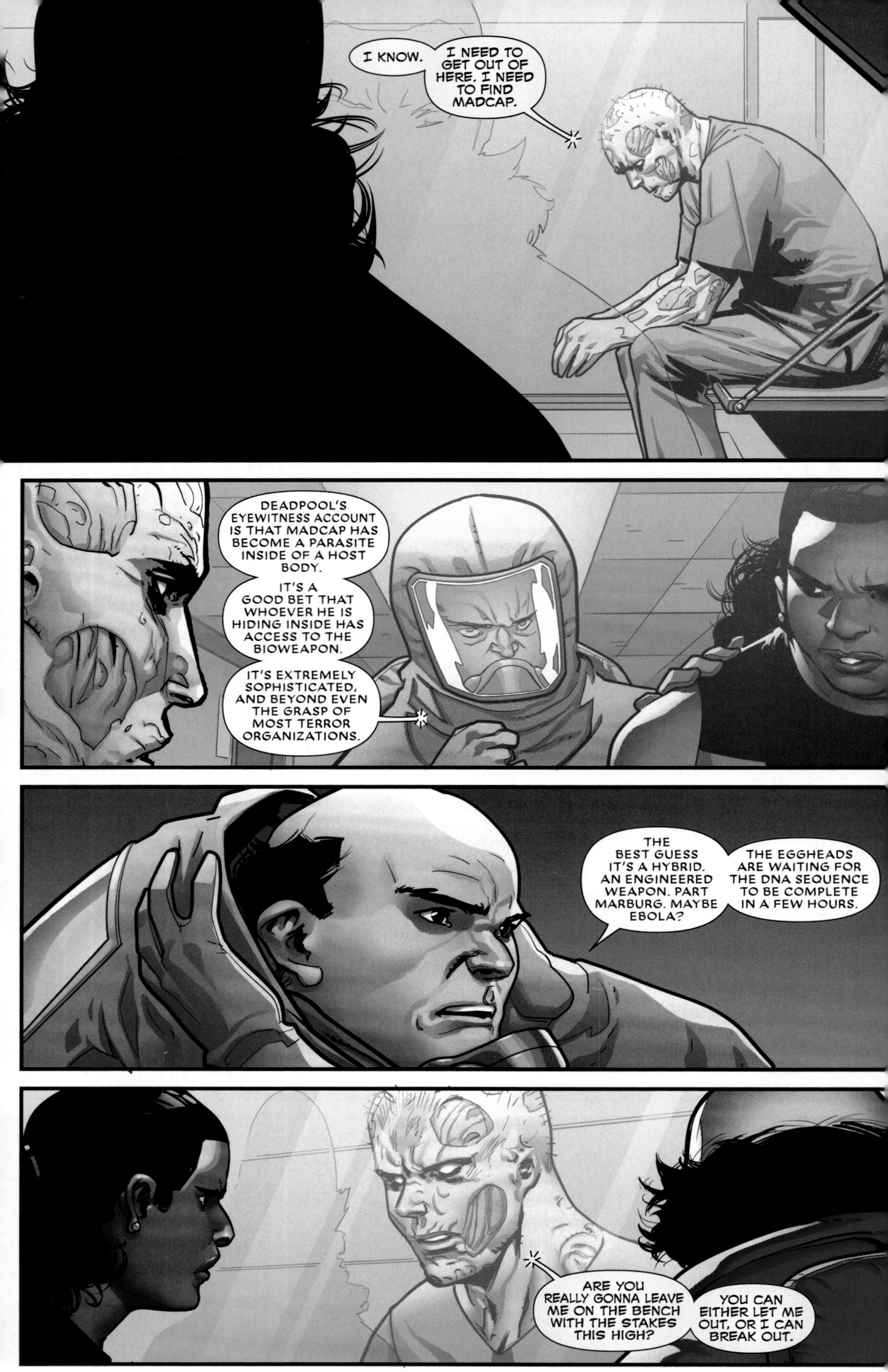
I KNOW.
I NEED TO GET OUT OF HERE. I NEED TO FIND MADCAP.
DEADPOOL'S EYEWITNESS ACCOUNT IS THAT MADCAP HAS BECOME A PARASITE INSIDE OF A HOST BODY.
IT'S A GOOD BET THAT WHOEVER HE IS HIDING INSIDE HAS ACCESS TO THE BIOWEAPON.
IT'S EXTREMELY SOPHISTICATED, AND BEYOND EVEN THE GRASP OF MOST TERROR ORGANIZATIONS.
THE BEST GUESS IT'S A HYBRID. AN ENGINEERED WEAPON. PART MARBURG. MAYBE EBOLA?
THE EGGHEADS ARE WAITING FOR THE DNA SEQUENCE TO BE COMPLETE IN A FEW HOURS.
ARE YOU REALLY GONNA LEAVE ME ON THE BENCH WITH THE STAKES THIS HIGH?
YOU CAN EITHER LET ME OUT, OR I CAN BREAK OUT.

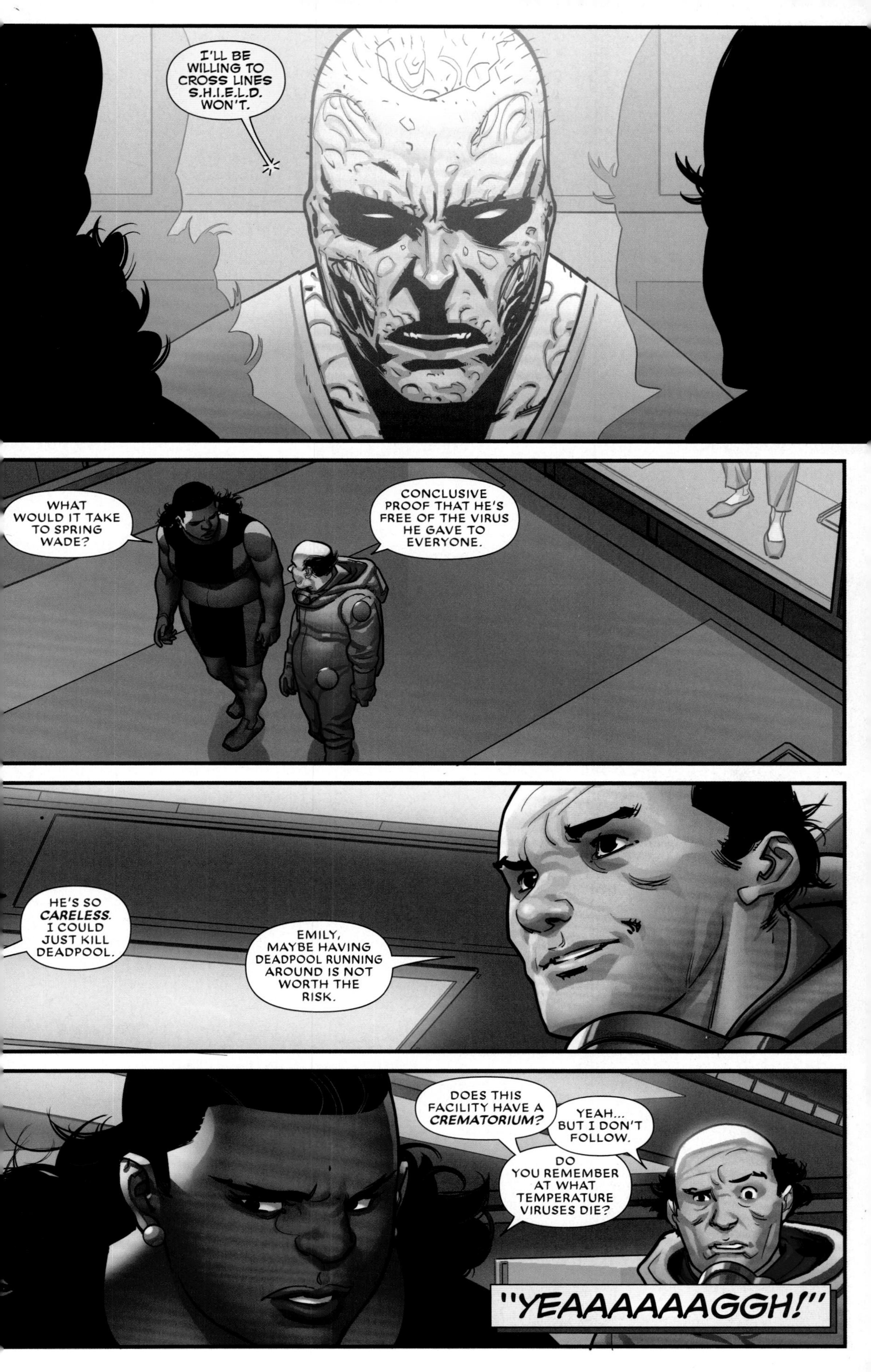
I'LL BE WILLING TO CROSS LINES S.H.I.E.L.D. WON'T.
WHAT WOULD IT TAKE TO SPRING WADE?
CONCLUSIVE PROOF THAT HE'S FREE OF THE VIRUS HE GAVE TO EVERYONE.
HE'S SO *CARELESS.* I COULD JUST KILL DEADPOOL.
EMILY, MAYBE HAVING DEADPOOL RUNNING AROUND IS NOT WORTH THE RISK.
DOES THIS FACILITY HAVE A *CREMATORIUM?*
YEAH... BUT I DON'T FOLLOW.
DO YOU REMEMBER AT WHAT TEMPERATURE VIRUSES DIE?
"YEAAAAAAGGH!"

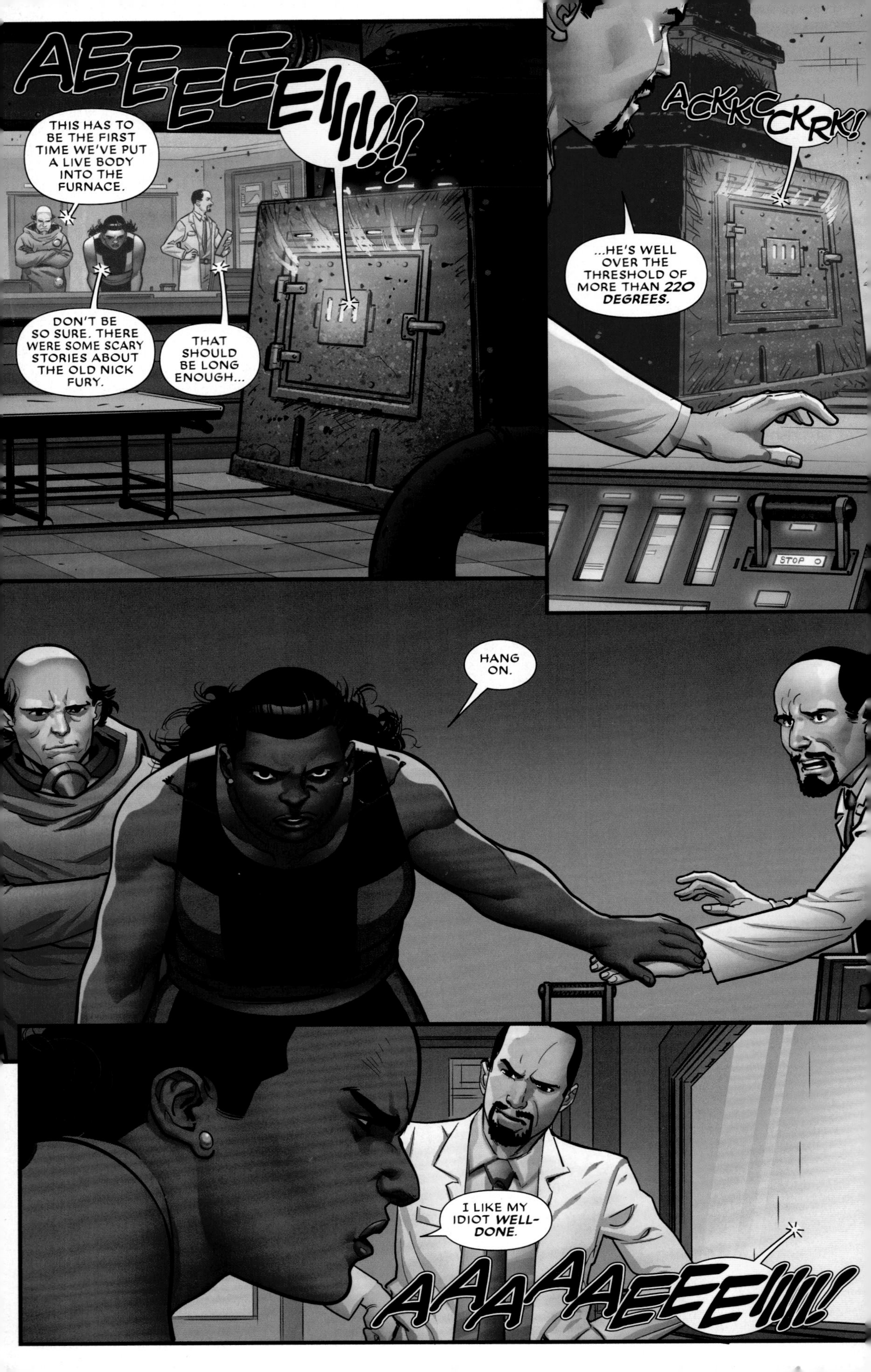
AEEEEEEIII!!!
THIS HAS TO BE THE FIRST TIME WE'VE PUT A LIVE BODY INTO THE FURNACE.
DON'T BE SO SURE. THERE WERE SOME SCARY STORIES ABOUT THE OLD NICK FURY.
THAT SHOULD BE LONG ENOUGH...
ACKKCCKRK!
...HE'S WELL OVER THE THRESHOLD OF MORE THAN 220 DEGREES.
STOP
HANG ON.
I LIKE MY IDIOT WELL-DONE.
AAAAAEEEIIII!

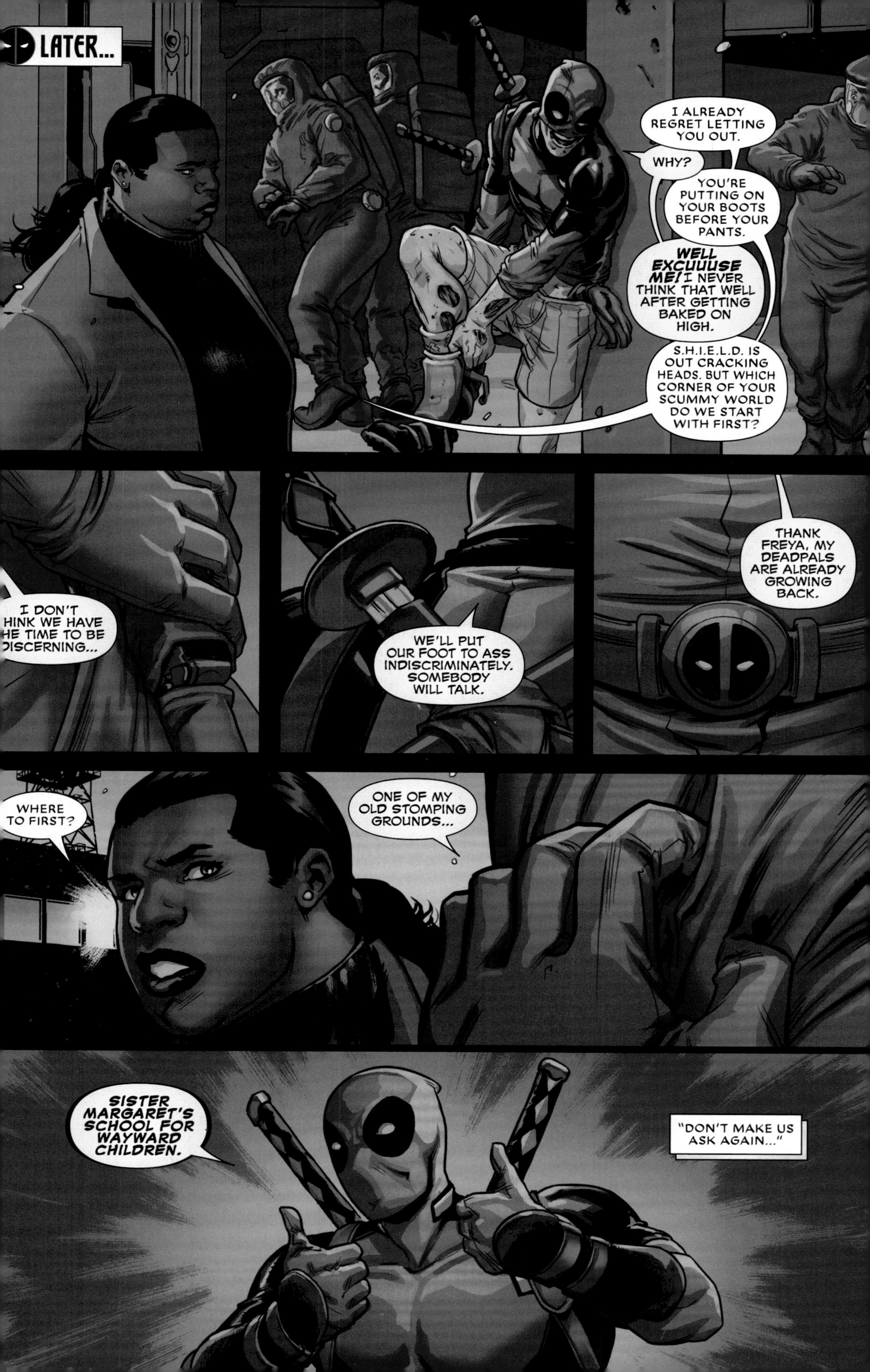
LATER...
I ALREADY REGRET LETTING YOU OUT.
WHY?
YOU'RE PUTTING ON YOUR BOOTS BEFORE YOUR PANTS.
WELL EXCUUUSE ME! I NEVER THINK THAT WELL AFTER GETTING BAKED ON HIGH.
S.H.I.E.L.D. IS OUT CRACKING HEADS. BUT WHICH CORNER OF YOUR SCUMMY WORLD DO WE START WITH FIRST?
I DON'T HINK WE HAVE HE TIME TO BE DISCERNING...
WE'LL PUT OUR FOOT TO ASS INDISCRIMINATELY. SOMEBODY WILL TALK.
THANK FREYA, MY DEADPALS ARE ALREADY GROWING BACK.
WHERE TO FIRST?
ONE OF MY OLD STOMPING GROUNDS...
SISTER MARGARET'S SCHOOL FOR WAYWARD CHILDREN.
"DON'T MAKE US ASK AGAIN..."

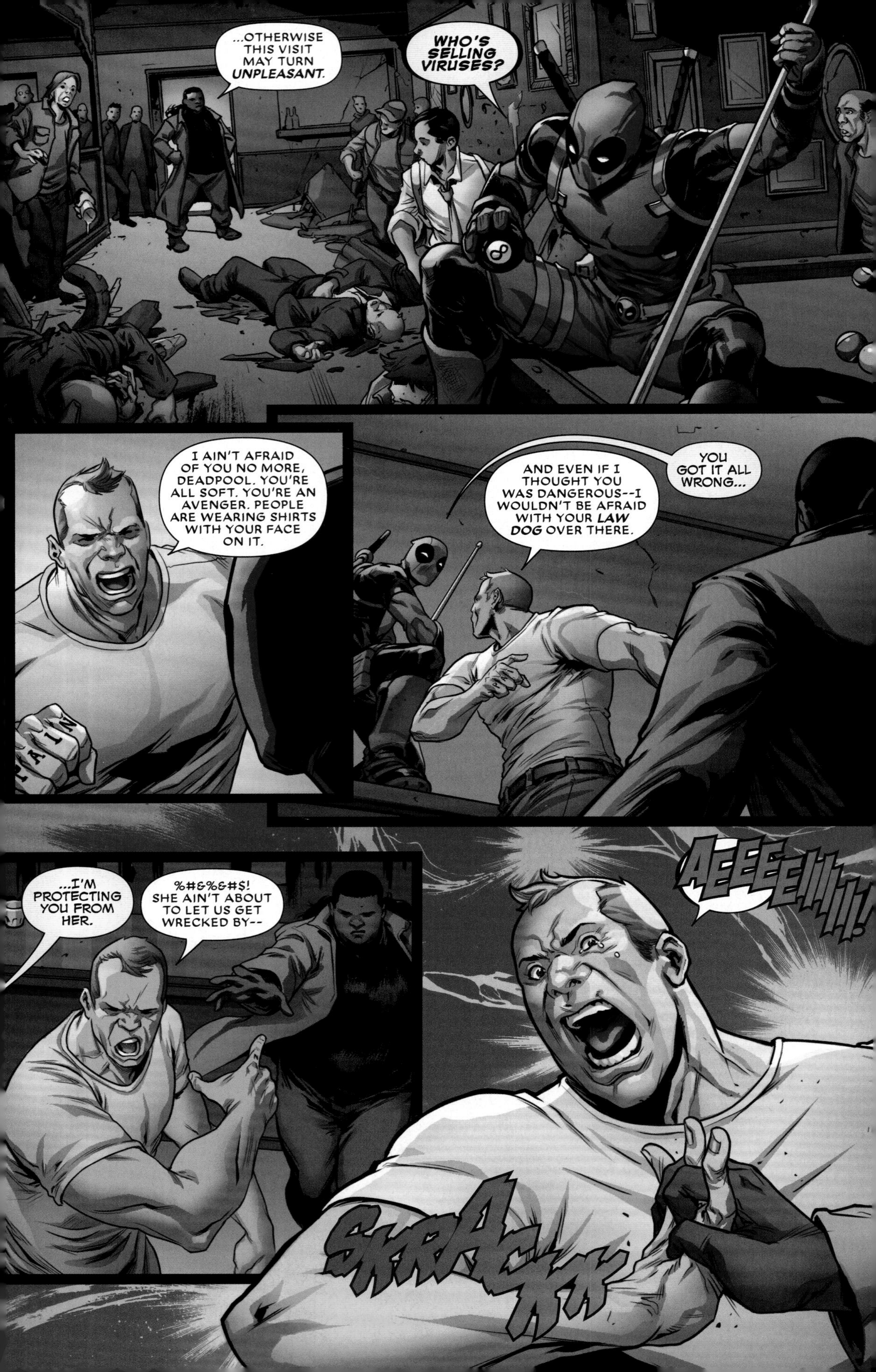
...OTHERWISE THIS VISIT MAY TURN UNPLEASANT.
WHO'S SELLING VIRUSES?
I AIN'T AFRAID OF YOU NO MORE, DEADPOOL. YOU'RE ALL SOFT. YOU'RE AN AVENGER. PEOPLE ARE WEARING SHIRTS WITH YOUR FACE ON IT.
AND EVEN IF I THOUGHT YOU WAS DANGEROUS--I WOULDN'T BE AFRAID WITH YOUR LAW DOG OVER THERE.
YOU GOT IT ALL WRONG...
...I'M PROTECTING YOU FROM HER.
%#&%&#$! SHE AIN'T ABOUT TO LET US GET WRECKED BY--
AEEEEIIIIII!
SKRACKK

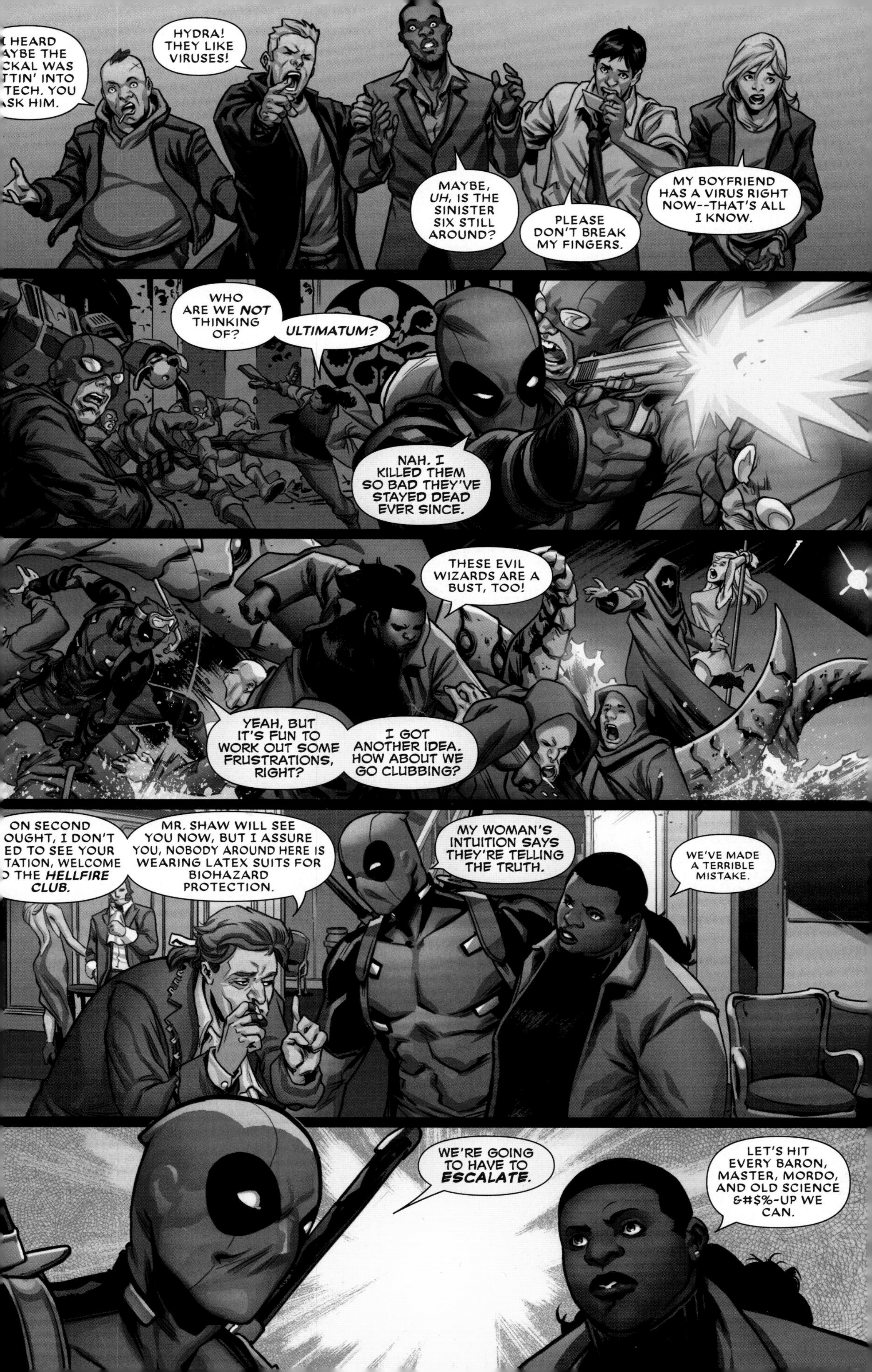

I HEARD AYBE THE CKAL WAS TTIN' INTO TECH. YOU ASK HIM.
HYDRA! THEY LIKE VIRUSES!
MAYBE, UH, IS THE SINISTER SIX STILL AROUND?
PLEASE DON'T BREAK MY FINGERS.
MY BOYFRIEND HAS A VIRUS RIGHT NOW--THAT'S ALL I KNOW.
WHO ARE WE NOT THINKING OF?
ULTIMATUM?
NAH. I KILLED THEM SO BAD THEY'VE STAYED DEAD EVER SINCE.
THESE EVIL WIZARDS ARE A BUST, TOO!
YEAH, BUT IT'S FUN TO WORK OUT SOME FRUSTRATIONS, RIGHT?
I GOT ANOTHER IDEA. HOW ABOUT WE GO CLUBBING?
ON SECOND OUGHT, I DON'T ED TO SEE YOUR TATION, WELCOME O THE HELLFIRE CLUB.
MR. SHAW WILL SEE YOU NOW, BUT I ASSURE YOU, NOBODY AROUND HERE IS WEARING LATEX SUITS FOR BIOHAZARD PROTECTION.
MY WOMAN'S INTUITION SAYS THEY'RE TELLING THE TRUTH.
WE'VE MADE A TERRIBLE MISTAKE.
WE'RE GOING TO HAVE TO ESCALATE.
LET'S HIT EVERY BARON, MASTER, MORDO, AND OLD SCIENCE &#$%-UP WE CAN.

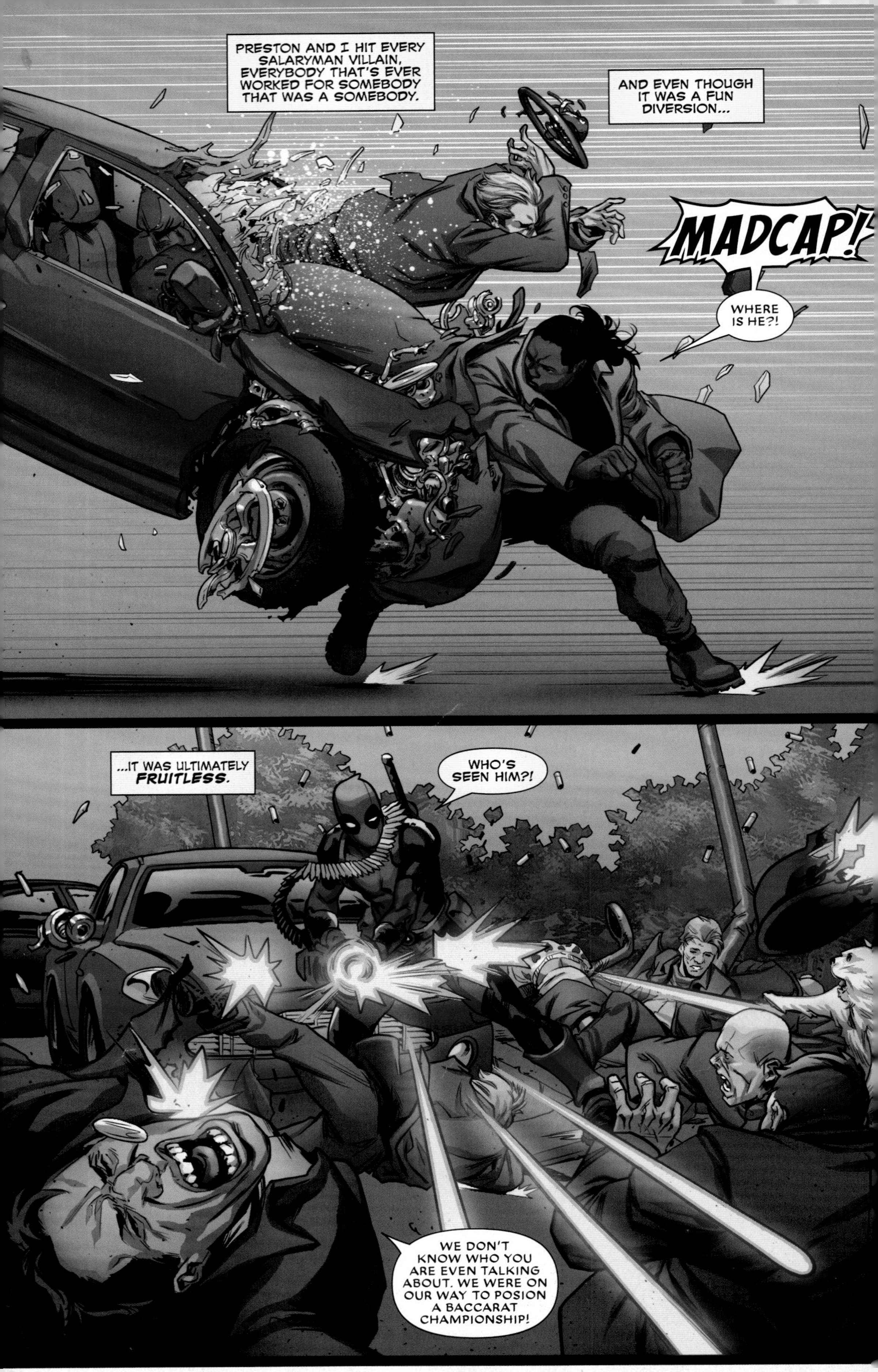
PRESTON AND I HIT EVERY SALARYMAN VILLAIN, EVERYBODY THAT'S EVER WORKED FOR SOMEBODY THAT WAS A SOMEBODY.
AND EVEN THOUGH IT WAS A FUN DIVERSION...
MADCAP!
WHERE IS HE?!
...IT WAS ULTIMATELY FRUITLESS.
WHO'S SEEN HIM?!
WE DON'T KNOW WHO YOU ARE EVEN TALKING ABOUT. WE WERE ON OUR WAY TO POSION A BACCARAT CHAMPIONSHIP!

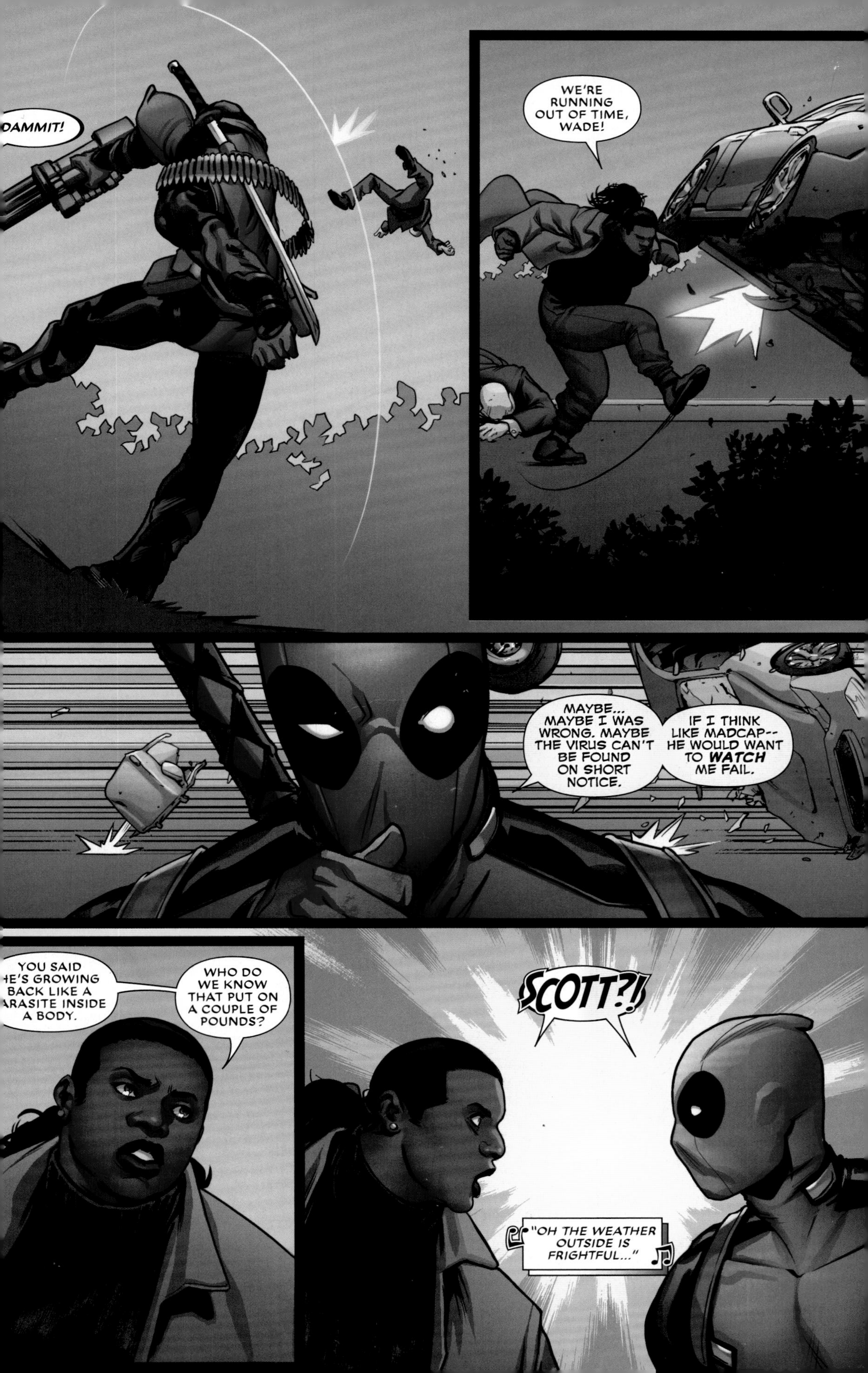
DAMMIT!
WE'RE RUNNING OUT OF TIME, WADE!
MAYBE... MAYBE I WAS WRONG. MAYBE THE VIRUS CAN'T BE FOUND ON SHORT NOTICE.
IF I THINK LIKE MADCAP-- HE WOULD WANT TO WATCH ME FAIL.
YOU SAID HE'S GROWING BACK LIKE A PARASITE INSIDE A BODY.
WHO DO WE KNOW THAT PUT ON A COUPLE OF POUNDS?
SCOTT?!
"OH THE WEATHER OUTSIDE IS FRIGHTFUL..."

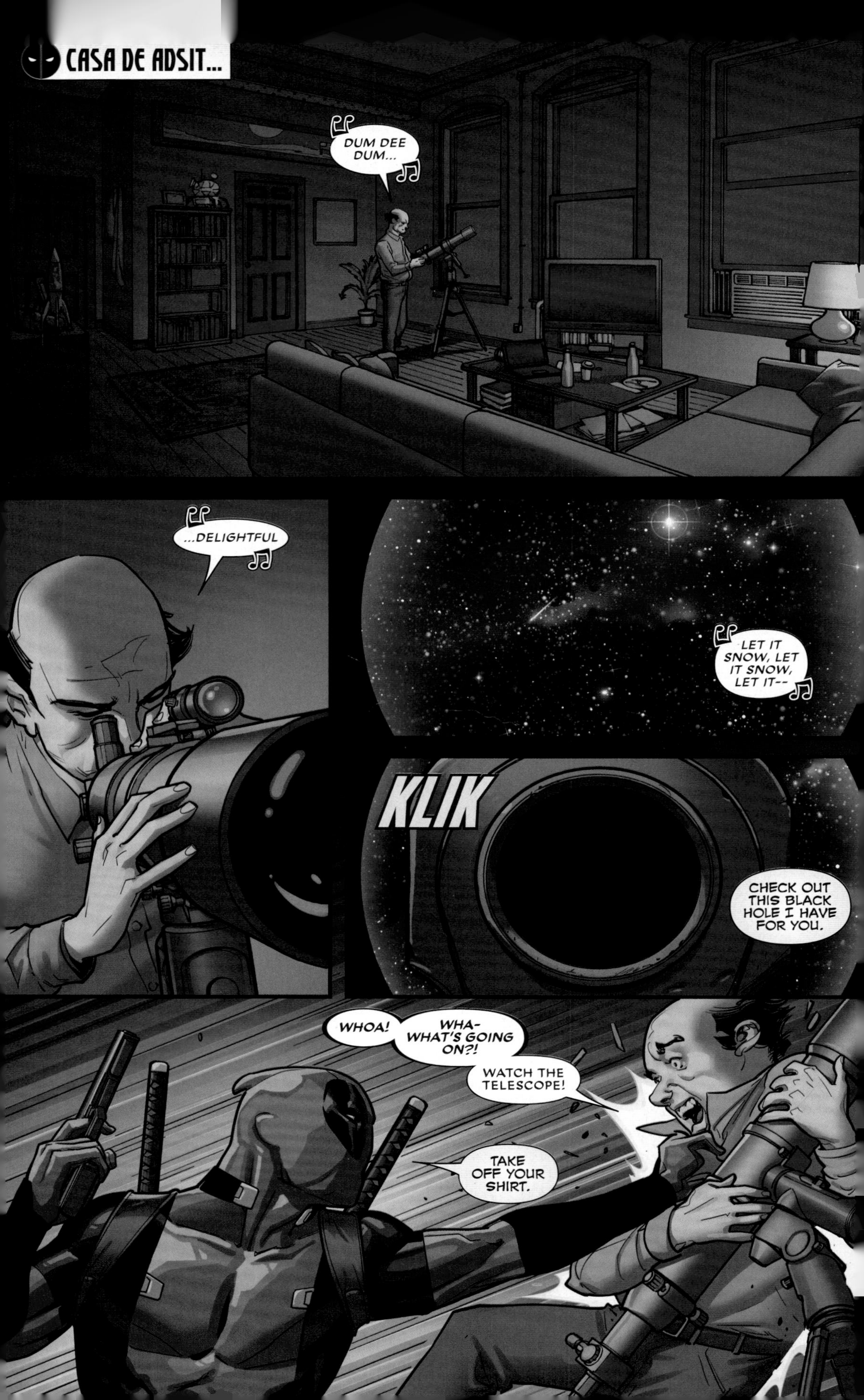
CASA DE ADSIT...
DUM DEE DUM...
...DELIGHTFUL
LET IT SNOW, LET IT SNOW, LET IT--
KLIK
CHECK OUT THIS BLACK HOLE I HAVE FOR YOU.
WHOA!
WHA-WHAT'S GOING ON?!
WATCH THE TELESCOPE!
TAKE OFF YOUR SHIRT.

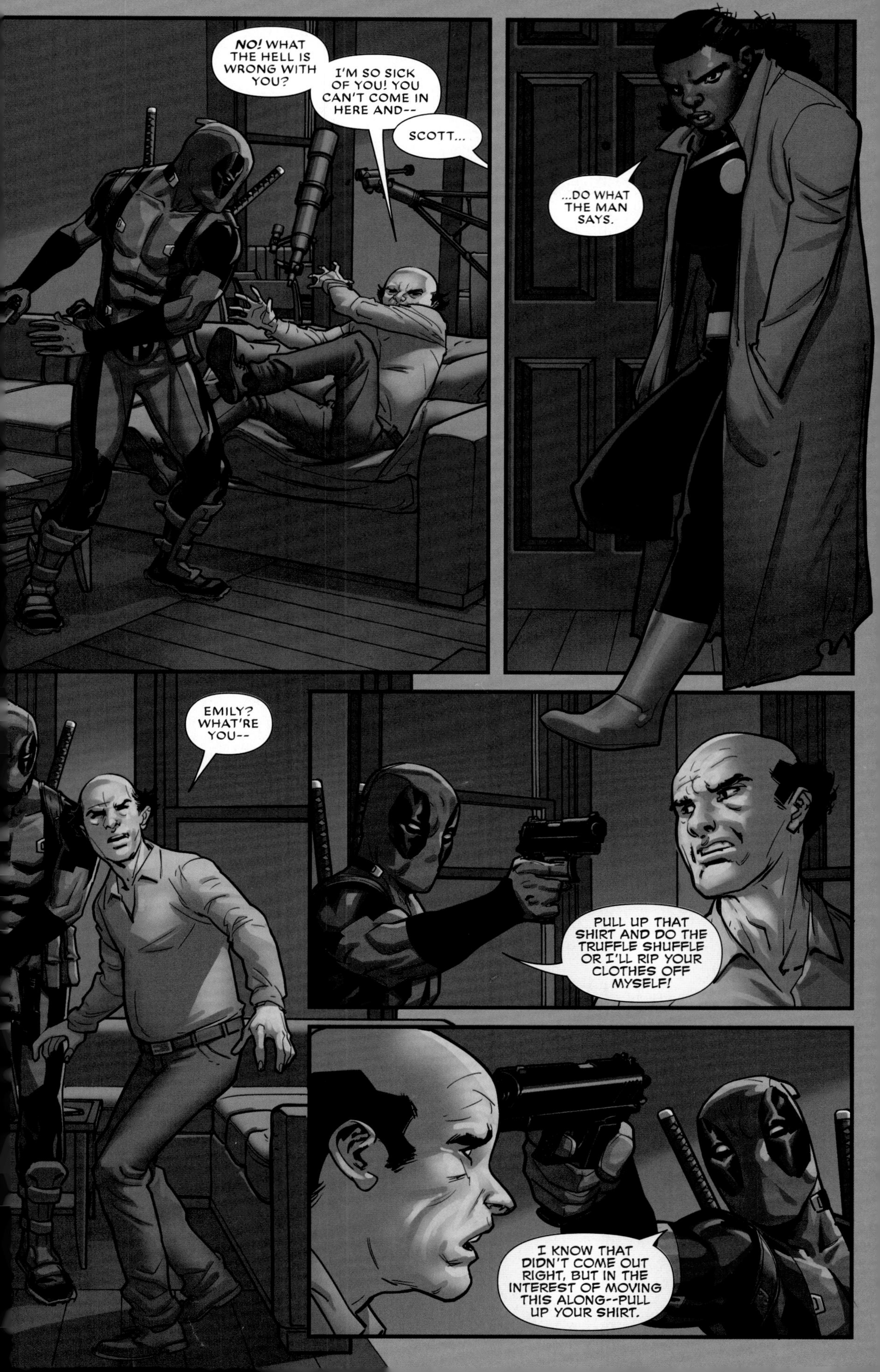
NO! WHAT THE HELL IS WRONG WITH YOU?
I'M SO SICK OF YOU! YOU CAN'T COME IN HERE AND--
SCOTT...
...DO WHAT THE MAN SAYS.
EMILY? WHAT'RE YOU--
PULL UP THAT SHIRT AND DO THE TRUFFLE SHUFFLE OR I'LL RIP YOUR CLOTHES OFF MYSELF!
I KNOW THAT DIDN'T COME OUT RIGHT, BUT IN THE INTEREST OF MOVING THIS ALONG--PULL UP YOUR SHIRT.

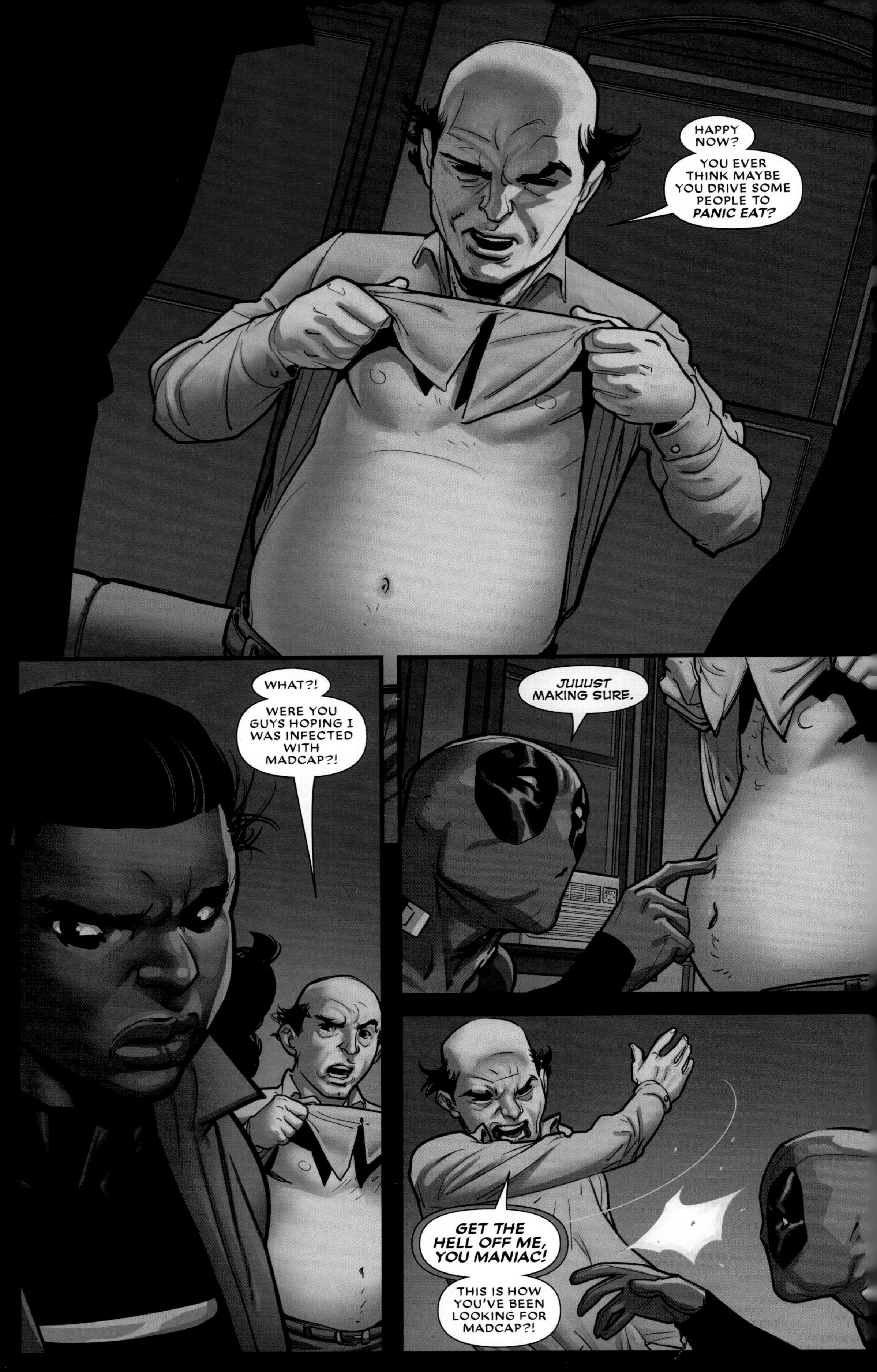
HAPPY NOW?
YOU EVER THINK MAYBE YOU DRIVE SOME PEOPLE TO *PANIC EAT?*
WHAT?!
WERE YOU GUYS HOPING I WAS INFECTED WITH MADCAP?!
JUUUST MAKING SURE.
GET THE HELL OFF ME, YOU MANIAC!
THIS IS HOW YOU'VE BEEN LOOKING FOR MADCAP?!

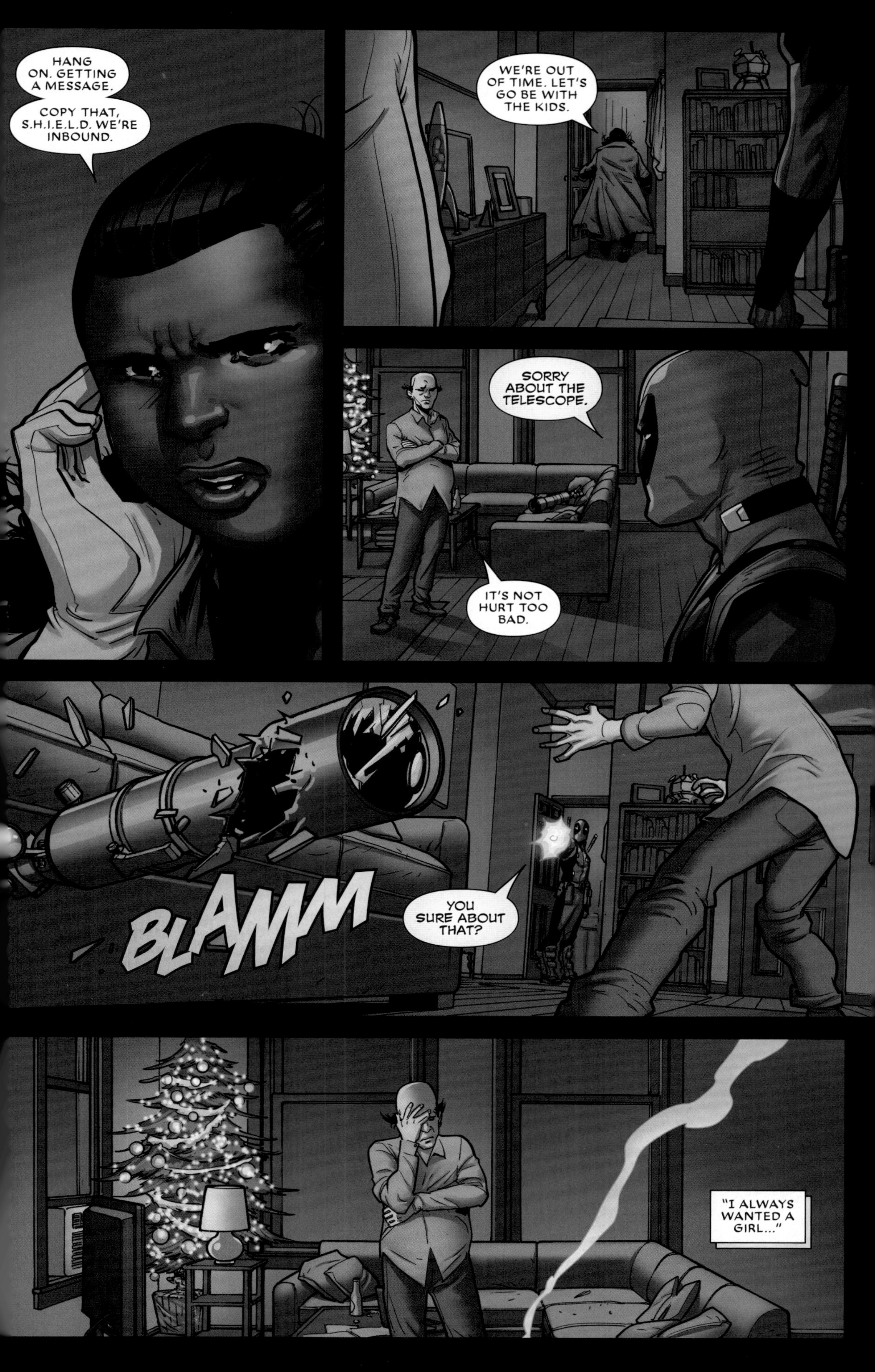
HANG ON. GETTING A MESSAGE.
COPY THAT, S.H.I.E.L.D. WE'RE INBOUND.
WE'RE OUT OF TIME. LET'S GO BE WITH THE KIDS.
SORRY ABOUT THE TELESCOPE.
IT'S NOT HURT TOO BAD.
BLAMM
YOU SURE ABOUT THAT?
"I ALWAYS WANTED A GIRL..."

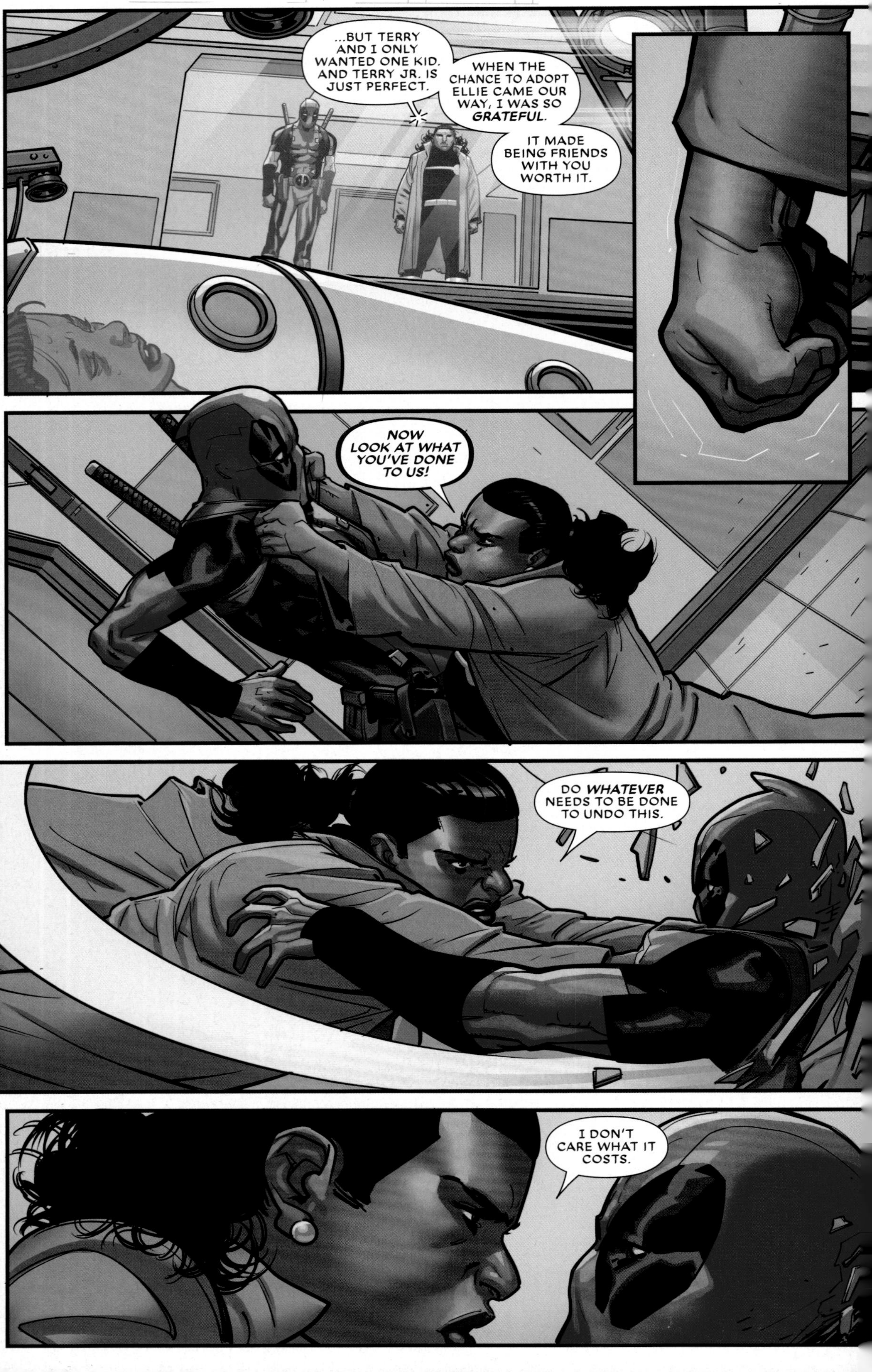
...BUT TERRY AND I ONLY WANTED ONE KID. AND TERRY JR. IS JUST PERFECT.
WHEN THE CHANCE TO ADOPT ELLIE CAME OUR WAY, I WAS SO *GRATEFUL*.
IT MADE BEING FRIENDS WITH YOU WORTH IT.
NOW LOOK AT WHAT YOU'VE DONE TO US!
DO *WHATEVER* NEEDS TO BE DONE TO UNDO THIS.
I DON'T CARE WHAT IT COSTS.

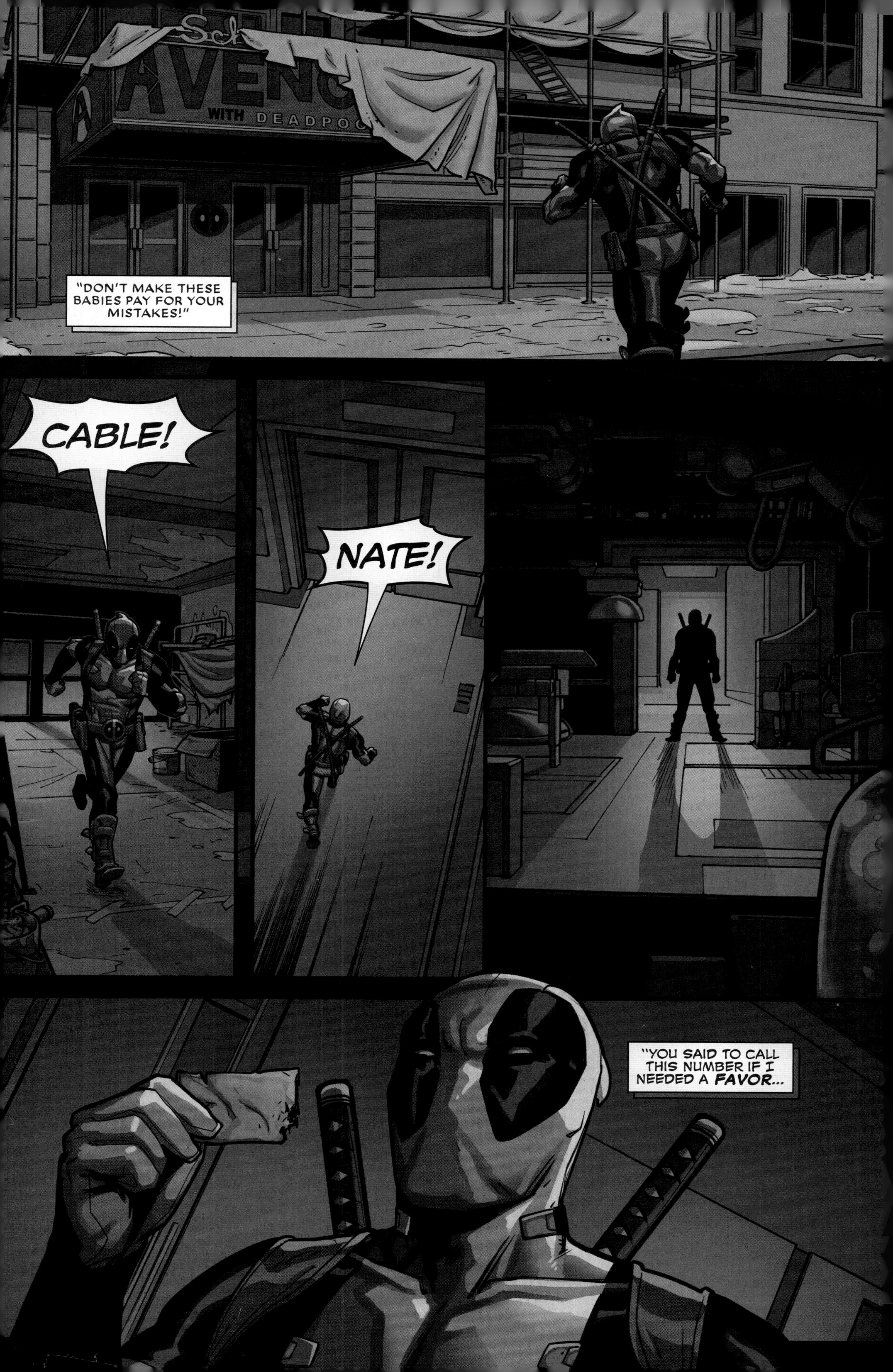
AVENG
WITH DEADPOO
"DON'T MAKE THESE BABIES PAY FOR YOUR MISTAKES!"
CABLE!
NATE!
"YOU SAID TO CALL THIS NUMBER IF I NEEDED A FAVOR...

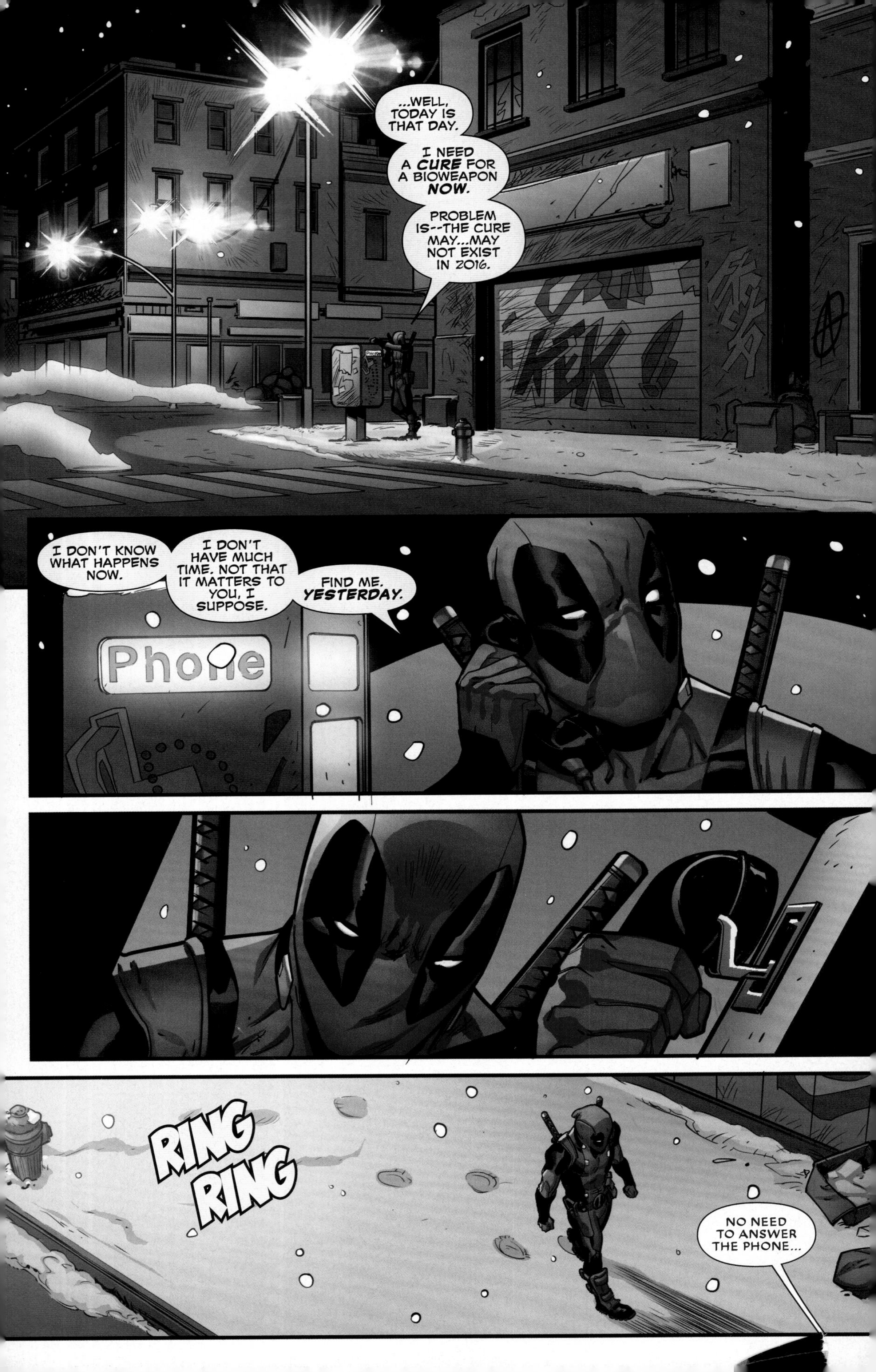
...WELL, TODAY IS THAT DAY.
I NEED A CURE FOR A BIOWEAPON NOW.
PROBLEM IS--THE CURE MAY...MAY NOT EXIST IN 2016.
I DON'T KNOW WHAT HAPPENS NOW.
I DON'T HAVE MUCH TIME. NOT THAT IT MATTERS TO YOU, I SUPPOSE.
FIND ME. YESTERDAY.
Phone
RING RING
NO NEED TO ANSWER THE PHONE...

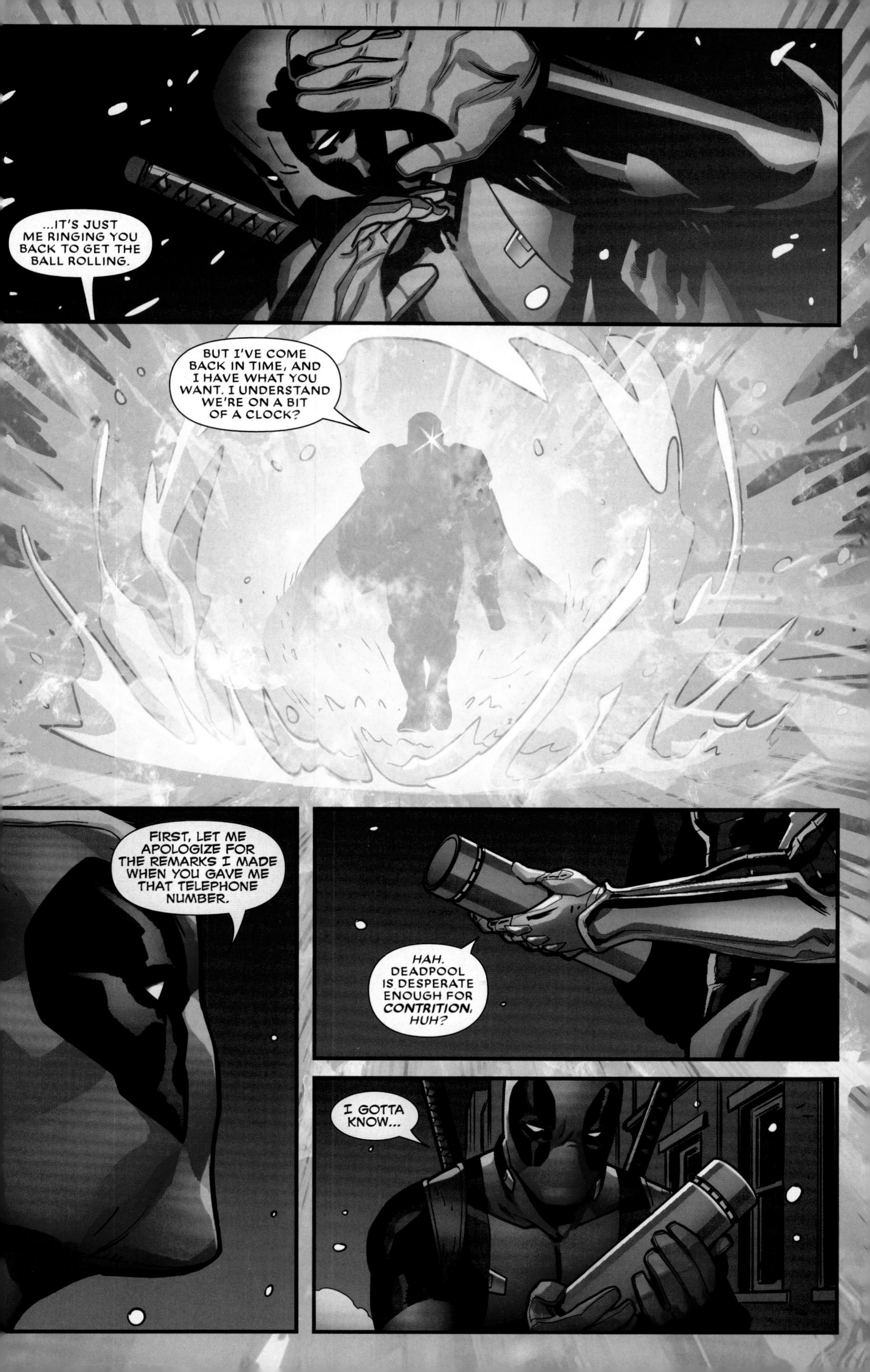
...IT'S JUST ME RINGING YOU BACK TO GET THE BALL ROLLING.
BUT I'VE COME BACK IN TIME, AND I HAVE WHAT YOU WANT. I UNDERSTAND WE'RE ON A BIT OF A CLOCK?
FIRST, LET ME APOLOGIZE FOR THE REMARKS I MADE WHEN YOU GAVE ME THAT TELEPHONE NUMBER.
HAH. DEADPOOL IS DESPERATE ENOUGH FOR CONTRITION, HUH?
I GOTTA KNOW...

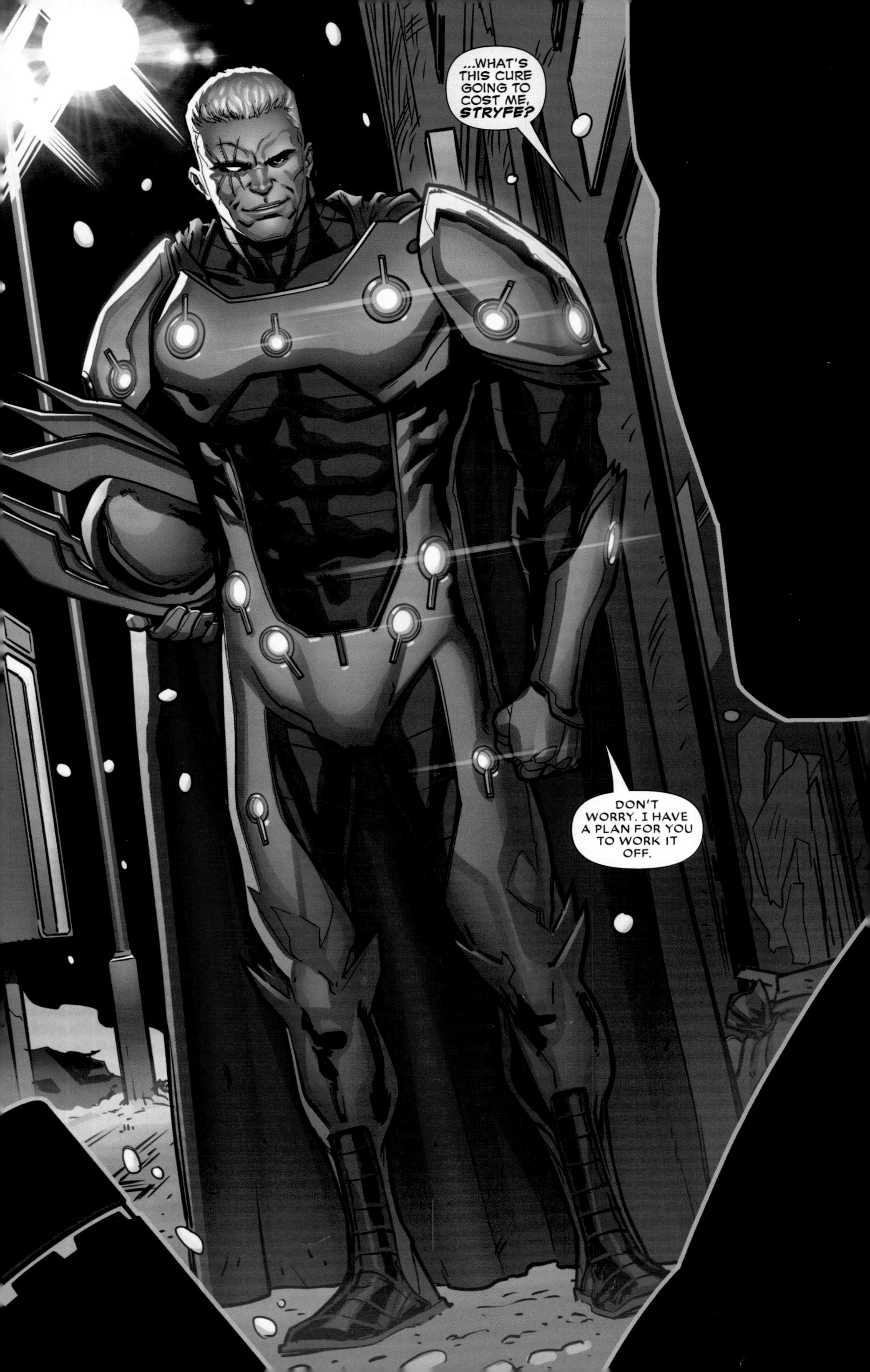
...WHAT'S THIS CURE GOING TO COST ME, STRYFE?
DON'T WORRY. I HAVE A PLAN FOR YOU TO WORK IT OFF.

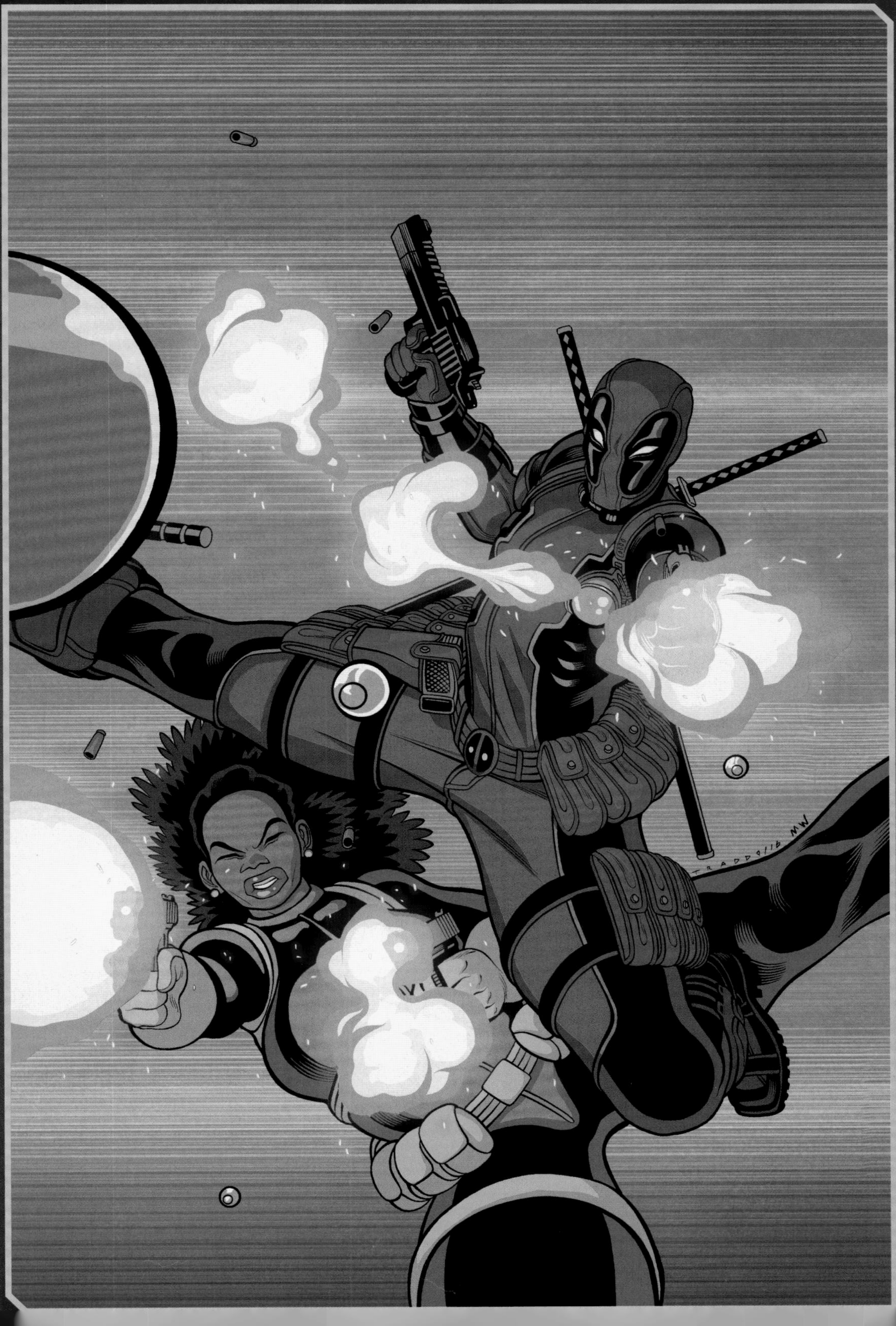

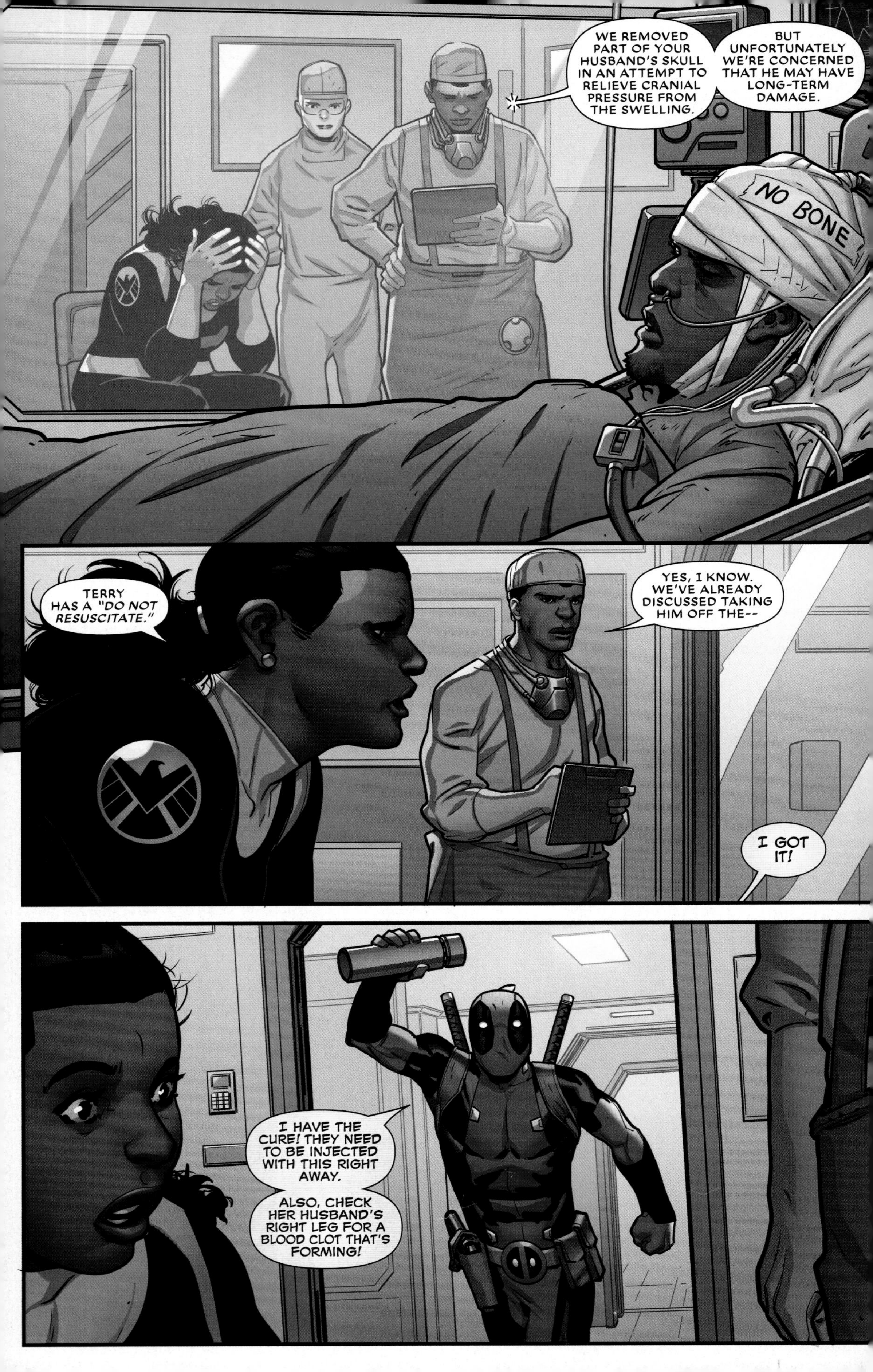

WE REMOVED PART OF YOUR HUSBAND'S SKULL IN AN ATTEMPT TO RELIEVE CRANIAL PRESSURE FROM THE SWELLING.
BUT UNFORTUNATELY WE'RE CONCERNED THAT HE MAY HAVE LONG-TERM DAMAGE.
NO BONE
TERRY HAS A "DO NOT RESUSCITATE."
YES, I KNOW. WE'VE ALREADY DISCUSSED TAKING HIM OFF THE--
I GOT IT!
I HAVE THE CURE! THEY NEED TO BE INJECTED WITH THIS RIGHT AWAY.
ALSO, CHECK HER HUSBAND'S RIGHT LEG FOR A BLOOD CLOT THAT'S FORMING!

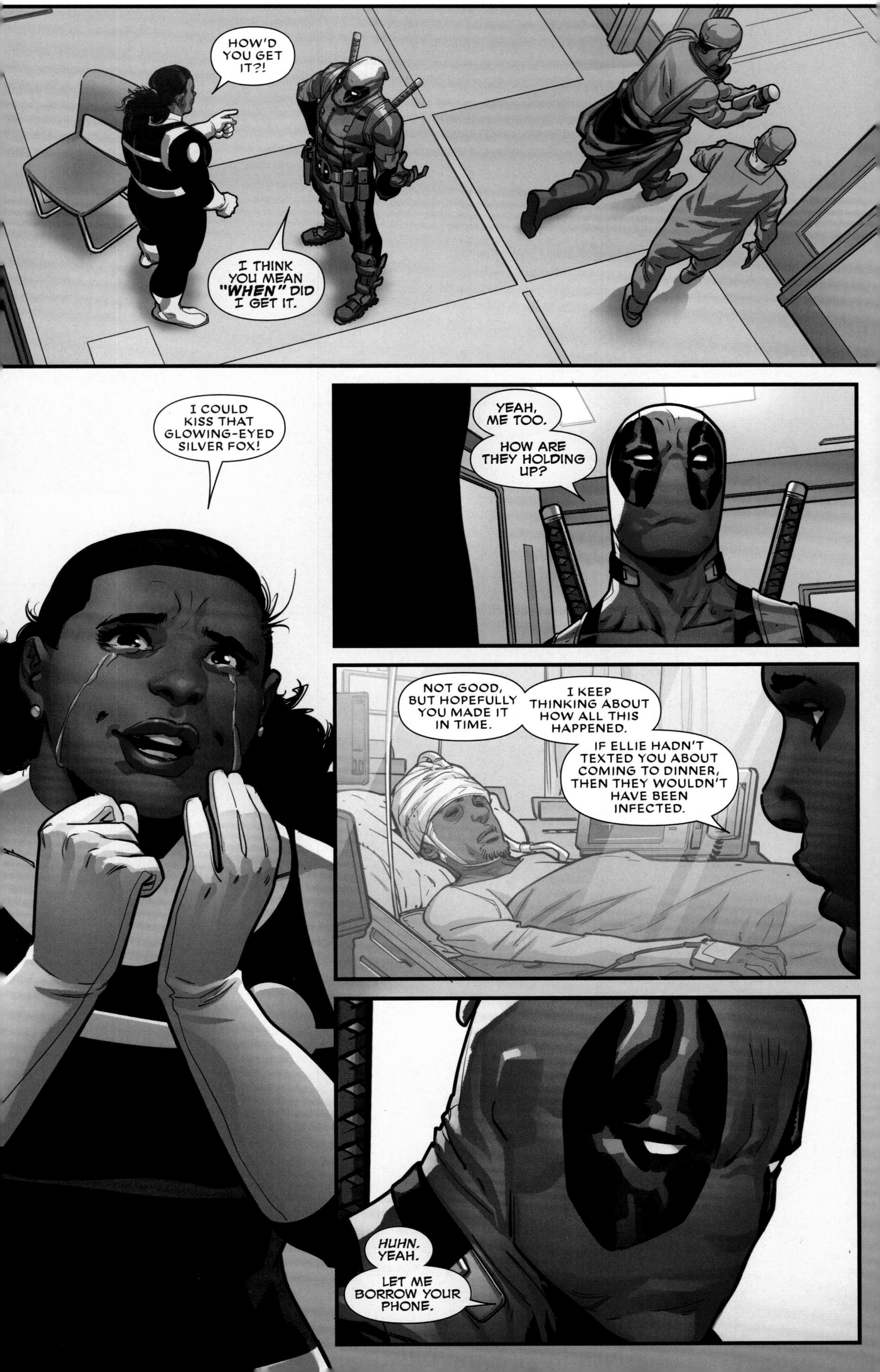
HOW'D YOU GET IT?!
I THINK YOU MEAN "WHEN" DID I GET IT.
I COULD KISS THAT GLOWING-EYED SILVER FOX!
YEAH, ME TOO.
HOW ARE THEY HOLDING UP?
NOT GOOD, BUT HOPEFULLY YOU MADE IT IN TIME.
I KEEP THINKING ABOUT HOW ALL THIS HAPPENED.
IF ELLIE HADN'T TEXTED YOU ABOUT COMING TO DINNER, THEN THEY WOULDN'T HAVE BEEN INFECTED.
HUHN. YEAH.
LET ME BORROW YOUR PHONE.

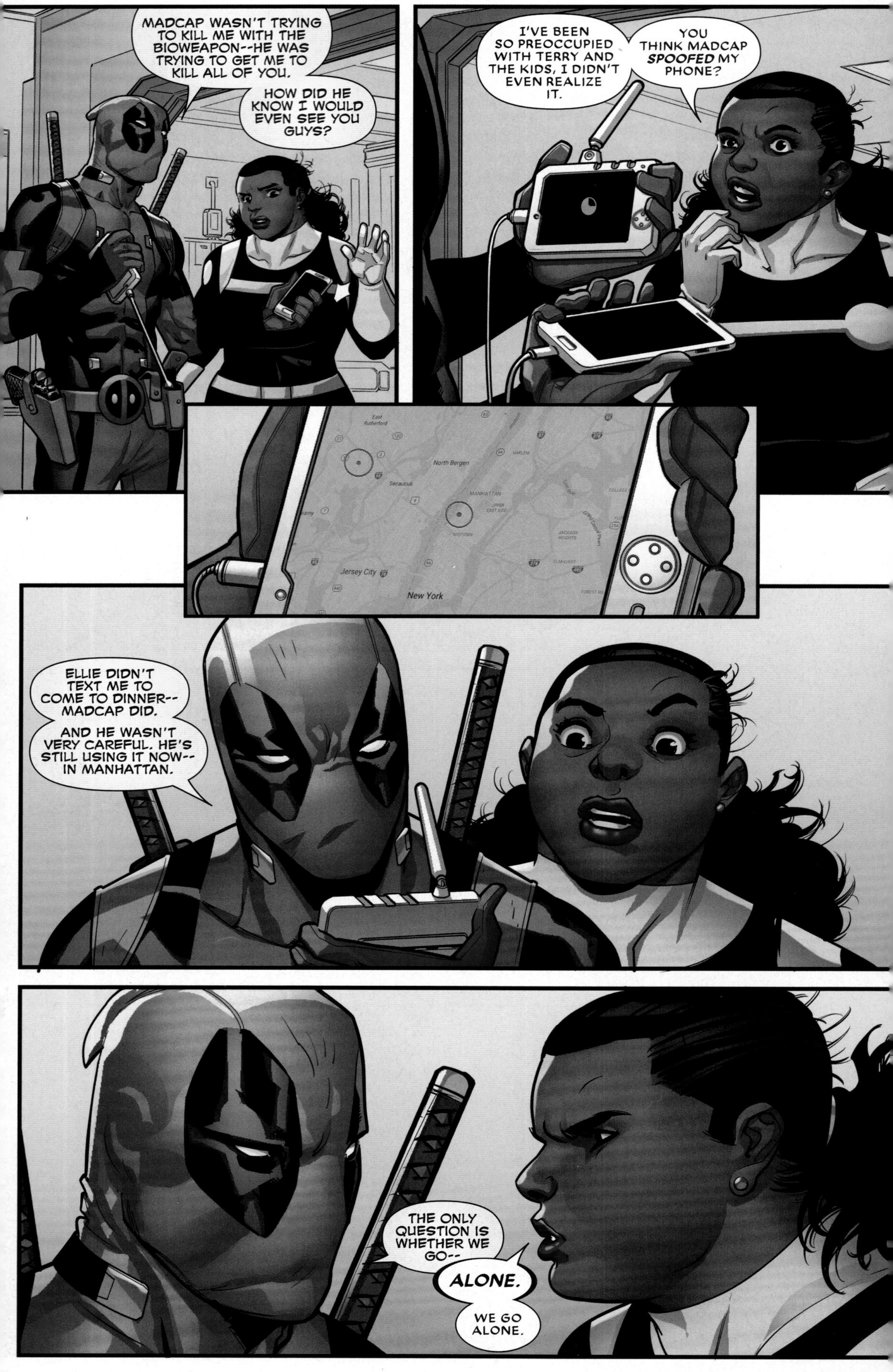

MADCAP WASN'T TRYING TO KILL ME WITH THE BIOWEAPON--HE WAS TRYING TO GET ME TO KILL ALL OF YOU.
HOW DID HE KNOW I WOULD EVEN SEE YOU GUYS?
I'VE BEEN SO PREOCCUPIED WITH TERRY AND THE KIDS, I DIDN'T EVEN REALIZE IT.
YOU THINK MADCAP *SPOOFED* MY PHONE?
East Rutherford
North Bergen
Secaucus
MANHATTAN
Jersey City
New York
ELLIE DIDN'T TEXT ME TO COME TO DINNER--MADCAP DID.
AND HE WASN'T VERY CAREFUL. HE'S STILL USING IT NOW--IN MANHATTAN.
THE ONLY QUESTION IS WHETHER WE GO--
ALONE.
WE GO ALONE.

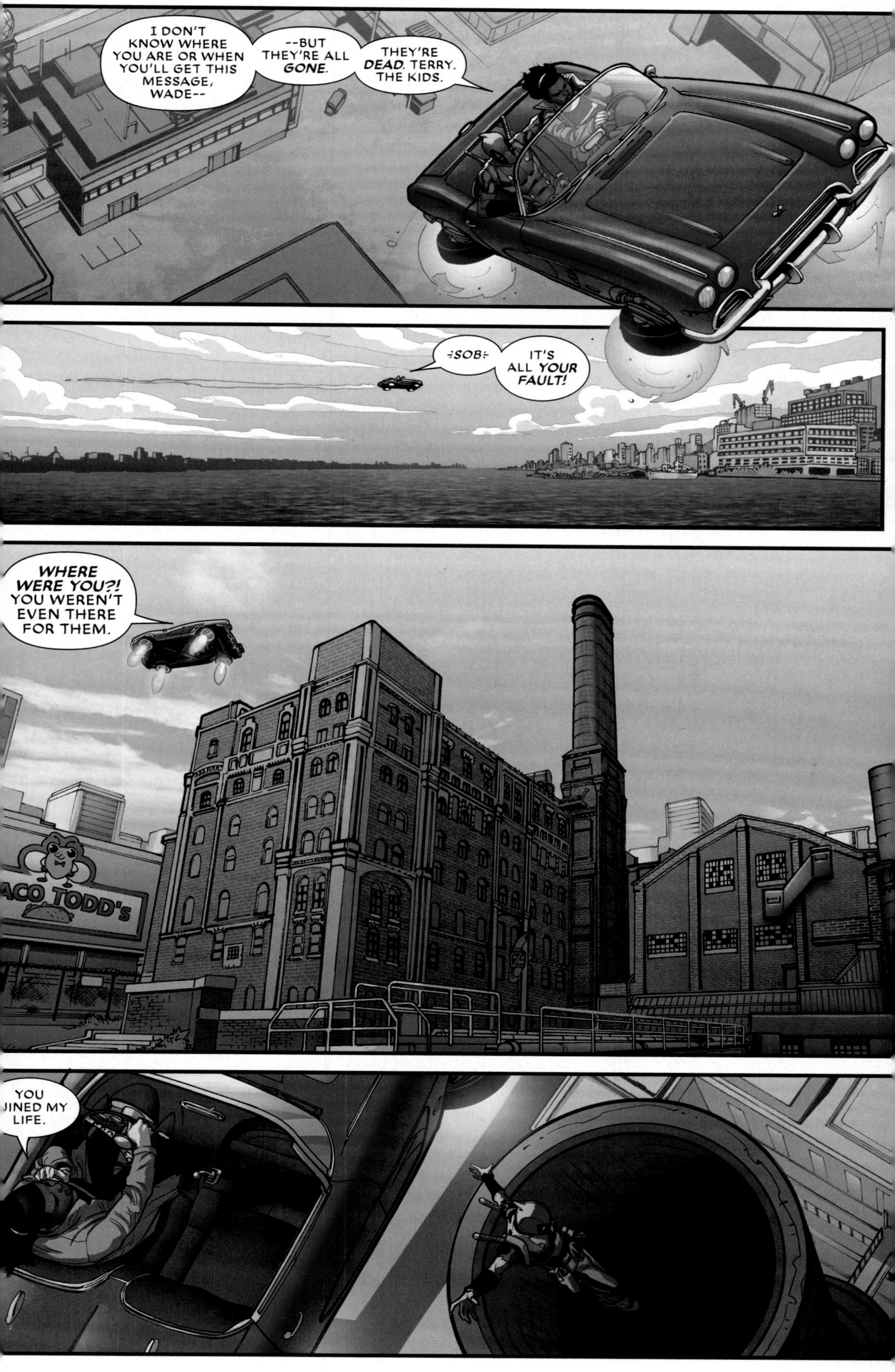
I DON'T KNOW WHERE YOU ARE OR WHEN YOU'LL GET THIS MESSAGE, WADE--
--BUT THEY'RE ALL *GONE*.
THEY'RE *DEAD*. TERRY. THE KIDS.
-SOB-
IT'S ALL *YOUR FAULT!*
WHERE WERE YOU?! YOU WEREN'T EVEN THERE FOR THEM.
ACO TODD'S
YOU UINED MY LIFE.

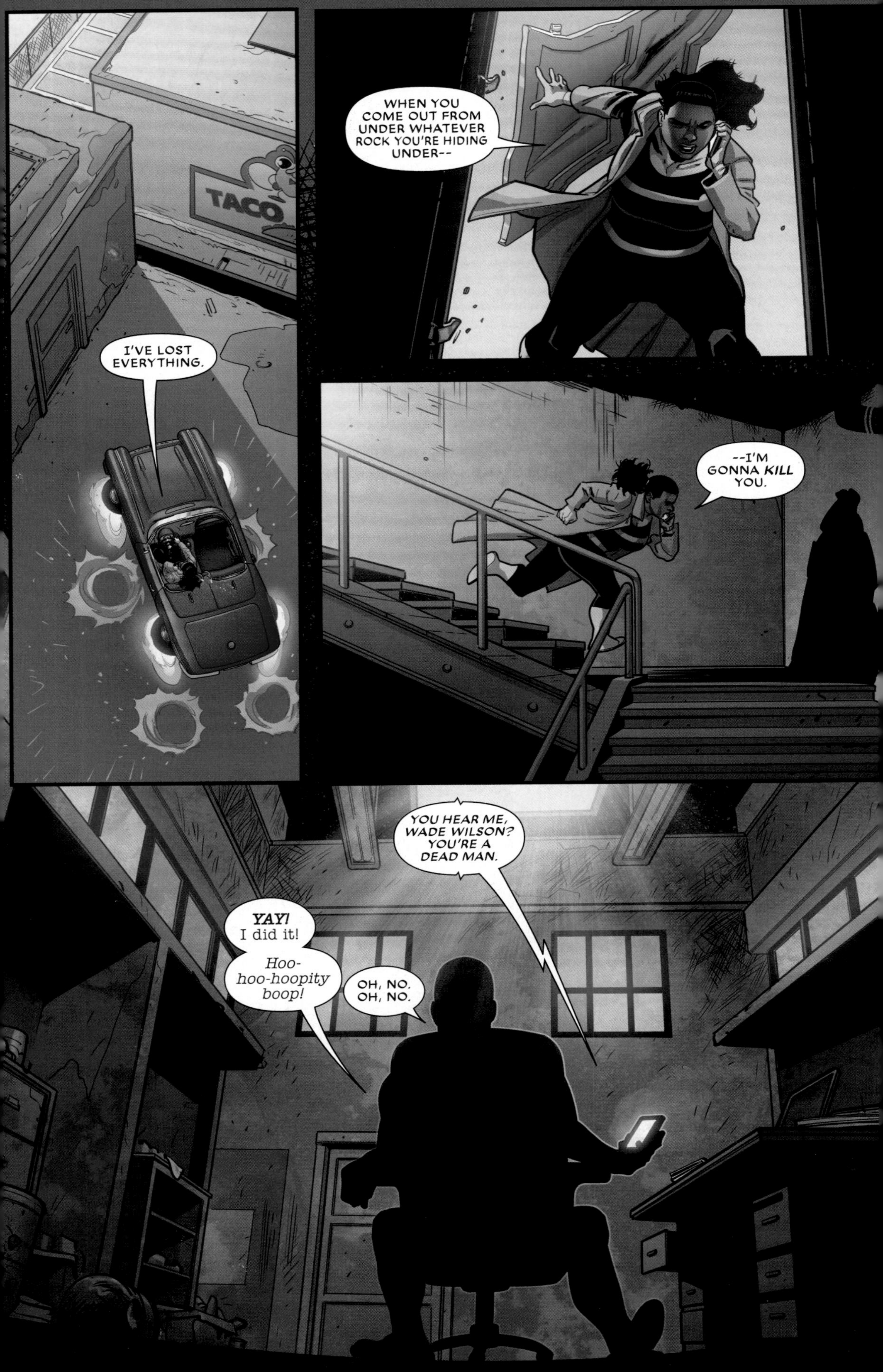
TACO
WHEN YOU COME OUT FROM UNDER WHATEVER ROCK YOU'RE HIDING UNDER--
I'VE LOST EVERYTHING.
--I'M GONNA *KILL* YOU.
YOU HEAR ME, WADE WILSON? YOU'RE A DEAD MAN.
YAY! I did it!
Hoo-hoo-hoopity boop!
OH, NO. OH, NO.

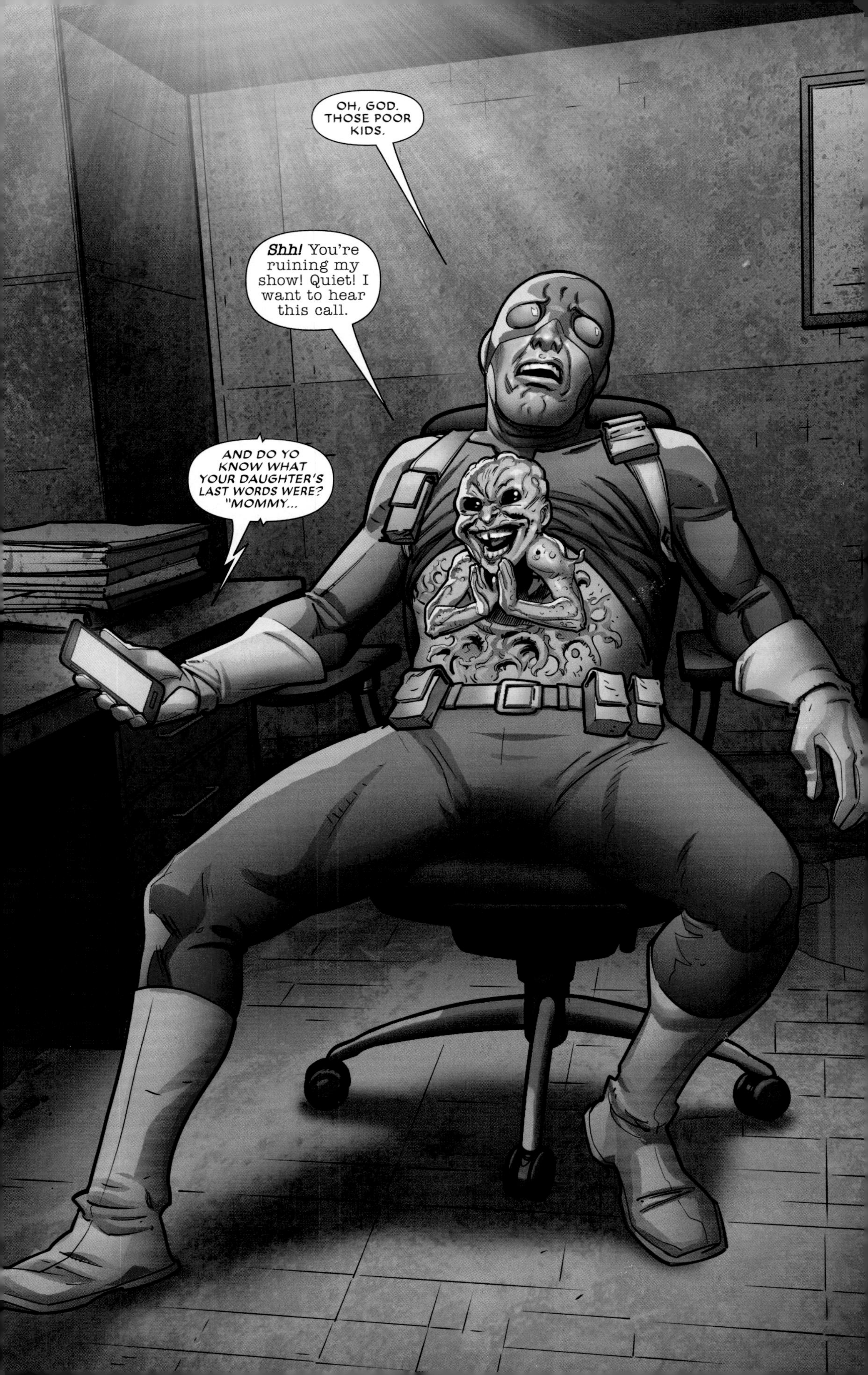
OH, GOD. THOSE POOR KIDS.
Shh! You're ruining my show! Quiet! I want to hear this call.
AND DO YO KNOW WHAT YOUR DAUGHTER'S LAST WORDS WERE? "MOMMY...

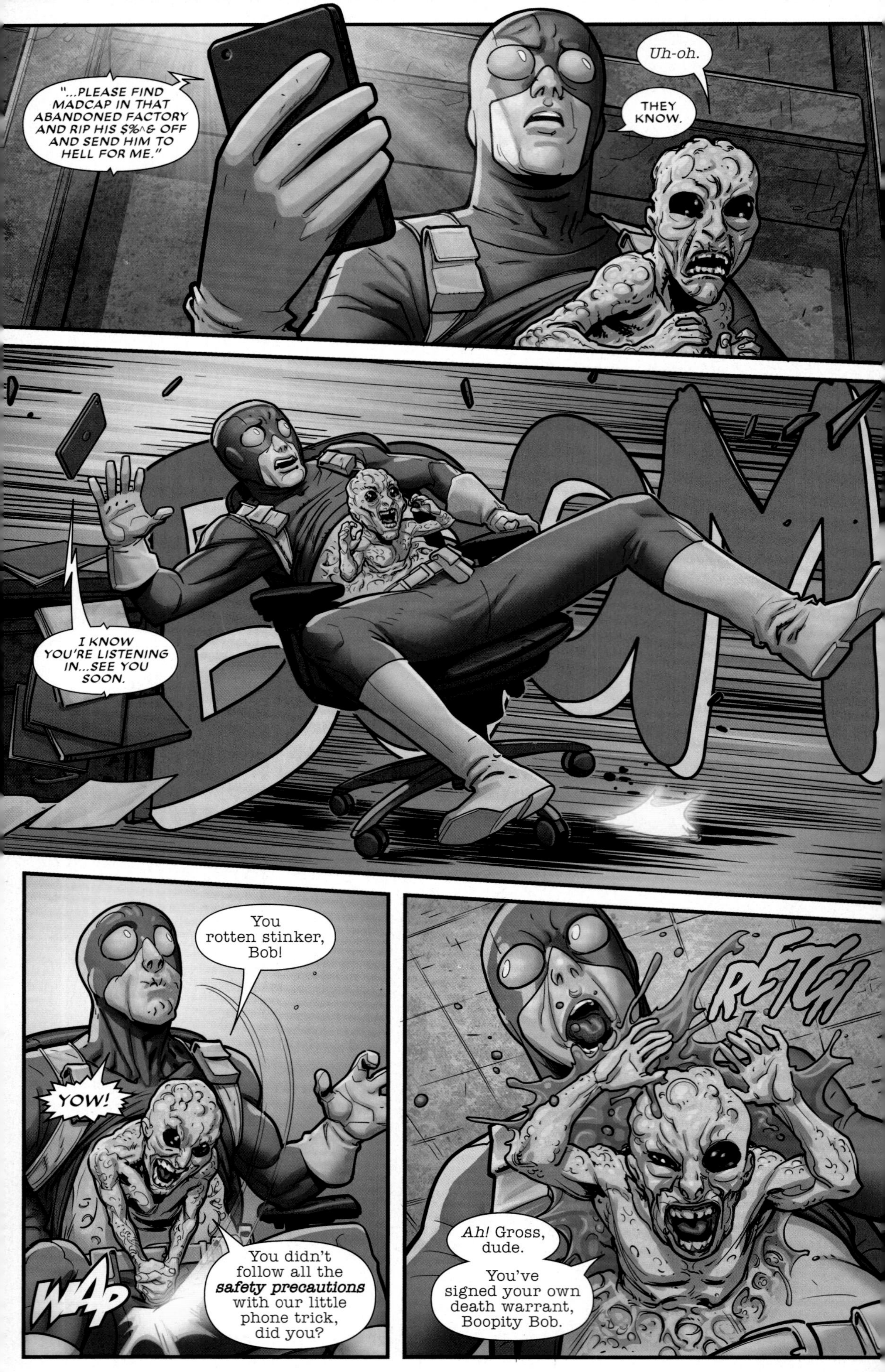
"...PLEASE FIND MADCAP IN THAT ABANDONED FACTORY AND RIP HIS $%^& OFF AND SEND HIM TO HELL FOR ME."
Uh-oh.
THEY KNOW.
I KNOW YOU'RE LISTENING IN...SEE YOU SOON.
You rotten stinker, Bob!
YOW!
You didn't follow all the safety precautions with our little phone trick, did you?
WAP
RETCH
Ah! Gross, dude.
You've signed your own death warrant, Boopity Bob.

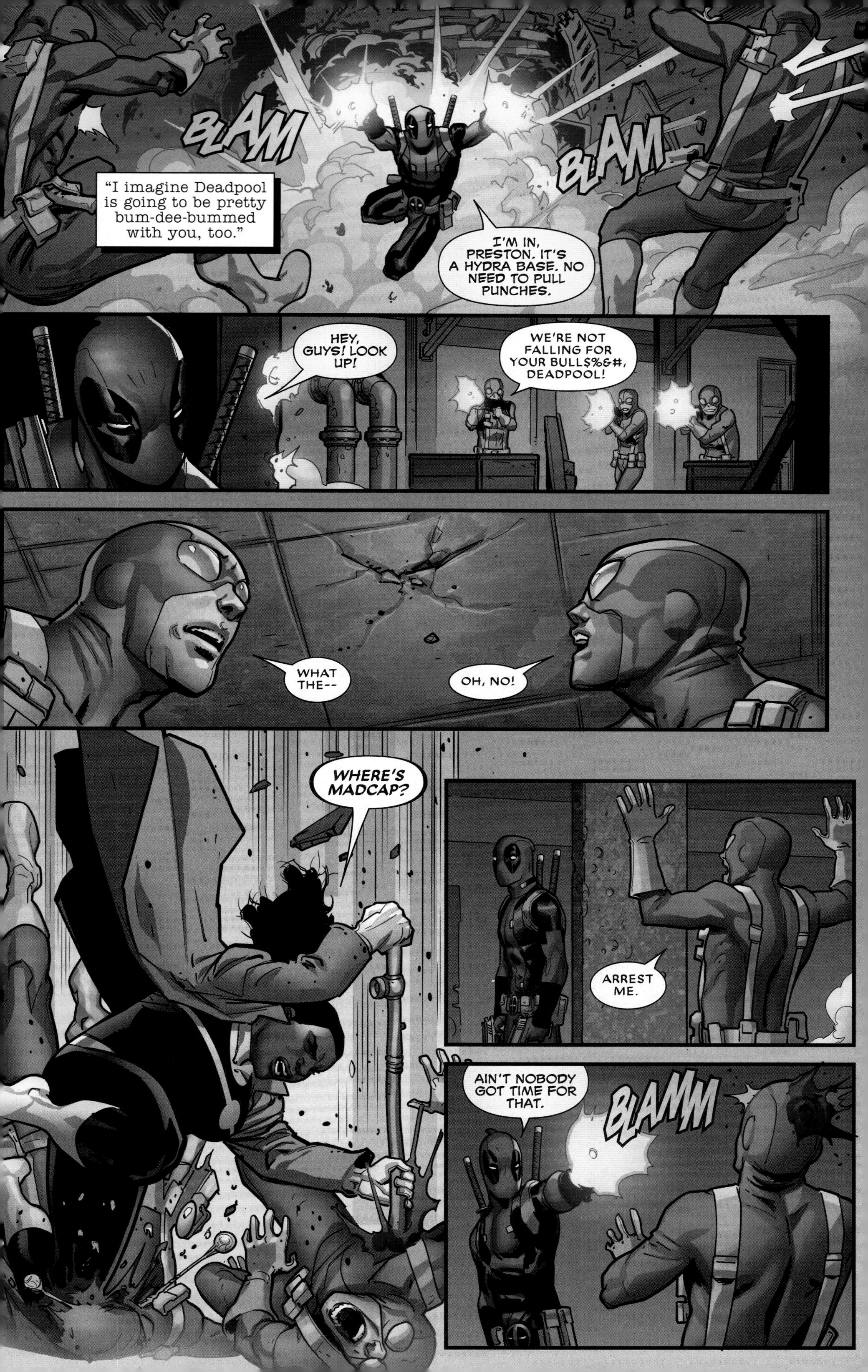
BLAM
"I imagine Deadpool is going to be pretty bum-dee-bummed with you, too."
BLAM
I'M IN, PRESTON. IT'S A HYDRA BASE. NO NEED TO PULL PUNCHES.
HEY, GUYS! LOOK UP!
WE'RE NOT FALLING FOR YOUR BULL$%&#, DEADPOOL!
WHAT THE--
OH, NO!
WHERE'S MADCAP?
ARREST ME.
AIN'T NOBODY GOT TIME FOR THAT.
BLAMM

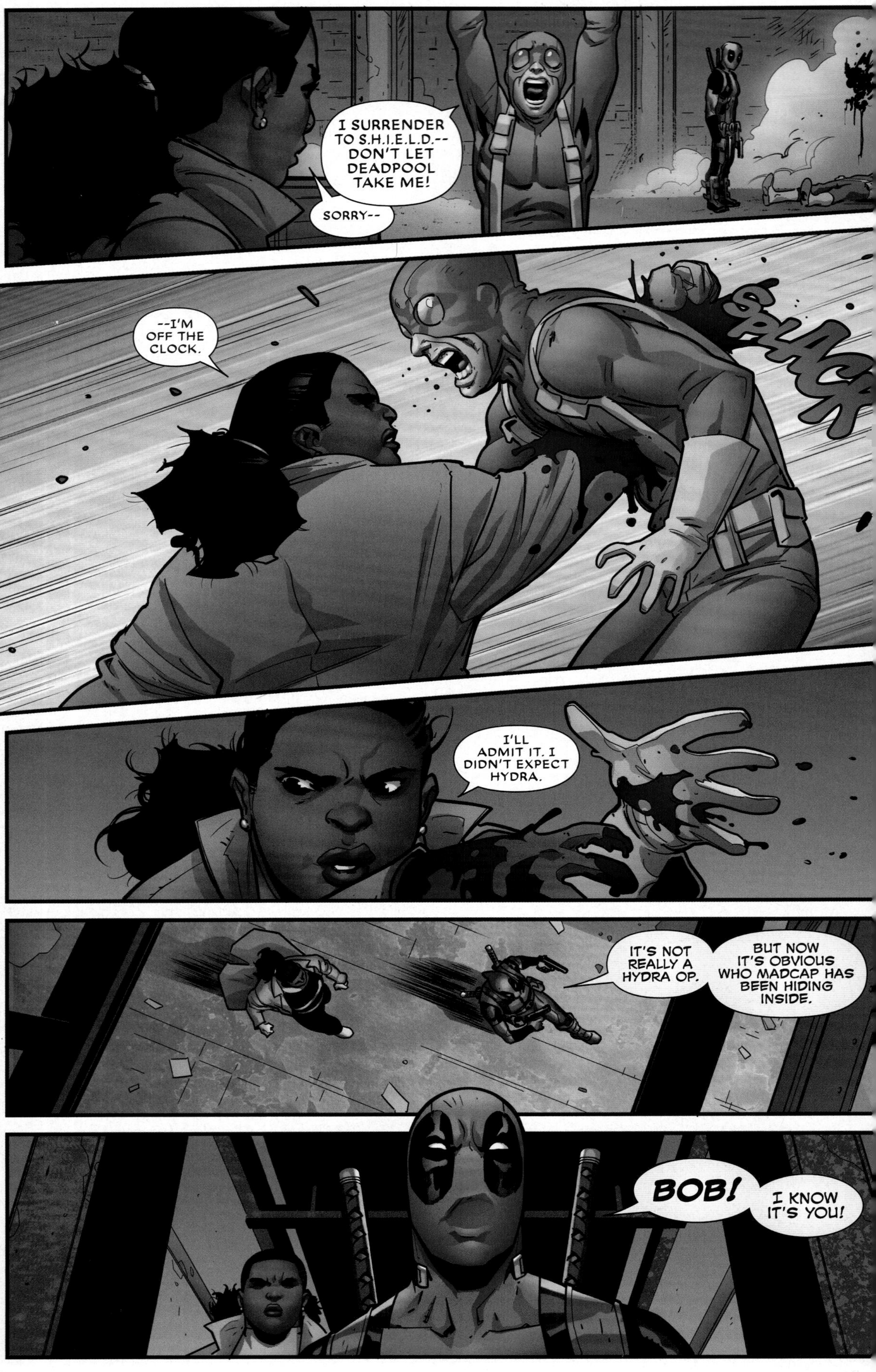
I SURRENDER TO S.H.I.E.L.D.-- DON'T LET DEADPOOL TAKE ME!
SORRY--
--I'M OFF THE CLOCK.
SPLACK
I'LL ADMIT IT. I DIDN'T EXPECT HYDRA.
IT'S NOT REALLY A HYDRA OP.
BUT NOW IT'S OBVIOUS WHO MADCAP HAS BEEN HIDING INSIDE.
BOB!
I KNOW IT'S YOU!

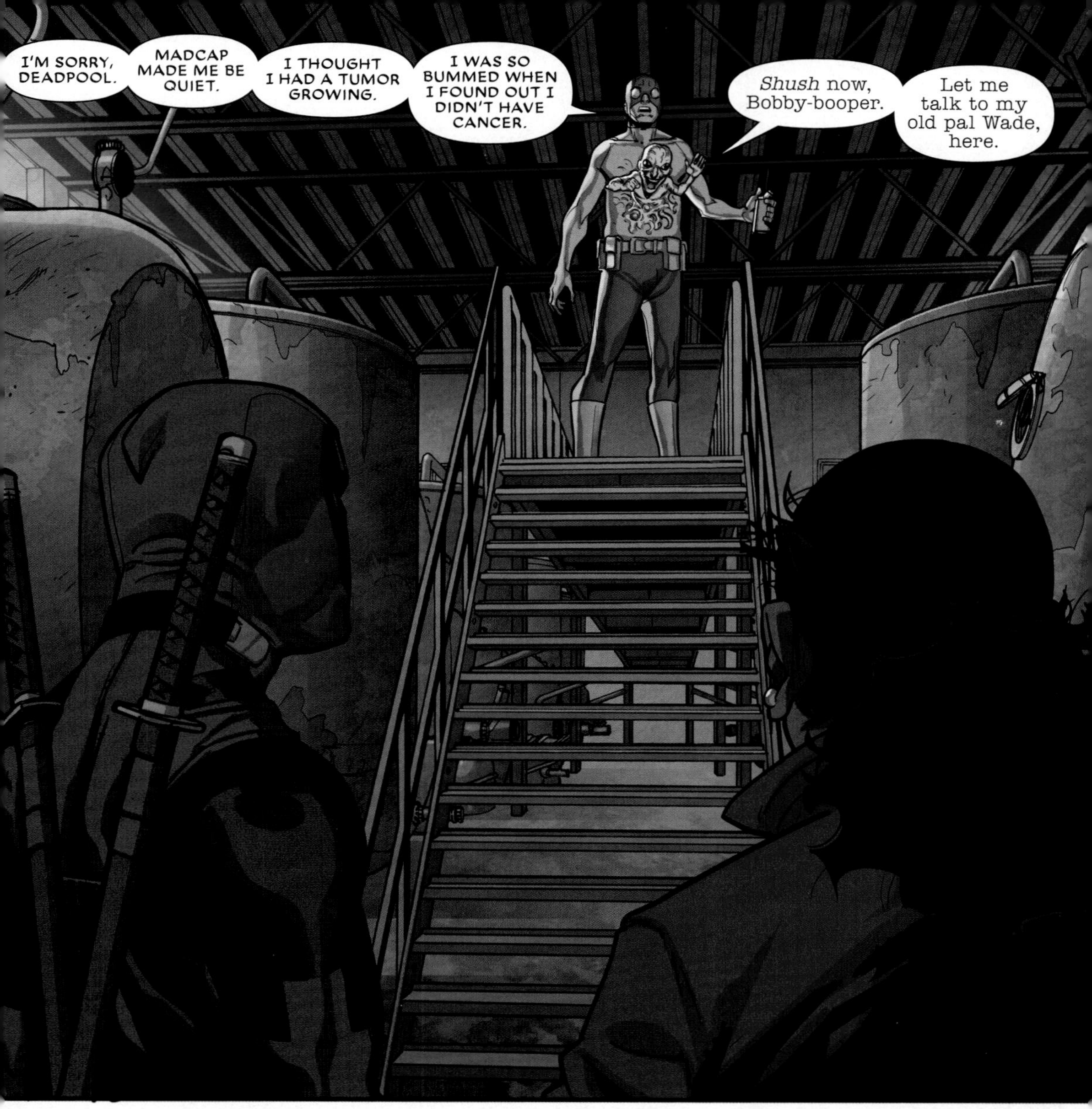
I'M SORRY, DEADPOOL.
MADCAP MADE ME BE QUIET.
I THOUGHT I HAD A TUMOR GROWING.
I WAS SO BUMMED WHEN I FOUND OUT I DIDN'T HAVE CANCER.
Shush now, Bobby-booper.
Let me talk to my old pal Wade, here.

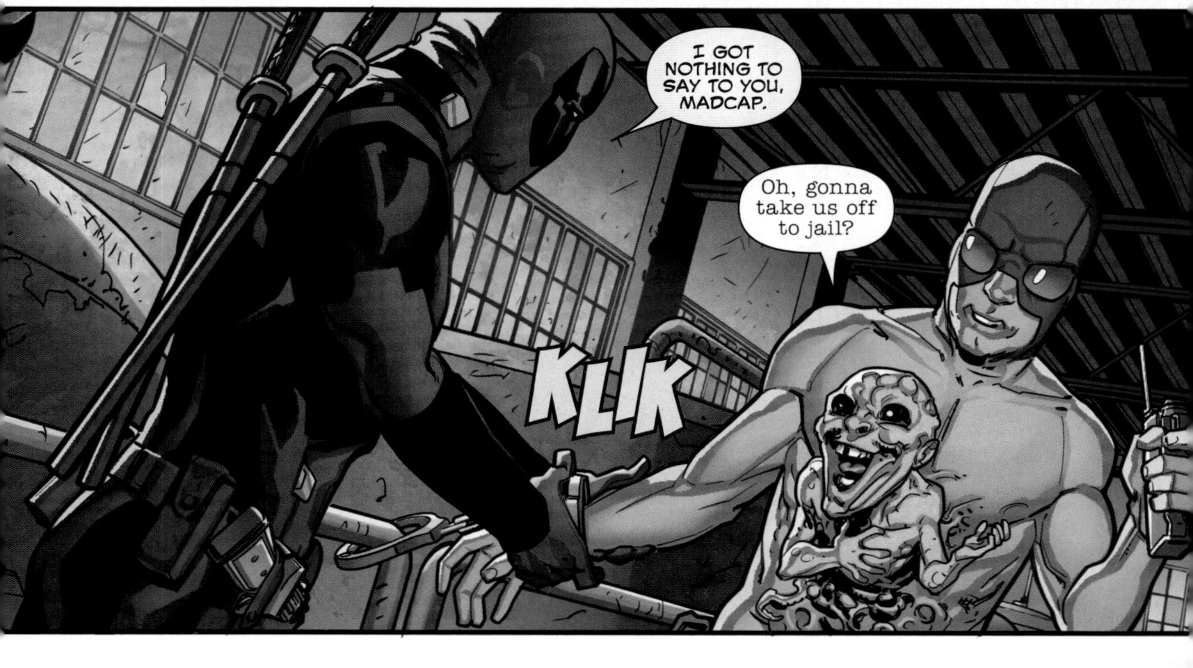
I GOT NOTHING TO SAY TO YOU, MADCAP.
Oh, gonna take us off to jail?
KLIK

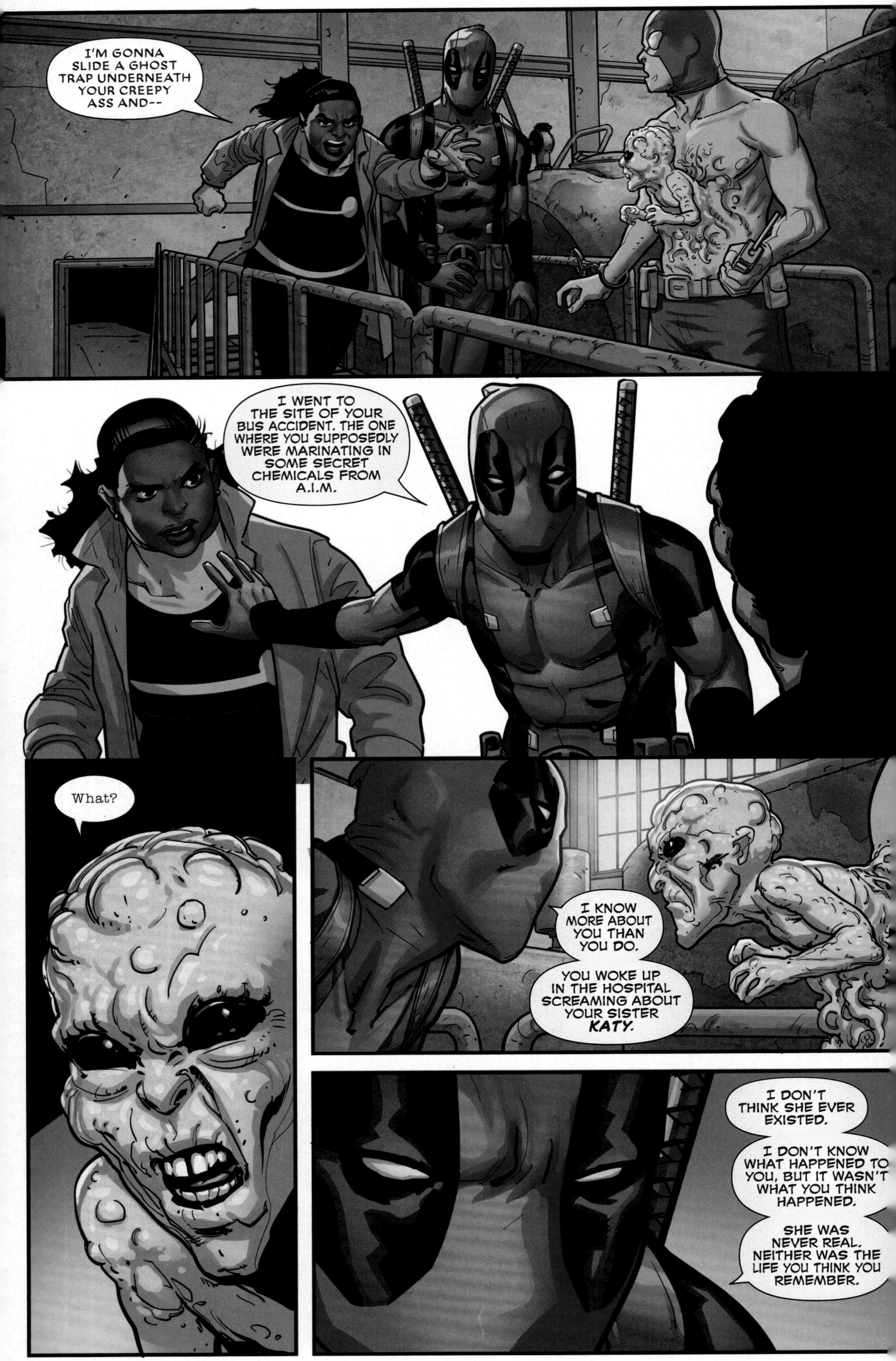

I'M GONNA SLIDE A GHOST TRAP UNDERNEATH YOUR CREEPY ASS AND--
I WENT TO THE SITE OF YOUR BUS ACCIDENT. THE ONE WHERE YOU SUPPOSEDLY WERE MARINATING IN SOME SECRET CHEMICALS FROM A.I.M.
What?
I KNOW MORE ABOUT YOU THAN YOU DO.
YOU WOKE UP IN THE HOSPITAL SCREAMING ABOUT YOUR SISTER *KATY*.
I DON'T THINK SHE EVER EXISTED.
I DON'T KNOW WHAT HAPPENED TO YOU, BUT IT WASN'T WHAT YOU THINK HAPPENED.
SHE WAS NEVER REAL. NEITHER WAS THE LIFE YOU THINK YOU REMEMBER.

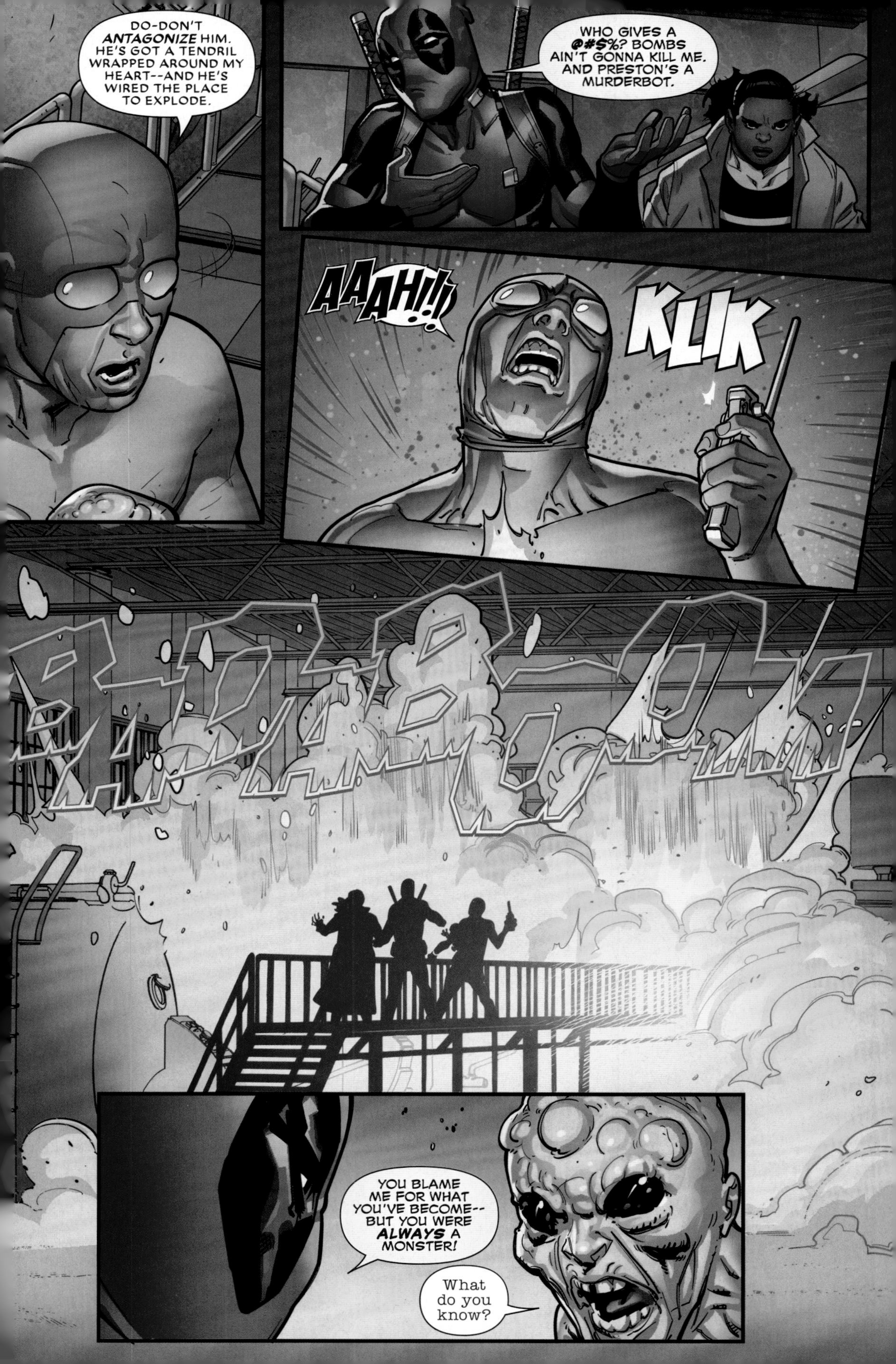
DO-DON'T ANTAGONIZE HIM. HE'S GOT A TENDRIL WRAPPED AROUND MY HEART--AND HE'S WIRED THE PLACE TO EXPLODE.
WHO GIVES A @#$%? BOMBS AIN'T GONNA KILL ME. AND PRESTON'S A MURDERBOT.
AAAH!!!
KLIK
YOU BLAME ME FOR WHAT YOU'VE BECOME--BUT YOU WERE ALWAYS A MONSTER!
What do you know?

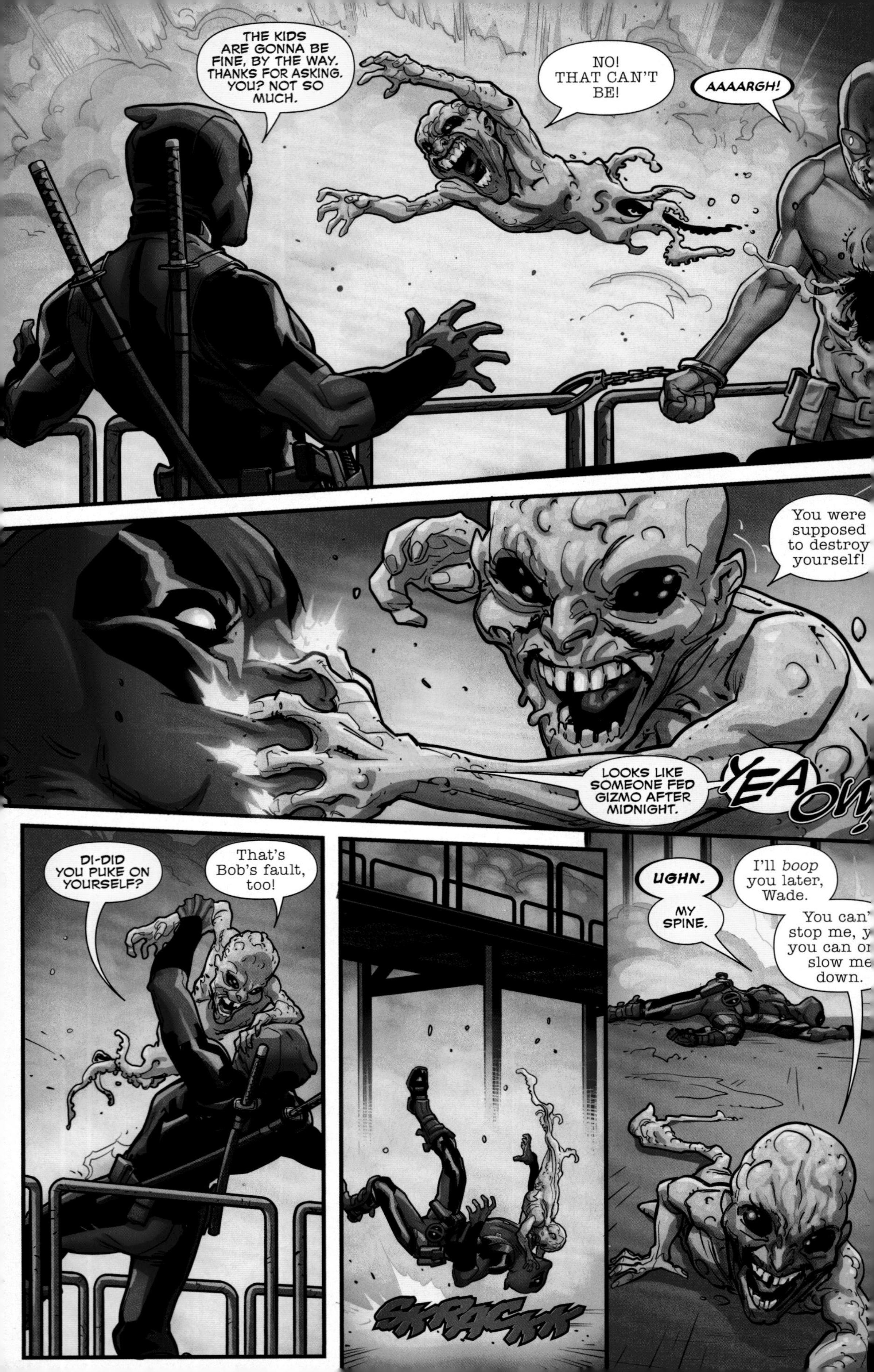

THE KIDS ARE GONNA BE FINE, BY THE WAY. THANKS FOR ASKING. YOU? NOT SO MUCH.
NO! THAT CAN'T BE!
AAAARGH!
You were supposed to destroy yourself!
LOOKS LIKE SOMEONE FED GIZMO AFTER MIDNIGHT.
YEAOW!
DI-DID YOU PUKE ON YOURSELF?
That's Bob's fault, too!
SKRACKK
UGHN.
MY SPINE.
I'll *boop* you later, Wade.

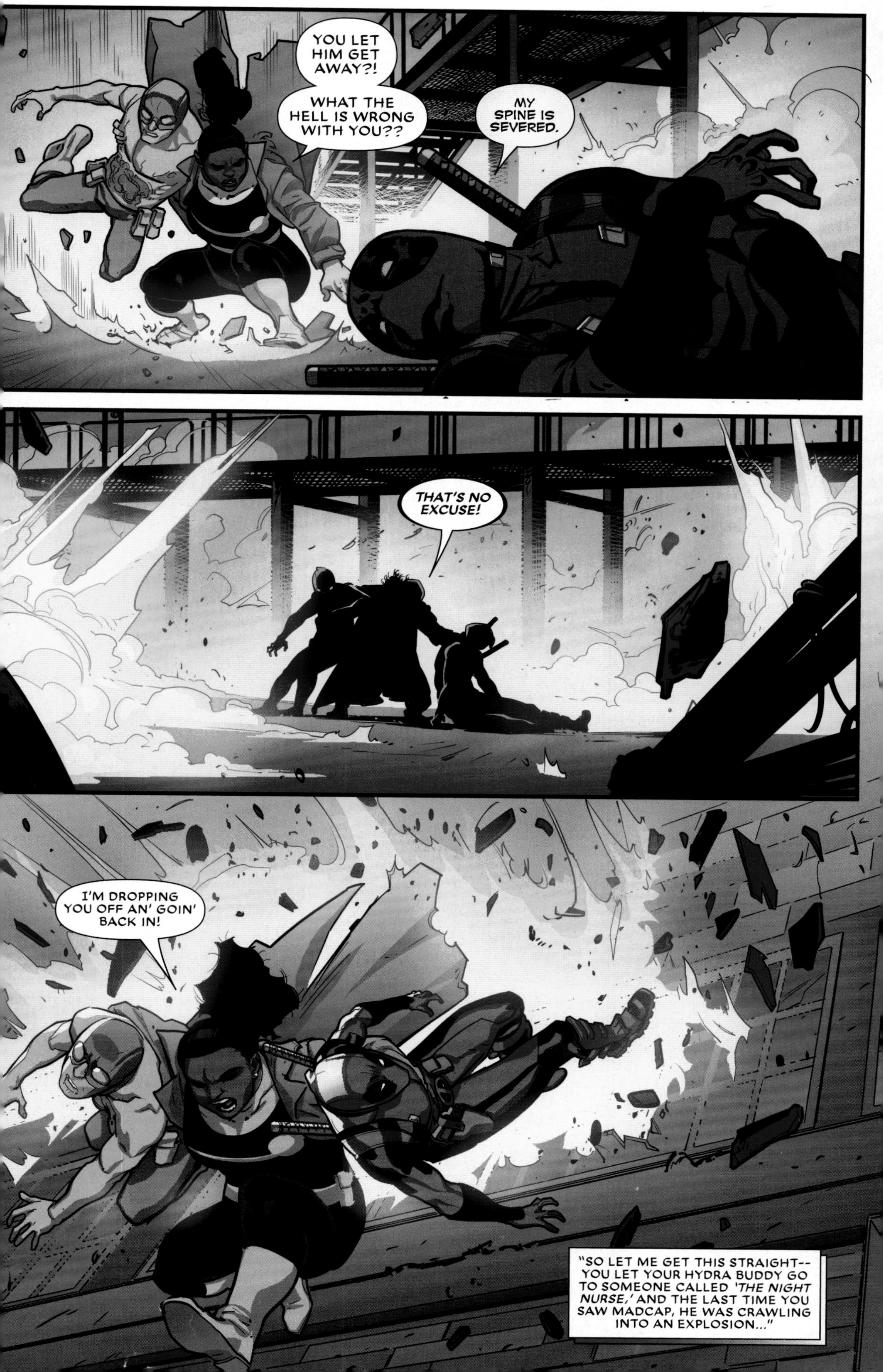
YOU LET HIM GET AWAY?!
WHAT THE HELL IS WRONG WITH YOU??
MY SPINE IS SEVERED.
THAT'S NO EXCUSE!
I'M DROPPING YOU OFF AN' GOIN' BACK IN!
"SO LET ME GET THIS STRAIGHT-- YOU LET YOUR HYDRA BUDDY GO TO SOMEONE CALLED 'THE NIGHT NURSE,' AND THE LAST TIME YOU SAW MADCAP, HE WAS CRAWLING INTO AN EXPLOSION..."

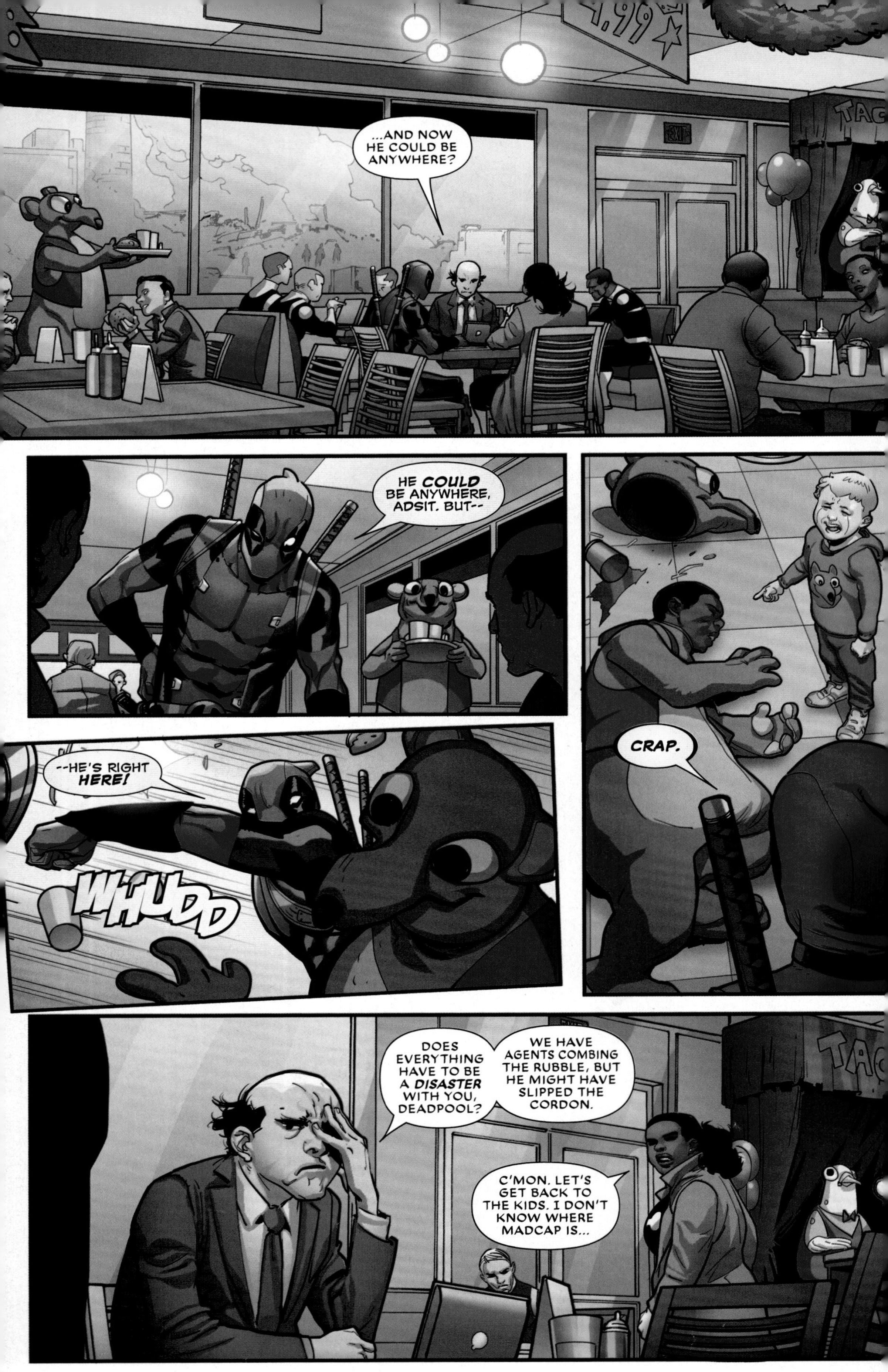
4.99
EXIT
TACO
...AND NOW HE COULD BE ANYWHERE?
HE COULD BE ANYWHERE, ADSIT. BUT--
--HE'S RIGHT HERE!
WHUDD
CRAP.
DOES EVERYTHING HAVE TO BE A DISASTER WITH YOU, DEADPOOL?
WE HAVE AGENTS COMBING THE RUBBLE, BUT HE MIGHT HAVE SLIPPED THE CORDON.
C'MON. LET'S GET BACK TO THE KIDS. I DON'T KNOW WHERE MADCAP IS...

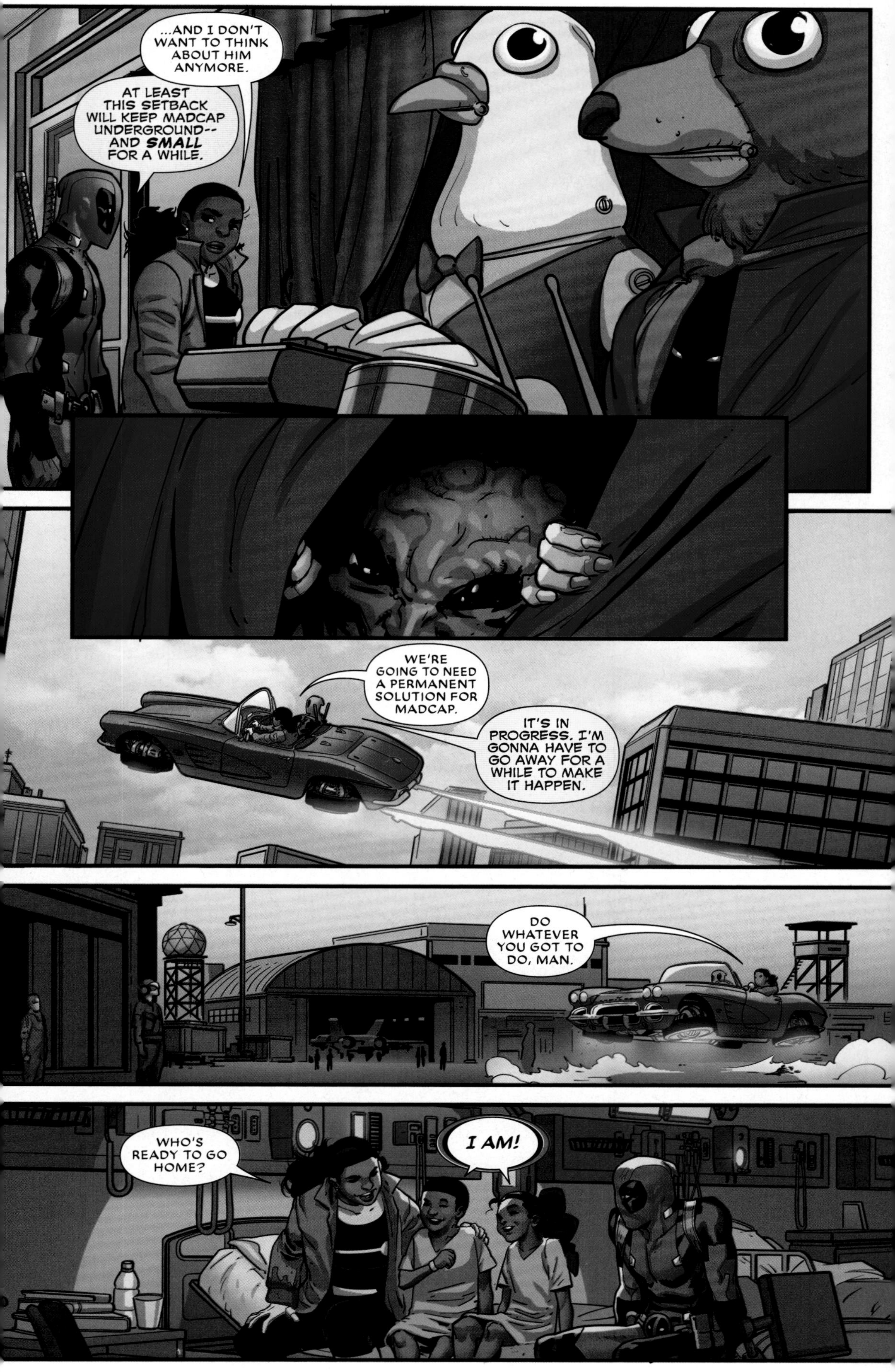
...AND I DON'T WANT TO THINK ABOUT HIM ANYMORE.
AT LEAST THIS SETBACK WILL KEEP MADCAP UNDERGROUND-- AND SMALL FOR A WHILE.
WE'RE GOING TO NEED A PERMANENT SOLUTION FOR MADCAP.
IT'S IN PROGRESS. I'M GONNA HAVE TO GO AWAY FOR A WHILE TO MAKE IT HAPPEN.
DO WHATEVER YOU GOT TO DO, MAN.
WHO'S READY TO GO HOME?
I AM!

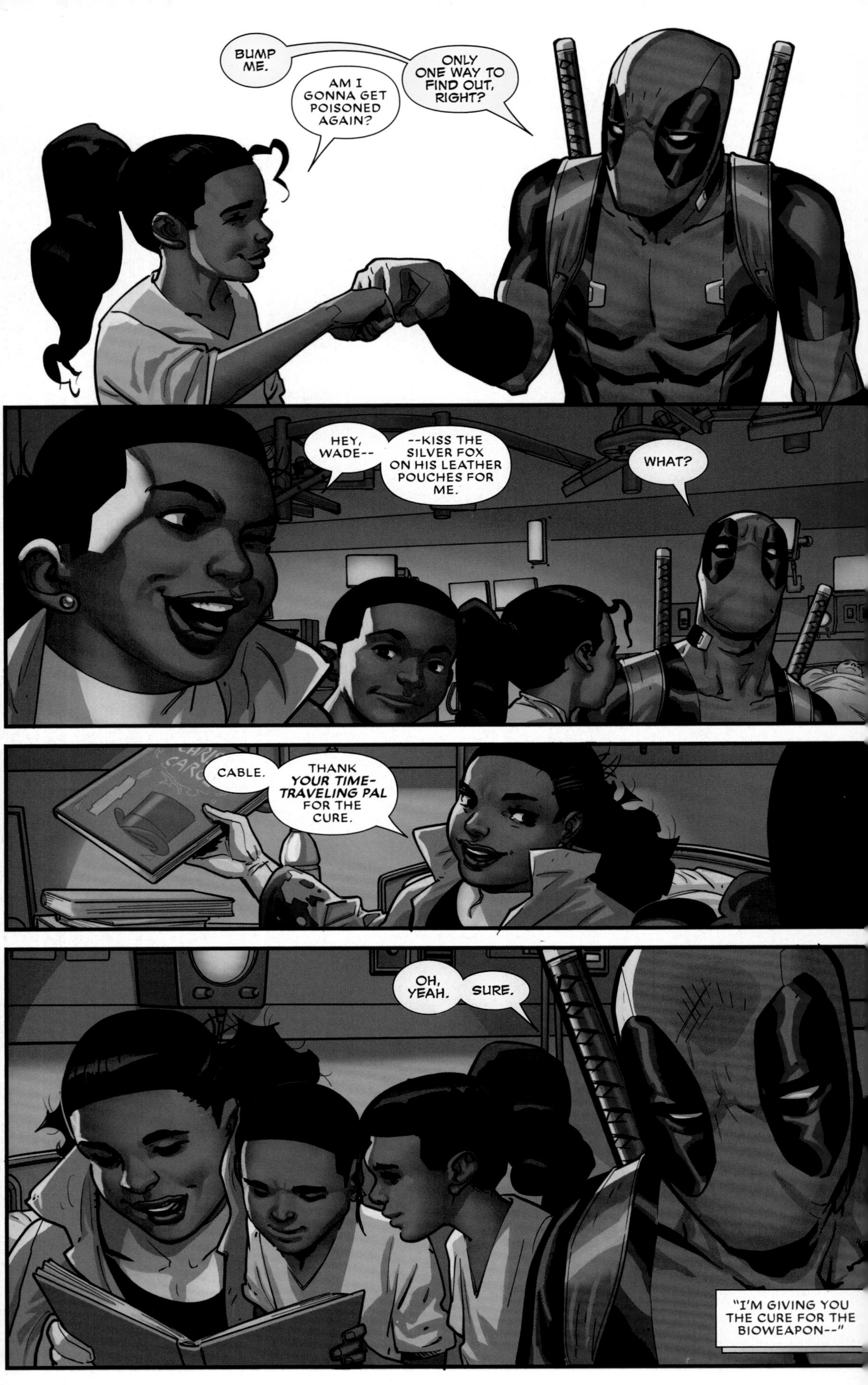
BUMP ME.
AM I GONNA GET POISONED AGAIN?
ONLY ONE WAY TO FIND OUT, RIGHT?
HEY, WADE--
--KISS THE SILVER FOX ON HIS LEATHER POUCHES FOR ME.
WHAT?
CABLE.
THANK *YOUR TIME-TRAVELING PAL* FOR THE CURE.
OH, YEAH.
SURE.
"I'M GIVING YOU THE CURE FOR THE BIOWEAPON--"

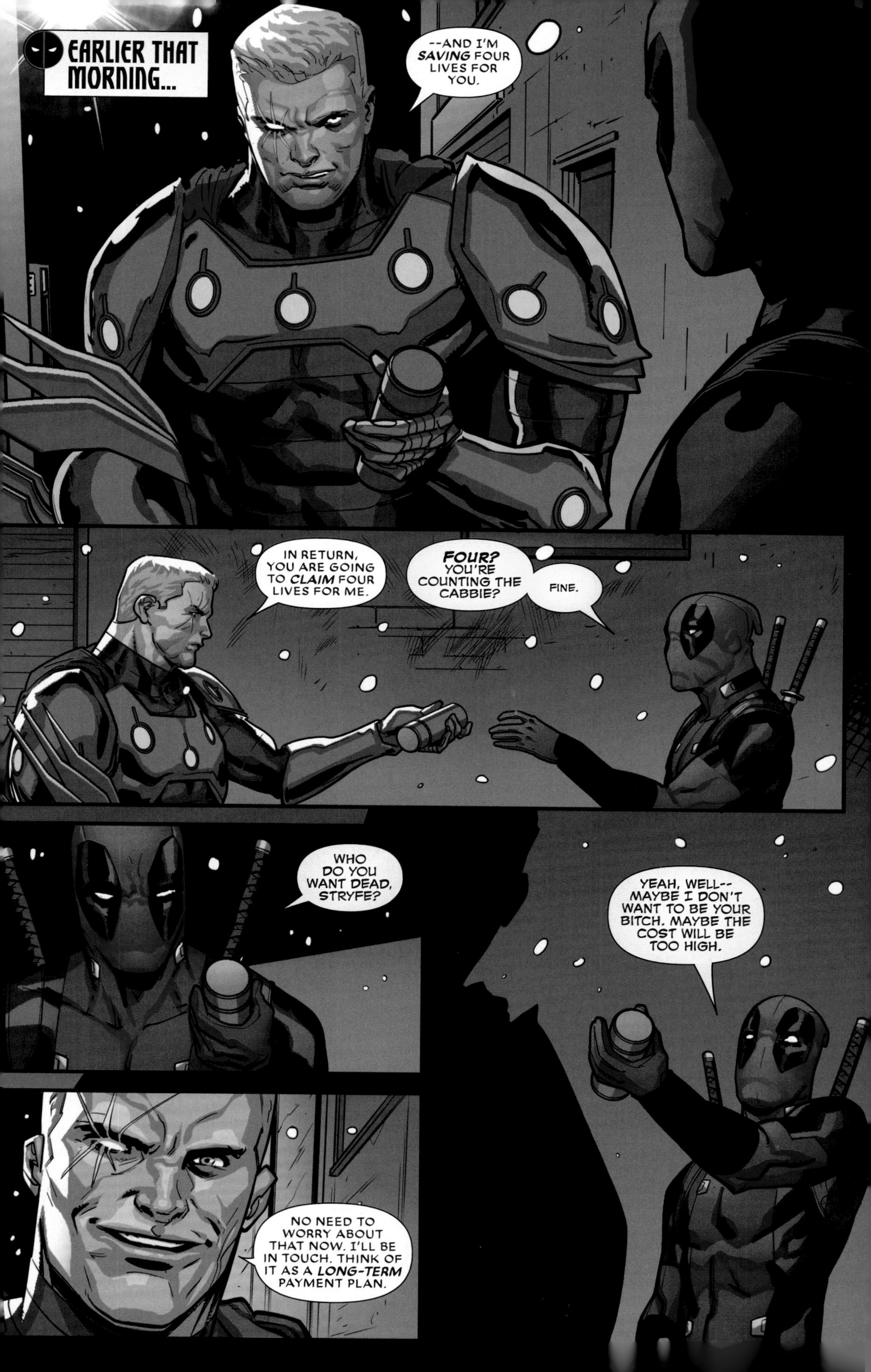
EARLIER THAT MORNING...
--AND I'M SAVING FOUR LIVES FOR YOU.
IN RETURN, YOU ARE GOING TO CLAIM FOUR LIVES FOR ME.
FOUR? YOU'RE COUNTING THE CABBIE?
FINE.
WHO DO YOU WANT DEAD, STRYFE?
YEAH, WELL-- MAYBE I DON'T WANT TO BE YOUR BITCH. MAYBE THE COST WILL BE TOO HIGH.
NO NEED TO WORRY ABOUT THAT NOW. I'LL BE IN TOUCH. THINK OF IT AS A LONG-TERM PAYMENT PLAN.

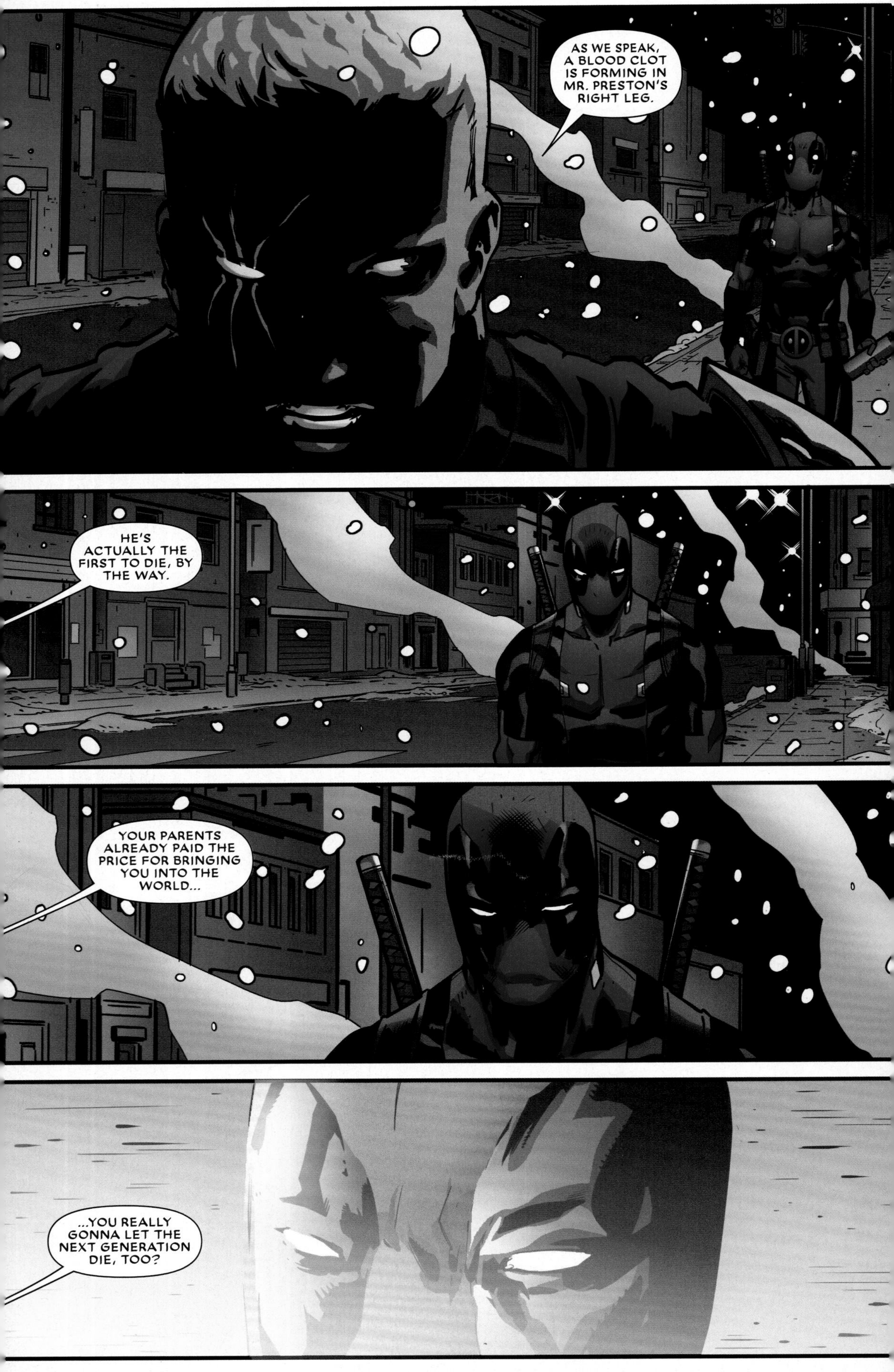
AS WE SPEAK, A BLOOD CLOT IS FORMING IN MR. PRESTON'S RIGHT LEG.
HE'S ACTUALLY THE FIRST TO DIE, BY THE WAY.
YOUR PARENTS ALREADY PAID THE PRICE FOR BRINGING YOU INTO THE WORLD...
...YOU REALLY GONNA LET THE NEXT GENERATION DIE, TOO?

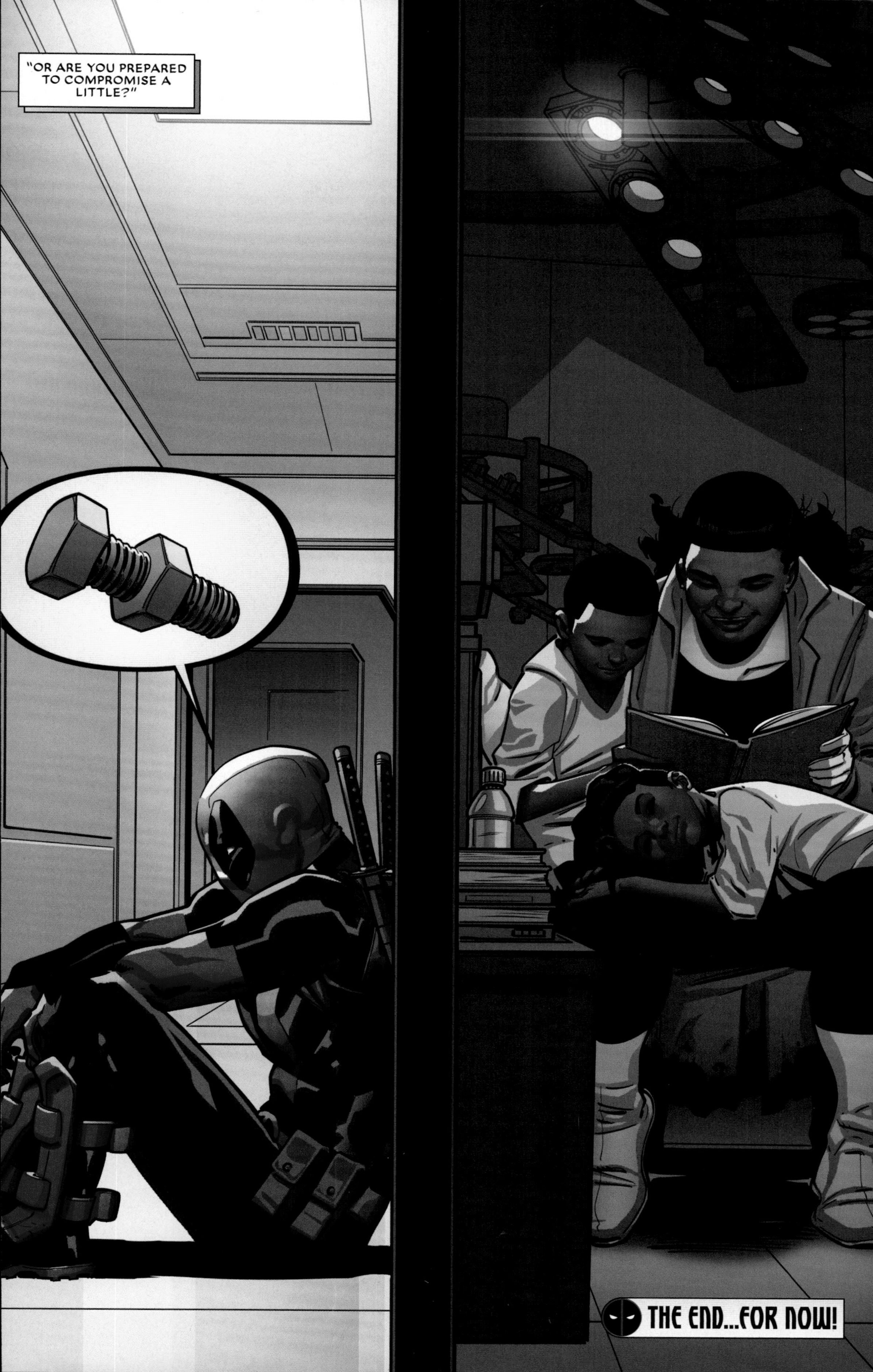
"OR ARE YOU PREPARED TO COMPROMISE A LITTLE?"
THE END...FOR NOW!

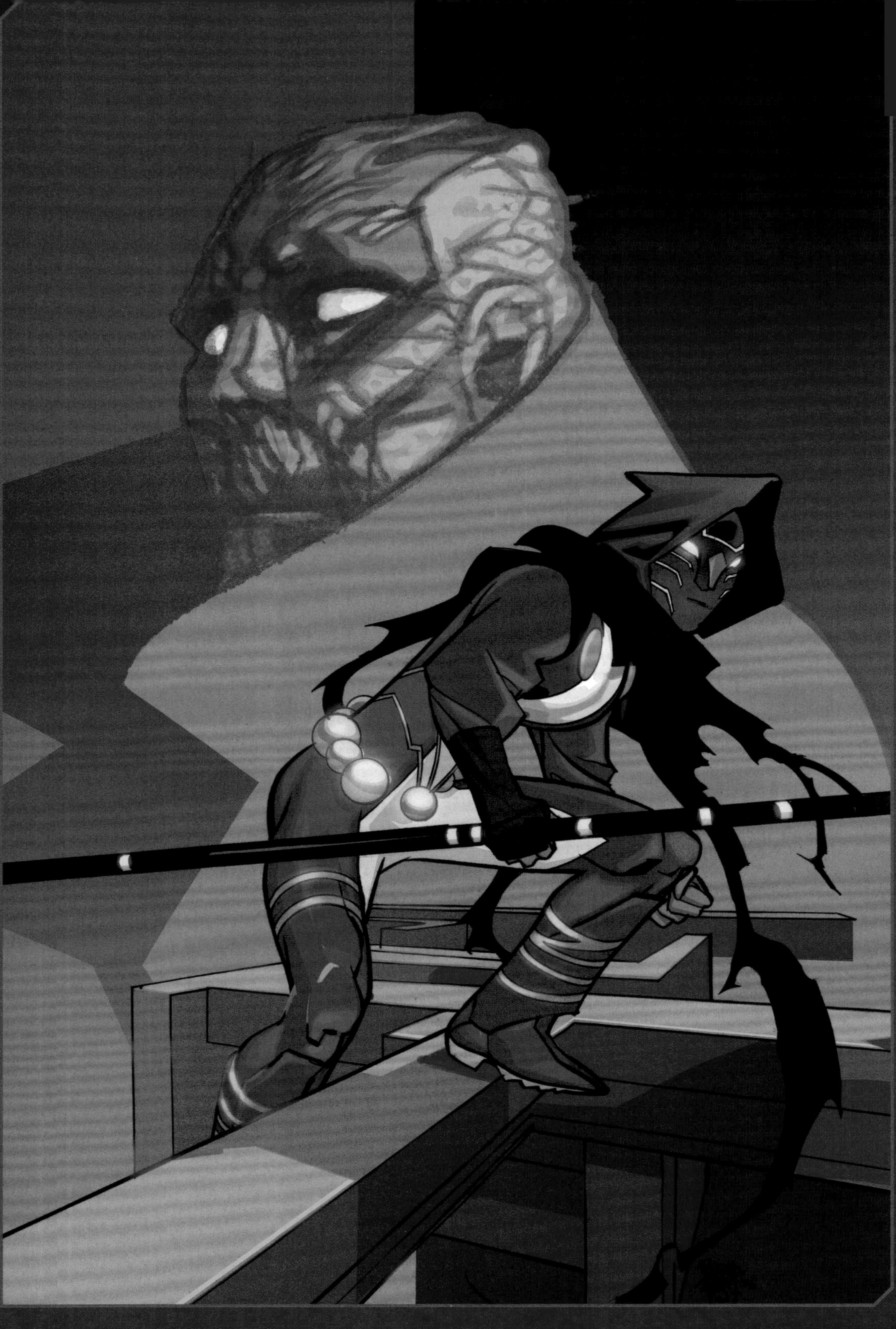

#25 variant by PASQUAL FERRY & DAVE McCAIG

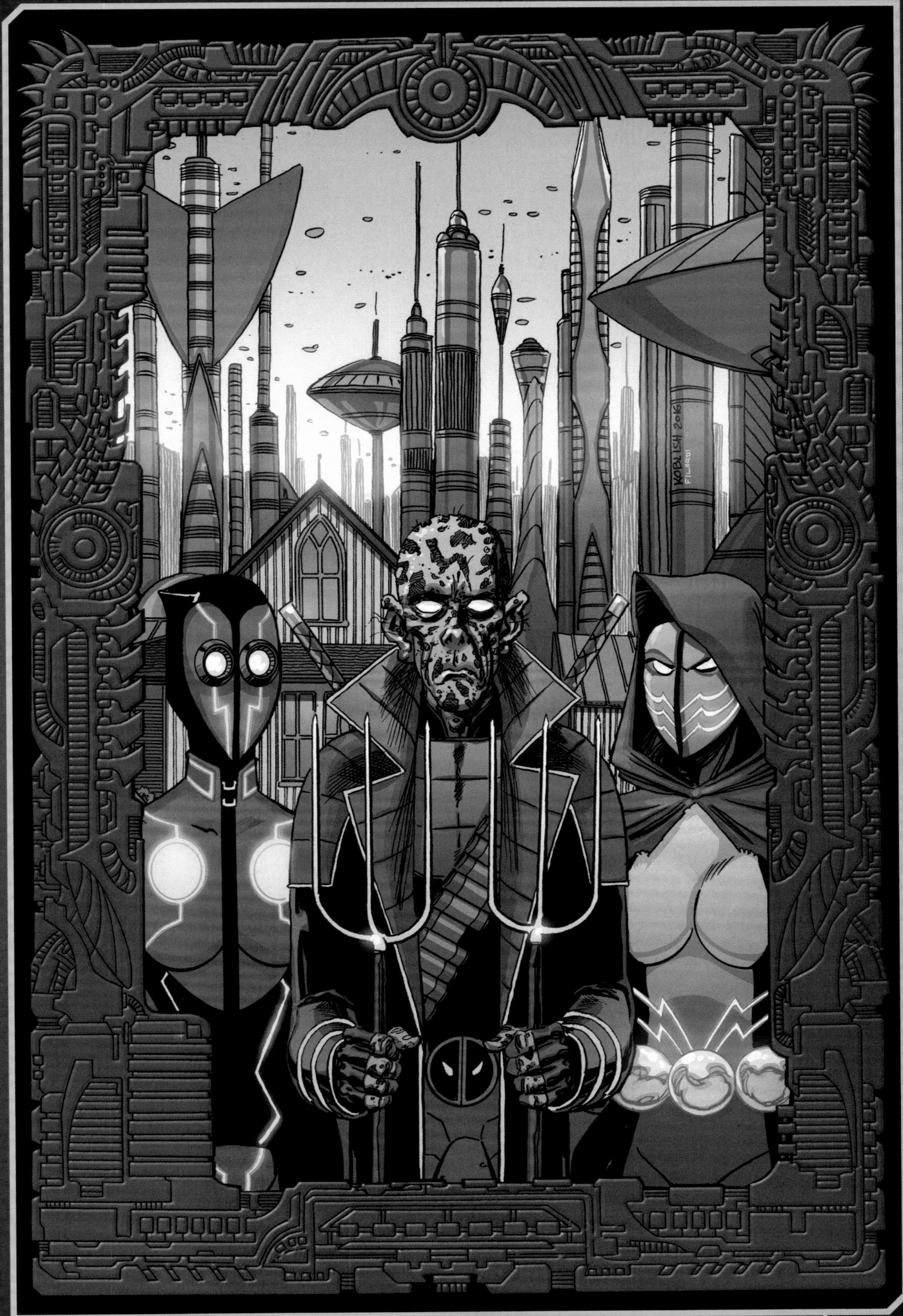
KOBLISH 2016

POSSIBLY THE MOST SKILLED MERCENARY OF THE CENTURY, AND DEFINITELY THE MOST DANGEROUS, WARDA WILSON WREAKS HAVOK ACROSS THE WORLD OF 2099, REBELLING AGAINST SOCIETY AND DOING THINGS HER OWN WAY. DAUGHTER OF A FAST-TALKING MERCENARY WITH A HEALING FACTOR AND A DEMONIC SUCCUBUS QUEEN, WARDA HAS NEVER FIT IN ANYWHERE...SO SHE MAKES HER HOME ON THE OUTSIDE, LIVING BY HER OWN RULES. CALL HER THE MERC WITH THE MOUTH...CALL HER THE REGENERATIN' DEGENERATE...CALL HER...

DEADPOOL

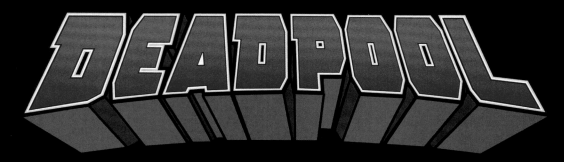

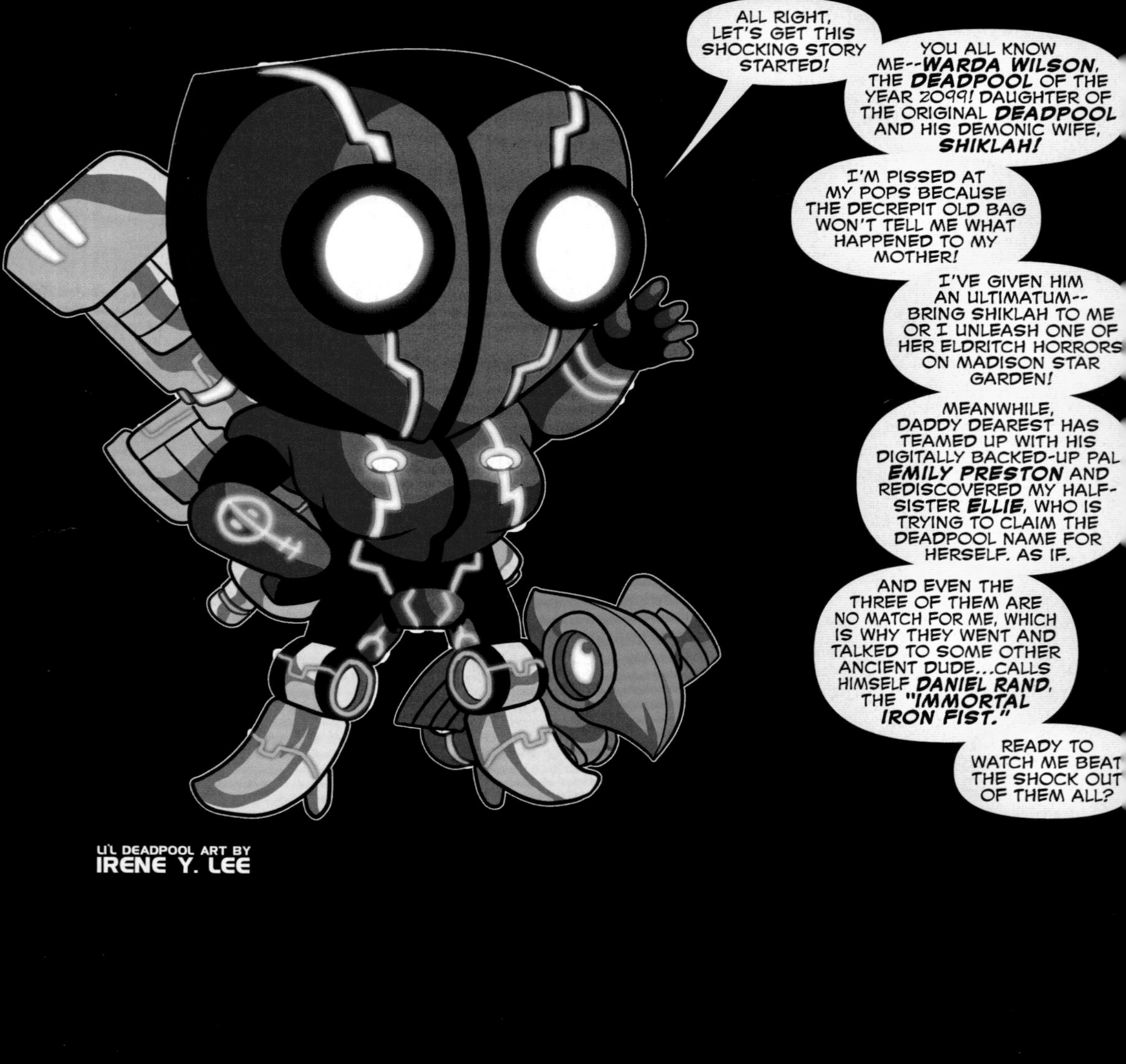
ALL RIGHT, LET'S GET THIS SHOCKING STORY STARTED!
YOU ALL KNOW ME--WARDA WILSON, THE DEADPOOL OF THE YEAR 2099! DAUGHTER OF THE ORIGINAL DEADPOOL AND HIS DEMONIC WIFE, SHIKLAH!
I'M PISSED AT MY POPS BECAUSE THE DECREPIT OLD BAG WON'T TELL ME WHAT HAPPENED TO MY MOTHER!
I'VE GIVEN HIM AN ULTIMATUM-- BRING SHIKLAH TO ME OR I UNLEASH ONE OF HER ELDRITCH HORRORS ON MADISON STAR GARDEN!
MEANWHILE, DADDY DEAREST HAS TEAMED UP WITH HIS DIGITALLY BACKED-UP PAL EMILY PRESTON AND REDISCOVERED MY HALF-SISTER ELLIE, WHO IS TRYING TO CLAIM THE DEADPOOL NAME FOR HERSELF. AS IF.
AND EVEN THE THREE OF THEM ARE NO MATCH FOR ME, WHICH IS WHY THEY WENT AND TALKED TO SOME OTHER ANCIENT DUDE...CALLS HIMSELF DANIEL RAND, THE "IMMORTAL IRON FIST."
READY TO WATCH ME BEAT THE SHOCK OUT OF THEM ALL?

LI'L DEADPOOL ART BY
IRENE Y. LEE

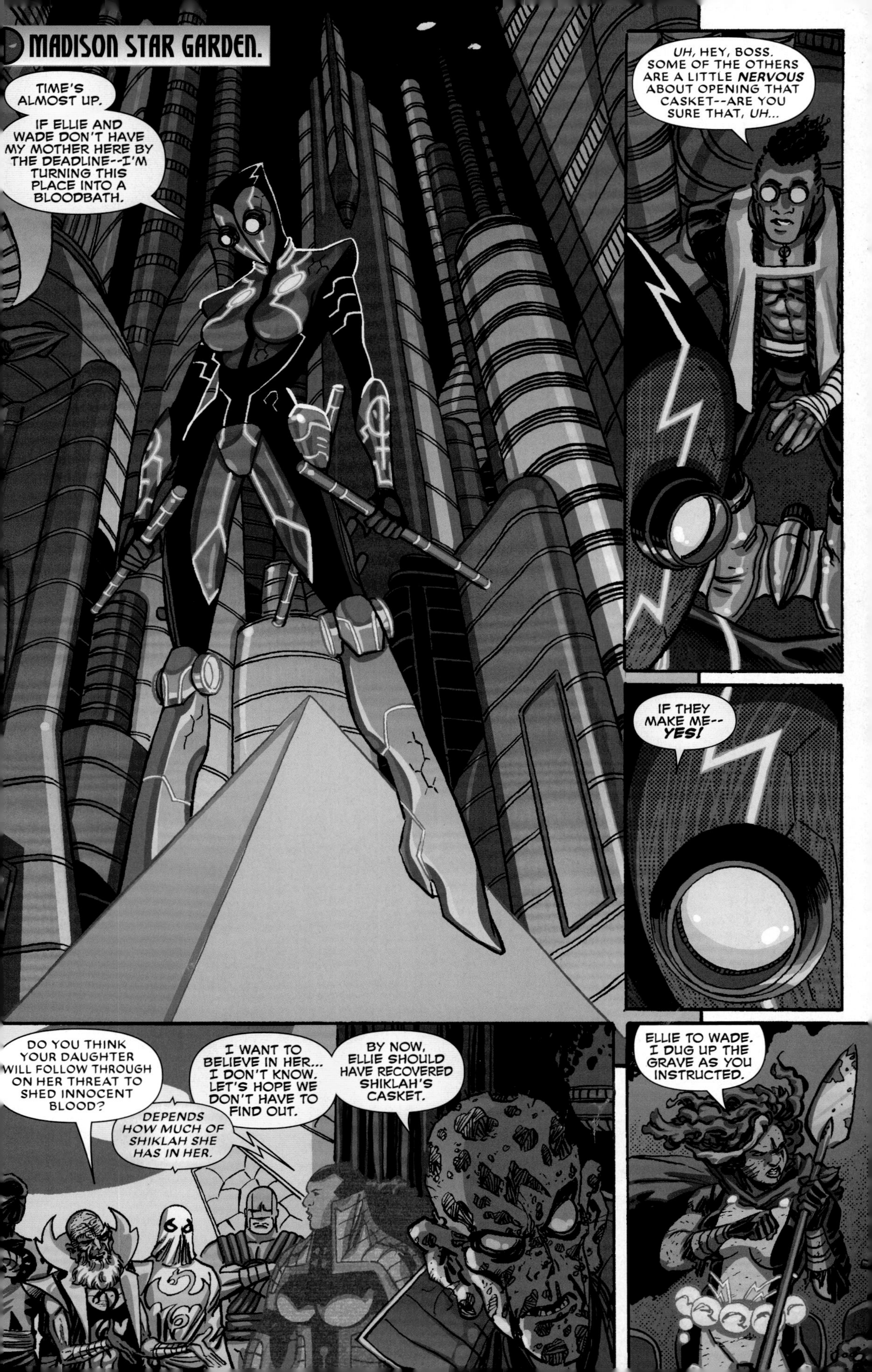
MADISON STAR GARDEN.
TIME'S ALMOST UP.
IF ELLIE AND WADE DON'T HAVE MY MOTHER HERE BY THE DEADLINE--I'M TURNING THIS PLACE INTO A BLOODBATH.
UH, HEY, BOSS. SOME OF THE OTHERS ARE A LITTLE NERVOUS ABOUT OPENING THAT CASKET--ARE YOU SURE THAT, UH...
IF THEY MAKE ME-- YES!
DO YOU THINK YOUR DAUGHTER WILL FOLLOW THROUGH ON HER THREAT TO SHED INNOCENT BLOOD?
DEPENDS HOW MUCH OF SHIKLAH SHE HAS IN HER.
I WANT TO BELIEVE IN HER... I DON'T KNOW. LET'S HOPE WE DON'T HAVE TO FIND OUT.
BY NOW, ELLIE SHOULD HAVE RECOVERED SHIKLAH'S CASKET.
ELLIE TO WADE. I DUG UP THE GRAVE AS YOU INSTRUCTED.

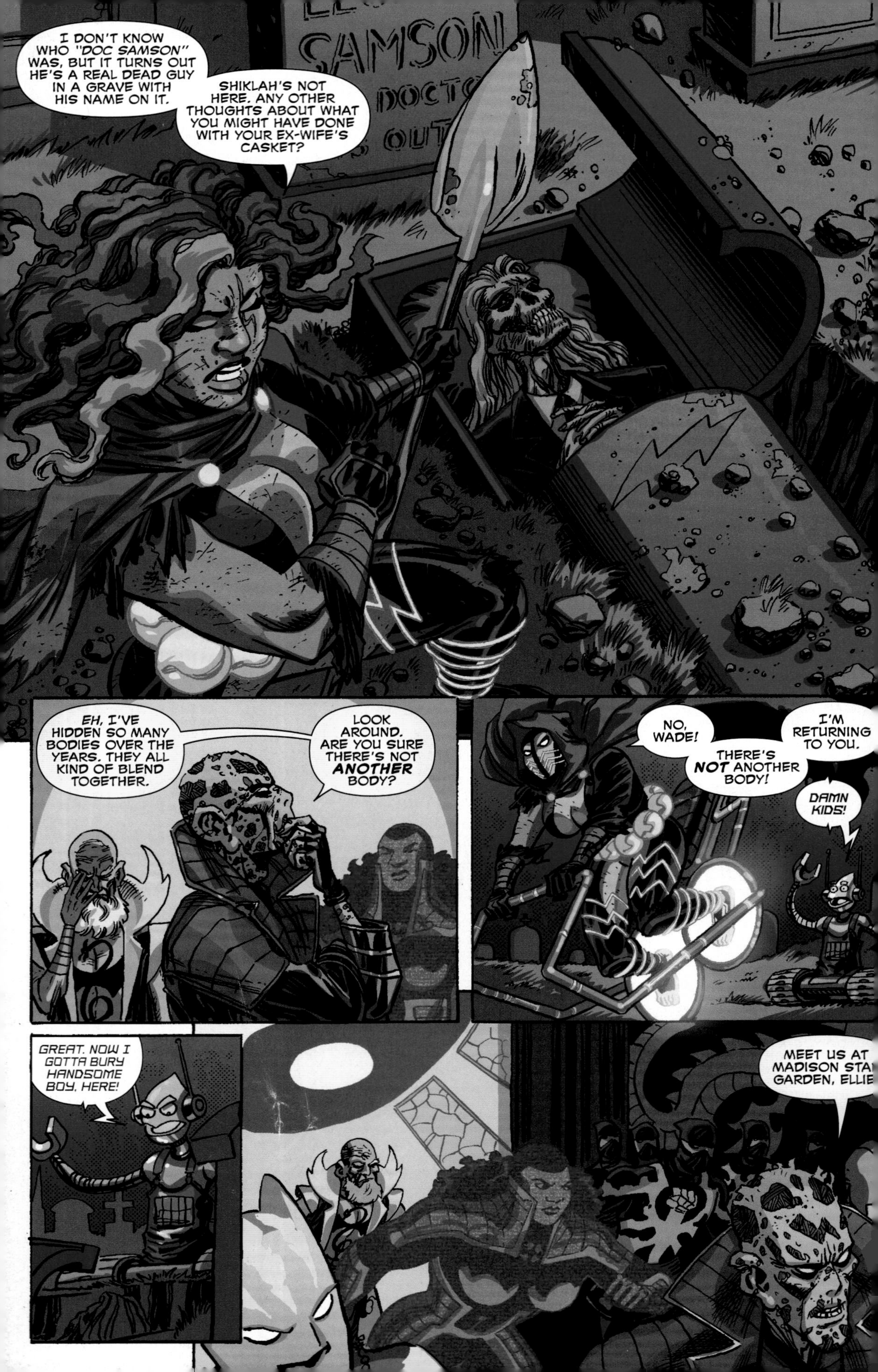
SAMSON
DOCTO
OUT
I DON'T KNOW WHO "DOC SAMSON" WAS, BUT IT TURNS OUT HE'S A REAL DEAD GUY IN A GRAVE WITH HIS NAME ON IT.
SHIKLAH'S NOT HERE. ANY OTHER THOUGHTS ABOUT WHAT YOU MIGHT HAVE DONE WITH YOUR EX-WIFE'S CASKET?
EH, I'VE HIDDEN SO MANY BODIES OVER THE YEARS. THEY ALL KIND OF BLEND TOGETHER.
LOOK AROUND. ARE YOU SURE THERE'S NOT ANOTHER BODY?
NO, WADE!
THERE'S NOT ANOTHER BODY!
I'M RETURNING TO YOU.
DAMN KIDS!
GREAT. NOW I GOTTA BURY HANDSOME BOY, HERE!
MEET US AT MADISON STA GARDEN, ELLIE

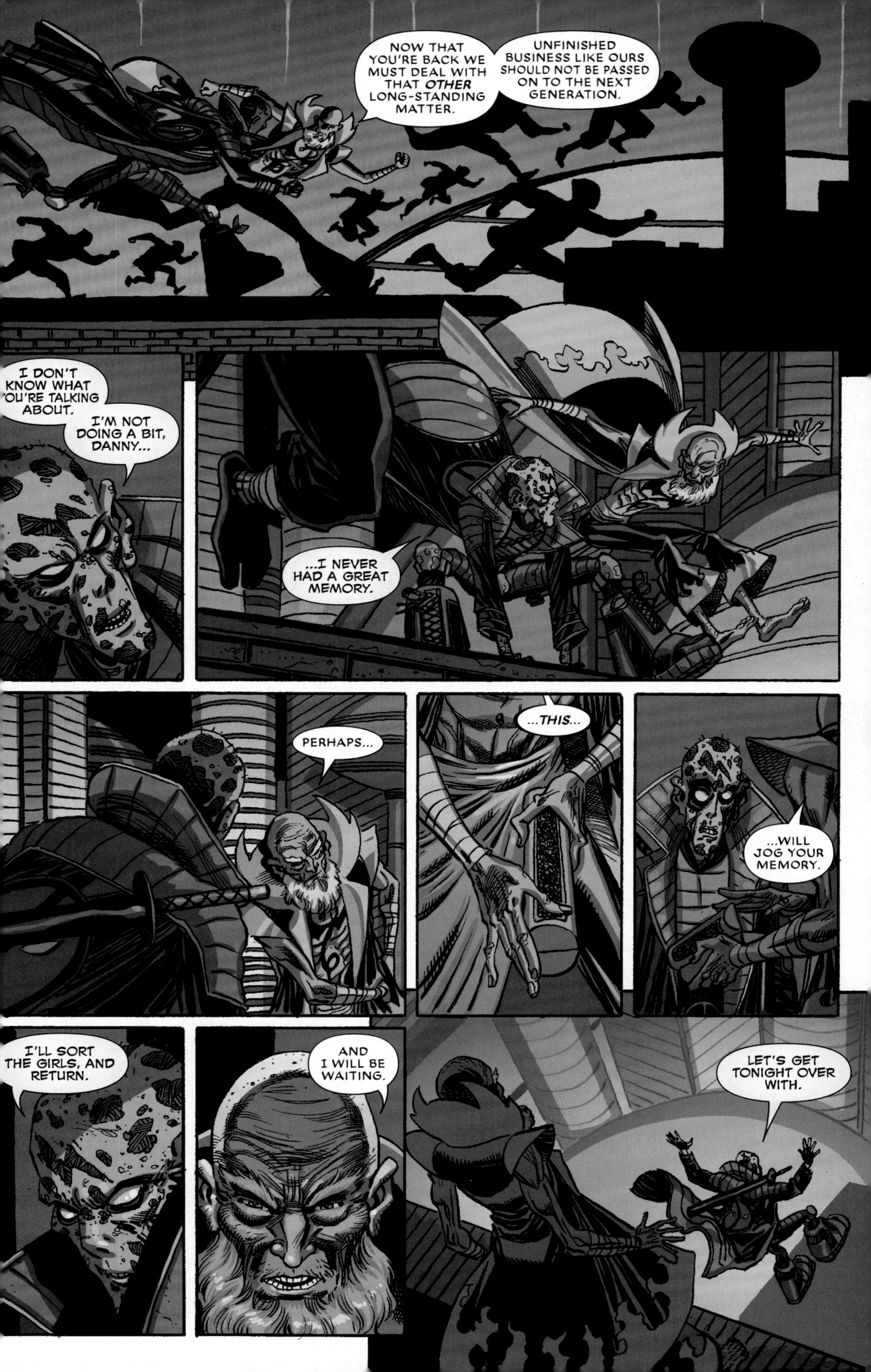
NOW THAT YOU'RE BACK WE MUST DEAL WITH THAT OTHER LONG-STANDING MATTER.
UNFINISHED BUSINESS LIKE OURS SHOULD NOT BE PASSED ON TO THE NEXT GENERATION.
I DON'T KNOW WHAT YOU'RE TALKING ABOUT.
I'M NOT DOING A BIT, DANNY...
...I NEVER HAD A GREAT MEMORY.
PERHAPS...
...THIS...
...WILL JOG YOUR MEMORY.
I'LL SORT THE GIRLS, AND RETURN.
AND I WILL BE WAITING.
LET'S GET TONIGHT OVER WITH.

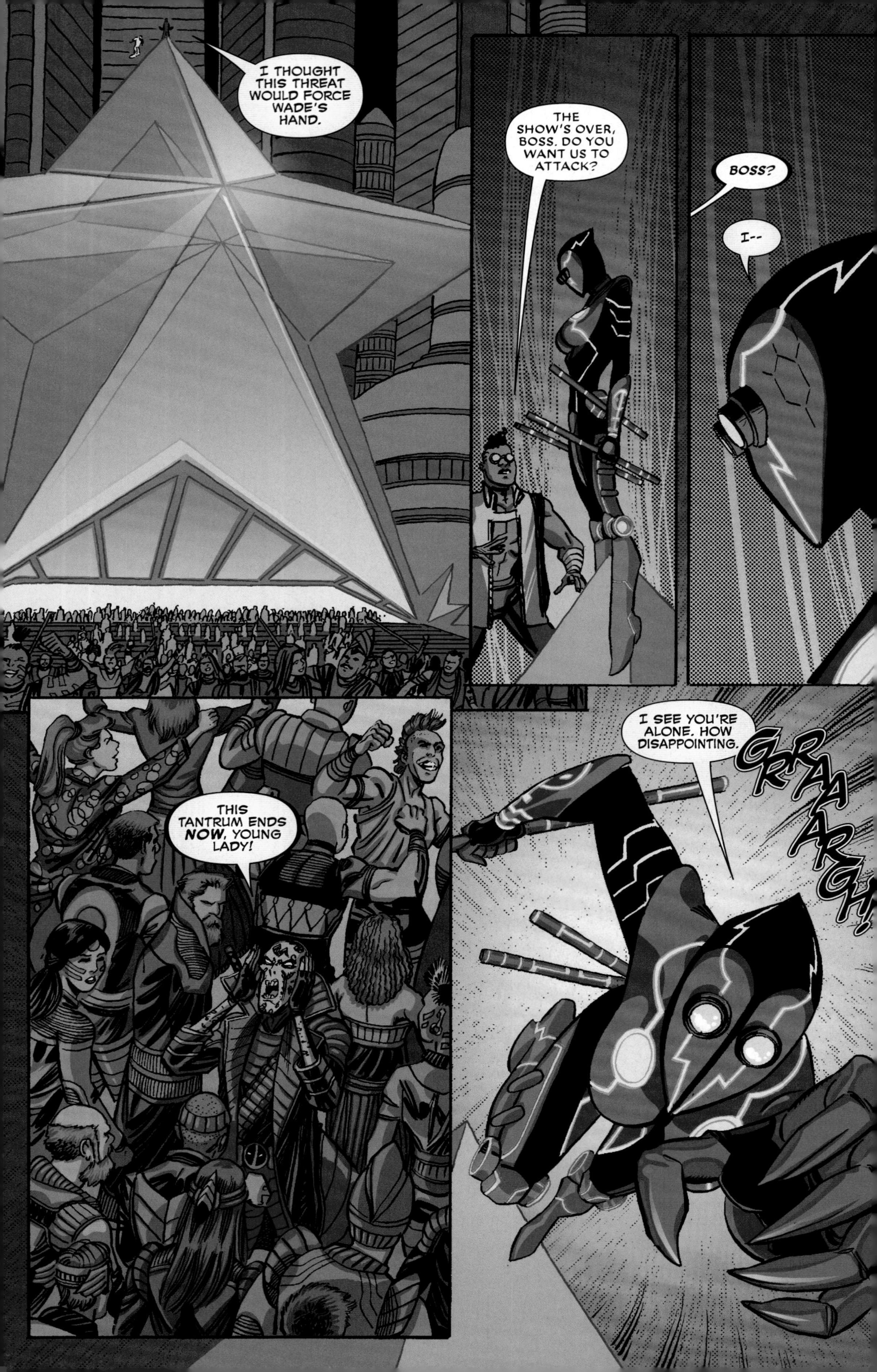
I THOUGHT THIS THREAT WOULD FORCE WADE'S HAND.
THE SHOW'S OVER, BOSS. DO YOU WANT US TO ATTACK?
BOSS?
I--
THIS TANTRUM ENDS **NOW**, YOUNG LADY!
I SEE YOU'RE ALONE. HOW DISAPPOINTING.
GRRAAAARGH!

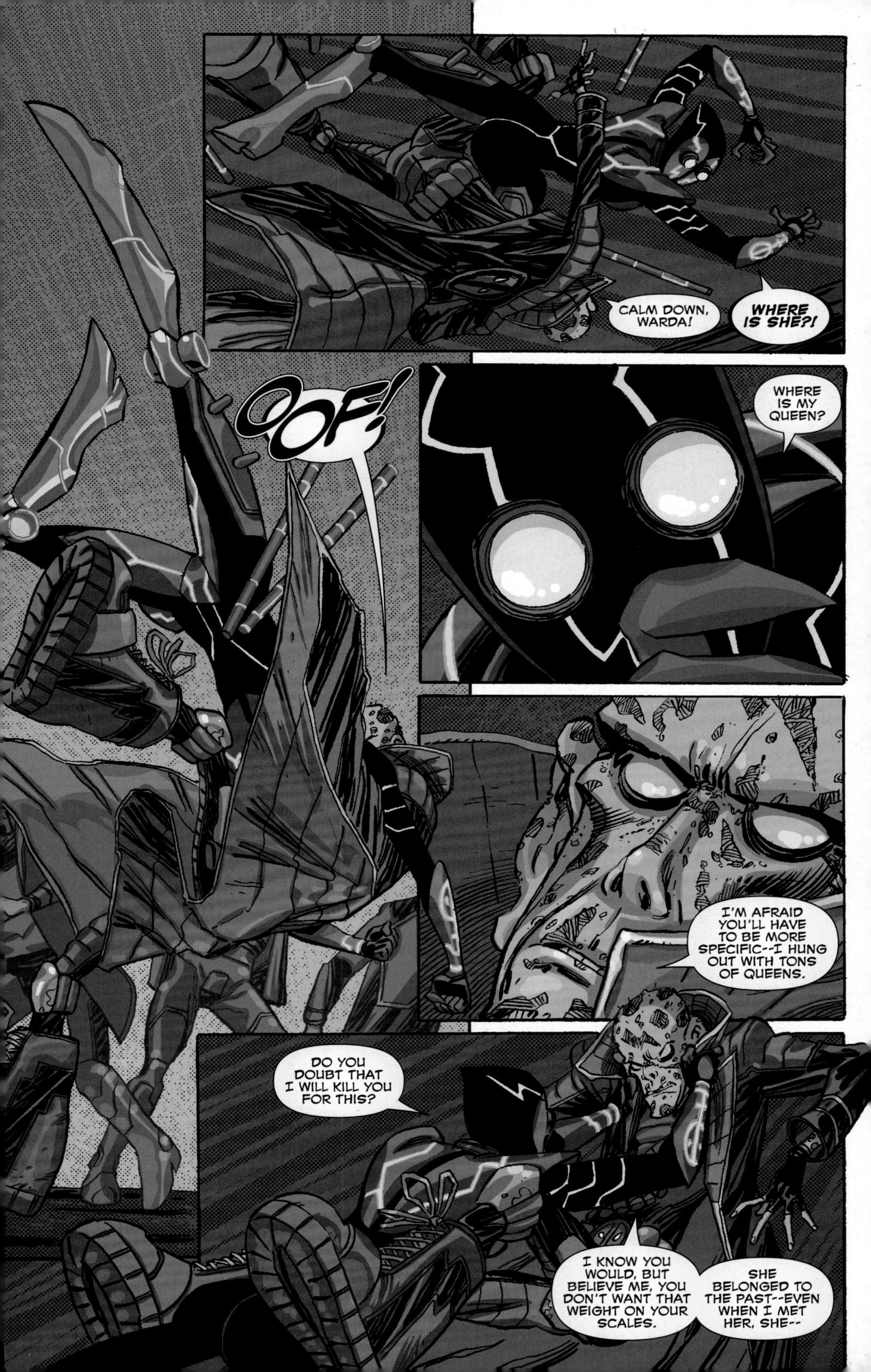

CALM DOWN, WARDA!
WHERE IS SHE?!
OOF!
WHERE IS MY QUEEN?
I'M AFRAID YOU'LL HAVE TO BE MORE SPECIFIC--I HUNG OUT WITH TONS OF QUEENS.
DO YOU DOUBT THAT I WILL KILL YOU FOR THIS?
I KNOW YOU WOULD, BUT BELIEVE ME, YOU DON'T WANT THAT WEIGHT ON YOUR SCALES.
SHE BELONGED TO THE PAST--EVEN WHEN I MET HER, SHE--

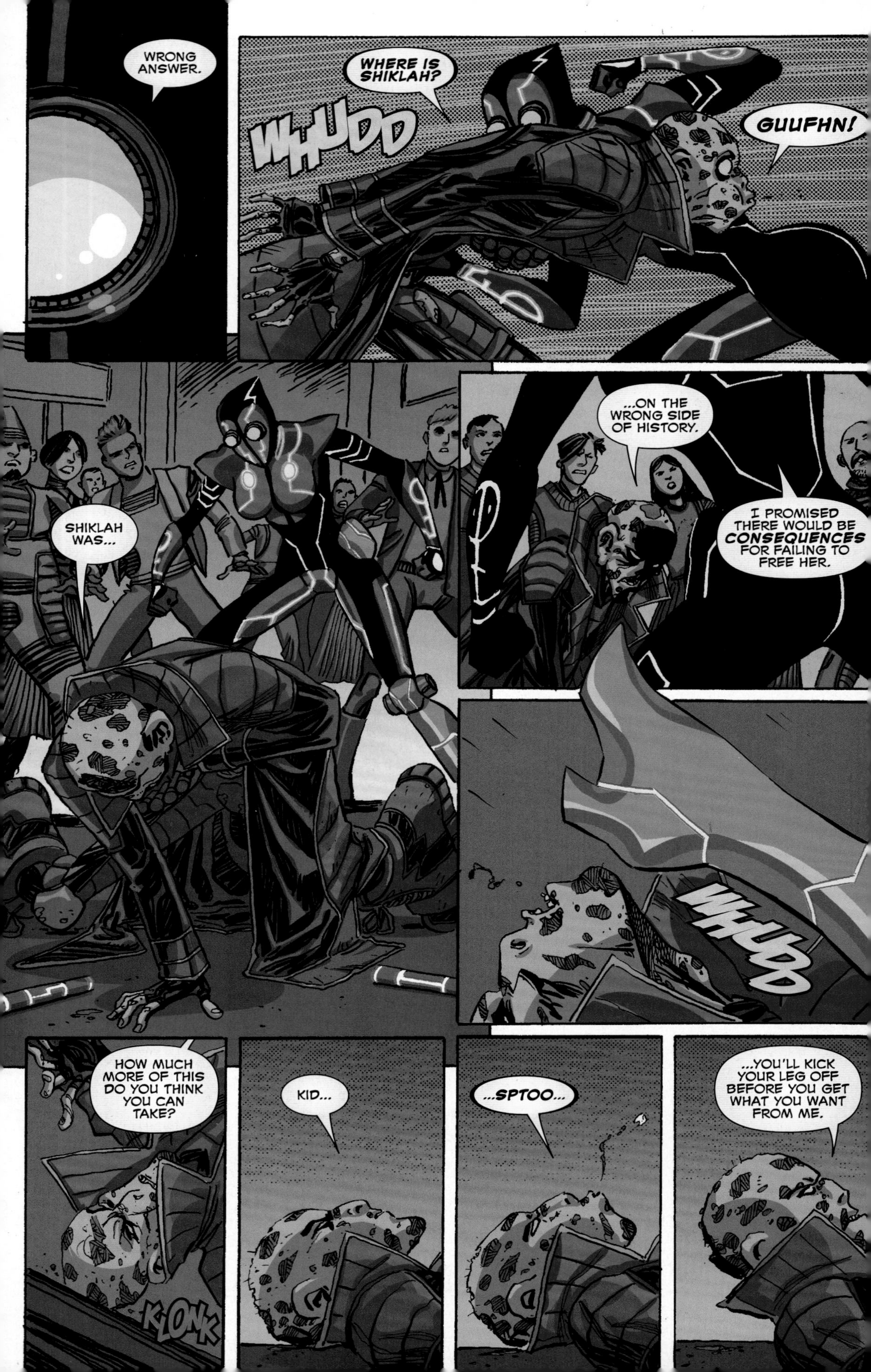
WRONG ANSWER.
WHERE IS SHIKLAH?
WHUDD
GUUFHN!
SHIKLAH WAS...
...ON THE WRONG SIDE OF HISTORY.
I PROMISED THERE WOULD BE CONSEQUENCES FOR FAILING TO FREE HER.
WHUDD
HOW MUCH MORE OF THIS DO YOU THINK YOU CAN TAKE?
KLONK
KID...
...SPTOO...
...YOU'LL KICK YOUR LEG OFF BEFORE YOU GET WHAT YOU WANT FROM ME.

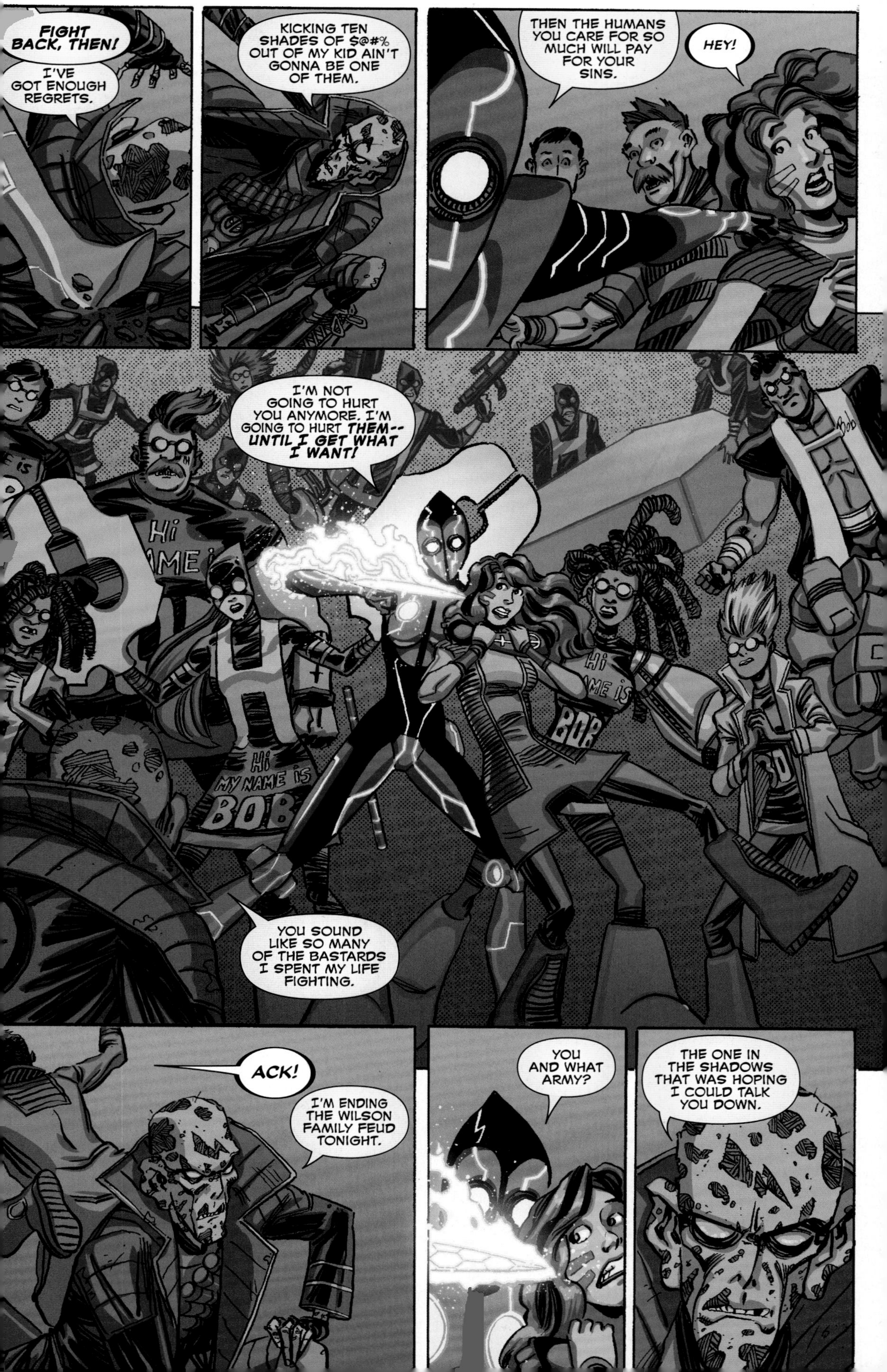
FIGHT BACK, THEN!
I'VE GOT ENOUGH REGRETS.
KICKING TEN SHADES OF $@#% OUT OF MY KID AIN'T GONNA BE ONE OF THEM.
THEN THE HUMANS YOU CARE FOR SO MUCH WILL PAY FOR YOUR SINS.
HEY!
I'M NOT GOING TO HURT YOU ANYMORE. I'M GOING TO HURT THEM-- UNTIL I GET WHAT I WANT!
Hi MY NAME is BOB
YOU SOUND LIKE SO MANY OF THE BASTARDS I SPENT MY LIFE FIGHTING.
ACK!
I'M ENDING THE WILSON FAMILY FEUD TONIGHT.
YOU AND WHAT ARMY?
THE ONE IN THE SHADOWS THAT WAS HOPING I COULD TALK YOU DOWN.

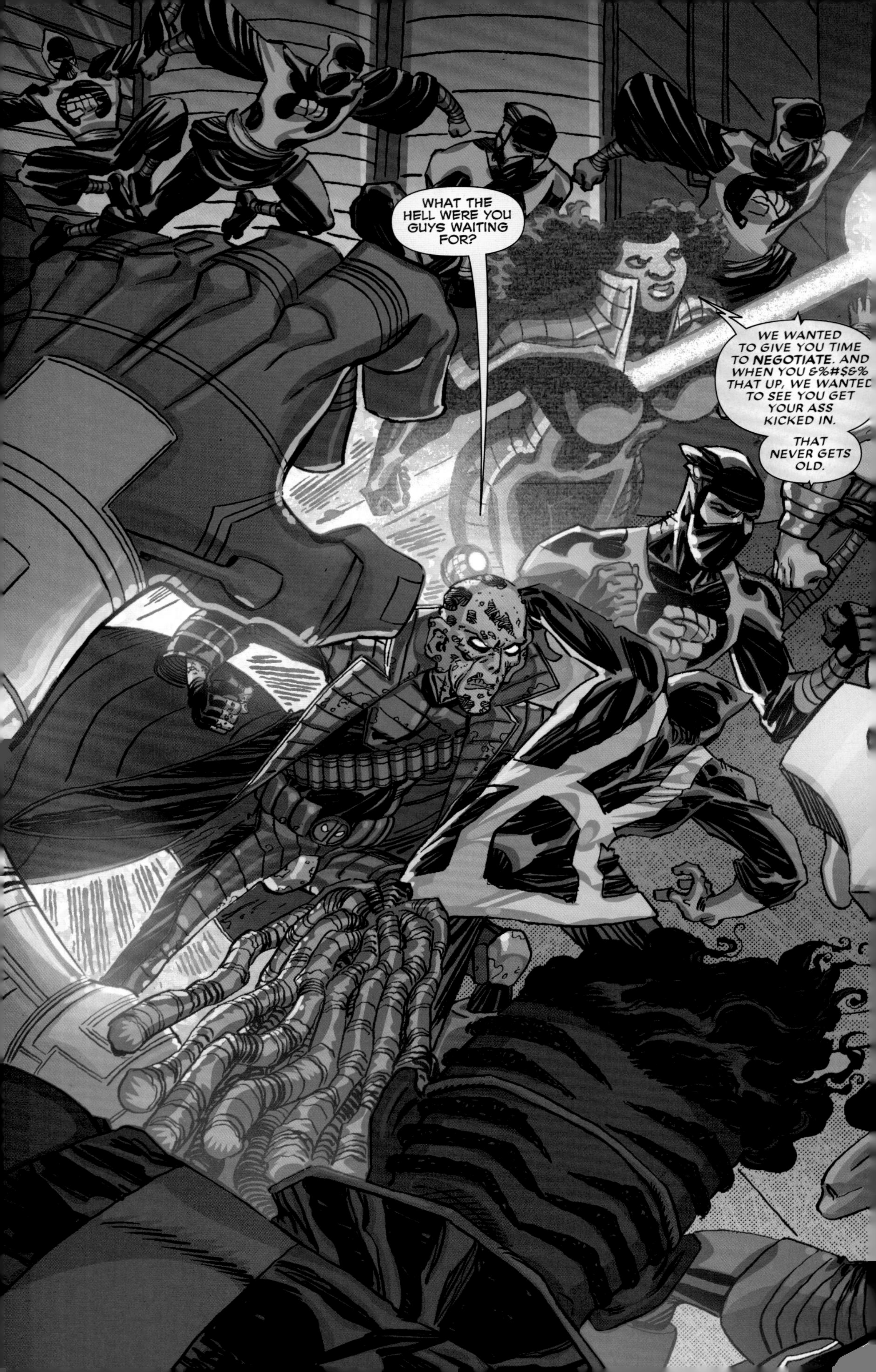
WHAT THE HELL WERE YOU GUYS WAITING FOR?
WE WANTED TO GIVE YOU TIME TO NEGOTIATE. AND WHEN YOU &%#$&% THAT UP, WE WANTED TO SEE YOU GET YOUR ASS KICKED IN.
THAT NEVER GETS OLD.

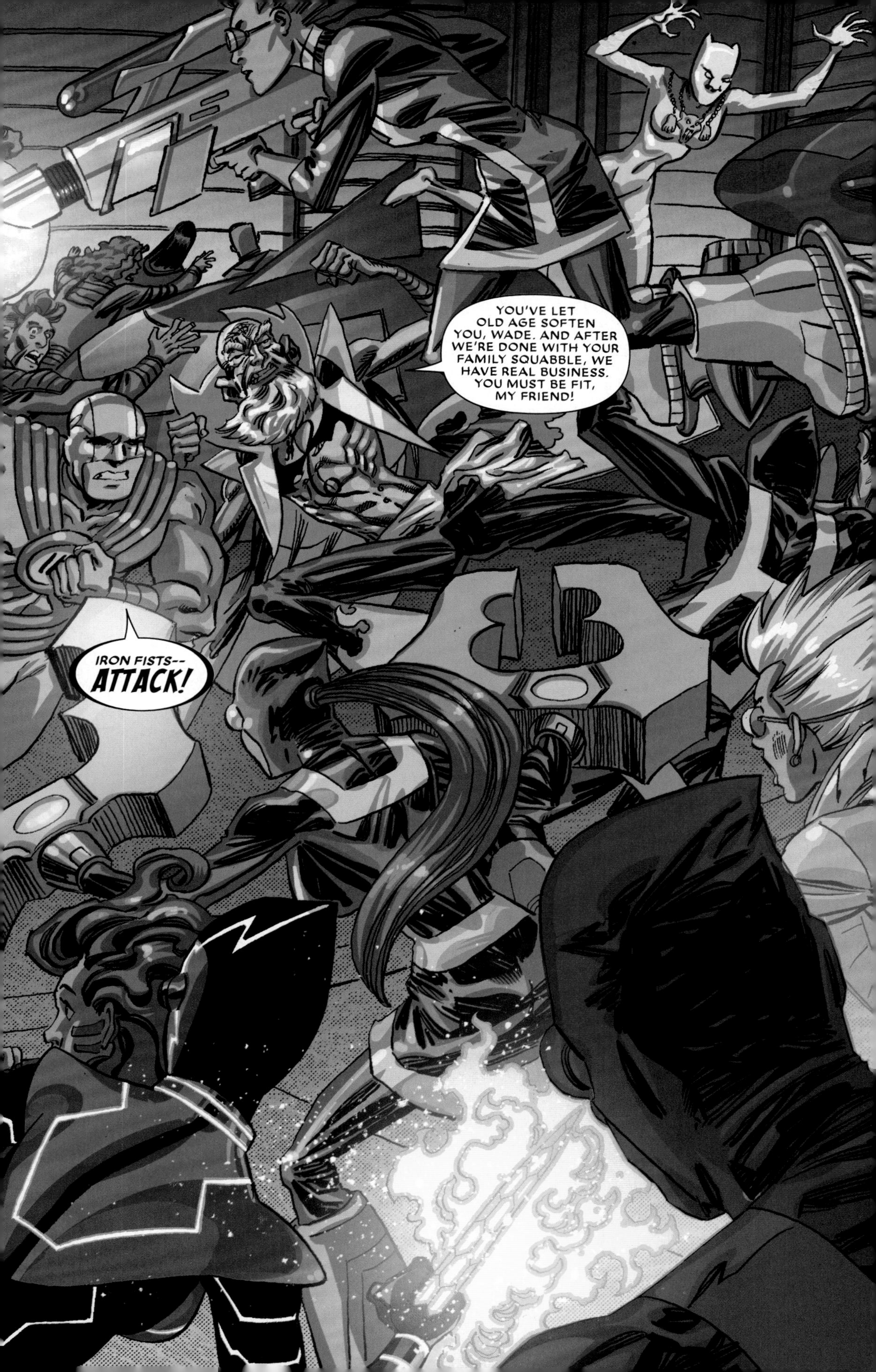
YOU'VE LET OLD AGE SOFTEN YOU, WADE. AND AFTER WE'RE DONE WITH YOUR FAMILY SQUABBLE, WE HAVE REAL BUSINESS. YOU MUST BE FIT, MY FRIEND!
IRON FISTS-- ATTACK!

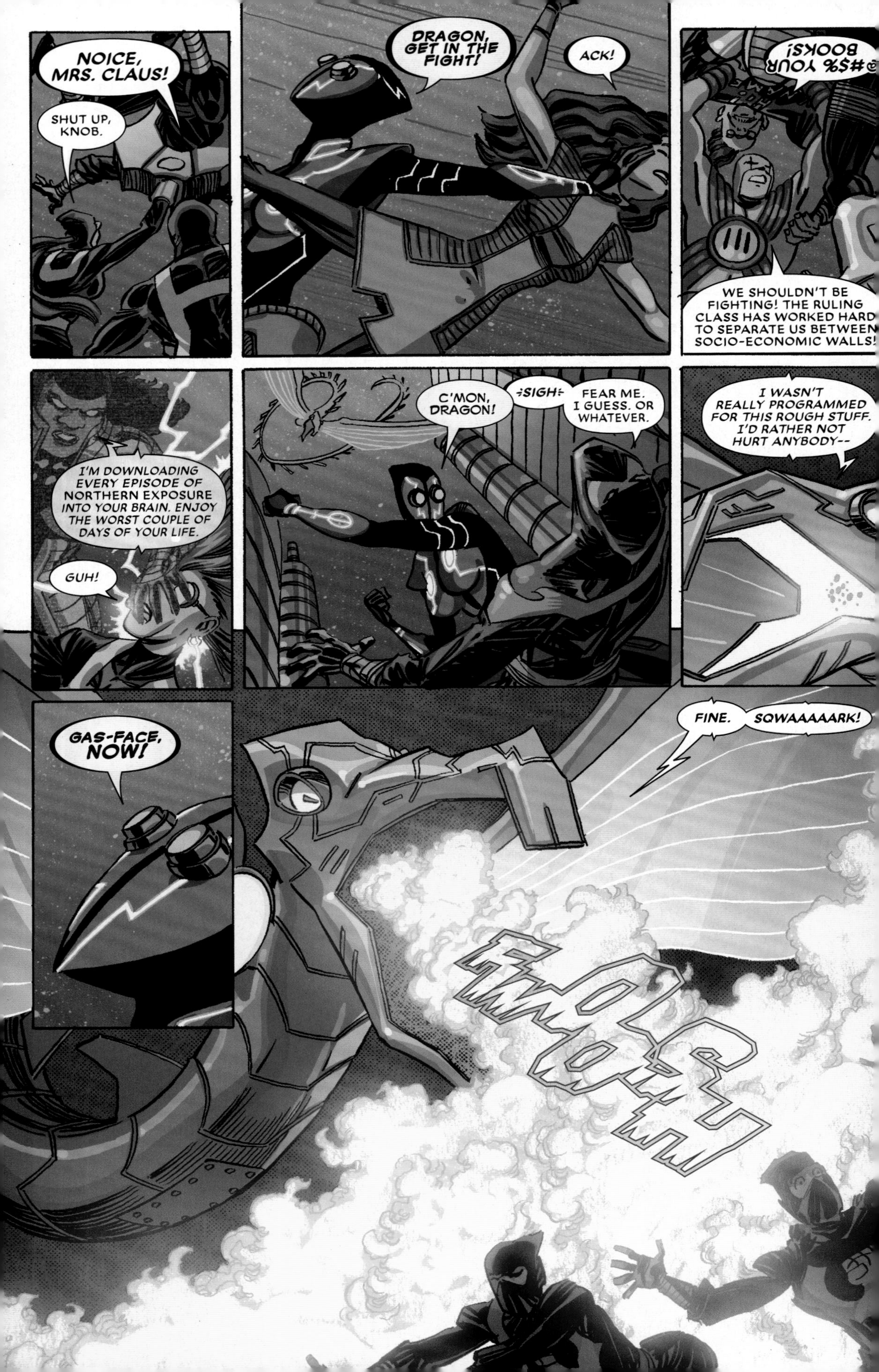
NOICE, MRS. CLAUS!
SHUT UP, KNOB.
DRAGON, GET IN THE FIGHT!
ACK!
@#$% YOUR BOOKS!
WE SHOULDN'T BE FIGHTING! THE RULING CLASS HAS WORKED HARD TO SEPARATE US BETWEEN SOCIO-ECONOMIC WALLS!
I'M DOWNLOADING EVERY EPISODE OF NORTHERN EXPOSURE INTO YOUR BRAIN. ENJOY THE WORST COUPLE OF DAYS OF YOUR LIFE.
GUH!
C'MON, DRAGON!
-SIGH-
FEAR ME. I GUESS. OR WHATEVER.
I WASN'T REALLY PROGRAMMED FOR THIS ROUGH STUFF. I'D RATHER NOT HURT ANYBODY--
GAS-FACE, NOW!
FINE.
SQWAAAAARK!
FOOSH

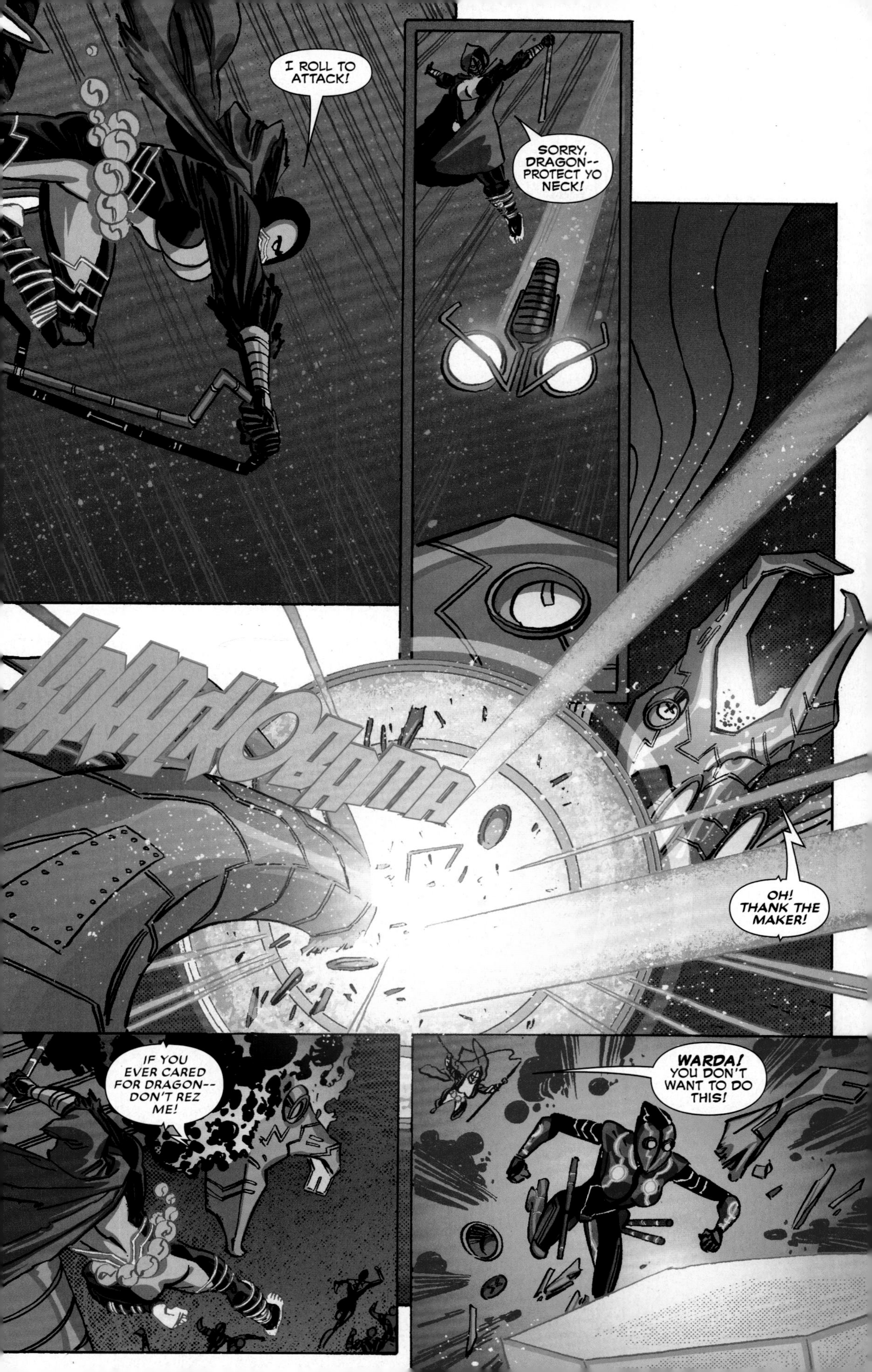
I ROLL TO ATTACK!
SORRY, DRAGON-- PROTECT YO NECK!
KAHADKOHAMA
OH! THANK THE MAKER!
IF YOU EVER CARED FOR DRAGON-- DON'T REZ ME!
WARDA! YOU DON'T WANT TO DO THIS!

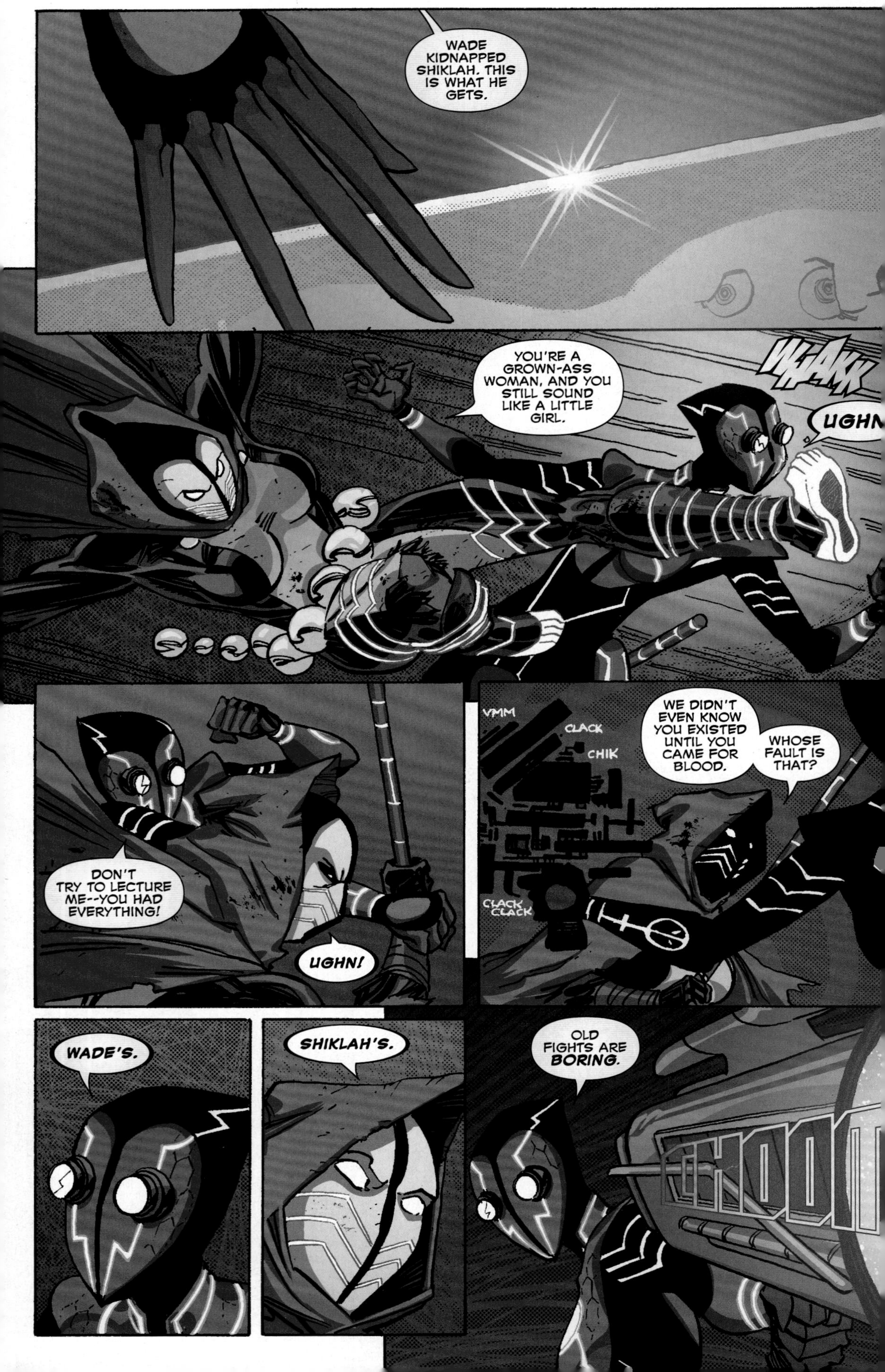

WADE KIDNAPPED SHIKLAH. THIS IS WHAT HE GETS.
YOU'RE A GROWN-ASS WOMAN, AND YOU STILL SOUND LIKE A LITTLE GIRL.
UGHN
DON'T TRY TO LECTURE ME--YOU HAD EVERYTHING!
UGHN!
VMM
CLACK
CHIK
CLACK CLACK
WE DIDN'T EVEN KNOW YOU EXISTED UNTIL YOU CAME FOR BLOOD.
WHOSE FAULT IS THAT?
WADE'S.
SHIKLAH'S.
OLD FIGHTS ARE BORING.

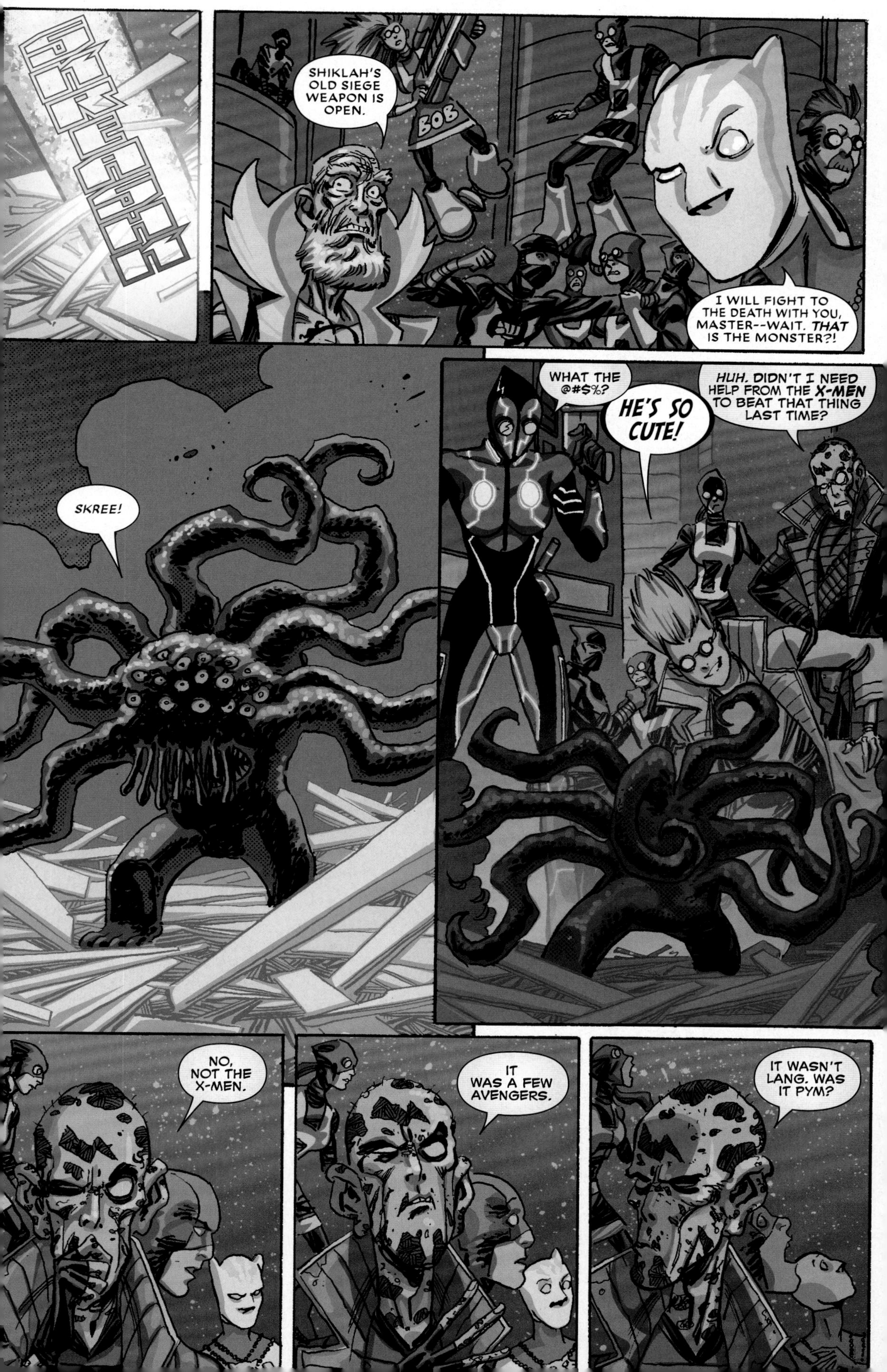
SHIKLAH'S OLD SIEGE WEAPON IS OPEN.
I WILL FIGHT TO THE DEATH WITH YOU, MASTER--WAIT. *THAT* IS THE MONSTER?!
SKREE!
WHAT THE @#$%?
HE'S SO CUTE!
HUH. DIDN'T I NEED HELP FROM THE *X-MEN* TO BEAT THAT THING LAST TIME?
NO, NOT THE X-MEN.
IT WAS A FEW AVENGERS.
IT WASN'T LANG. WAS IT PYM?

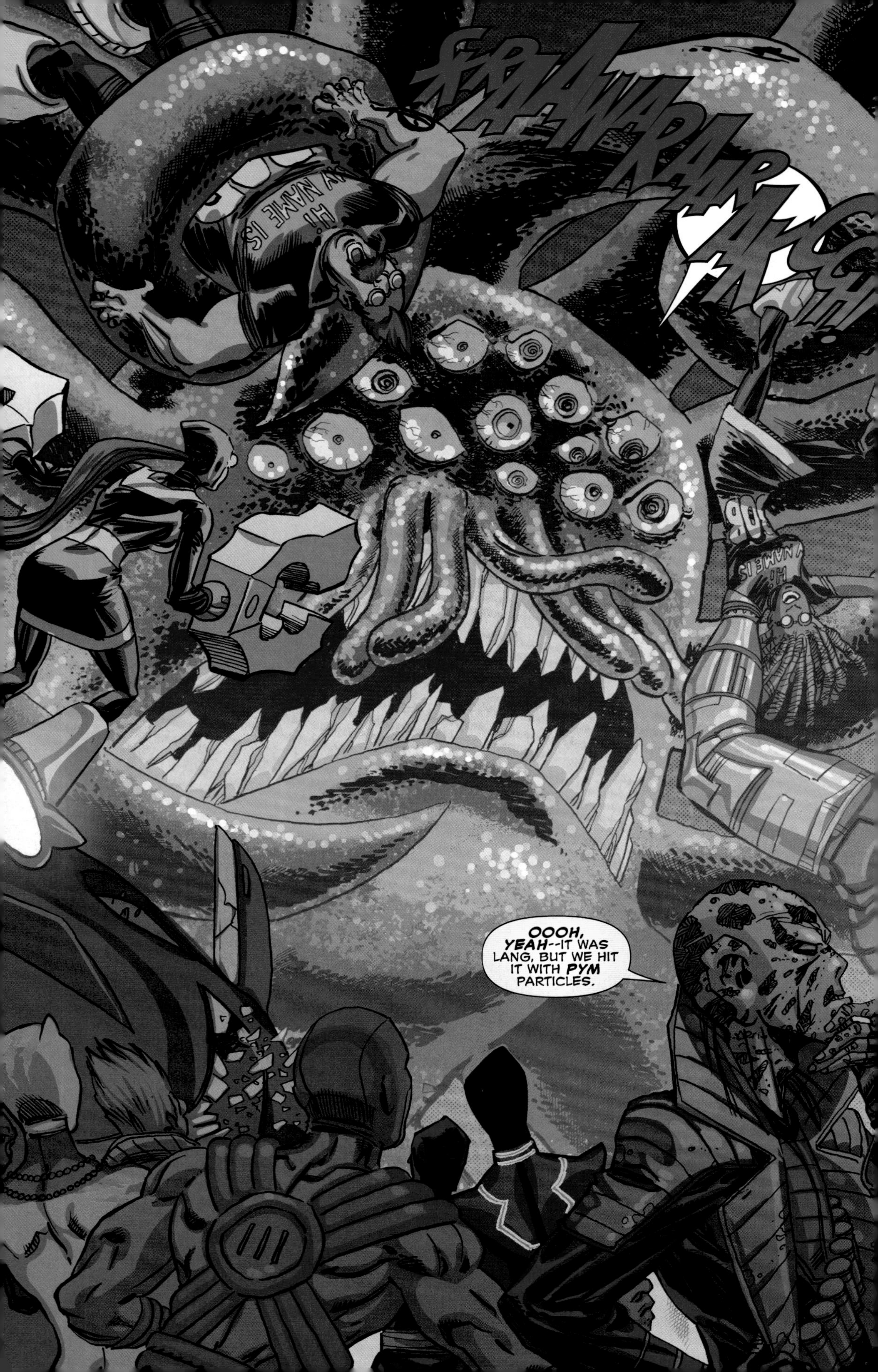
OOOH, YEAH--IT WAS LANG, BUT WE HIT IT WITH PYM PARTICLES.

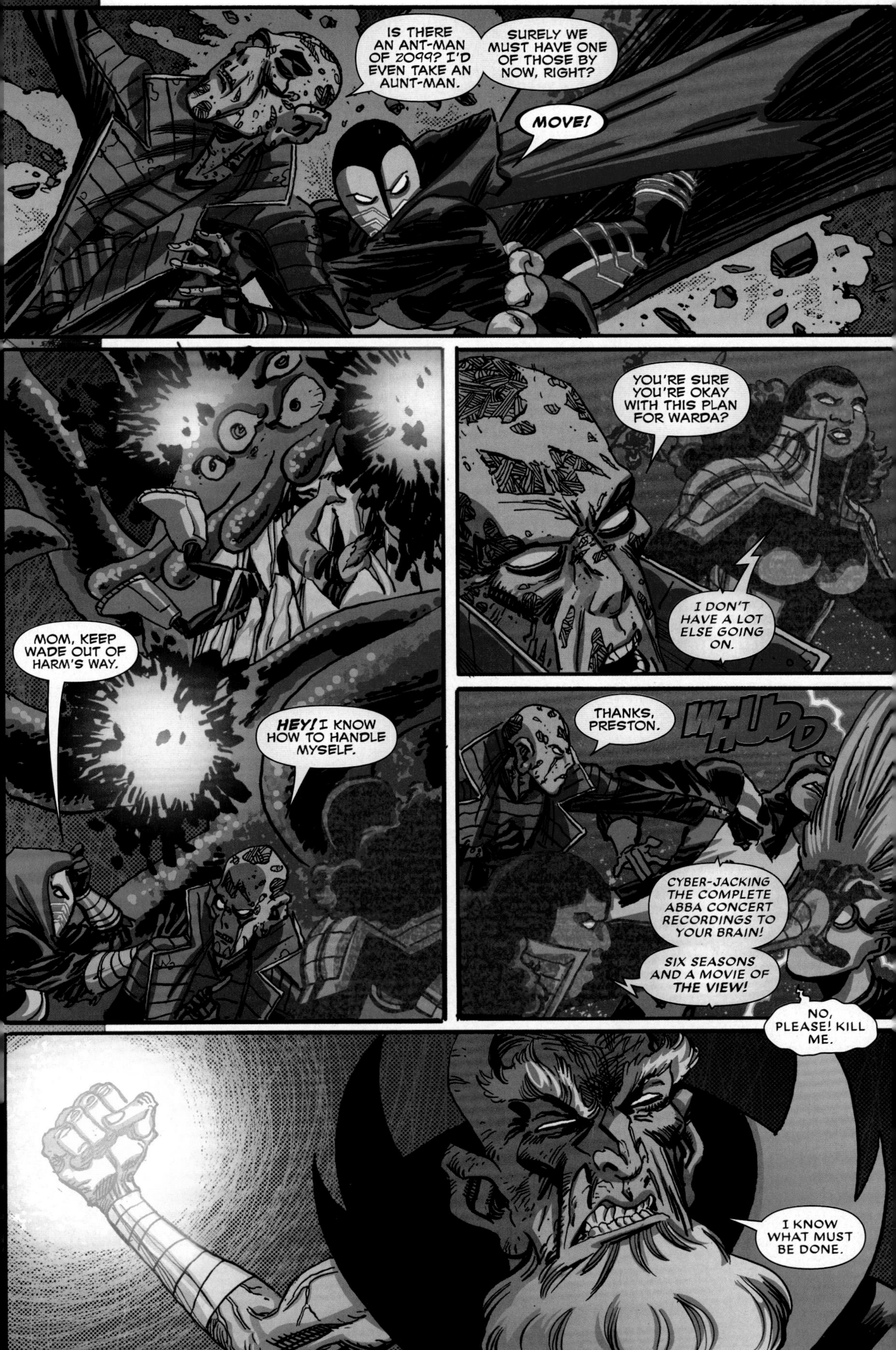
IS THERE AN ANT-MAN OF 2099? I'D EVEN TAKE AN AUNT-MAN.
SURELY WE MUST HAVE ONE OF THOSE BY NOW, RIGHT?
MOVE!
MOM, KEEP WADE OUT OF HARM'S WAY.
HEY! I KNOW HOW TO HANDLE MYSELF.
YOU'RE SURE YOU'RE OKAY WITH THIS PLAN FOR WARDA?
I DON'T HAVE A LOT ELSE GOING ON.
THANKS, PRESTON.
WHUDD
CYBER-JACKING THE COMPLETE ABBA CONCERT RECORDINGS TO YOUR BRAIN!
SIX SEASONS AND A MOVIE OF THE VIEW!
NO, PLEASE! KILL ME.
I KNOW WHAT MUST BE DONE.

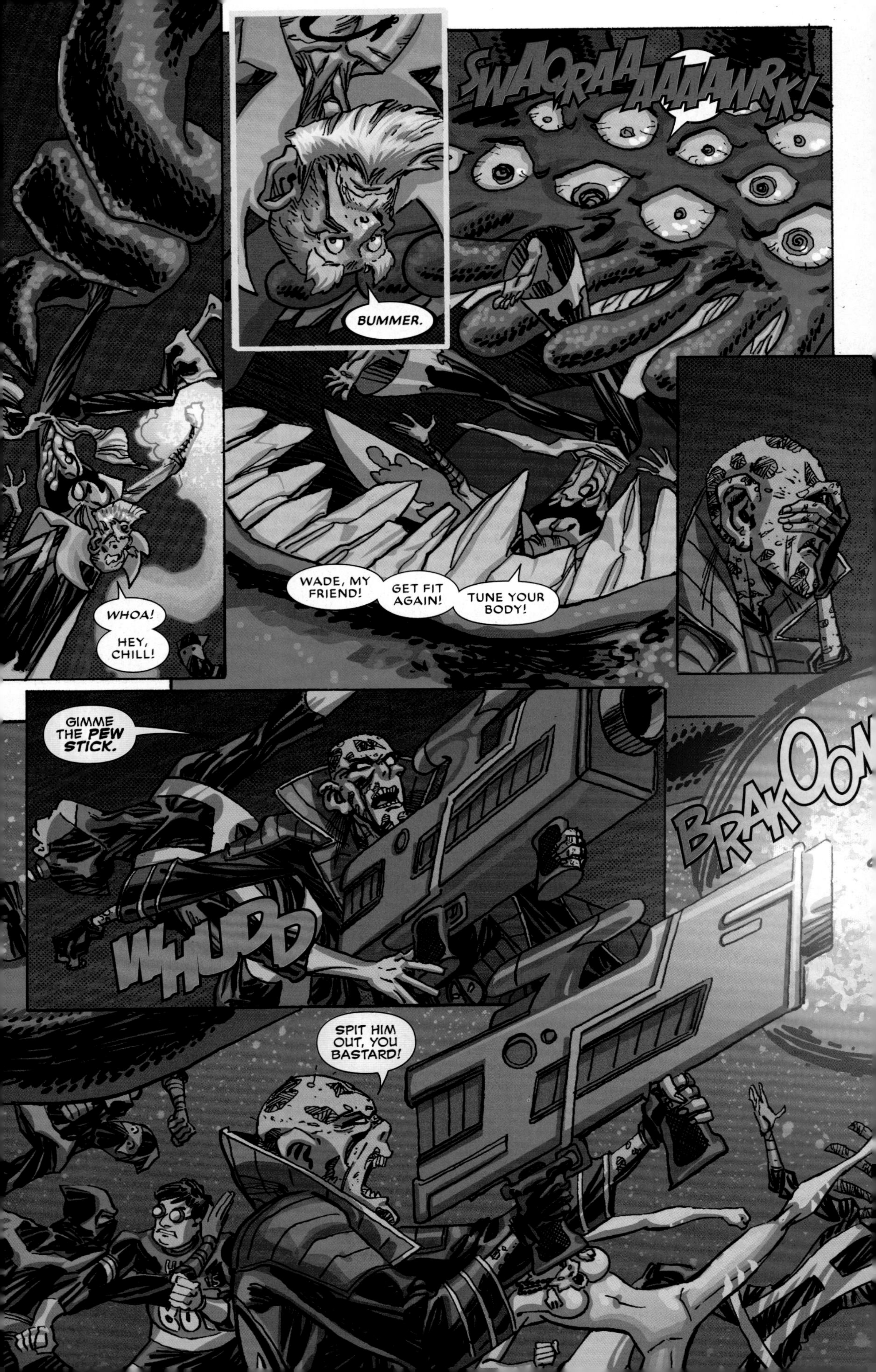
SWAQRAAAAAAWRK!
BUMMER.
WHOA!
HEY, CHILL!
WADE, MY FRIEND!
GET FIT AGAIN!
TUNE YOUR BODY!
GIMME THE PEW STICK.
WHUDD
BRAKOOM
SPIT HIM OUT, YOU BASTARD!

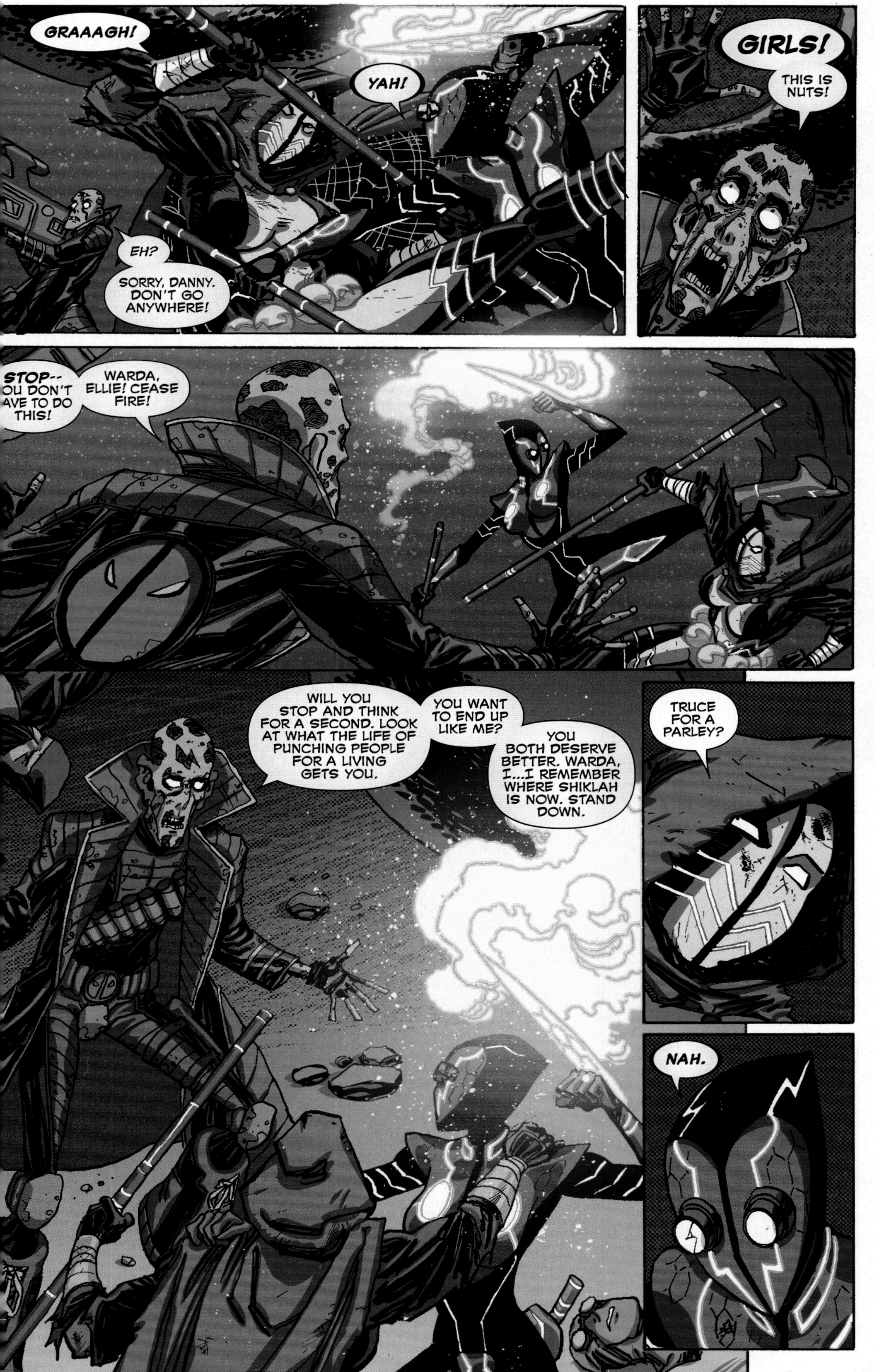
GRAAAGH!
YAH!
EH?
SORRY, DANNY. DON'T GO ANYWHERE!
GIRLS!
THIS IS NUTS!
STOP-- OU DON'T AVE TO DO THIS!
WARDA, ELLIE! CEASE FIRE!
WILL YOU STOP AND THINK FOR A SECOND. LOOK AT WHAT THE LIFE OF PUNCHING PEOPLE FOR A LIVING GETS YOU.
YOU WANT TO END UP LIKE ME?
YOU BOTH DESERVE BETTER. WARDA, I...I REMEMBER WHERE SHIKLAH IS NOW. STAND DOWN.
TRUCE FOR A PARLEY?
NAH.

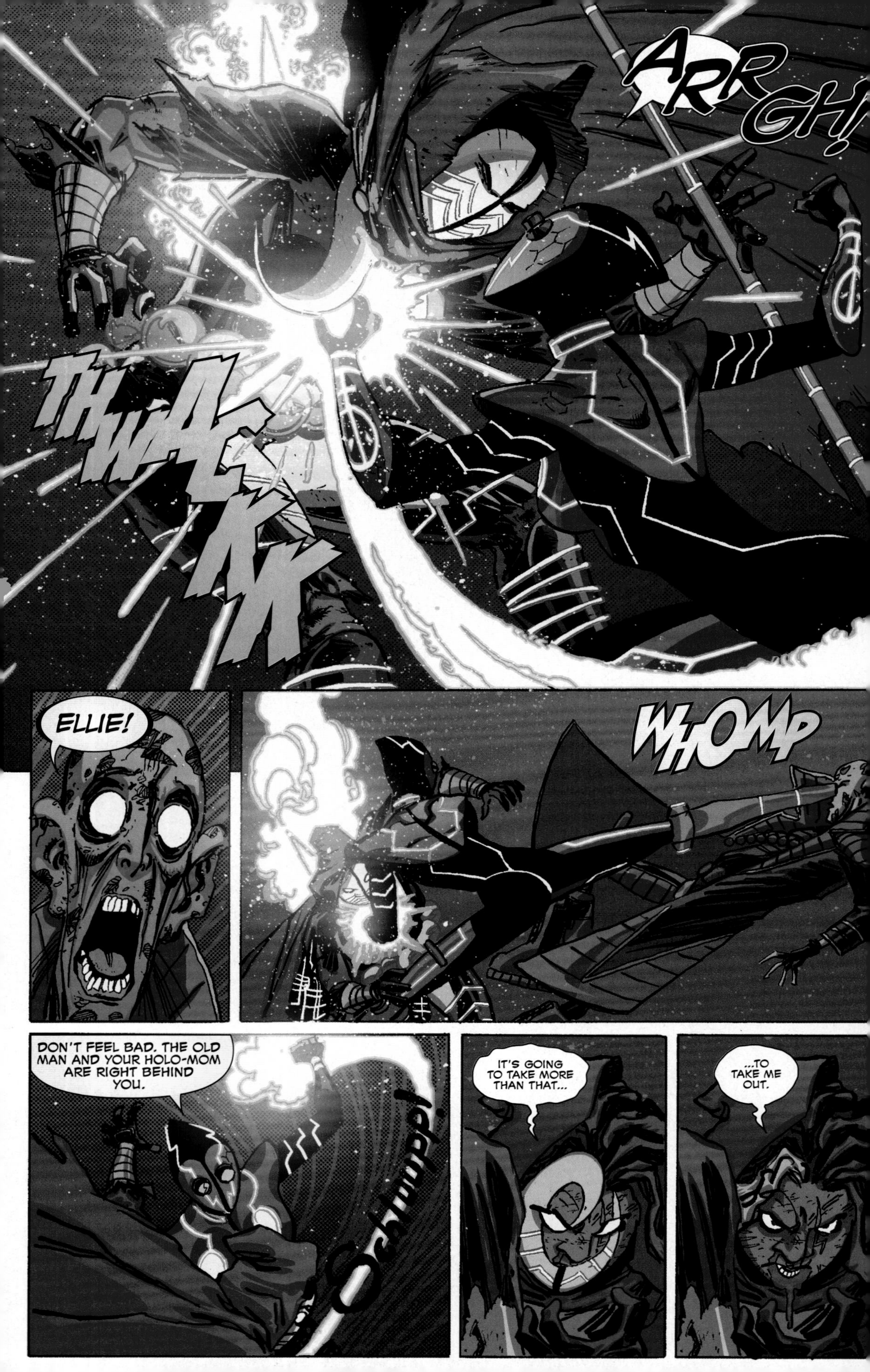
ARRGH!
THWACK
ELLIE!
WHOMP
DON'T FEEL BAD. THE OLD MAN AND YOUR HOLO-MOM ARE RIGHT BEHIND YOU.
SCHUPP!
IT'S GOING TO TAKE MORE THAN THAT...
...TO TAKE ME OUT.

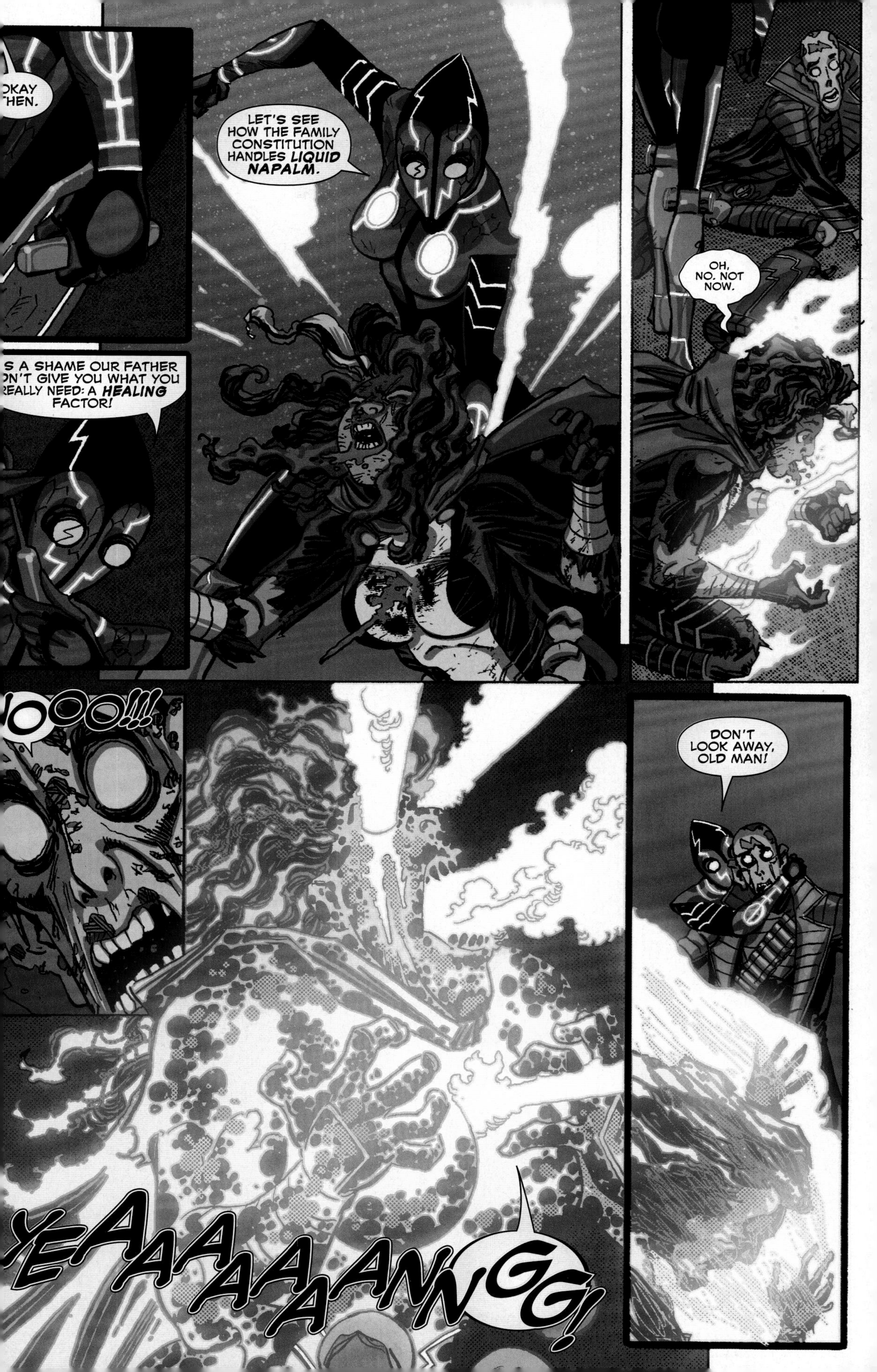
OKAY THEN.
LET'S SEE HOW THE FAMILY CONSTITUTION HANDLES LIQUID NAPALM.
OH, NO. NOT NOW.
S A SHAME OUR FATHER N'T GIVE YOU WHAT YOU REALLY NEED: A HEALING FACTOR!
OOO!!!
DON'T LOOK AWAY, OLD MAN!
YEAAAAAAAANNGG!

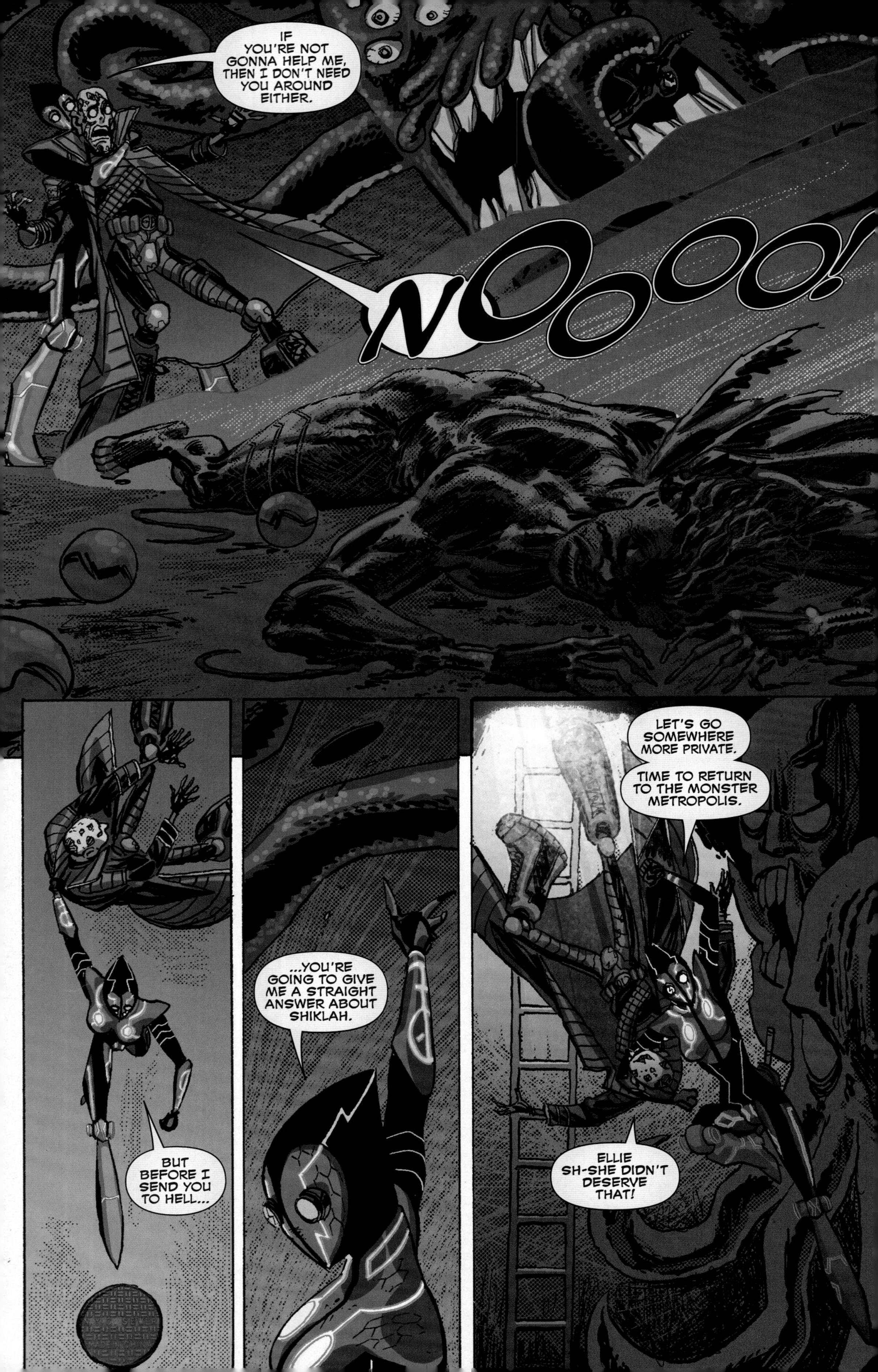
IF YOU'RE NOT GONNA HELP ME, THEN I DON'T NEED YOU AROUND EITHER.
NOOOOO!
BUT BEFORE I SEND YOU TO HELL...
...YOU'RE GOING TO GIVE ME A STRAIGHT ANSWER ABOUT SHIKLAH.
LET'S GO SOMEWHERE MORE PRIVATE.
TIME TO RETURN TO THE MONSTER METROPOLIS.
ELLIE SH-SHE DIDN'T DESERVE THAT!

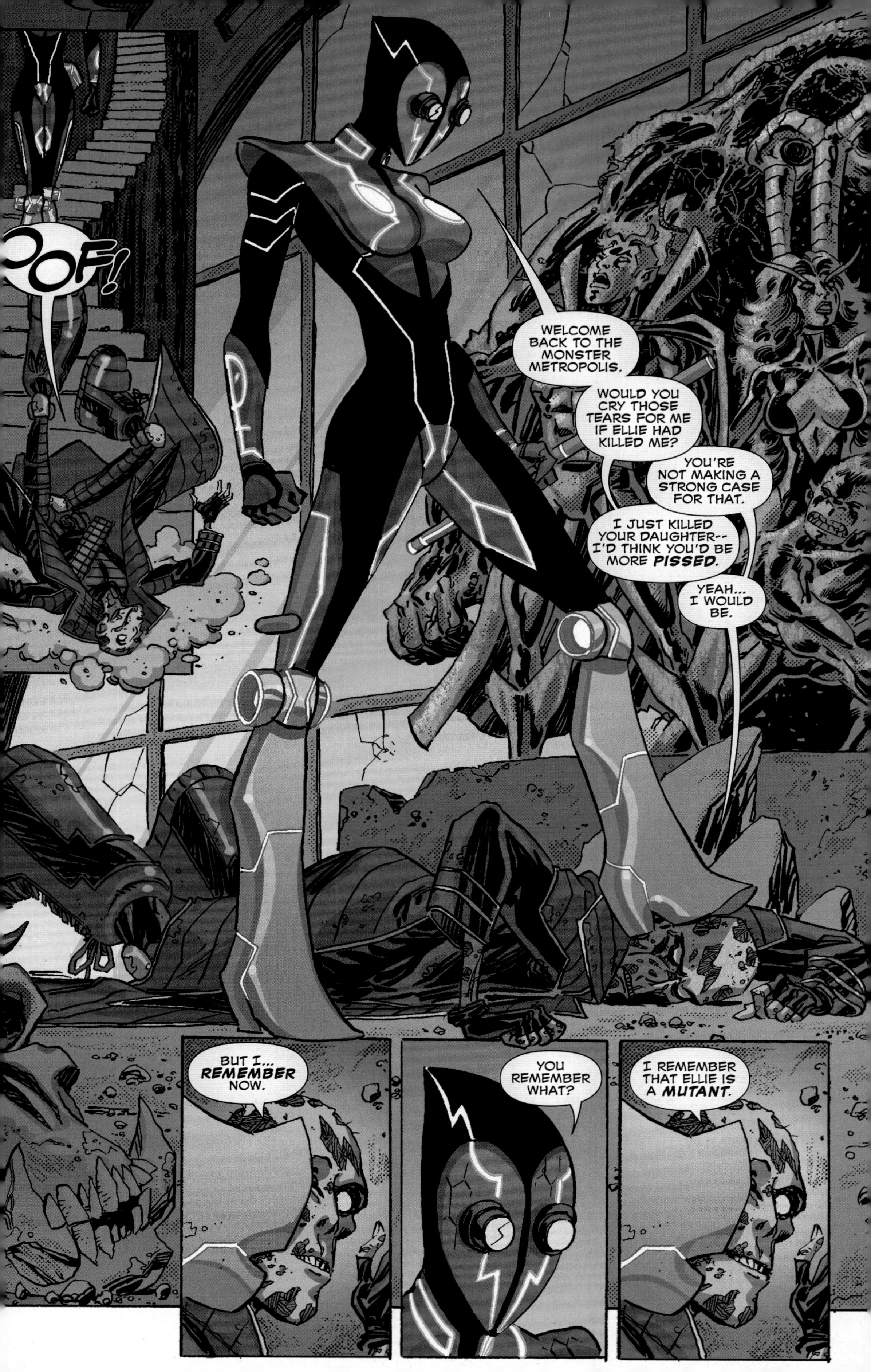

OOF!
WELCOME BACK TO THE MONSTER METROPOLIS.
WOULD YOU CRY THOSE TEARS FOR ME IF ELLIE HAD KILLED ME?
YOU'RE NOT MAKING A STRONG CASE FOR THAT.
I JUST KILLED YOUR DAUGHTER-- I'D THINK YOU'D BE MORE PISSED.
YEAH... I WOULD BE.
BUT I... REMEMBER NOW.
YOU REMEMBER WHAT?
I REMEMBER THAT ELLIE IS A MUTANT.

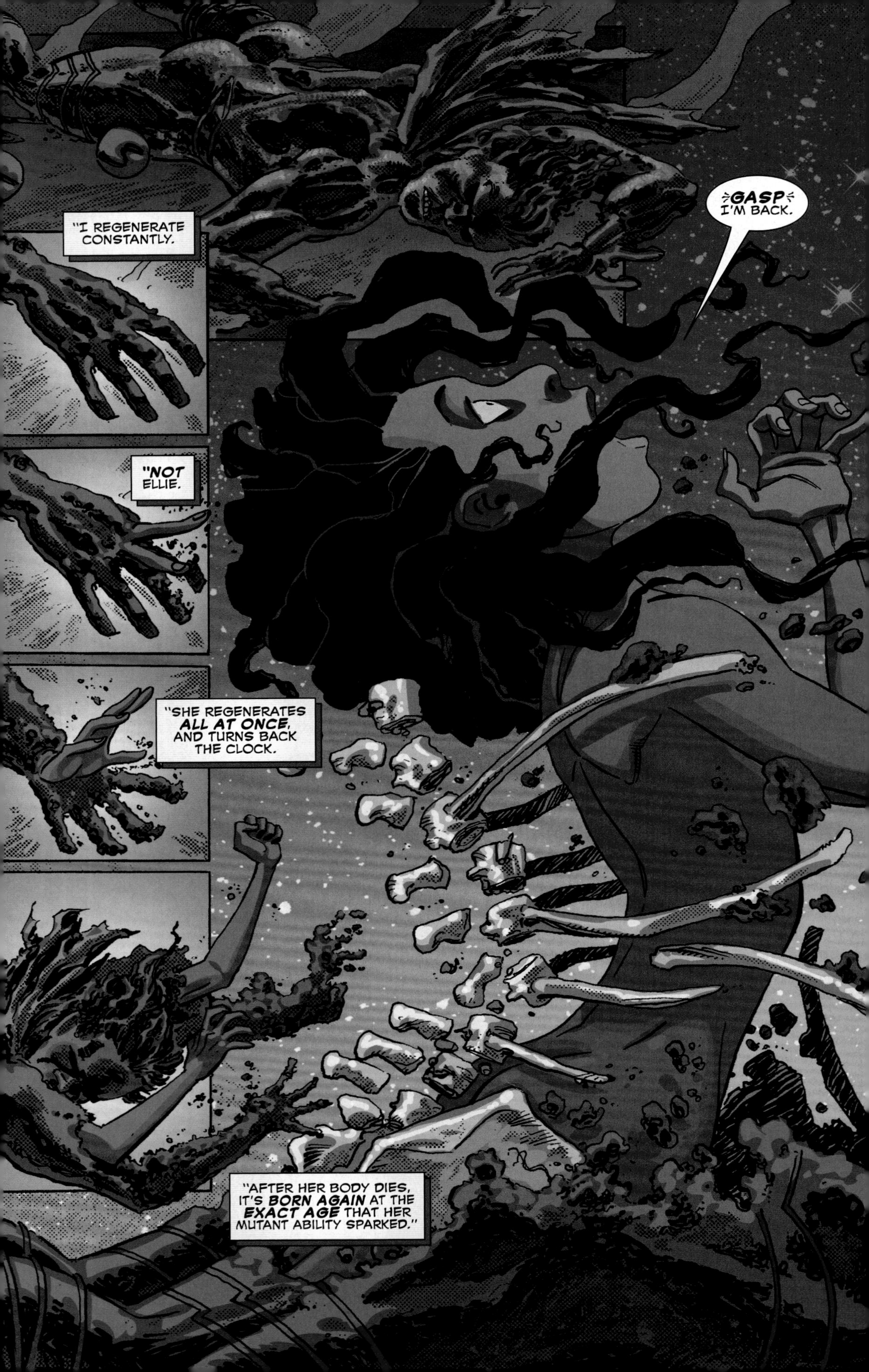

"I REGENERATE CONSTANTLY.
≠GASP≠ I'M BACK.
"NOT ELLIE.
"SHE REGENERATES ALL AT ONCE, AND TURNS BACK THE CLOCK.
"AFTER HER BODY DIES, IT'S BORN AGAIN AT THE EXACT AGE THAT HER MUTANT ABILITY SPARKED."

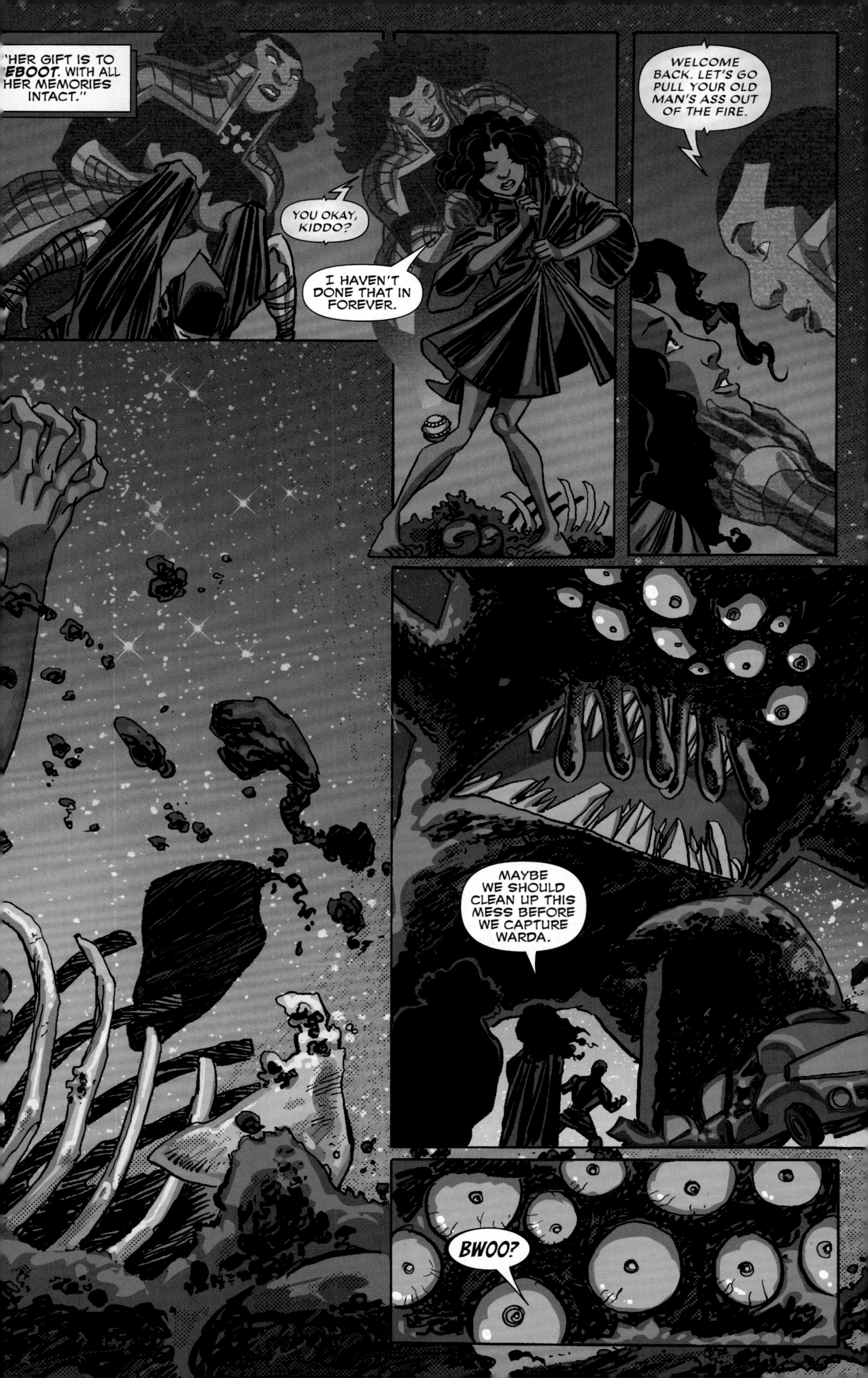
"HER GIFT IS TO REBOOT. WITH ALL HER MEMORIES INTACT."
YOU OKAY, KIDDO?
I HAVEN'T DONE THAT IN FOREVER.
WELCOME BACK. LET'S GO PULL YOUR OLD MAN'S ASS OUT OF THE FIRE.
MAYBE WE SHOULD CLEAN UP THIS MESS BEFORE WE CAPTURE WARDA.
BWOO?

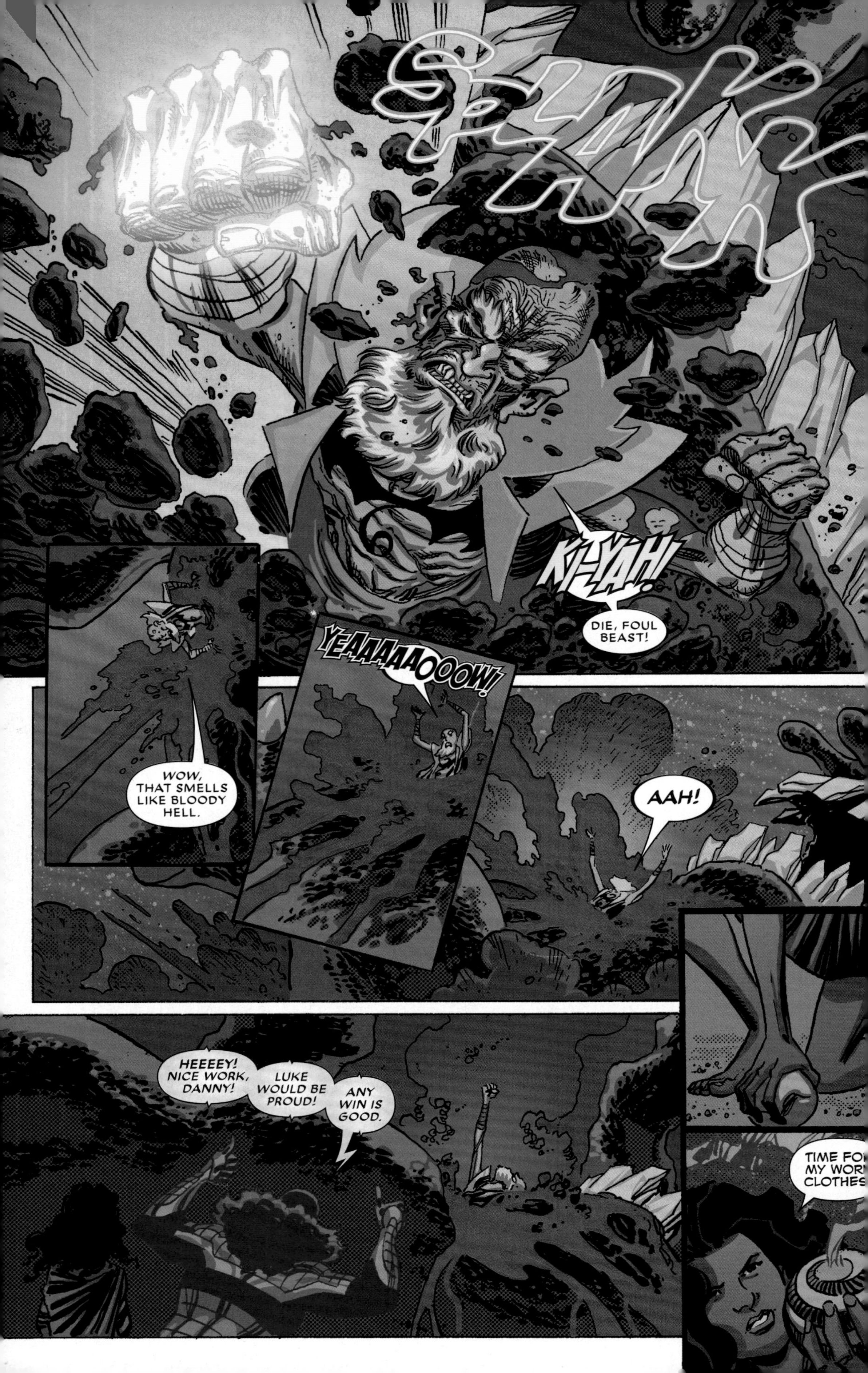

KI-YAH!
DIE, FOUL BEAST!
WOW, THAT SMELLS LIKE BLOODY HELL.
YEAAAAAOOOW!
AAH!
HEEEEY! NICE WORK, DANNY!
LUKE WOULD BE PROUD!
ANY WIN IS GOOD.

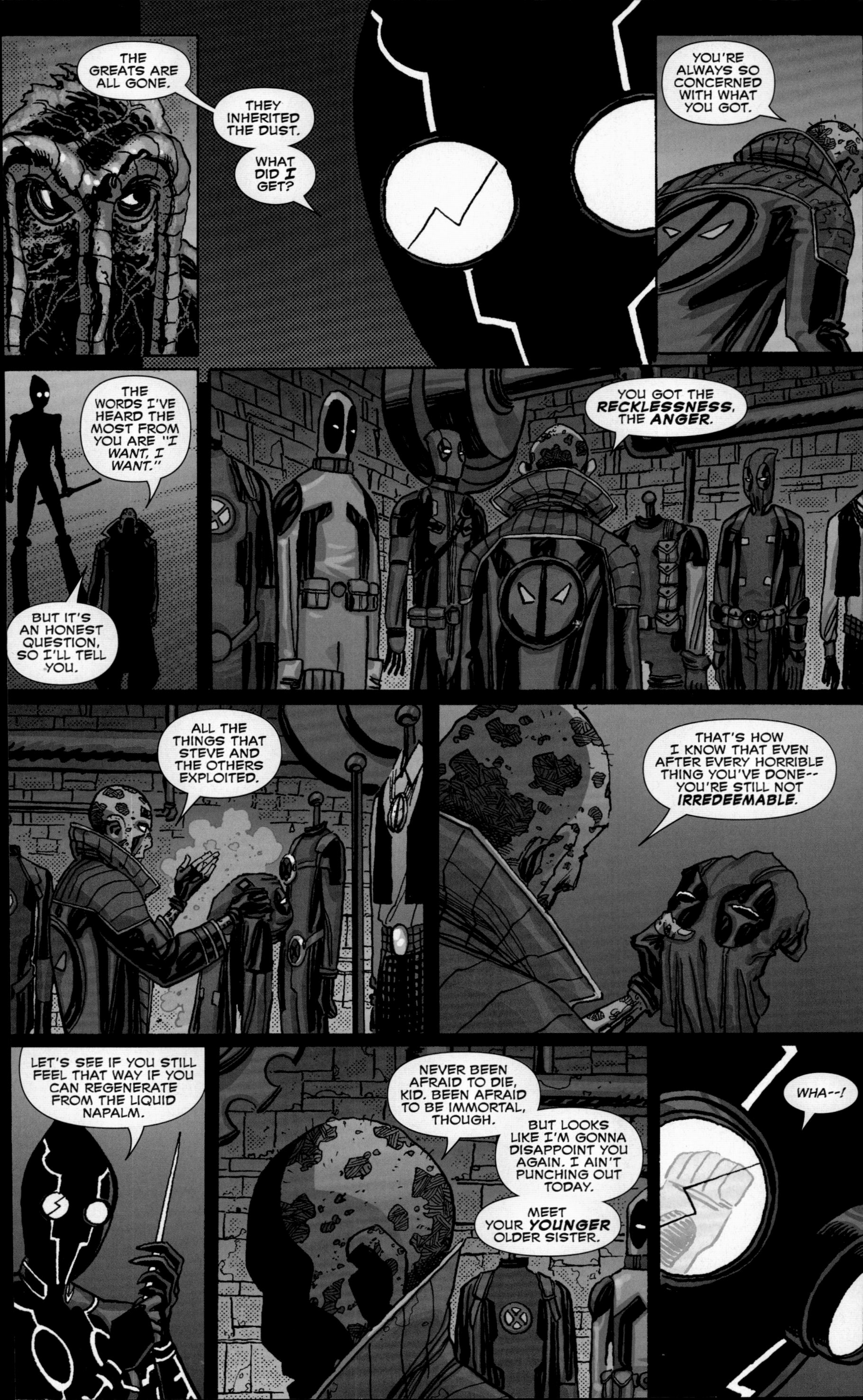

THE GREATS ARE ALL GONE.
THEY INHERITED THE DUST.
WHAT DID *I* GET?
YOU'RE ALWAYS SO CONCERNED WITH WHAT YOU GOT.
THE WORDS I'VE HEARD THE MOST FROM YOU ARE "I WANT, I WANT."
BUT IT'S AN HONEST QUESTION, SO I'LL TELL YOU.
YOU GOT THE ***RECKLESSNESS***, THE ***ANGER***.
ALL THE THINGS THAT STEVE AND THE OTHERS EXPLOITED.
THAT'S HOW I KNOW THAT EVEN AFTER EVERY HORRIBLE THING YOU'VE DONE-- YOU'RE STILL NOT ***IRREDEEMABLE***.
LET'S SEE IF YOU STILL FEEL THAT WAY IF YOU CAN REGENERATE FROM THE LIQUID NAPALM.
NEVER BEEN AFRAID TO DIE, KID. BEEN AFRAID TO BE IMMORTAL, THOUGH.
BUT LOOKS LIKE I'M GONNA DISAPPOINT YOU AGAIN. I AIN'T PUNCHING OUT TODAY.
MEET YOUR ***YOUNGER*** OLDER SISTER.
WHA--!

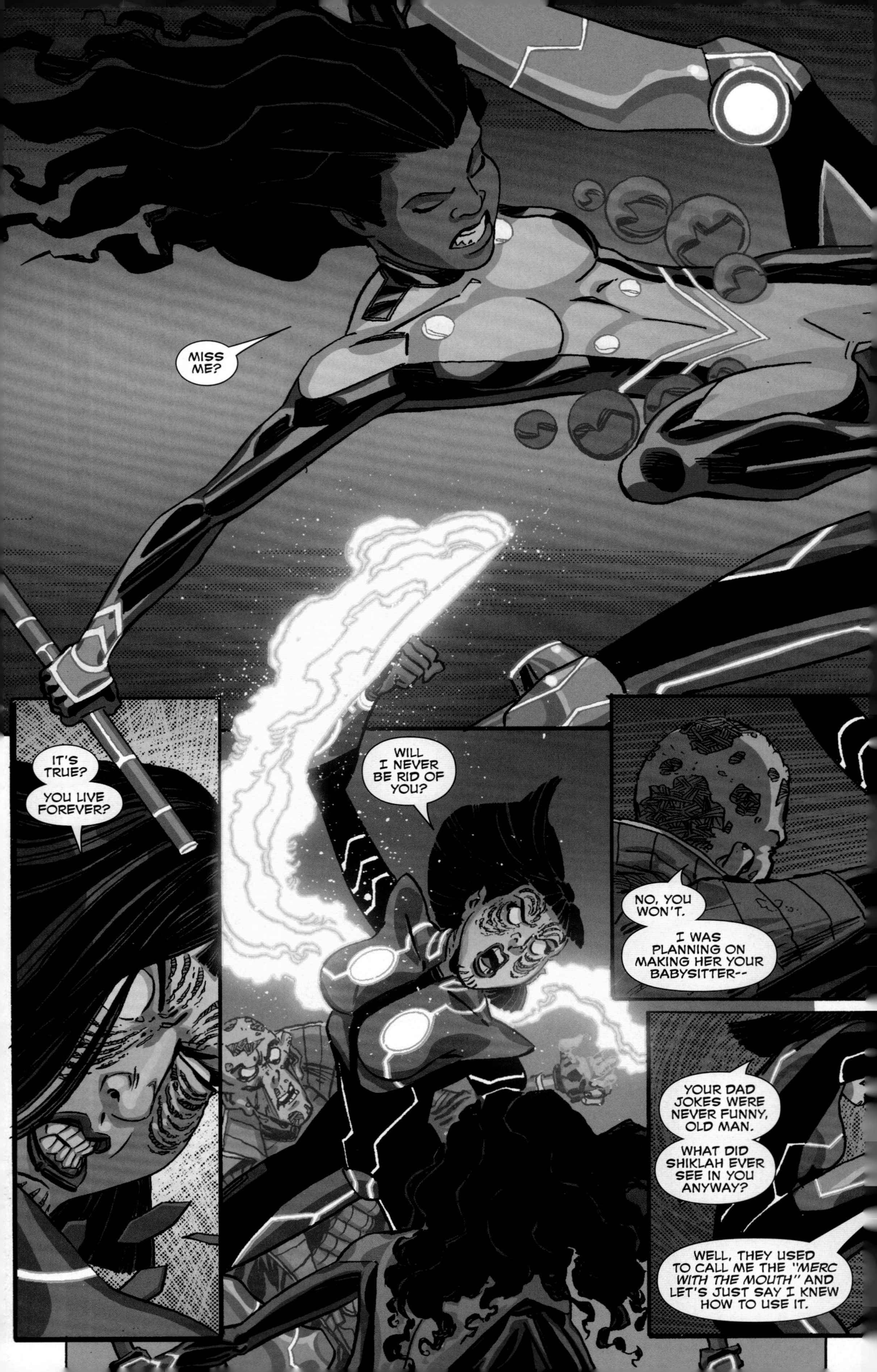
MISS ME?
IT'S TRUE?
YOU LIVE FOREVER?
WILL I NEVER BE RID OF YOU?
NO, YOU WON'T.
I WAS PLANNING ON MAKING HER YOUR BABYSITTER--
YOUR DAD JOKES WERE NEVER FUNNY, OLD MAN.
WHAT DID SHIKLAH EVER SEE IN YOU ANYWAY?
WELL, THEY USED TO CALL ME THE "*MERC WITH THE MOUTH*" AND LET'S JUST SAY I KNEW HOW TO USE IT.

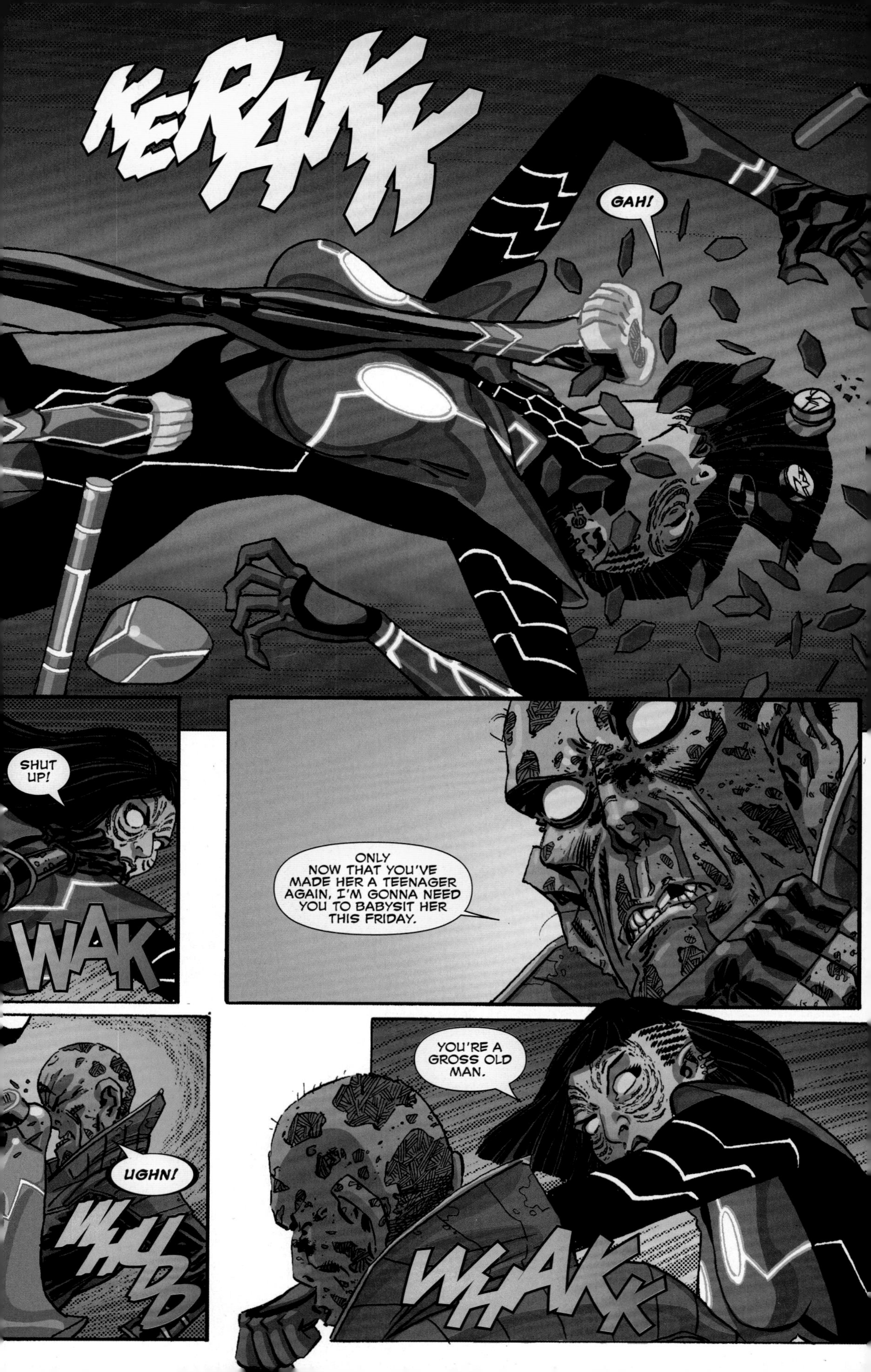
KERAKK
GAH!
SHUT UP!
WAK
ONLY NOW THAT YOU'VE MADE HER A TEENAGER AGAIN, I'M GONNA NEED YOU TO BABYSIT HER THIS FRIDAY.
UGHN!
WHUD
YOU'RE A GROSS OLD MAN.
WHAKK

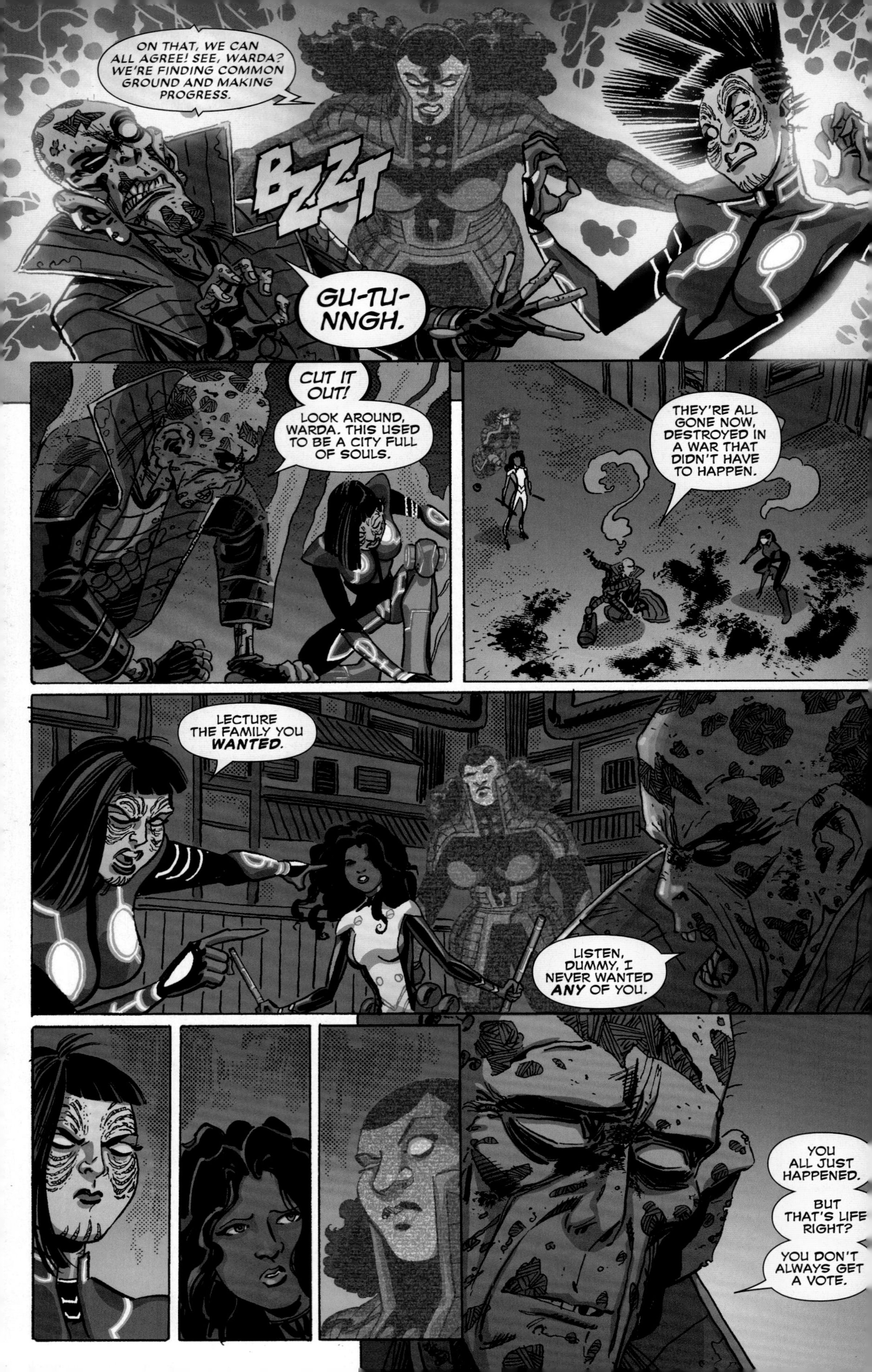
ON THAT, WE CAN ALL AGREE! SEE, WARDA? WE'RE FINDING COMMON GROUND AND MAKING PROGRESS.
BZZT
GU-TU-NNGH.
CUT IT OUT!
LOOK AROUND, WARDA. THIS USED TO BE A CITY FULL OF SOULS.
THEY'RE ALL GONE NOW, DESTROYED IN A WAR THAT DIDN'T HAVE TO HAPPEN.
LECTURE THE FAMILY YOU WANTED.
LISTEN, DUMMY, I NEVER WANTED ANY OF YOU.
YOU ALL JUST HAPPENED.
BUT THAT'S LIFE RIGHT?
YOU DON'T ALWAYS GET A VOTE.

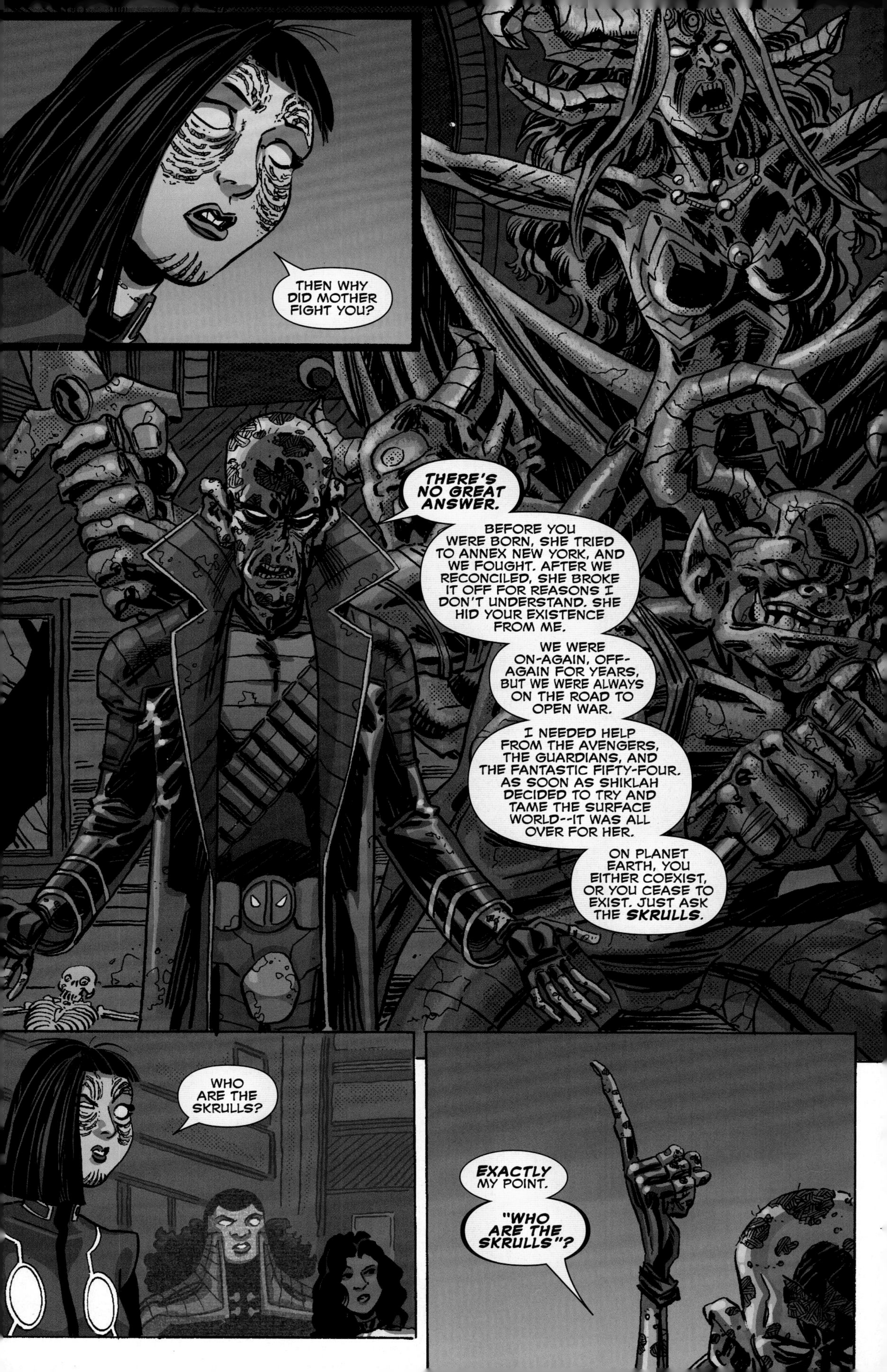
THEN WHY DID MOTHER FIGHT YOU?
THERE'S NO GREAT ANSWER.
BEFORE YOU WERE BORN, SHE TRIED TO ANNEX NEW YORK, AND WE FOUGHT. AFTER WE RECONCILED, SHE BROKE IT OFF FOR REASONS I DON'T UNDERSTAND. SHE HID YOUR EXISTENCE FROM ME.
WE WERE ON-AGAIN, OFF-AGAIN FOR YEARS, BUT WE WERE ALWAYS ON THE ROAD TO OPEN WAR.
I NEEDED HELP FROM THE AVENGERS, THE GUARDIANS, AND THE FANTASTIC FIFTY-FOUR. AS SOON AS SHIKLAH DECIDED TO TRY AND TAME THE SURFACE WORLD--IT WAS ALL OVER FOR HER.
ON PLANET EARTH, YOU EITHER COEXIST, OR YOU CEASE TO EXIST. JUST ASK THE SKRULLS.
WHO ARE THE SKRULLS?
EXACTLY MY POINT.
"WHO ARE THE SKRULLS"?

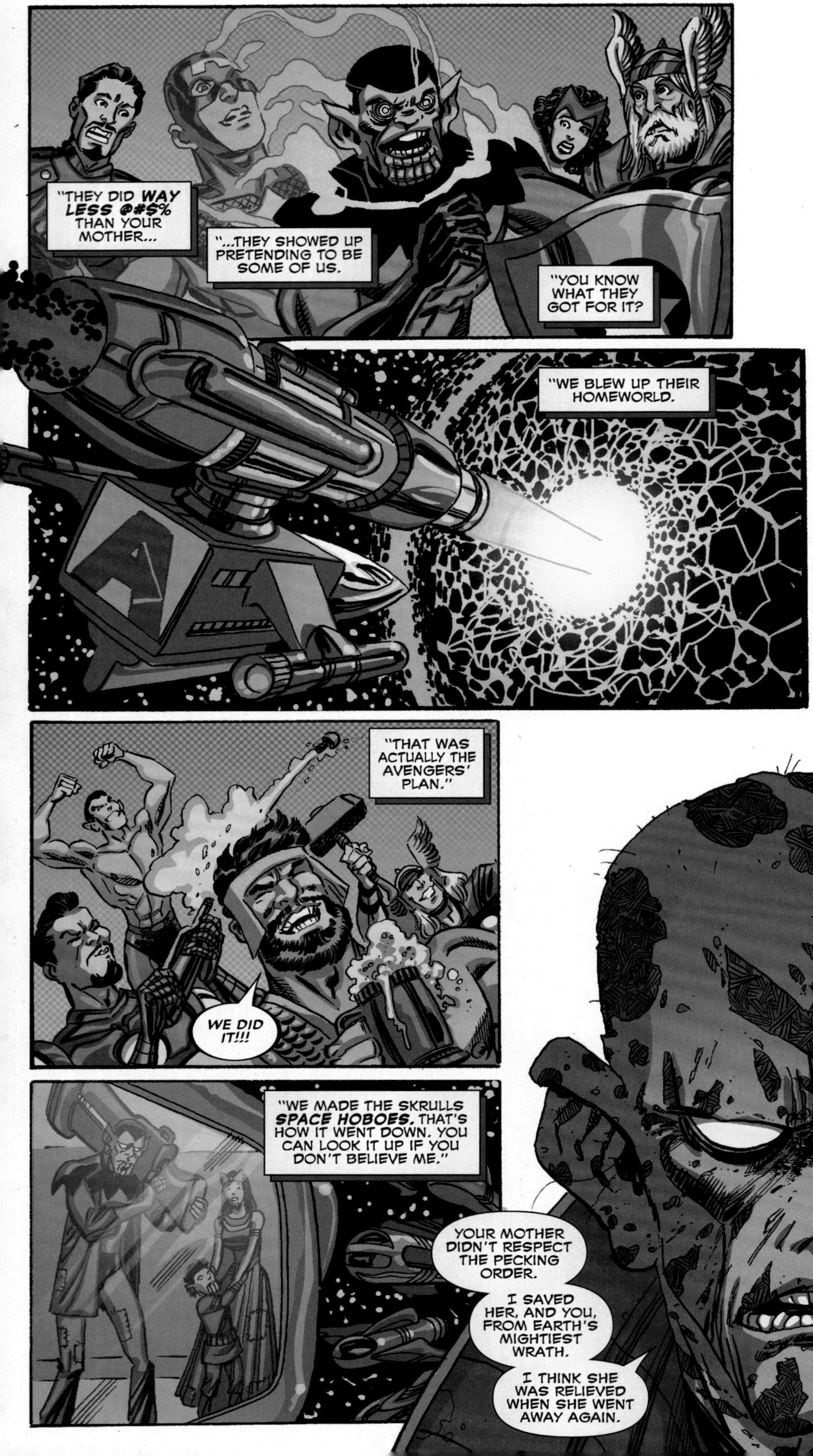
"THEY DID WAY LESS @#$% THAN YOUR MOTHER...
"...THEY SHOWED UP PRETENDING TO BE SOME OF US.
"YOU KNOW WHAT THEY GOT FOR IT?
"WE BLEW UP THEIR HOMEWORLD.
"THAT WAS ACTUALLY THE AVENGERS' PLAN."
WE DID IT!!!
"WE MADE THE SKRULLS SPACE HOBOES. THAT'S HOW IT WENT DOWN. YOU CAN LOOK IT UP IF YOU DON'T BELIEVE ME."
YOUR MOTHER DIDN'T RESPECT THE PECKING ORDER.
I SAVED HER, AND YOU, FROM EARTH'S MIGHTIEST WRATH.
I THINK SHE WAS RELIEVED WHEN SHE WENT AWAY AGAIN.

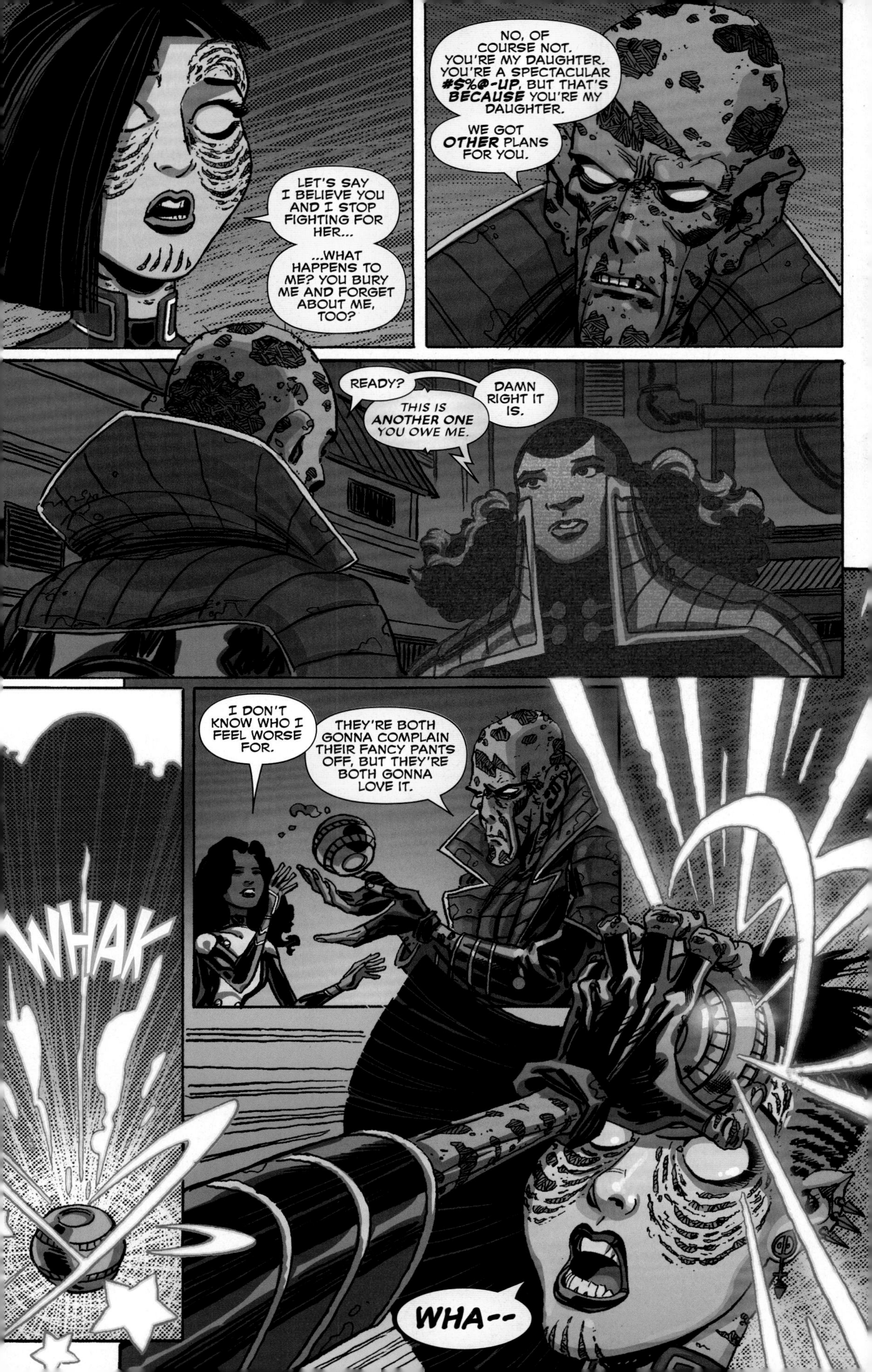
LET'S SAY I BELIEVE YOU AND I STOP FIGHTING FOR HER...
...WHAT HAPPENS TO ME? YOU BURY ME AND FORGET ABOUT ME, TOO?
NO, OF COURSE NOT. YOU'RE MY DAUGHTER. YOU'RE A SPECTACULAR #$%@-UP, BUT THAT'S BECAUSE YOU'RE MY DAUGHTER.
WE GOT OTHER PLANS FOR YOU.
READY?
DAMN RIGHT IT IS.
THIS IS ANOTHER ONE YOU OWE ME.
I DON'T KNOW WHO I FEEL WORSE FOR.
THEY'RE BOTH GONNA COMPLAIN THEIR FANCY PANTS OFF, BUT THEY'RE BOTH GONNA LOVE IT.
WHAK
WHA--

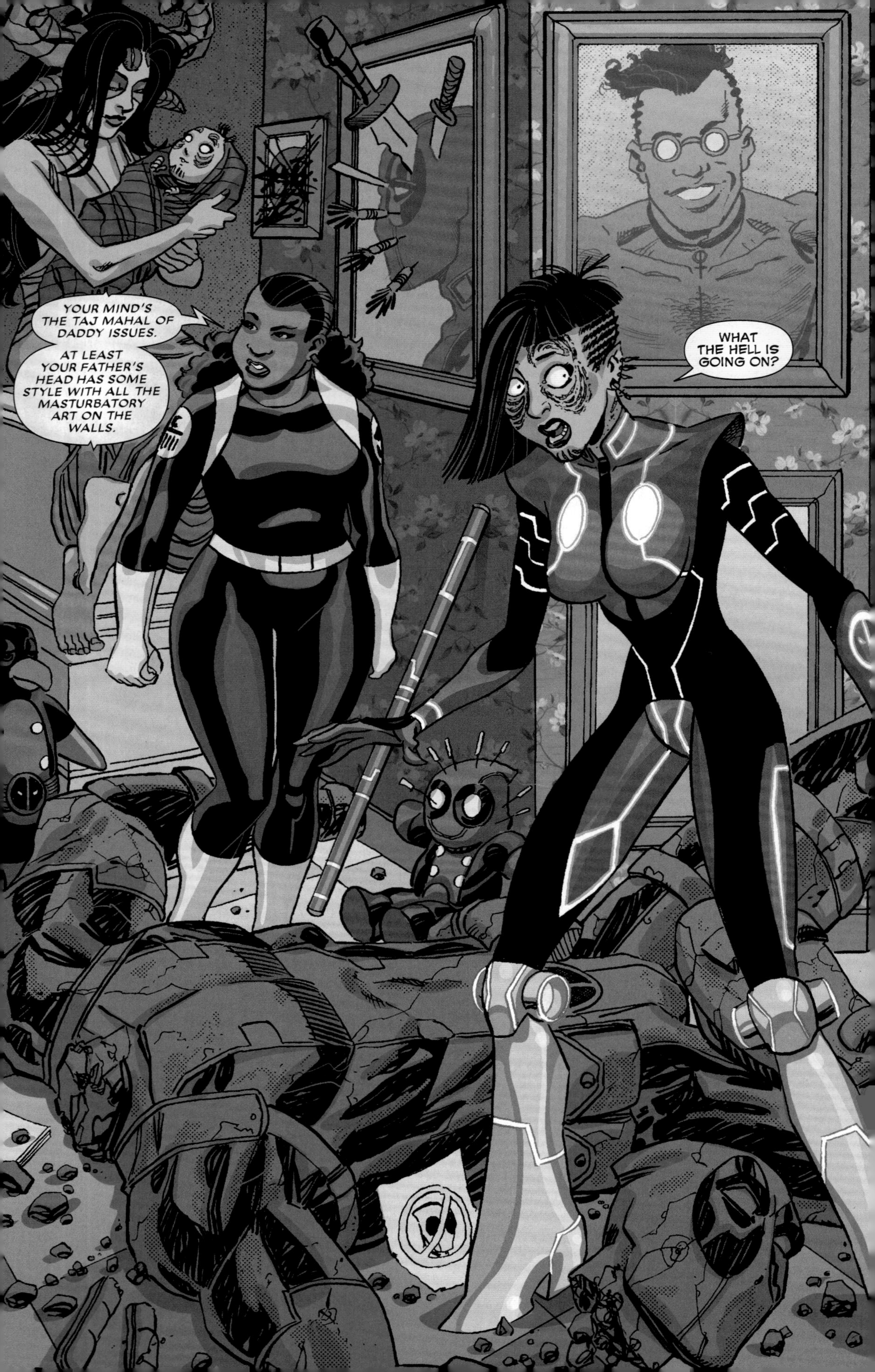
YOUR MIND'S THE TAJ MAHAL OF DADDY ISSUES.
AT LEAST YOUR FATHER'S HEAD HAS SOME STYLE WITH ALL THE MASTURBATORY ART ON THE WALLS.
WHAT THE HELL IS GOING ON?

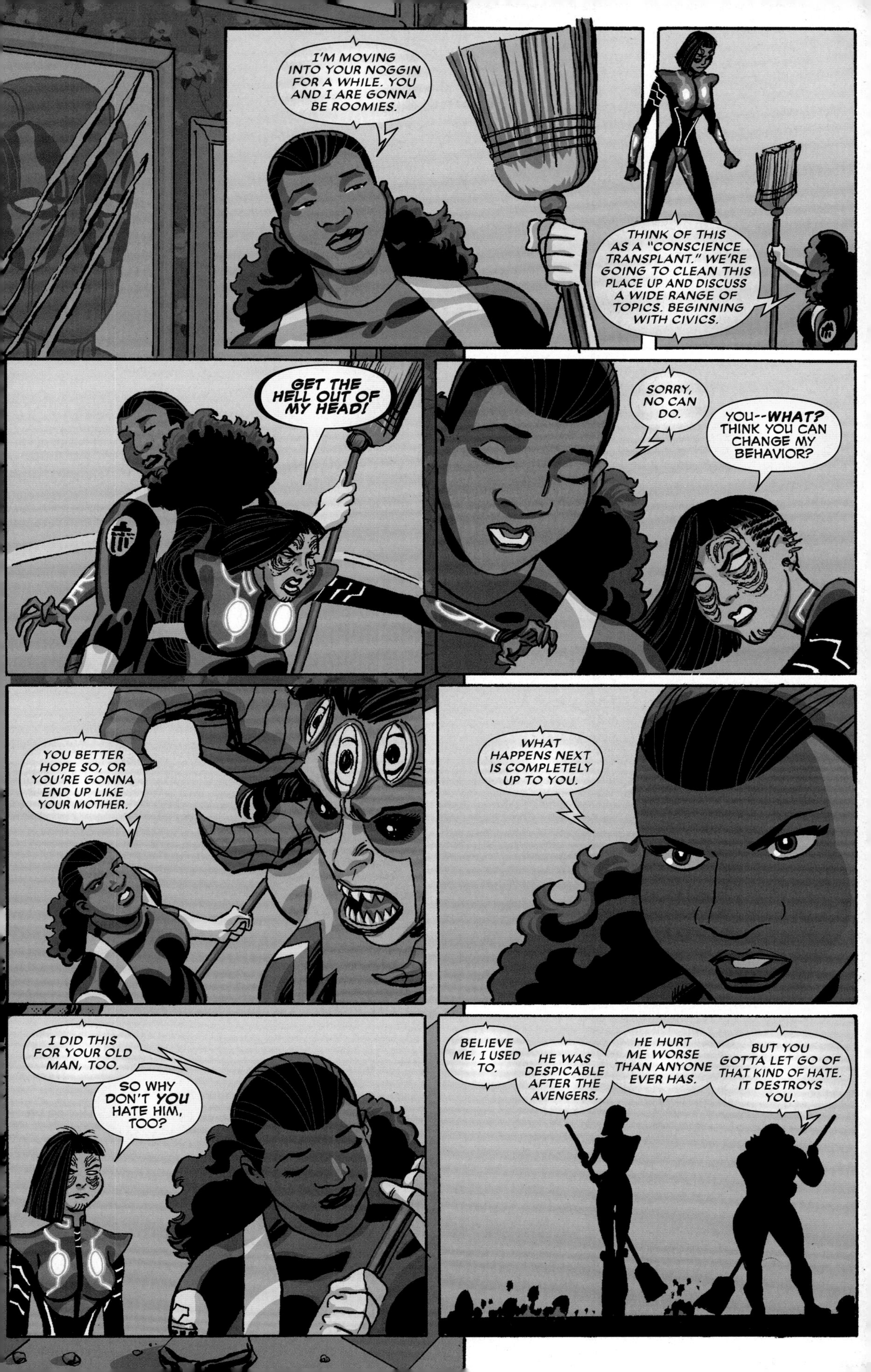

I'M MOVING INTO YOUR NOGGIN FOR A WHILE. YOU AND I ARE GONNA BE ROOMIES.
THINK OF THIS AS A "CONSCIENCE TRANSPLANT." WE'RE GOING TO CLEAN THIS PLACE UP AND DISCUSS A WIDE RANGE OF TOPICS. BEGINNING WITH CIVICS.
GET THE HELL OUT OF MY HEAD!
SORRY, NO CAN DO.
YOU--WHAT? THINK YOU CAN CHANGE MY BEHAVIOR?
YOU BETTER HOPE SO, OR YOU'RE GONNA END UP LIKE YOUR MOTHER.
WHAT HAPPENS NEXT IS COMPLETELY UP TO YOU.
I DID THIS FOR YOUR OLD MAN, TOO.
SO WHY DON'T YOU HATE HIM, TOO?
BELIEVE ME, I USED TO.
HE WAS DESPICABLE AFTER THE AVENGERS.
HE HURT ME WORSE THAN ANYONE EVER HAS.
BUT YOU GOTTA LET GO OF THAT KIND OF HATE. IT DESTROYS YOU.

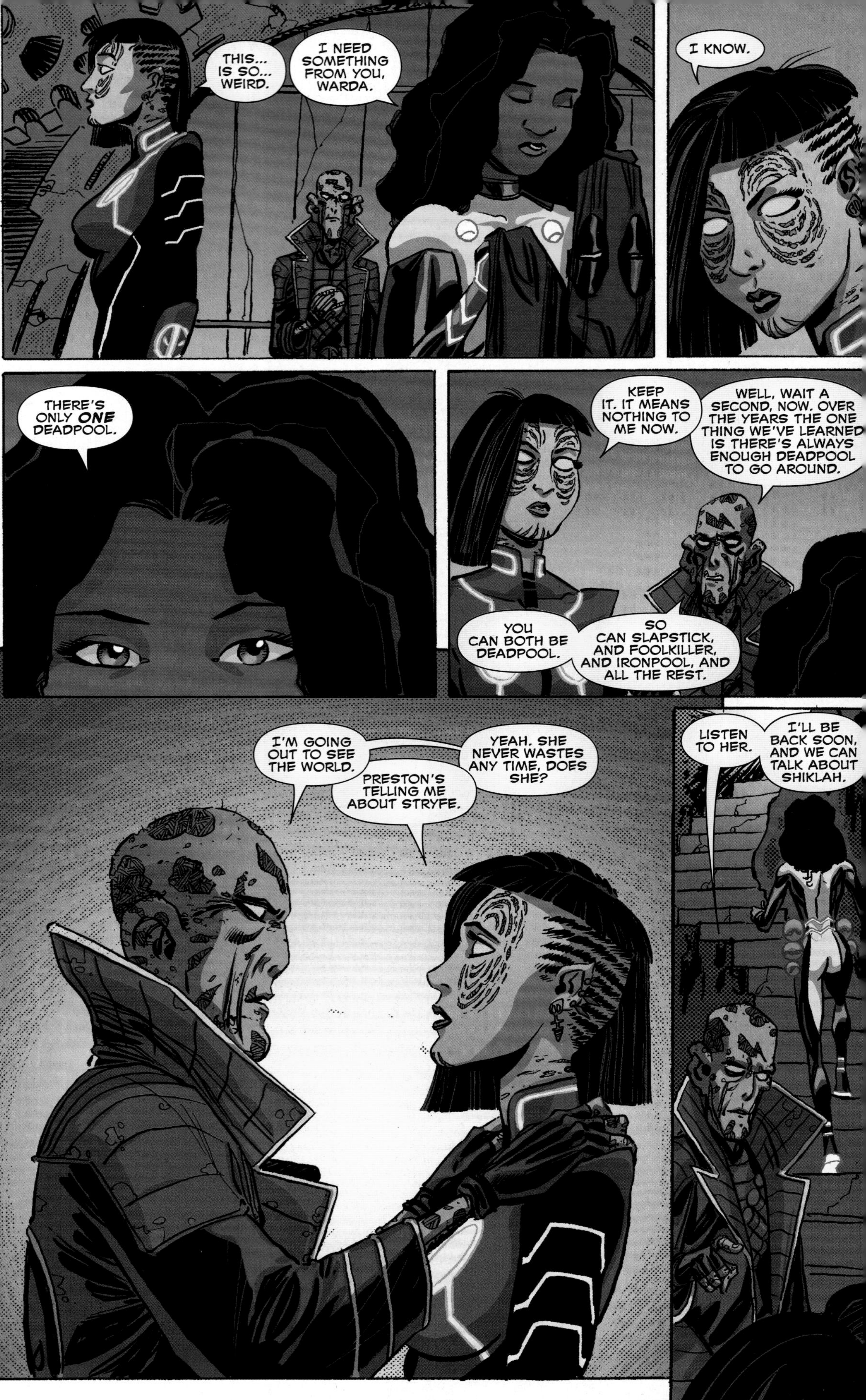
THIS... IS SO... WEIRD.
I NEED SOMETHING FROM YOU, WARDA.
I KNOW.
THERE'S ONLY ONE DEADPOOL.
KEEP IT. IT MEANS NOTHING TO ME NOW.
WELL, WAIT A SECOND, NOW. OVER THE YEARS THE ONE THING WE'VE LEARNED IS THERE'S ALWAYS ENOUGH DEADPOOL TO GO AROUND.
YOU CAN BOTH BE DEADPOOL.
SO CAN SLAPSTICK, AND FOOLKILLER, AND IRONPOOL, AND ALL THE REST.
I'M GOING OUT TO SEE THE WORLD.
YEAH. SHE NEVER WASTES ANY TIME, DOES SHE?
PRESTON'S TELLING ME ABOUT STRYFE.
LISTEN TO HER.
I'LL BE BACK SOON, AND WE CAN TALK ABOUT SHIKLAH.

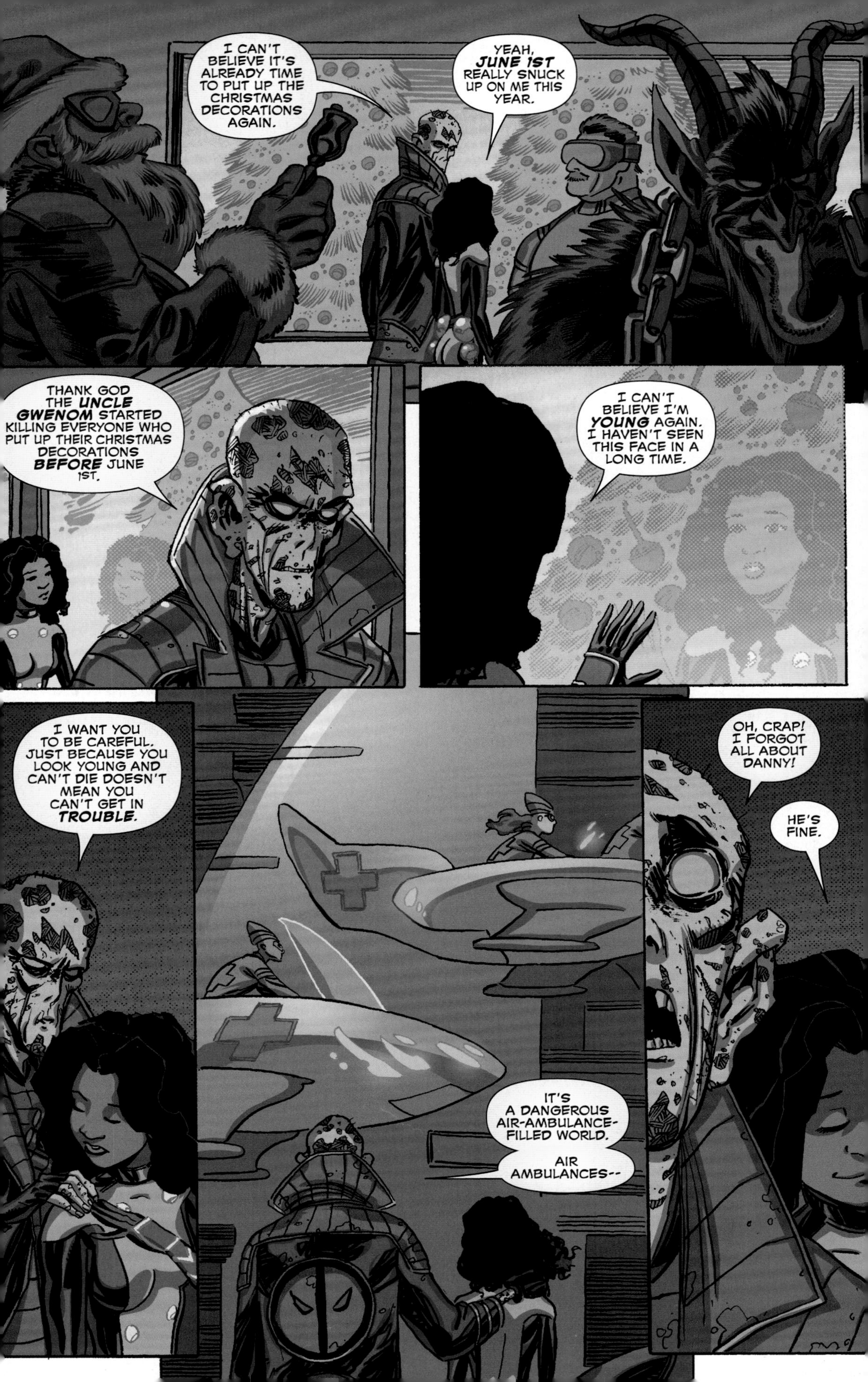
I CAN'T BELIEVE IT'S ALREADY TIME TO PUT UP THE CHRISTMAS DECORATIONS AGAIN.
YEAH, JUNE 1ST REALLY SNUCK UP ON ME THIS YEAR.
THANK GOD THE UNCLE GWENOM STARTED KILLING EVERYONE WHO PUT UP THEIR CHRISTMAS DECORATIONS BEFORE JUNE 1ST.
I CAN'T BELIEVE I'M YOUNG AGAIN. I HAVEN'T SEEN THIS FACE IN A LONG TIME.
I WANT YOU TO BE CAREFUL. JUST BECAUSE YOU LOOK YOUNG AND CAN'T DIE DOESN'T MEAN YOU CAN'T GET IN TROUBLE.
IT'S A DANGEROUS AIR-AMBULANCE-FILLED WORLD.
AIR AMBULANCES--
OH, CRAP! I FORGOT ALL ABOUT DANNY!
HE'S FINE.

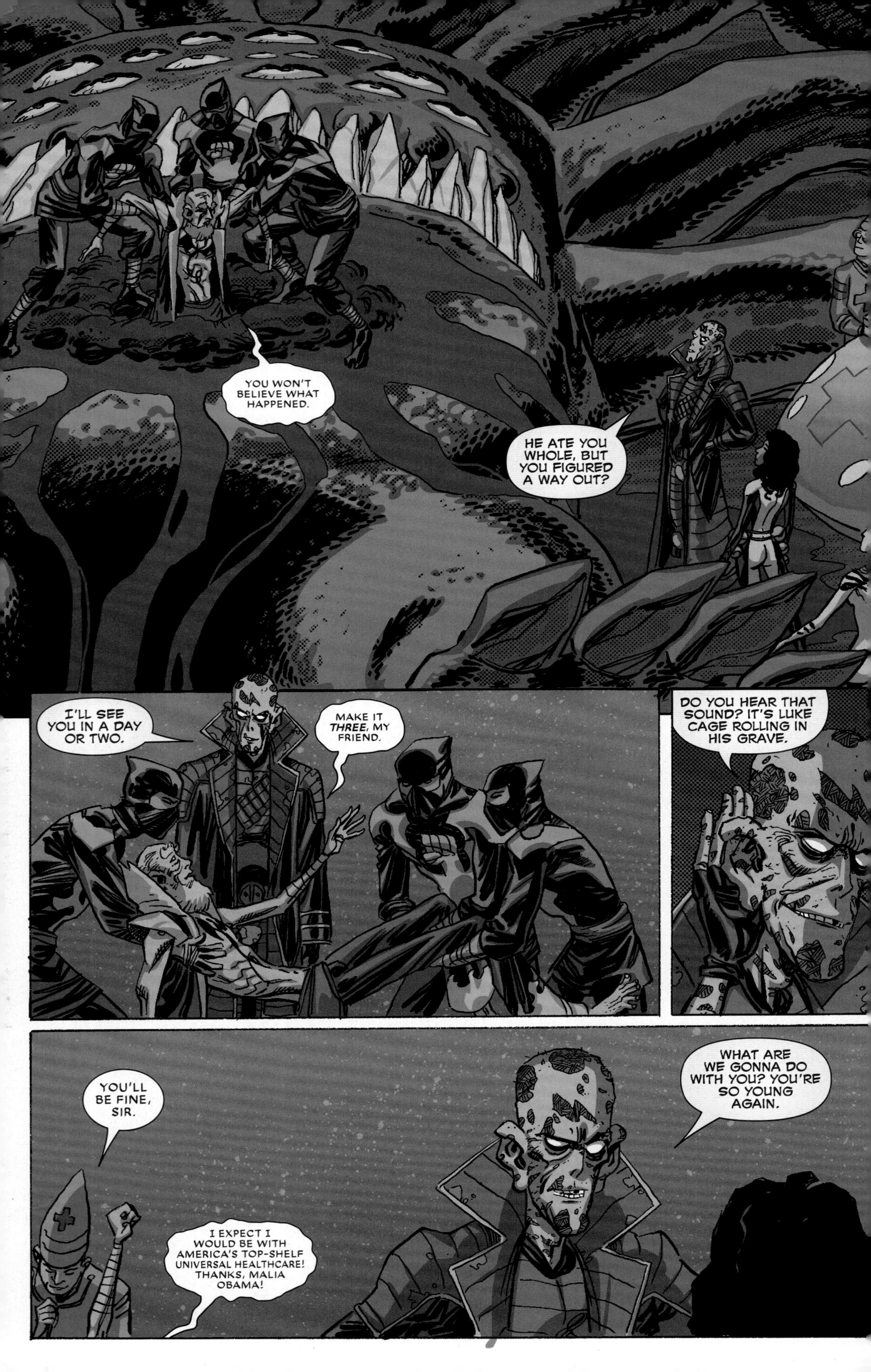
YOU WON'T BELIEVE WHAT HAPPENED.
HE ATE YOU WHOLE, BUT YOU FIGURED A WAY OUT?
I'LL SEE YOU IN A DAY OR TWO.
MAKE IT *THREE*, MY FRIEND.
DO YOU HEAR THAT SOUND? IT'S LUKE CAGE ROLLING IN HIS GRAVE.
YOU'LL BE FINE, SIR.
I EXPECT I WOULD BE WITH AMERICA'S TOP-SHELF UNIVERSAL HEALTHCARE! THANKS, MALIA OBAMA!
WHAT ARE WE GONNA DO WITH YOU? YOU'RE SO YOUNG AGAIN.

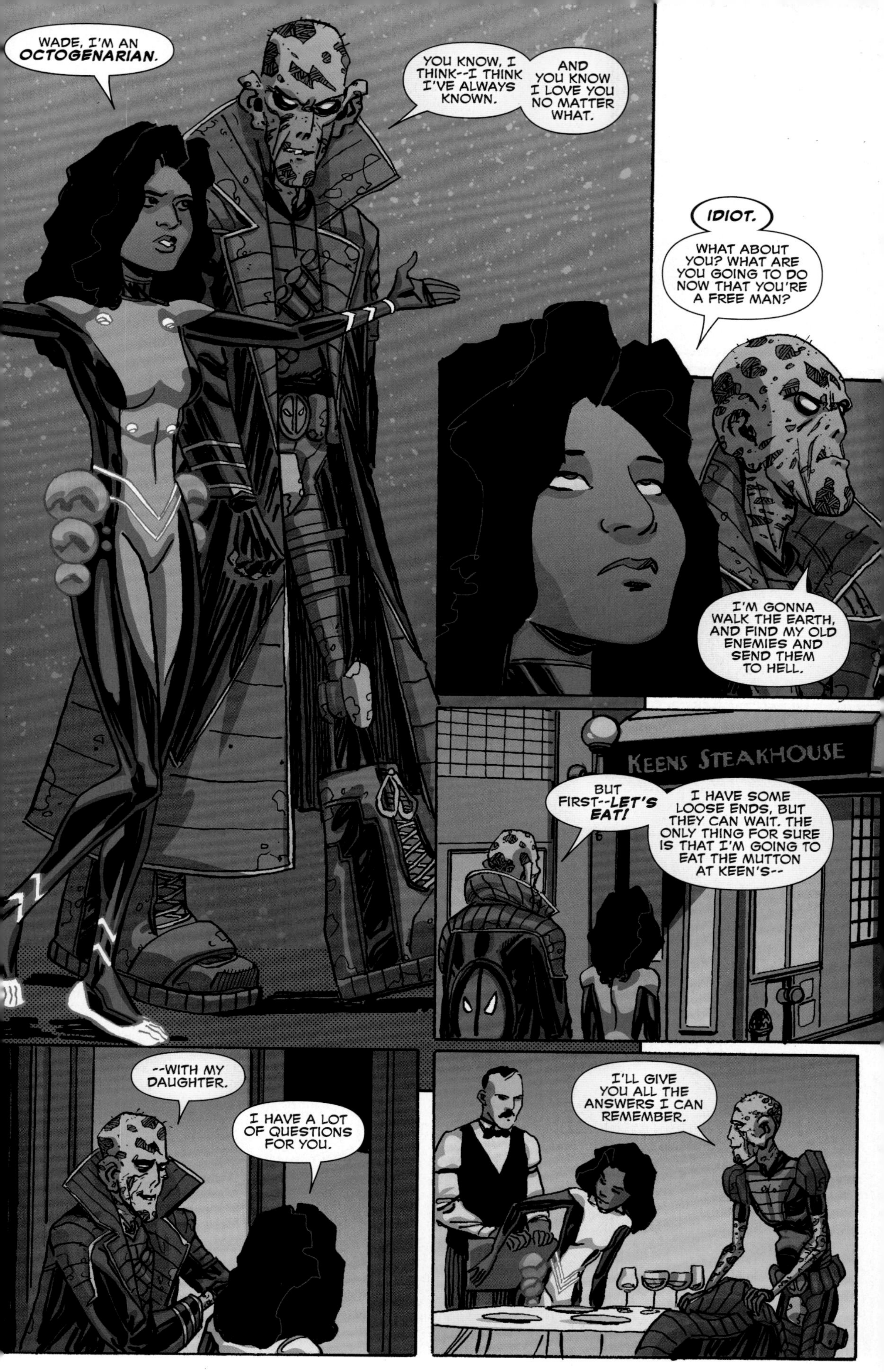
WADE, I'M AN OCTOGENARIAN.
YOU KNOW, I THINK--I THINK I'VE ALWAYS KNOWN.
AND YOU KNOW I LOVE YOU NO MATTER WHAT.
IDIOT.
WHAT ABOUT YOU? WHAT ARE YOU GOING TO DO NOW THAT YOU'RE A FREE MAN?
I'M GONNA WALK THE EARTH, AND FIND MY OLD ENEMIES AND SEND THEM TO HELL.
KEENS STEAKHOUSE
I HAVE SOME LOOSE ENDS, BUT THEY CAN WAIT. THE ONLY THING FOR SURE IS THAT I'M GOING TO EAT THE MUTTON AT KEEN'S--
BUT FIRST--LET'S EAT!
--WITH MY DAUGHTER.
I HAVE A LOT OF QUESTIONS FOR YOU.
I'LL GIVE YOU ALL THE ANSWERS I CAN REMEMBER.

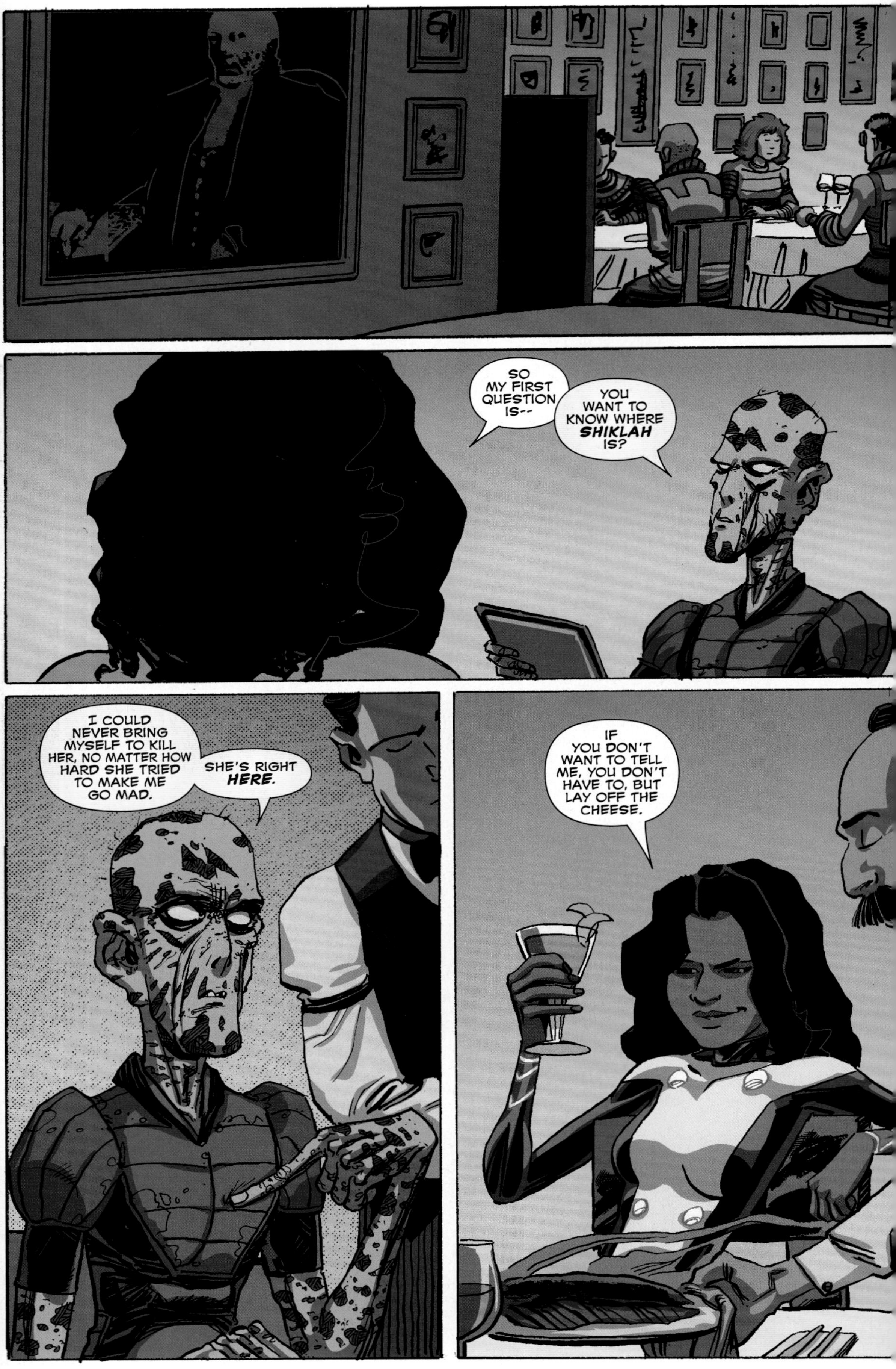
SO MY FIRST QUESTION IS--
YOU WANT TO KNOW WHERE SHIKLAH IS?
I COULD NEVER BRING MYSELF TO KILL HER, NO MATTER HOW HARD SHE TRIED TO MAKE ME GO MAD.
SHE'S RIGHT HERE.
IF YOU DON'T WANT TO TELL ME, YOU DON'T HAVE TO, BUT LAY OFF THE CHEESE.

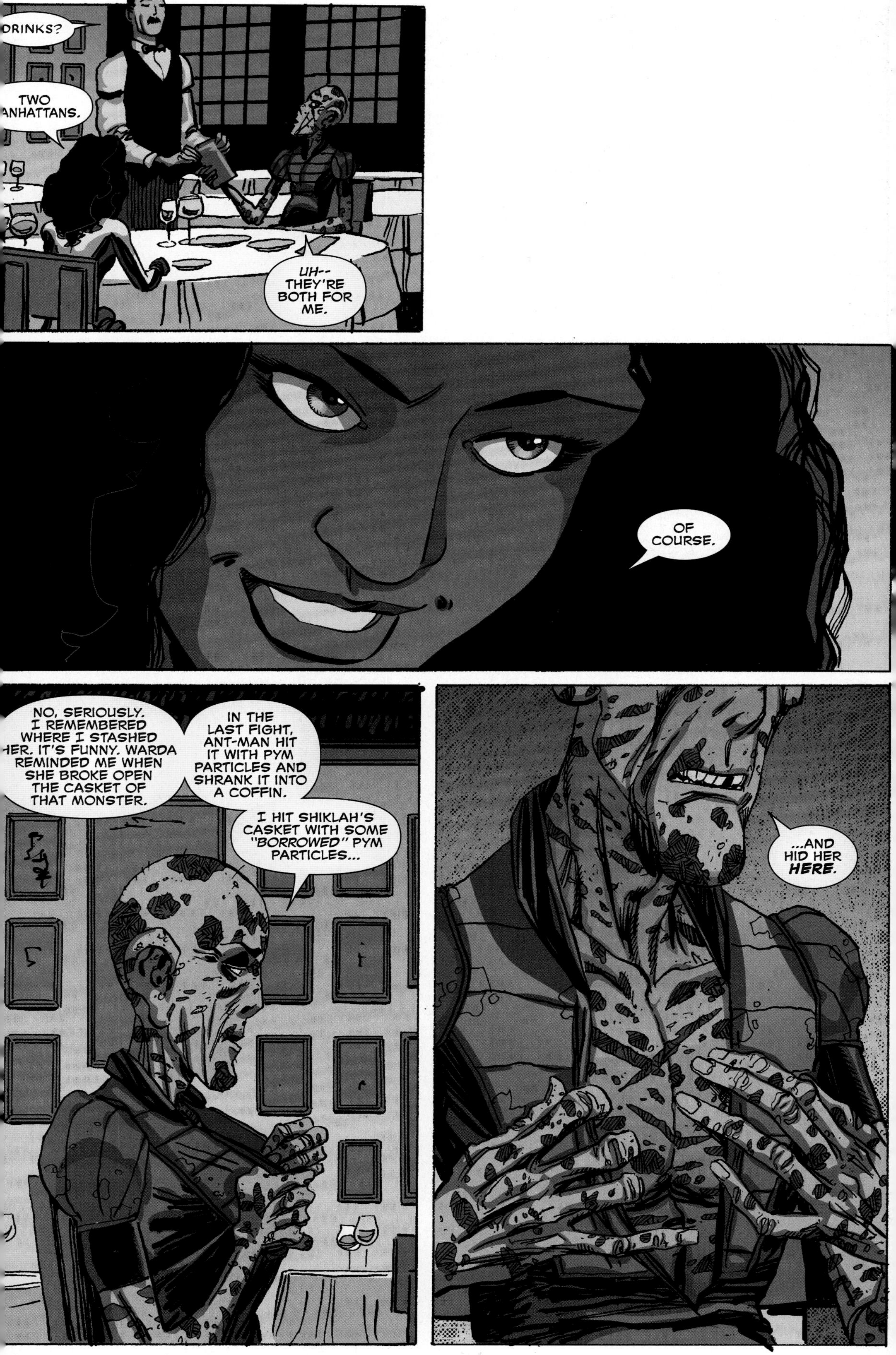
DRINKS?
TWO MANHATTANS.
UH-- THEY'RE BOTH FOR ME.
OF COURSE.
NO, SERIOUSLY. I REMEMBERED WHERE I STASHED HER. IT'S FUNNY. WARDA REMINDED ME WHEN SHE BROKE OPEN THE CASKET OF THAT MONSTER.
IN THE LAST FIGHT, ANT-MAN HIT IT WITH PYM PARTICLES AND SHRANK IT INTO A COFFIN.
I HIT SHIKLAH'S CASKET WITH SOME "BORROWED" PYM PARTICLES...
...AND HID HER HERE.

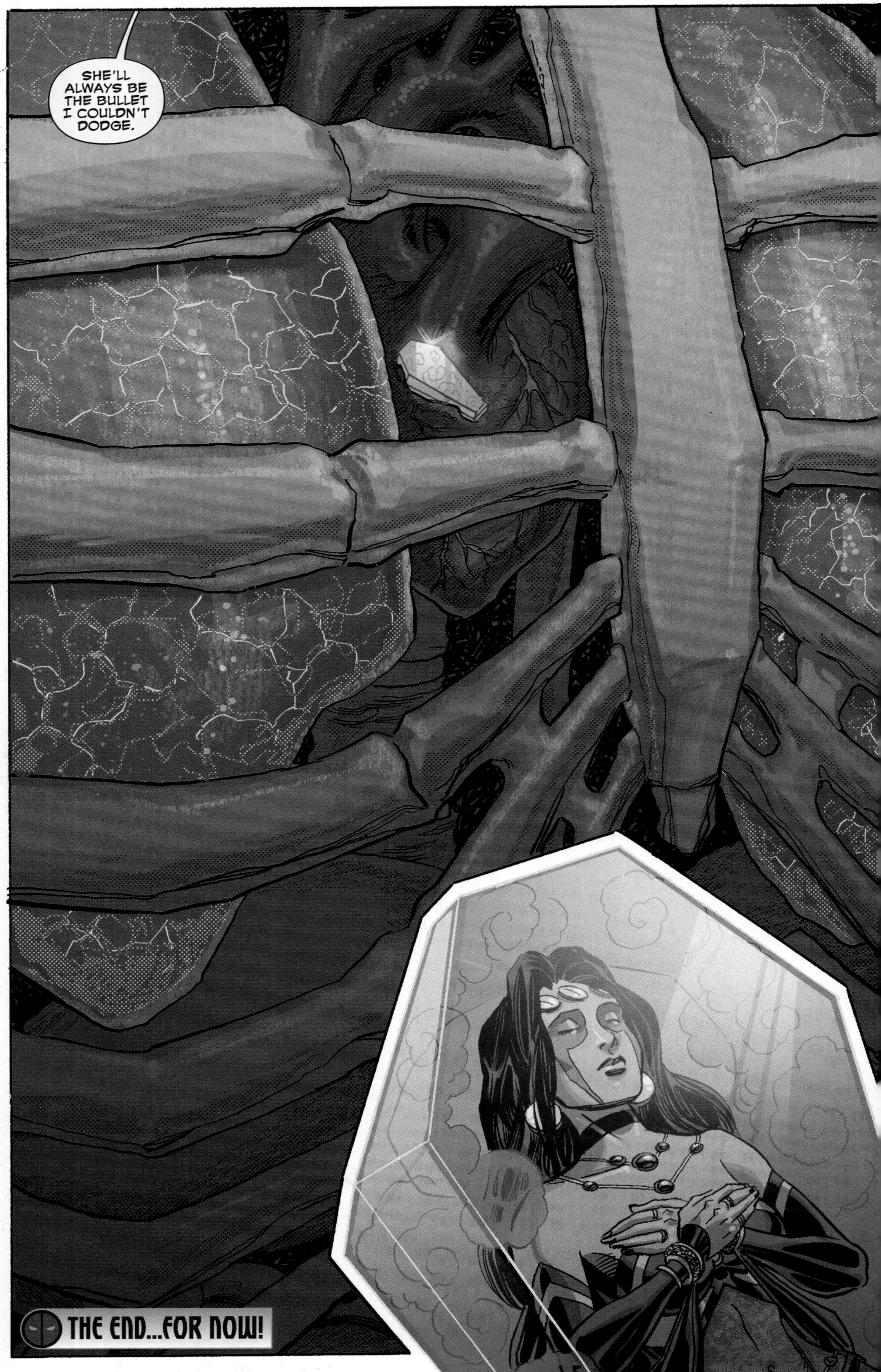
SHE'LL ALWAYS BE THE BULLET I COULDN'T DODGE.
THE END...FOR NOW!

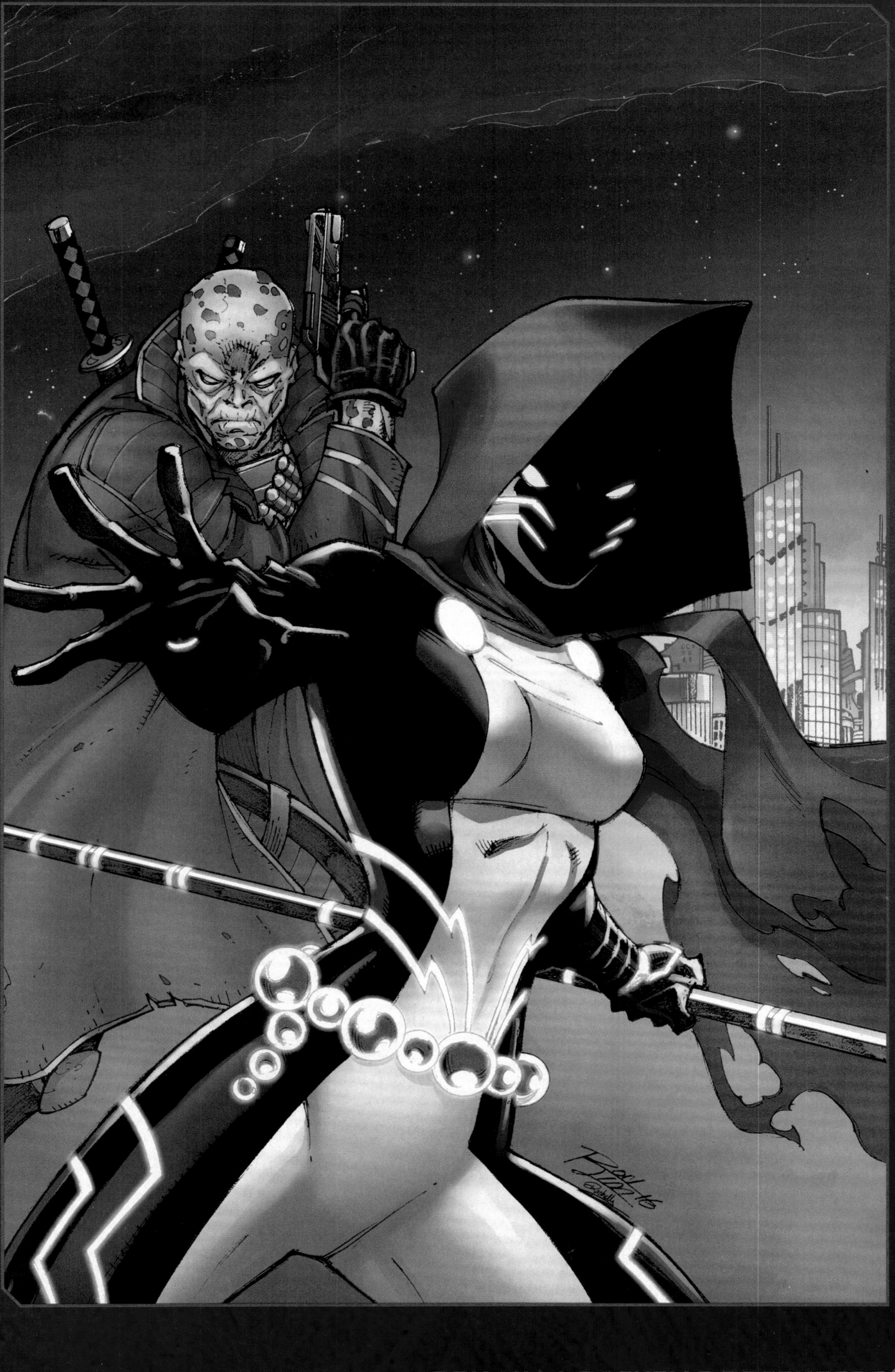

#75 Variant by RON LIM & RACHELLE ROSENBERG

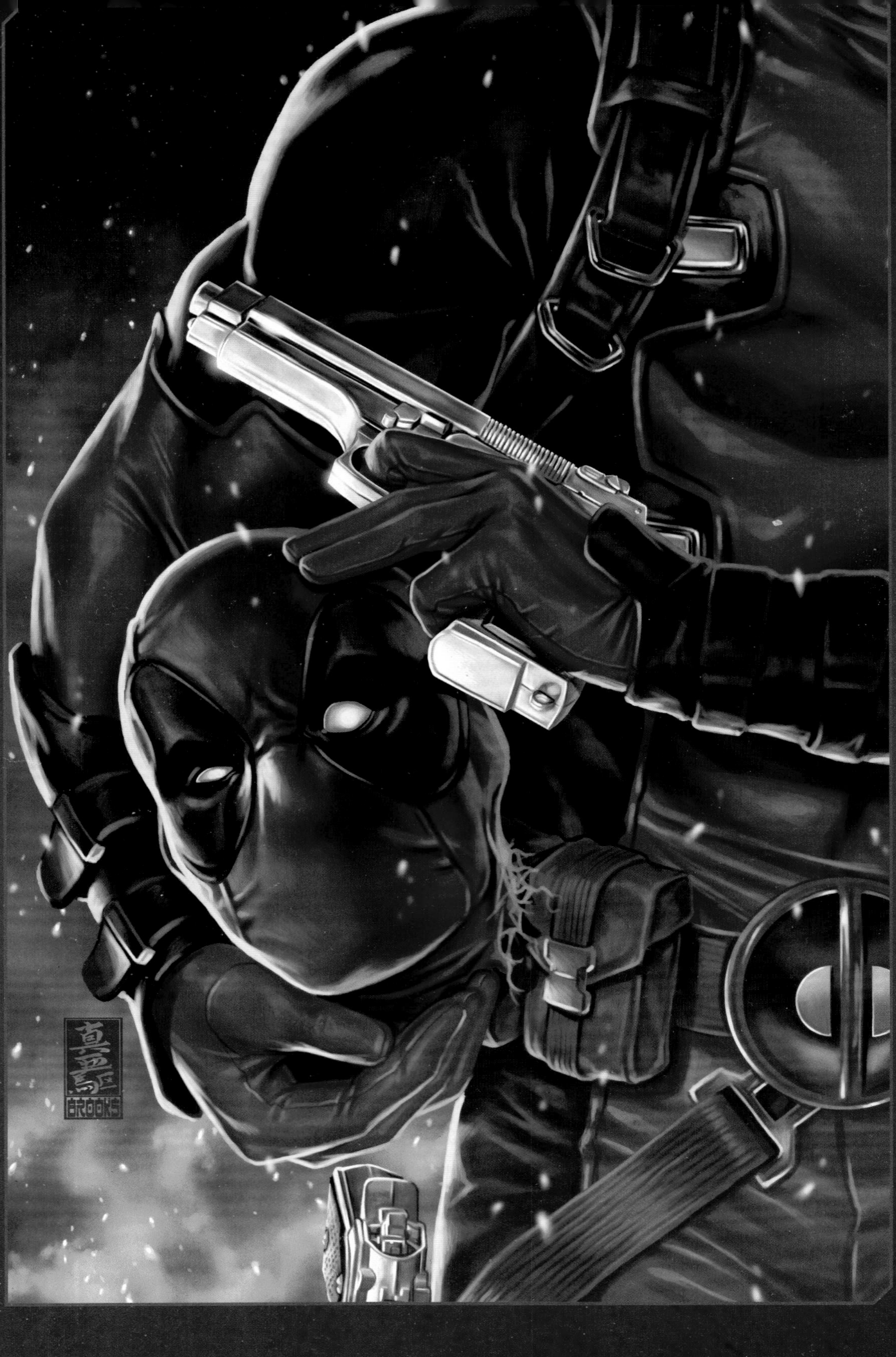

#25 variant by MARK BROOKS

THE W[...]EATEST CO[...]MAGAZINE!

DEADPOOL

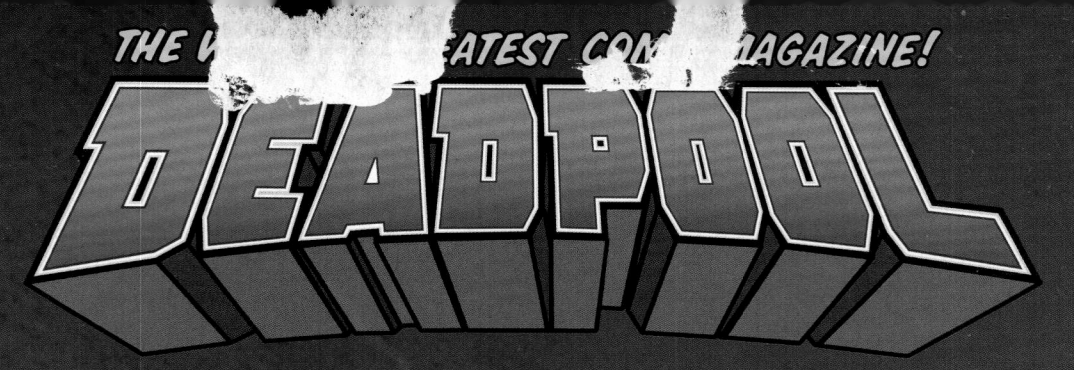

PATIENCE: ZERO

GERRY DUGGAN
writer

ISSUES #20-24

MATTEO LOLLI WITH **PAOLO VILLANELLI** [#23]
pencilers

MATTEO LOLLI [#20-22] &
CHRISTIAN DALLA VECCHIA [#23-24]
WITH **PAOLO VILLANELLI** [#23]
inkers

GURU-eFX
color artist

TRADD MOORE & MATTHEW WILSON
cover art

ISSUE #25

SCOTT KOBLISH
artist

NICK FILARDI
color artist

SCOTT KOBLISH & NICK FILARDI
cover art

VC's JOE SABINO
letterer

HEATHER ANTOS
assistant editor

JORDAN D. WHITE
editor

Special Thanks to DR. WILLIAM DEUBERT, Psychologist

collection editor JENNIFER GRÜNWALD
assistant editor CAITLIN O'CONNELL
associate managing editor KATERI WOODY
editor, special projects MARK D. BEAZLEY
vp production & special projects JEFF YOUNGQUIST
svp print, sales & marketing DAVID GABRIEL
book designer ADAM DEL RE

editor in chief AXEL ALONSO
chief creative officer JOE QUESADA
president DAN BUCKLEY
executive producer ALAN FINE

DEADPOOL created by ROB LIEFELD & FABIAN NICIEZA

DEADPOOL: WORLD'S GREATEST VOL. 6 — PATIENCE: ZE[...] [...]N# 978-1-302-90243-8. Published by MARVEL WORLDWIDE, INC., a subsidiary of MARVEL ENTERTAINMENT, LLC. OFFICE[...] [...]een any of the names, characters, persons, and/or institutions in this magazine with those of any living or dead person or [...] [...]AN BUCKLEY, President, Marvel Entertainment; JOE QUESADA, Chief Creative Officer; TOM BREVOORT, SVP of Publishing; D[...] [...]nagement & Development, Asia; DAVID GABRIEL, SVP of Sales & Marketing, Publishing; JEFF YOUNGQUIST, VP of Producti[...] [...] Publishing Operations; SUSAN CRESPI, Production Manager; STAN LEE, Chairman Emeritus. For information regarding ad[...] [...]is@marvel.com. For Marvel subscription inquiries, please call 888-511-5480. **Manufactured between 3/3/2017 and 4/4[...]**

10 9 8 7 6 5 4 3 2 1

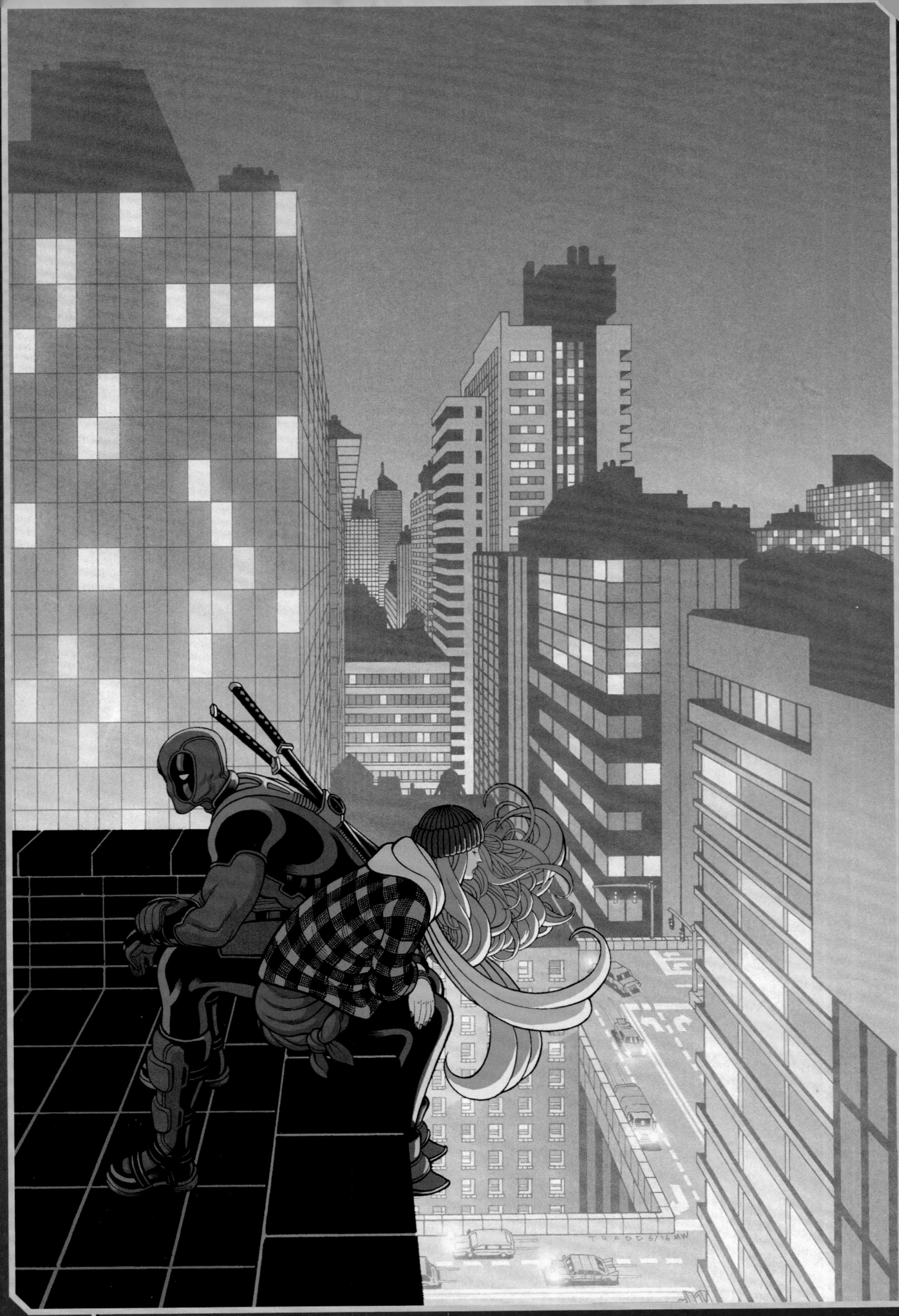
TRADD 6/16 MW

20 | THE NEVER-ENDING STRUGGLE